D0221229

FEARFUL WARRIORS

FEARFUL WARRIORS

A Psychological Profile of
U.S.–Soviet Relations

Ralph K. White

THE FREE PRESS
A Division of Macmillan, Inc.
NEW YORK

Collier Macmillan Publishers
LONDON

Copyright © 1984 by The Free Press
A Division of Macmillan, Inc.

All rights reserved. No part of this book may be reproduced
or transmitted in any form or by any means, electronic or
mechanical, including photocopying, recording, or by any
information storage and retrieval system, without permission
in writing from the Publisher.

The Free Press
A Divison of Macmillan, Inc.
866 Third Avenue, New York, N.Y. 10022

Collier Macmillan Canada, Inc.

Printed in the United States of America

printing number
1 2 3 4 5 6 7 8 9 10

Library of Congress Cataloging in Publication Data
White, Ralph K.
    Fearful warriors.

    Bibliography: p.
    Includes index.
    1. United States—Foreign relations—Soviet Union—
Psychological aspects.   2. Soviet Union—Foreign
relations—United States—Psychological aspects.
I. Title.
E183.8.S65W48   1984   327.73047   83-49001
ISBN 0-02-933760-7

E
183
.8
.S65 W48
1984

Library
UNIVERSITY OF UTAH

''In our time only a madman can start a war, and he himself will perish in its flames.''

Khrushchev

Contents

Preface   ix

1. Introduction   1

Part I.   THE PRESENT SITUATION

2. Empathizing with the Soviet Government   9

3. Soviet Power   31

4. Soviet Intentions   37

5. More Plausible Scenarios for the Outbreak of Nuclear War   53

6. Three Unpromising Approaches to Peace   67

7. The Case for Minimal Deterrence   80

8. The Case for Drastic Tension-reduction   87

Part II.   POLITICAL PSYCHOLOGY: MOTIVES AND PERCEPTIONS

9. War-promoting Motives   109

10. War-promoting Perceptions   135

11. The Chief Corrective: Realistic Empathy   160

12. Unmotivated, Cognitive Errors   168

Part III.   COMPARATIVE HISTORY

13. The First World War   189

14. The Second World War   210

15. The East–West Conflict   227

16. The Three Conflicts Compared   255

Part IV. PREVENTION

17. Forms of Minimal Deterrence   273

18. Forms of Drastic Tension-reduction: Arms Control   295

19. Other Ways to Reduce Tension   315

20. Eventual World Federation   320

21. Persuading the American People   328

22. Grounds for Hope   344

References
                                                               350

Index
                                                               363

Preface

The "madness" that is carrying the world closer and closer to nuclear war has at its core a psychological explanation: Each side, though fundamentally afraid, misperceives the nature of the danger it faces. Each side imagines that it faces an inherently, implacably aggressive enemy when actually it faces an enemy as fearful as itself—an enemy driven mainly by fear to do the things that lead to war. That is the central theme of this book.

It follows that if we, the human race, want to avoid a nuclear catastrophe, our most urgent task is to promote realistic empathy, on each side of the East–West conflict, with fear on the other side. While certain kinds of armed deterrence are needed, they must be combined with a many-sided program of tension-reduction, and the chief focus of the tension-reduction should be to promote full recognition of the other superpower's fear.

The title of the book, *Fearful Warriors*, states its central theme in two words. The Soviet Union and the United States are warriors in the sense that, while hating and fearing war, both are doing things, such as building enormously redundant arsenals of first-strike nuclear weapons, that bring war steadily closer. They are warriors also in that each is likely to become a warrior in the most literal sense unless present trends are stopped and drastically reversed. They are fearful in that both are doing war-promoting things mainly because of fear.

While this theme and its practical implications are central, the book is actually a good deal broader than its title suggests. Its broader goal is ambitious: to study systematically the causes of war in general and the problems of how to prevent war. In doing so it draws heavily from other disciplines, especially history and political science. While the book is designed for the general reader, it is interdisciplinary enough to be used as a text in college-level interdisciplinary courses in peace studies or the causes and prevention of war.

CHAPTER ONE

Introduction

What Can We Do?

Many have pictured the ultimate horrors of nuclear war and have made a thoroughly convincing case.

Some critics insist that Jonathan Schell (1982) exaggerated when he suggested that an all-out nuclear exchange could mean the literal extinction of the human race. Perhaps he did exaggerate. The Last Epidemic may not necessarily kill everyone. Perhaps as many as a million would survive, miserably, in out-of-the-way parts of the earth—roughly one-four-thousandth of the present world population. Perhaps many millions more.

The main point is that that is too many horrible deaths. The prospect of 99 percent extinction, or even 50 percent, is enough. It is more than enough if accompanied by the nearly total extinction of civilized human life as we know it for most of those who survive. It is enough to convince millions of those now alive that no other need is as urgent as the need to avoid nuclear war. It is enough to galvanize into action those whose only contribution so far has been a wringing of hands.

But how?

At that point there is a confusion of counsels. Some say that even a nuclear freeze, which appears at first sight to be the simplest and most obvious step toward avoiding nuclear war, would actually increase the danger. President Reagan argues that it would "freeze us into a position of inferiority," which would tempt our implacable enemies to strike first and precipitate precisely the catastrophe we all want to avoid. Is he right? Is he partly right? Are there other things we could do that would unequivocally reduce the danger? If so, what?

Schell's own idea of prevention is world government. Is he right? If so, are there psychologically realistic ways of attacking the seemingly insuperable obstacle of national self-centeredness?

Those are only some of the questions that arise when our minds move from the emotion of horror at the thought of nuclear war to practical thinking about how to prevent it—and how to prevent any kind of war, since almost any kind could become nuclear.

The Paradox of Unwanted War

The moment we move toward action we run into a psychological puzzle of the first magnitude. Everyone seems to hate war. Everyone talks peace, peace, peace. To judge by what they say, almost everyone in every country wants peace (at least if he can have it on fair, "acceptable" terms). Yet all over the world nations are preparing for war, pursuing arms policies that are often economically backbreaking and that in the aggregate seem both likely to produce war and likely, if they do, to make it colossally destructive. Small wars repeatedly occur (Cambodia, Iran–Iraq, Lebanon, the Falkland Islands), some of which could trigger large ones, and a possible gigantic East–West conflict seems to come closer and closer.

Why?

The question has been acute ever since the failure of the diagnosis and the prediction contained in Norman Angell's *The Great Illusion*, published in 1910 and widely read and applauded. The "great illusion," he argued, was that war might possibly benefit the country that started it; according to Angell war had already become so expensive and destructive that no sane nation could undertake it. He was right that it had already become prohibitively destructive; he was wrong in thinking that its destructiveness would prevent it. The history of the seventy-odd years since then speaks for itself. The paradox of wars that no one should have wanted did not begin with the invention of nuclear or thermonuclear weapons. It was there all along.

A fundamental attack on the problem therefore requires first of all raising this rock-bottom question: When people say they hate war and talk peace, peace, peace, can we take their words at face value? Are they fully honest with us or with themselves? Or, along with all its horrors, is there something powerfully attractive in war? Sigmund Freud (1924), Robert Ardrey (1963), Konrad Lorenz (1966), and others tell us that there is. According to them, something primitive in man urges him toward it, unconsciously if not consciously. There is a basic animal impulse of "aggression" in the human species that often overrides rational self-interest.

But this explanation is partial at best. Those who stress it sometimes forget that in addition to anger and the impulse to hurt others there is another elemental emotion, *fear*. In animal evolution the principle of self-preservation is at least as basic as the urge to fight with other members of the same species. The fittest survive partly because they escape from danger most of the time, and fight to the death, in most species, only rarely.

In the modern world, with nuclear destruction looming in the background, one would think that the emotion of fear and the impulse to preserve oneself and one's family from pain and death would be enough to prevent the mutual destruction of war if the two primitive emotions were simply and directly pitted against each other. Even leaving aside such additional motives as conscience, sympathy, and enlightened economic self-interest, fear for self and family should be enough to prevent war. It is not. Fighting in clear national self-defense could certainly be attributed to a fairly simple kind of fear, extended to the "collective self," but that explanation too breaks down when applied to the nation or nations on the more aggressive side. The essential paradox therefore remains: The great majority of all human beings want peace (on balance) but often wage war.

Another explanation that probably represents a part of the truth is the "devil theory" of war. According to it, some men do want war for its own sake, for the power and profit it may give them, or both. Hitler is a prime example. Others are then forced to fight in self-defense. In this view, favored by nationalists everywhere, Nazis, Communists, capitalists, or the rulers of rival nations are essentially evil and are the essential cause of war.

It would be a mistake to dismiss this view simply by calling it a "good guys and bad guys" interpretation or a "black-and-white picture" of the world. There *are* "bad guys" (or at least dangerous fanatics), and aggression does occur. When Hitler's troops march into Prague or when Soviet tanks roll into Hungary, Czechoslovakia, or Afghanistan, it may not be the highest wisdom to stay above the battle, to declare that "probably each side is right from its own point of view" and do nothing. Anger is sometimes realistic and healthy. Churchill was realistic when he called Hitler a "bloodthirsty guttersnipe." On the other hand, if there is in fact a "military–industrial complex" in the United States (or other capitalist countries) that consciously promotes wars in Vietnam and elsewhere for the greater power and profit of men in Wall Street and the Pentagon, Americans would be wise, for the sake of their own survival, to recognize that situation and do something about it.

Nevertheless, the prevailing assumption that wars occur *primarily* because evil men want them and that those of us who regard ourselves as peaceful good guys are therefore free from further responsibility, is, in the light of all the evidence to be presented in this book, a gross distortion. The evidence indicates that in the modern world the great majority of the men and women involved in the decisions that lead to war—followers as well as leaders—make those decisions not because they want war or because they are exceptionally evil, but for other psychological reasons that urgently need analysis.

At this point psychology and psychiatry can supplement the other sorts of knowledge possessed by the historian, the political scientist, and the practitioner of international affairs. If in our nuclear age "only a madman could start a war," the problem of war becomes grist also for the psychologist's and psychiatrist's mill, since madness in all its forms and degrees, including the everyday madness of ordinary people, is in their bailiwick. The proposition that "war itself is madness," while perhaps in a sense quite true, is by no means enough. We need a concrete picture of what happens in the minds of men who sincerely (on balance) want peace but favor policies or make decisions that in fact, usually without their desire or intention, lead to war.

Such a picture obviously cannot be drawn by psychologists alone. Complex and hotly controversial questions about what policies "in fact" lead to war must be raised and debated, chiefly by historians, political scientists, and experienced diplomats, before the psychologist can appropriately inquire into the mental processes of those who favor the policies that have been debated. But at that point psychologists (including this one), if they also have an interdisciplinary approach that includes much study of history from a psychological point of view, should have a special contribution to make. They should, and sometimes do, have the advantage of systematic study of human motivation in general, including the less conscious as well as the more conscious motives; and they should have the advantage of intensive study of what is sometimes called "misperception" or "cognitive distortion"—a variegated process that is accentuated in the psychotic but that pervades everyday living as well.

The successful, supposedly realistic makers of foreign policy and the ordinary citizens who elect or applaud them are not free from misperception. Therefore the knowledge that often exists in the minds of psychologists, psychiatrists, and psychologically oriented political scientists with regard to the nature and sources of misperception may provide a number of clues to the resolution of our basic paradox—the question of why normally sane and peaceloving human beings, without intending the consequences, so often involve themselves step by step in actions that lead to war. In other words, why they so often misjudge the probable effects of their own actions.

Diagnosis Before Prescription

Given a danger so enormous and a paradox so formidable, there is clearly a need for a broad, systematic attack on the problem of war's causes and prevention—with its causes put first and, in the study of its causes, with as much objectivity as, being human, we can manage to achieve.

The breadth of the problem calls for an equally broad, and certainly interdisciplinary, attack on it. At least nineteen overlapping subjects of study are relevant: history (especially comparative history), political science, economics, sociology, anthropology, social psychology (especially its very new subdiscipline, political psychology), psychiatry, ethology, philosophy, semantics, geopolitics, Soviet studies, American studies, Middle East studies, negotiation and mediation, public opinion research, communications research, military strategy, and military technology. To master all of them would be a superhuman task, far beyond the scope of this writer, who can claim professional competence in only one of them, social psychology (and its subdiscipline, political psychology). What this book tries to do, rather, is pull together some of the more relevant parts of each of them to make a semicoherent whole.

There is also an urgent need to work toward objectivity, to the limited extent to which objectivity—which is not the same as neutrality—is possible on such an emotion-packed subject as this. The emotion implicit in the two previous sections of this introduction needs to be sternly held in check while attention is concentrated on a careful examination of the available evidence as to what causes what. Action can come later. Both peace emotions and patriotic emotions, along with the preconceptions associated with them, must be pushed into the very back of our minds while we study the evidence and while we actually focus especially on new evidence that counts against what we have previously been thinking. For instance, peace activists who have been giving top priority to arms control might give special attention to the facts that have led both Salvador de Madariaga and Barbara Tuchman to believe that excessive distrust causes excessive arms, more than the other way around. Deterrence activists who abhor "appeasement," without clearly defining it, might give special attention to the problem of defining it clearly, noting the words of that arch-opponent of appeasement, Winston Churchill: "Appeasement in itself may be good or bad depending on circumstances. . . . Appeasement from strength is magnanimous and noble and might be the surest and perhaps the only path to world peace" (quoted by Fulbright, 1966). A good physician diagnoses first, making use of all he knows about a particular patient and all his accumulated knowledge of disease processes and health-promoting processes, before prescribing remedies.

Part I of this book, "The Present Situation," is analogous to a physician's examination of a patient, the patient in this case being the human race, especially the United States and the USSR in the last two decades of the twentieth century. Part II, "Political Psychology: Motives and Misperceptions," and Part III, "Comparative History," are analogous to a physician's training and past experience. Part IV, "Prevention," is analogous to the treatment then prescribed.

PART I

The Present Situation

CHAPTER TWO

Empathizing with the Soviet Government

For anyone caught in a conflict, a resolution of that conflict begins with an attempt to understand how the conflict looks from the other fellow's point of view. In our case the "other fellows" who matter most are the men who govern the USSR, and our first task, underlying everything that comes later in this book, must be an attempt to empathize realistically with them.

Two words in that statement, "empathize" and "govern," call for definition and some discussion.

A sharp distinction is made here between empathy and sympathy. Although the two words are often used almost interchangeably, empathy will be defined for the purposes of this book as a realistic *understanding* of the thoughts and feelings of others, while sympathy will be defined, in accordance with its Greek derivation, as *feeling with* others—being happy because they are or unhappy because they are—which often implies doing what one can to help them. Empathy is cognitive, in the language of psychology; sympathy is affective.

While the two processes often occur together and are often related as cause and effect, each facilitating the other, the distinction between them is important, and it is especially important when the "others" are an opposing group in an acute conflict situation. It is extremely difficult if not impossible to "feel with" such an opponent, chiefly because its hostility to one's own group is so genuine and often so genuinely dangerous. A plea for warm-hearted sympathy with the men in the Kremlin would be psychologically naive. We could not achieve it even if we tried, and there is no need to try. A plea for realistic empathy with them, though, is not naive. It is vital. If we do not clearly recognize their hostility to us, we will not be tough in the ways we should be tough,

Note: This chapter is a modified version of an article published under the title "Empathizing with the Rulers of the USSR" (White, 1982).

9

and if we do not clearly recognize the ways in which they are human beings like us, with thoughts and feelings resembling ours, we will not be reasonable and cooperative in the ways we must be in order to survive.

The word "govern" also calls for discussion. Governing in the Soviet Union is not the same as in the United States. It is far closer to total control. As most of us see the Soviet system (with good reason) it is as inefficient economically as it is undemocratic politically. It is still essentially totalitarian, as it was in the days of Stalin's one-man rule and his mammoth Gulag Archipelago, though without his special kind of sadism, and now oligarchic rather than autocratic. Those who govern are still grimly determined to cling to the essentials of their own power both in the USSR and in the outlying but adjacent areas (Eastern Europe, Afghanistan, Mongolia) that they now control. In this respect the term "mirror-image," made familiar by Urie Bronfenbrenner (1961; cf. White, 1965; Frank, 1967, pp. 115–36), breaks down. There are significant psychological differences between them and our own elected leaders, along with many similarities, and in our effort to see their humanity there is no need to lean over backward and ignore those differences. The real similarities, though, need to be understood too.

In any case, those who govern—not the general Soviet public—make the decisions on which war and peace may depend. If we want realistic ways to prevent war, they are the ones it is most urgent to understand.

Their Underlying Insecurity

The first and perhaps the most important thesis in this book is that the Soviet decision-makers are driven mainly by a deeply ingrained sense of insecurity in their foreign policies and defense policies. Their aggressive behavior, when they are aggressive, is more defensive than offensive in its underlying motivation. So is the steady military build-up that has been going on at least since 1963. Therefore, if we want peace, their insecurity—not a grim determination to conquer the world—is the most important obstacle that the West needs to understand and try to overcome.

The most accurate word here is insecure, not frightened. The

Soviet decision-makers are not shaking in their shoes. For one thing they are tough individuals, with more than a touch of *machismo*. (We Americans have more than a touch of it too.) For another, they have been impressed and reassured by the fact that the West has not attacked them since 1945, or used against them the immense nuclear superiority that it has had for many years. And, in the third place, the armies and the weapons that they now possess have given the Soviets confidence in their ability to deter, or, if necessary, to hold their own against any future aggressor.

Nevertheless, many kinds of evidence suggest that they have an underlying sense of anxiety which these sources of reassurance enable them to push into the back of their minds but which would quickly leap into the front of their minds if the sources of reassurance were not there. They feel an emotional *need* for the reassurance that their strength and that their control of contiguous territory give them.

One kind of evidence of this anxiety is the testimony of respected Western students of Soviet affairs, including many who have intimate first-hand knowledge of the USSR.

George Kennan, perhaps the best known of all Western experts on the USSR, says that he sees in the Kremlin "a group of troubled men . . . prisoners of certain ingrained peculiarities of the Russian statesmanship of past ages—the congenital sense of insecurity, the lack of inner self-confidence . . ." (1982, p. 153).

Robert C. Tucker, author of *The Soviet Political Mind*: "From the standpoint of the latter-day Stalinists . . . to imagine that it is possible to come to terms with the other side strategically, if only on the question of steps to survival, is to misunderstand the changeless nature of the enemy" (1971, p. 251).

Adam Ulam, author of *The Rivals*: "It was not until 1947 that the Soviets became convinced through a most amazing misunderstanding that the United States had an elaborate plan to undermine the Soviet empire" (1971, p. 99).

Robert Kaiser, in *Russia: the People and the Power*: "A siege mentality has infected the leaders of Soviet society since its birth in 1917" (1976, p. 500).

Craig Whitney, the *New York Times* Bureau Chief in Moscow in 1980, speaks of a general "sense of isolation and insecurity. . . . They have basic misperceptions about the West, and at times of crisis they tend to listen to fears and ideologies, not facts'' (1980, pp. 91, 30).

Strobe Talbott, the editor and translator of *Khrushchev Remembers* and *Times*'s diplomatic correspondent in Moscow, writing with his colleague Bruce Nelan: ''What the United States sees—and seeks—as 'containment' of Soviet power, the Kremlin sees and fears as 'encirclement' by its enemies. That fear has driven Soviet foreign policy since 1917'' (1980, p. 18).

Another body of evidence is provided by Russian history. For more than a thousand years it has been largely a history of foreign invasions. In the midst of a vast plain, with no natural barriers to protect it such as we in America have had, Russia-in-Europe has repeatedly fallen prey to invaders. The Germans in the days of Alexander Nevsky; the Tartar conquest, which began in 1237 and effectively cut Russia off from European civilization for more than two centuries (Pares, 1947, pp. 7, 54–102); the Turks; the Poles (*ibid.*, pp. 141, 165); the Swedes (*ibid.*, pp. 189–97); the French under Napoleon; the British and French in the Crimea; the Germans in World War I, for Russia a disaster; and the Germans again, with results still more disastrous, in World War II (Halle, 1967, p. 14). Besides, although most Americans have forgotten it or never knew it, the United States and its allies had troops in Russia in 1918–20.

It has not by any means been wholly one-sided. Russia joined in the partitioning of Poland and in the East occupied the relatively empty wastes of Siberia, comparable to our American West. It has also expanded elsewhere (the Caucasus, Central Asia), especially in the nineteenth century, when all the Great Powers were engaged in colonial competition and Britain's expansion far exceeded Russia's (Karpovich, 1951). Recently, of course, there has been the occupation of the Baltic states (again) and Eastern Europe, though there is a strong case (below, Chapter 15) for interpreting the occupation of Eastern Europe as primarily defensive in motivation after the extreme trauma of Hitler's invasion of the USSR. Nothing said here should be interpreted as indicating that either Czarist Russia or Communist Russia has been less aggressive or expansionist than most of the other Great Powers. On the other hand, the evidence has not shown either one to be more so. And, when Russia has expanded, it has probably always had defensive as well as purely power-oriented reasons for doing so. That is, in addition to their expectable human relishing of power and prestige for their own sake, the Russians have always had in the back of their minds the thought that in controlling borderlands they were establishing buffers between themselves and potentially aggressive enemies.

In any case there is every reason to think that *their* conception of their past is overwhelmingly in terms of long-suffering, stubborn, and in the long run successful self-defense. From Tolstoy's description of the battle of Borodino against Napoleon's Grand Army to present-day novels and films of the defense of Stalingrad against Hitler's legions their memories cling not to glorious conquests (of which there have been very few) but to the central theme of defending Mother Russia against foreign invaders. Like many other peoples, and perhaps more than most, the Russians have a strong tendency to focus selectively on the episodes in their history that cast no doubt on either their virtue or their virility. The homeland, the motherland, the *rodina*, is precious and must be defended. Ordinary Russians will look at you in amazement if you suggest that their role in a war could be anything but self-defense.

There is much other evidence in support of the thesis that Soviet motivation is basically more defensive than offensive. It includes for instance the evidence that in overall military strength the Soviet Union (with only about 6% of the world's population and not much more than half of America's GNP, leaving aside Western Europe's) is by no means clearly superior to the combination of its various present and potential enemies, including most of Western Europe, China, and perhaps Japan as well as the United States; the old ideology of world revolution has faded in Soviet minds; the United States, like the USSR, has since 1950 done a number of things, mainly defensive in purpose, that could look offensive to its chief opponent; and, in accord with their own black-and-white picture (the reverse of ours) the Soviet rulers and public have tended to put the worst possible interpretation on our ambiguous actions. Elaboration of all of these propositions will have to be postponed to later chapters, especially Chapters 8, 10, and 16.

There are three questions, though, that cannot be postponed, because, quite legitimately, they are uppermost in American minds today. They are: What about Afghanistan? What about the Soviet arms build-up since 1963, which to us seems far greater than the Soviet Union needs for self-defense? And what about the shooting down of the Korean airliner in 1983? Can ''empathy'' square any of these with the hypothesis of defensive motivation?

It can.

Afghanistan

The essential question about Afghanistan is not whether the armed intervention by the Soviet Union should be called aggression. It should.[1] The psychologically interesting question is whether the motivation behind the action, from the Soviet government's own point of view, was mainly defensive—as defensive as, for example, the motivation of the United States in Vietnam.[2]

That is not a far-fetched comparison, and in our task of empathizing realistically with the Soviet rulers it may be useful, since we ourselves went through the Vietnam experience, believing—at least most of us did, at least at the beginning—that our own motives were strictly defensive.

There are a number of interesting similarities, the chief one being that in each case a superpower intervened by force in support of an unpopular government threatened by a formidable popular revolt. Another is that the superpower had helped to install the unpopular government in the first place. Americans had something to do with establishing Diem in Saigon in 1954 and much to do with keeping him in power after that; the Soviet Union, we have much reason to suspect, had much to do with the ''April revolution'' in Kabul in April 1978, when, apparently, a small minority group consisting mainly of urban Marxist intellectuals and left-wing army officers seized power. (It may well be that Soviet support for that coup was more blameworthy, in the sense of being less readily explained by defensive motives, and also more of a blunder, than any of the later Soviet actions that flowed from it.) From that point on there was in each case a sense

[1]The definition of aggression proposed in this book (Chapter 15) is ''the use or threat of force, in territory not clearly one's own, without clear evidence that a majority of the emotionally involved people in that territory want such intervention.'' By that definition the Soviet action was clearly an act of aggression.

[2]For a detailed discussion of America's motivation in Vietnam, see White (1970, pp. 182–237). For a high-level Soviet view of the USSR's motivation in Afghanistan, see Arbatov (1982, pp. 177–78). The judgment of American observers appears later in this chapter. See also Arnold (1982).

of commitment—and an investment of national pride, prestige, and credibility hinging on the outcome—that carried the intervening nation on and on in spite of mounting regrets that the whole affair had ever been started.

Another similarity, psychologically fundamental, is that in both cases the world situation was seen by the intervening power, rightly or wrongly, as threatening enough to justify drastic action.

During the years 1962–65, when the United States in Vietnam was becoming more and more involved and committed, most of the interested American public, and especially America's leaders, saw an advancing Communist movement threatening the entire Free World. We saw it using new "Chinese" techniques of subversion and guerrilla warfare that the West was only beginning to understand and learn how to combat effectively. The four-year Soviet threat to Berlin, 1958–62, and the Cuban missile crisis of 1962, were freshly remembered events, and the idea of a domino process, resembling the spread of a fire, an epidemic, or a spreading cancer, was widely accepted. Ngo Dinh Diem appeared to be not exactly a democratic leader, but a firm ruler, valiantly trying to hold back the Communist tide and deserving America's help in doing so.

What we did not remember, or think much about, was the Vietnamese people. Feeling that they did not really matter much when compared with the world-wide Communist menace, most of us contented ourselves with the proposition (not really based on evidence) that the Vietnamese peasants "couldn't care less" about which side won, as long as peace came soon; then we forgot about that last provision and prolonged the war for several years, in opposition to what we ourselves thought the Vietnamese people wanted. And, chiefly because we were not really thinking about the Vietnamese people, we lost the war.

Something similar can be reasonably inferred about the psychology of the Soviets in their thinking about the world context of Afghanistan. After high hopes of détente and lasting peace during the Nixon Administration, they saw four years go by, 1975–79, during which, mysteriously (from their point of view), American actions deflated those hopes. Their own armament, which in their eyes probably was simply catching up with America's and NATO's hitherto always overweening strategic strength, was continuing at a steady pace of about a 3 percent annual increase. But (naturally rationalizing all their own dubious actions during the same period) they saw (as they apparently interpreted it) America giving up mutually beneficial trade opportunities in order to interfere with their internal affairs by way of the Jackson–Vanik amendment on behalf of Jews who wanted to emigrate; they saw America, after fine initial cooperation between Vance and Gromyko, totally excluding them from the peacemaking process in the Middle East, which was far from America but just next to their own border; they saw America sidling up to their arch-enemy, China; they saw President Carter stepping up America's arms program to a figure much higher than an annual increase of 3 percent, though probably in their eyes they were just beginning to be equal to the United States in strategic strength; they saw SALT II, on which they had sweated blood with their American counterparts, dying in Congress; they saw the dread prospect of Pershing II missiles and cruise missiles. All *before* Afghanistan.

And all exaggerated and one-sided, of course. We from our perspective may judge that all of it was grossly exaggerated threat-perception, to a point that might almost be called paranoid. It was nevertheless more or less natural and expectable, given both what America did and the inevitably distorted perception of those things by Soviet decision-makers. Nor would it be surprising if, against this background, most of the men in the Kremlin decided that détente was dead, that President Carter had finally succumbed to the baleful influence of the military-industrial complex (called by them the capitalist and militarist "ruling circles in America"), and that they must fall back upon their own military strength in order to be safe, plus, of course, keeping friendly nations on their borders.

It was in this anxiety-filled psychological context that the Afghan situation went from bad to worse. Hafizullah Amin, a strong-willed but impractical, ultra-left dictator, was making the situation steadily worse, prematurely (as seasoned Moscow authorities saw it) pushing such things as land reform and rights for women, and needlessly provoking the fiercely independent Afghan nationalists and the Islamic fundamentalists. He refused to listen to what Moscow thought was its sane, prudent advice. It was natural for the Politburo to begin to see images of the future in which Afghanistan would fall into anarchy, break up into its ethnic parts, and the vultures of capitalism and feudalism—Pakistan, the CIA, and China—would be right on hand to pick up the pieces. Something *had* to be done. Amin had to be done away with, and Babrak Karmal, the leader of the saner faction, the Parcham faction, within the coalition that had engineered the April Revolution in 1978, who after all had as much right to lead as Amin had, could be brought back from exile. He could lead the reform movement, toward moderation, that would restore order and keep a friendly nation, rather than a disintegrated and then hostile nation, on the southern border of the USSR, next to its Moslem republics.

There is a real parallel, here, to the situation in Vietnam in 1965, just before America began to send in its own troops on a large scale. Washington at that time saw the Viet Cong riding high, the shaky military government of Diem's successors in danger of imminent collapse, and if it did collapse the probability of a domino process extending at least to Laos and Cambodia and possibly much further (*Pentagon Papers*, 1971, pp. xix, 106). Less realistically, there was in Washington selective inattention to the disconcerting evidence, already available, that most of the really emotionally involved people in South Vietnam hated the Saigon government and saw the Viet Cong either as good or as the lesser evil (White, 1970, pp. 37–103).

Similarly, in 1979, just before the Kremlin began to use its troops in Afghanistan, there was a realistic Soviet perception that the Islamic, antiforeign, antiatheist rebellion was riding high, that the shaky leftist government of Amin in Kabul was in danger of imminent collapse, and that if or when it did collapse the influence of the USSR would suffer throughout the Middle East, conceivably including the neighboring Islamic parts of the USSR itself. That would seriously hurt Soviet pride if not Soviet security. Less realistically, there was probably selective inattention to available evidence that the opposition to land reform and to "socialism" was not confined to reactionary mullahs and infiltrators from Pakistan, supposedly paid by the CIA, but might include most of the emotionally involved people in the country itself.

There are other interesting psychological similarities. Like the Politburo, the decision-makers in Washington in 1963 were sorely tempted to replace an incompetent leader (Diem in their case, Amin in the Soviet case) whose incompetence and unmanageability seemed likely to lead to humiliating defeat. Perhaps we did have a hand in the death of Diem; perhaps not. The Soviets quite probably did have a hand in the death of Amin, with a particularly repulsive pretext that "the government" in Kabul, which presumably meant Amin and not the Parcham faction opposed to him, had asked for Soviet armed intervention. Like the men in the Kremlin, the men in Washington, including President Johnson, covered their intervention with the dubious claim that they were protecting an allied nation from a danger originating mainly outside its borders. Like them, the men in Washington covered an antidemocratic action with a bit of semantic legerdemain: Johnson announced that "South Vietnam" had asked for American help—not Ky or Thieu or the Saigon government, but "South Vietnam" had done it—a blurring of the important distinction between the government and the people. Similarly, the men in Moscow said that "Afghanistan" had asked for Soviet help—not Babrak Karmal, not the Parcham faction within the group that had engineered the April Revolution, or even the Kabul government, but "Afghanistan," with a similar blurring of the important distinction between government and people.

Naturally, since no two historical events are ever identical, there were differences as well as similarities, and some of the differences were important. Perhaps, but only perhaps, the chemical and biological weapons apparently now being used by the Soviet forces are more despicable than anything used by the United States or its allies in Vietnam. (We used napalm and agent orange, and our allies used widely attested torture.) More important, but not in our favor, is the fact that Afghanistan is on the border of the USSR while Vietnam is about as far from the United States as it could possibly be. Psychologically that is very important to the Russians, with their special sensitivity to the danger of having hostile rather than friendly or neutral nations on their border. Also important, and not necessarily in our favor, is the fact that the Kabul government was and is (in spite of its new moderation) leftist, while the Saigon government was rightist, much influenced by landowners who were opposing, not promulgating, drastic land reform. On that basis, Soviet observers could believe that the Babrak Karmal government is on the side of "the people" (though in fact most of "the people" reject it) while we in Vietnam were on the side of the exploiters of the people. That would be a gross distortion of our reasons for being there, but perhaps our turning our minds away from the fact that our allies in Vietnam were not on the side of the people was an equal distortion.

More fundamental than any of these other similarities and differences, however, is the psychological fact that in both cases the primary underlying motive appears to have been, in a sense, defensive. It is true that, by at least one definition of aggression, both were unequivocally acts of aggression. Probably, too, on a less conscious level, both were motivated in part by the normal nationalistic desire to expand, or retain, national power and prestige for their own sake—an unlovely motive that is unfortunately not confined to the two superpowers. Nevertheless, in both cases the primary underlying motive seems to have been defensive in the sense that the psychological context of the intervention, in the eyes of the interveners, was one of superpower competition for influence within the Third World—a competition in which national security was believed by each side to be basically, ultimately in danger because of the power and villainy of the superpower opponent—and there was perception, realistic or not, of an imminent, substantial loss of power and influence if intervention did not occur (Petrov, 1980, 30–34).

The practical consequences of America's present focus on the indubitable fact of Soviet aggression in Afghanistan, rather than on its mainly defensive motivation, are important. The belief of many Americans that the whole Middle East is in imminent danger of further Soviet expansionism is largely based on our interpretation of Soviet motivation in Afghanistan. Our present insistence on hurting our own economy in order to be at least equal to the Russians in the economy-breaking nuclear arms race has been much influenced by it. Therefore, it is appropriate to end this discussion with some examples of interpretation of the Soviet intervention by Americans who speak with special authority, either as knowledgeable observers who were in Moscow in the early stages of the intervention or as highly respected students of the psychology of the Soviet rulers. What were they saying, shortly after the initial armed intervention occurred? (Some have already been quoted on the more general question of Soviet insecurity.)

Craig Whitney, the *New York Times* Bureau Chief in Moscow, was speaking about a general "sense of isolation and insecurity that helped push them into Afghanistan" (1980, p. 91).

Strobe Talbott, *Time* correspondent, writing with his colleague Bruce Nelan, was saying "They have moved into Afghanistan primarily because the Moslem insurgency there threatened to turn a friendly neighbor into an unfriendly one. . . . The Afghan rebellion is doubly dangerous because it has Chinese backing. . . . One reason why détente has all but failed is that the Soviets believe the Carter Administration is rushing headlong into an alliance with China. That raises the old specter of encirclement'' (1980, p. 18).

Jerry Hough, a specialist on the Soviet government, on the basis of conversations he had between December 17, 1979, and January 12, 1980, with Soviet foreign-affairs specialists in Moscow, was saying: ''The usual answer given by Soviet scholars was that Afghanistan had long been in the Soviet sphere of influence and that a collapse of a Communist regime on the Soviet border could not be tolerated, especially when it would be replaced by a fundamentalist Islamic regime that might arouse fellow Moslems in the Central Asian republics of the Soviet Union'' (1980, p. 202).

George Kennan was saying: ''In the official American interpretation of what occurred in Afghanistan, no serious account appears to have been taken of such specific factors as geographical proximity, ethnic affinity of peoples on both sides of the border, and political instability in what is, after all, a border country of the Soviet Union. Now specific factors of that nature, all suggesting defensive rather than offensive impulses, may not be all there was to Soviet motivation, nor would they have sufficed to justify the action, but they were related to it'' (1980, p. 7).

The theme of geographical proximity came up repeatedly. Whitney wrote: ''The other day a Russian arms-control official asked: 'If Mexico, on your southern border, were suddenly in danger of being taken over by Communist infiltrators from Cuba, wouldn't you react? Of course you would, and we would understand' '' (1980, p. 32). For further evidence, see Guroff and Grant, 1981.

The main point of this whole discussion is not to mitigate the responsibility of the men in the Kremlin for their aggression in Afghanistan. It *was* aggression, as well as a major blunder. The main point is rather to raise a question about their reasons for doing it. That question has great relevance to any predictions about their future behavior. Considering their various motives, is there any good reason to infer that, like Hitler in 1938–39, they have embarked on a far-reaching career of conquest?

As a step toward realistic empathy, let us ask the same question of ourselves. Considering the defensive motives behind our intervention in Vietnam, is there any good reason to think t. like Hitler, *we* were then embarking on a far-reaching career conquest? The question answers itself. We were not. Therefore the similar action of the Soviet decision-makers does not prove that they were. Their primary motive was fear, comparable to ours in Vietnam.

The Soviet Arms Buildup

As in the case of the Soviet aggression in Afghanistan, there is no question here as to the reality of the fact that is to be interpreted. The steady, strong Soviet buildup of nuclear arms since the Cuban missile crisis of 1962 is a fact that the West has to face and somehow cope with. How we should cope, though, depends primarily on why they have done it. Does it, as a great many in the West believe, indicate a new determination, or underline an old determination, to dominate the world by force of arms? Or is it mainly based on the Soviet decision-makers' underlying sense of insecurity—an enormously exaggerated sense of insecurity, from our point of view, but perhaps quite genuine? Does it resemble Hitler's buildup in the 1930s, which was almost certainly a conscious preparation for a war of conquest? Or our own nuclear buildup since 1945, the motives of which, we have every reason to believe, have been essentially defensive?

That is a psychological question, and it is crucial. We cannot think realistically about the nature of the nuclear arms race or about how to stop and reverse that race unless we first have a sound, educated guess as to the motives behind the race on the other side.

The next two chapters take up several aspects of the question in some detail. Only a broad, general answer will be attempted here.

It is this: The bulk of the evidence indicates that the underlying Soviet motives are primarily, though by no means entirely, defensive. Fear, not coldblooded aggression, is the primary reason for the Soviet arms buildup, as it is of ours.

First, though, two concessions must be made to the viewpoint of those who feel that a further nuclear buildup by the West is needed. One concession (to be elaborated in the next chapter, on "Soviet Power") is that the overall strength of the USSR, considering conventional as well as nuclear strength, is now in all probability somewhat greater than that of the United States. The other is that their strength is much greater than they actually need for defense.

Stated most simply, the reason for regarding their overall strength as greater is that, while in nuclear arms the present situation is a controversial, ambiguous standoff, there is a clear and general consensus that in conventional arms the USSR is at least somewhat stronger.

In strategic nuclear weapons the two superpowers are close enough together so that the question of which is ahead is almost meaningless, because each has much more than enough to deter the other from starting a nuclear exchange if the other has any rationality left (see Chapter 3). Either side could cut back to a fraction of its present nuclear strength, unilaterally if necessary, and still—*if* it preserved a potent second-strike capability in the form of nuclear-armed submarines and a few good bombers—be almost as effective in deterring a nuclear attack by the other side as it is now. There would still be "strategic stability."

In conventional arms, which represent a much more probable type of war, the picture is quite different. In that context superiority and inferiority still mean something, and the Soviet Union's conventional land forces—troops, tanks, artillery, tactical air support, and logistic advantages if the war were fought close to the USSR—are far superior to those of the United States and have been, probably, since 1946. Naval forces, in which the United States is clearly superior, would be somewhat irrelevant if the war were fought on land. The USSR's conventional forces are completely adequate to defend the USSR if a conventional war were to be fought, in self-defense, on Soviet territory or in Eastern Europe. They are probably adequate to achieve a Soviet victory in a conventional war of offense in Western Europe, even against the relevant European NATO countries, the United States, and France. They are probably enough to win a conventional war of offense against China, even if supported by the United States and Japan. And they are almost certainly enough to win a quick decisive victory in a conventional war of offense in the Middle East against any combination of probable opponents.

That brings up the critically important question of probable allies of the United States. Georgy Arbatov, director of the Institute of U.S.A. and Canadian Studies in Moscow and presumably a key adviser to President Andropov, stresses this factor more than any other. According to him the "allegations" of American hard-liners with regard to Soviet superiority are "fantastic." They are the "biggest lie" of our time, chiefly because they ignore

> . . . some major politicogeographic realities, the most important of them being the fact that the Soviet Union under present circumstances has to regard as its potential adversaries not only the United States but also the NATO allies of the United States, Japan and China. As soon as one includes this factor in the equation, the picture becomes radically different. . . . According to the annual publication of the International Institute of Strategic Studies in London, *The Military Balance, 1981-82* . . ., the ratio of the Warsaw Treaty Organization and the NATO budgets is 1:1.5 in favor of NATO ($164.7 billion to $241 billion, correspondingly). If one brings Japan and China into the picture the correlation will be at least 1:2. Similar gaps in the numbers of troops, nuclear warheads and naval vessels are even bigger.

This lie is also "the most dangerous lie of our time . . ., for at present it is virtually the only rationale for the arms race" (Arbatov, 1982, pp. 179–80).

Let us leave aside for the moment the question of the accuracy of Arbatov's figures,[3] his undoubted role as a propagandist, and his probable tendency to worst-case thinking (comparable to that of many of our own military thinkers). The present point is that he ignores the extreme improbability that all of the Soviet Union's "potential adversaries" might unite in an attack on the USSR, or even in defense of each other. If the war were in Western Europe it seems extremely doubtful that China or Japan would fight; if it were in the Far East it seems very doubtful that the West European NATO countries or France would fight; and if it were in the Middle East it is doubtful that distant countries at either end of the enormous Eurasian continent would join in. The United States and Israel would probably be left to fight more or less alone, against the overwhelming superiority of the Soviet Union's troops, tanks, artillery, and logistic advantages, and— unless Moslem hostility due to America's position on the Arab-

[3]Comparisons of Soviet and Western spending figures are especially tricky and difficult and are not relied on in this discussion at all. See especially Cox (1982, pp. 103–8) and Stubbing (1982).

Israeli conflict were by then drastically reduced—probably without effective help from either Arabs or Iranians. If the United States in desperation were to resort to battlefield nuclear weapons, the Soviet Union would do the same, and the outcome, in military terms, would not be different.

Speaking geopolitically, the USSR does have the great advantage, in a conventional war, of its central position in the great Eurasian continent. On the offensive it could choose any one of the three great theaters of war and expect to face only some of the countries Arbatov calls ''potential adversaries.''

Arbatov has a point, however. The arms of America's NATO allies in Western Europe (plus France, which would presumably fight if Western Europe were invaded) should be included in any consideration of the Soviet Union's incentive to attack Western Europe. Along with the various other considerations that would discourage such an attack (see Chapter 4), and the probable full participation of the United States—which, as seen by the Soviets, could include first use of nuclear weapons even if we said we would not do it—there are many reasons to think the Soviet rulers are already adequately deterred from attacking Western Europe. Similarly, the formidable *defensive* strength of a combination of China, Japan, and the United States probably makes deterrence more than adequate in the Far East. It is only in the Middle East that the conventional superiority of the USSR seems decisively important (see Chapter 4).

A second concession is that present Soviet strength is probably much greater than the USSR actually needs for defense. If the West is fully deterred from a nuclear first strike and the USSR's conventional strength is greater than the West's or China's, is anything more needed for genuine Soviet self-defense? From our point of view certainly not, especially if we assume, as military men traditionally do, that in conventional warfare, other things being equal, the defense has a distinct advantage over the offense, usually estimated as at least 1.5:1 (e.g. Schlesinger, paraphrased by Blaker and Hamilton, 1982, p. 343). With its huge, well-trained army *and* the advantage of the defense in a conventional war, the USSR looks unquestionably safe—from our point of view.

Whether it looks equally safe from a Soviet point of view is a quite different question. At this point a real and sustained effort of empathy on our part is needed. Everything that has been said earlier in this chapter about the Soviets' underlying insecurity and their probable defensive reasons for intervening in Afghanistan is relevant here, including their conception of centuries of previous history in which Russia has been invaded from the east or from the west, and the testimony of such competent observers as George Kennan, Robert C. Tucker, Adam Ulam, Robert Kaiser, Craig Whitney, Jerry Hough, and Strobe Talbott. Robert Kaiser's reference to a "siege mentality which has infected the leaders of Soviet society since its birth in 1917" is corroborated by Helmut Sonnenfeldt and William Hyland (1979, p. 9), two Soviet specialists on whose expertise Henry Kissinger relied. It is noteworthy that the geopolitical perspective which makes the situation look especially dangerous from a Western point of view, if Soviet aggressiveness is assumed, looks equally dangerous from a Soviet point of view if Western-plus-Chinese aggressiveness is assumed. Strobe Talbott's comment bears repetition: "What the United States sees—and seeks—as 'containment' of Soviet power, the Kremlin sees and fears as 'encirclement' by its enemies. That fear has driven Soviet foreign policy since 1917" (1980, p. 18).

Long-term fear, then—fear of a future imbalance of power in which their encircling enemies could gain the power to overwhelm them—appears to be the primary reason for the Soviet strategic arms buildup. That is psychologically understandable. They have only about 6 percent of the world's population; they look out on a world in which most of the others have probably seemed to be basically, increasingly, and mysteriously hostile. Understandably, the Soviet decision-makers and public alike have probably had a feeling, not wholly unlike paranoia, that they had to fall back on their own strength in order to deter a concerted attack.

Within this picture of encircling enemies two countries have probably stood out in their minds. One has been the great economic and technological giant, the United States, whose technology they have always envied and emulated, which had a gross national product nearly twice their own, which had strong allies in Western Europe that were similarly economically advanced, which had a recent history of repeated major breakthroughs in the unthinkably terrifying weapons of modern warfare, and whose capitalist-and-militarist "ruling circles" were, according to their Marxist-Leninist ideology, inevitably aggressively hostile to the camp of "socialism." The other has been China, with a population more than three times their own, covetously (as they see it) eying the thinly populated eastern two-thirds of the USSR, ready to overflow into it as soon as China becomes strong enough to do so, industrious, bursting with disciplined energy, and quite capable of making good use of America's weapons and technology if the already budding collusion of the two nations were some day to reach fruition. Throw in Western Europe and a Japan that could again become militarized and aggressive, and the combination could indeed look fearsome.

A second motive behind their arms buildup, probably less important than fear but still important, has probably been the macho kind of pride—the kind of pride that has caused a great many Americans to insist that their own country must remain "number one" in the world, or "second to none."[4] One of the chief findings in the historical parts of this book (see Chapter 9) is that pride, especially wounded pride and fear of humiliation, is one of the two major, often not enough recognized, motives in international affairs, the other being fear. The Soviet Union is a prime example.

For instance, few Americans have empathized adequately with the kind of humiliation the Soviets must have felt at the time of the Cuban missile crisis. From their point of view there were at least two good reasons for placing missiles in Cuba. One, almost totally unknown even now to most of the American public (but see Lebow, 1981, pp. 64–65, and Hilsman, 1967, p. 164), is that from a Soviet standpoint the danger of an American nuclear first strike capability had suddenly become acute. They had just learned that expert satellite reconnaissance had enabled the United States to plot the exact locations of their ICBMs in the USSR, thereby almost eliminating the deterrent value of those ICBMs as second-strike weapons. If we put ourselves in the Soviet decision-makers' shoes and take into account their fears of America's hostile intentions, we can imagine how disturbing

---

[4]A Gallup Poll covering a national sample of Americans, conducted for Potomac Associates in 1976 (Watts and Free, 1976), provides a striking example of the macho spirit in the United States. The statement presented was: "The United States should maintain its dominant position as the world's most powerful nation at all costs, even going to the very brink of war if necessary." 52 percent agreed and only 41 percent disagreed. Other poll data (Yankelovich and Kaagan, 1981) suggest that the agreement would be even larger if the question were repeated now. See Chapter 9.

such a loss of deterrent power must have been. Intermediate-range missiles in Cuba must have seemed a promising way to restore, at least partially, their lost deterrent strength.

Another reason for putting in the missiles, in all probability, was a desire to deter the United States from again attacking the USSR's little protégé, Castro's Cuba, as it had done in effect in the Bay of Pigs episode a year and a half earlier. The desire to protect a protégé is something we Americans should understand, since we ourselves have felt it many times. We should find it easy to remember how we have felt about the small, faraway endangered countries we have aspired to protect, most notably South Korea, South Vietnam, and Israel. We should therefore find it easy to empathize with the Soviet decision-makers' feeling of humiliation when, to avoid a war on the other side of the ocean, they knuckled under to President Kennedy's threat—a type of threat that they had not resorted to when the United States installed similar weapons in various places around the Soviet periphery, including some in Turkey, which is closer to the border of the USSR than Cuba is to the border of the United States.

America's successful exclusion of them from the peacemaking process between Israel and the Arab states in the Middle East, which is on their doorstep and not on ours, must have been similarly humiliating.

That is not at all to say that a generous impulse to protect beleaguered little countries has been the mainspring of their actions either in Latin America or in the Middle East, though some of them may have imagined that it was. The desire to restore the strategic balance (which also served their pride) was probably a far more potent motive, and the desire to give Cuba protection was probably, to a large extent, a rationalization of their prideful desire to maintain, even as far away as the Western Hemisphere, a symbol of their own new status as a world power. But their sense of moral rightness in helping a small country defend itself against a big ''imperialist'' one must have added to their feeling of humiliation when they had to knuckle under to the big one.

Their sense of moral rightness should not be underestimated as a part of the total psychological pattern behind Soviet behavior in the Third World as a whole. Apparently they do believe, however mistakenly, that their competition with the West throughout the Third World is essentially on the side of economic underdogs and against the exploitation of those underdogs by American "economic imperialism." We have a right to suspect that such thoughts in their minds are mainly a rationalization of the macho type of pride, as they have a right to suspect that our talk about "defending the Free World," when we help right-wing dictators and oligarchies in South Korea, South Vietnam, Iran, or El Salvador, is mainly a rationalization of our macho pride in being and remaining "number one." Genuine idealism is probably as minor a factor in them as it is in us, or more so. It does not take much empathy, though, to recognize that if a person or nation knuckles under to what it perceives as intimidation by an opponent, while doing something that *feels* morally justified or even noble, the wound to pride can be deep. The fact that the big Soviet arms buildup began shortly after the Cuban missile crisis lends support to that interpretation.

In summary, the two major motives behind the Soviet military buildup have probably been a long-term fear of being eventually attacked by a coalition of strong enemies (unless those enemies continue to be deterred by Soviet strength), and a desire for at least equality with the United States in power and prestige—a motive that is here called macho pride.

Those may well be essentially the same as the major motives behind our own long strategic buildup.

(An additional Soviet motive could be a hope of eventual world-domination, but at most that is probably a far-off hope and a minor motive, for reasons that will be discussed at the end of Chapter 4.)

The Shooting Down of the Korean Airliner

The wave of intense anger that followed the Soviet shooting down of the Korean passenger plane in September 1983 has apparently set back, by months if not years, the previous movement in the West toward a reasonable, realistic accommodation with the USSR.

It should have had the opposite effect. It was a particularly clear example of the critically important role of fear in Soviet minds—party irrational, obsessive fear, of course, but still fear. If there had been any sizable amount of realistic empathy in the minds of the majority in the West it would have increased our desire to diminish the unhealthy kind of Soviet fear of us. Instead it evidently solidified our Bad Guy image of them and made us more inclined to frighten them still further by deploying our most deadly first-strike weapons. As the columnist Ellen Goodman put it, "We surely can't cure paranoia by making the victim more afraid" (1983, p. A21).

One step toward realism was provided by those Western commentators who used terms like paranoia to describe the long-standing, well-known Soviet obsession with secrecy and security. *Time* attributed the tragedy to a mixture of paranoia and bureaucratic rigidity. *Newsweek* attributed it to "a Soviet obsession with secrecy and deep-seated paranoia about borders." The simple little word "fear," which leaves open the question of how rational or irrational the fear is, would have been better. The trouble with applying psychiatric terms such as paranoia to a nation is that in the minds of the general public the connotations of outright insanity in such words are so strong that attempts at reasonable communication and persuasion seem doomed from the outset. The label "madman" precludes empathy and communication, almost as surely as the label "criminal" or "aggressor."

In this case what would realistic empathy consist of?

It could begin with recognition of the background reasons for fear that have been mentioned in this chapter and will be more adequately discussed in later chapters: Russia's history of being invaded many times, the terrible trauma of World War II, the partly genuine encirclement of the USSR by an intensely hostile China and a somewhat hostile West Europe as well as the by now intensely hostile United States, the baffling fact (from a Soviet standpoint) that the hostility of the United States since 1975 increased greatly even before Afghanistan and long before the plane incident. All of these have undoubtedly been misunderstood by the Soviet people and their government, and most of them have been exaggerated for psychological reasons that remain to be discussed, but that does not make the fear they have generated less real.

Empathy might then continue with specific recognition of three events in the field of air reconnaissance that the Soviet military must be much more aware of than most of us are: (1) At the outset of World War II the Nazi bombers destroyed about half of the Soviet air force on the ground, partly because of the efficiency of previous Nazi air reconnaissance; and (2) the downing of America's U-2 spy plane over central Russia in 1960 was not a single isolated incident. For four long years, 1956–60, the U-2 planes had been flying over the USSR and taking pictures, while the Soviets were unable to shoot them down. During those years the informed Soviet military men must have been seething with helpless chagrin at their inability to prevent such reconnaissance or to retaliate in kind. It was fortunate for American intelligence that the ending of the U-2 flights after the 1960 incident was quickly followed by satellite reconnaissance of comparable or greater effectiveness. This experience alone must have convinced the Soviet government that American intelligence is determined to discover as many Soviet military secrets as possible, and probably able, with its general technological superiority, to do so with frightening effectiveness. (3) The fact that another Korean plane in 1978 was able to "wander" a thousand miles into Soviet territory before being brought down was another humiliating experience that must have led to heightened suspicion of Korean planes and to an intensified policy of vigilance on the Soviet side.

How many Americans, even among those who once knew about the four-year history of U-2 flights, remembered it and thought about its relevance to their evaluation of the shooting down of the Korean airliner? Realistic empathy calls for conscious effort, and on both sides of the conflict such effort appears to be woefully lacking.

CHAPTER THREE

Soviet Power

Are They Ahead?

"Which side is ahead?" is not necessarily the fundamental question that the great majority on each side assumes it to be. The question as stated implies an assumption that is probably quite false: that the Bad Guys might deliberately resort to war, perhaps even nuclear war, if they felt themselves to be even somewhat stronger than the Good Guys. That is psychologically unrealistic in our nuclear era. When applied to questions of strategic strength it ignores the intense fear of any big war, especially nuclear war, now present on each side, and the likelihood that even a small nuclear force, if it was fairly invulnerable, would be enough to deter any rational opponent from a nuclear first strike.

Nevertheless, since a large majority of the people and their leaders on each side do assume that the Bad Guys are power-mad enough to risk annihilation once they feel strong enough to "win," it behooves peace activists to be familiar enough with the complexities and ambiguities of the power balance to discuss that subject with intelligence and realism. If they cannot, the maximal deterrers will simply stop listening.

A simple list of probable advantages and disadvantages on either side may be enough to bring out both the complexity and the ambiguity of the problem.[1]

SOVIET ADVANTAGES	WESTERN ADVANTAGES
In Nuclear War	
Great superiority in long-range theater nuclear forces (LRTNF) in Europe (SS-4s, SS-5s, SS-20s)	More warheads—the best single indicator of nuclear strength

[1]The evidence on which the list is based is derived mainly from the authoritative International Institute of Strategic Studies in London (1982), Anthony Cordesman (1982), Arthur Cox (1982, pp. 94–119), and various articles in Reichart and Sturm (1982).

SOVIET ADVANTAGES	WESTERN ADVANTAGES
Superiority in ICBM (SS-18 and SS-19 vs. Minuteman) launchers	Innovations: Pershing II, cruise missiles, D5 coming
Bombers and missiles, other than ICBMs, having longer range	More warheads *even after a Soviet first strike* and Western retaliation (Cordesman, 1982, p. 49)
Harder silos	Many more bombers
Better defense (surface-to-air missiles, radar, ABM)	Less vulnerable because more missiles in submarines
Advantage of first strike (including surprise) if willing to strike first; Steinbruner's (1981–82) ''nuclear decapitation''	Better electronic technology (computers, satellites, communication)
	Advantage of first strike if willing to do it; ''decapitation''

In Conventional War

	Reasons to expect Communist defeat or disastrous stalemate in any long war:
Great superiority in troops, tanks and artillery	
Western Europe held hostage by threat of conventional attack, with Soviet nuclear superiority in that theater (SS-20s) held in reserve to deter Western first use	USSR has only about 6% of world's population; other 94% mainly anti-Soviet, including China and almost all the more advanced countries
Geopolitical advantage: no comparably strong nations on periphery of Eurasian heartland; ability to attack them one theater at a time	West far ahead in overall economic, scientific, and technological strength
Decisive superiority in Middle East; enormous logistic problems there for the West	Geopolitical advantage: U.S., relatively invulnerable, can again be arsenal of democracy; naval superiority
Anti-imperialist feeling in Third World (especially Arabs and Iranians)	Fading of Communist ideology nearly everywhere, including USSR
Dedicated Communist cadres in some Third World countries (e.g. Vietnam, Cuba, Nicaragua); no Western counterpart	Reasons to expect high Soviet cost, if Western Europe (or China) is attacked, even if victory came fairly soon:

SOVIET ADVANTAGES	WESTERN ADVANTAGES
	Quality of Western weapons, including antitank weapons
	Quality of West German army
	Unreliability of East European troops
	General advantage (3 to 1? 1.5 to 1?) of defense over offense after first phase of conventional war

What is striking about this picture is its complexity (such a brief list does scant justice to its real complexity) and the number of intangible, unmeasurable factors it contains. Objectively speaking it is inconclusive. An honest, evidence-oriented person on either side, if he considered all these factors, would necessarily admit that he does not really know which side is ahead in the overall picture, though he might draw some more limited inferences, e.g. that the Soviet Union would undoubtedly be stronger in a purely conventional war fought in the Middle East, and that in other respects the two sides seem about equal (see also Chapter 2).

On the other hand, the list provides enough to fill with undue confidence anyone on either side who focused only or mainly on the factors favorable to his own side and to fill with undue alarm anyone who focused only or mainly on the factors favorable to the other side. Wishful thinking and worst-case thinking would distort the picture in opposite directions. Perhaps fortunately, worst-case thinking seems to predominate among the best-informed military men on both sides. Unfortunately, however, the effect of such worst-case thinking on the arms race can only be to accelerate it. For example, if Ronald Reagan's attention is focused mainly on the genuine Soviet advantages and if he means it when he describes the men in the Kremlin as power-mad Bad Guys and nothing else, he would certainly—and logically—conclude that it is imperative to arm just as strenuously as the state of the American economy permits. A Soviet decision-maker focusing mainly on the genuine Western advantages would necessarily be prompted to do likewise. With enough selective attention and inattention, diametrically opposite evaluations could easily be arrived at.

That is what seems to be happening now.

However, for all the dimness in the prospects for stopping or reversing the arms race, there is a bright side to the picture. Isn't it likely that the same worst-case thinking would powerfully deter both sides from deliberately starting either a nuclear or a conventional war? Isn't it likely that the deterrence each side is now so strenuously and expensively trying to create in the minds of its opponents already exists—to the extent that they are rational?

That brings up another key question.

Do the Soviet Decision-makers Think They Are Ahead?

Most of the evidence suggests that the men in the Kremlin do not think they are leading in the arms race. Worst-case thinking, rather than wishful thinking, apparently predominates in their minds, as it does in ours.

How can we tell what is going on in their minds? It goes without saying that we must look with the greatest skepticism at their words, especially when we know those words are intended for our eyes or ears. It goes without saying also that the official Communist line sets limits to what any Russian dares to say, especially in public. A propagandist is a propagandist. That includes even such an outstandingly intelligent and well-informed person as Georgy Arbatov, director of the Institute for U.S.A. and Canada Studies in Moscow.

There is nevertheless good reason to listen to such a person. A propagandist does not always lie. Seasoned propagandists know that credibility is a major asset, and as a rule they do not squander it unnecessarily (White, 1971, pp. 28–29; 1970, pp. 104–6). Certain checks also can and should be made: If we try to put ourselves in his shoes, is it plausible that he might really believe most if not all of what he says? Which parts of what he says is it plausible to think he may really believe? Do his countrymen say much the same thing when (as in the case of Soviet military men writing in Russian for other Soviet military men) their words are not intended primarily for foreign consumption? Most important, are his actions, or those of his country, consistent with his words?

Let us listen again to what Georgy Arbatov has to say on comparative military force and apply those checks. He has already been quoted at some length in Chapter 2. The nub of what he said is represented by these words: The "lie" of Soviet military superiority ignores

> . . . some major politicogeographic realities, the most impor-
> tant of them being the fact that the Soviet Union under present
> circumstances has to regard as its potential adversaries not only
> the United States but also the NATO allies of the United States,
> China and Japan. As soon as one includes this factor in the
> equation the picture becomes radically different. . . . The ratio
> of the Warsaw Treaty Organization and the NATO budgets is
> 1:1.5 in favor of NATO. If one brings Japan and China into the
> picture the correlation will be at least 1:2. [1982, pp. 179–80].

As might be expected of a seasoned propagandist writing for intelligent readers, Arbatov's tangible facts are essentially correct. He has quoted a highly respected Western source, the International Institute of Strategic Studies in London. As usual, the problem lies in his interpretation of those facts. Is it plausible that he really believes, and that the real Soviet decision-makers such as Yuri Andropov really believe, that Soviet military spending should be compared with that of the entire lineup of "potential adversaries," including both China and Japan? It is. Though that lineup is not familiar to Western minds, it is undoubtedly familiar to Soviet minds. It is consistent with what many Western observers in Moscow have called the "almost paranoid" feeling of Russians about Communist China. It is also reminiscent of the Russian "siege mentality" stressed by Robert Kaiser, the Soviet "sense of isolation" mentioned by Craig Whitney, and the fear of "encirclement" referred to by Strobe Talbott and Bruce Nelan (see Chapter 2)—all of them Americans intimately familiar with the Moscow scene. On this particular point Mr. Arbatov passes the test.

Do Soviet military men say similar things when writing in Russian for each other? Apparently they do. On the general point of whether they see themselves as militarily superior to their collective adversaries, their picture resembles Arbatov's. At least one respected American scholar who has thoroughly studied the Russian sources, Raymond Garthoff, has said that in his view the Soviet military men do not think they now surpass the West in strength; they think they have achieved a rough equality, but see it as precarious and probably temporary.[2] This is a crucial point. If we are talking about whether they are already confident that they could win a war or are already deterred by the thought that the West is too strong to be deliberately attacked, what matters is not the actual military balance but what they think it is.

Now our most important check: Are their actions consistent with their words? As of now the answer is clearly, ''Yes.'' Afghanistan is a possible exception, in spite of the reasons for thinking that its primary motivation was defensive (Chapter 2). Apart from their intervention in Afghanistan, however, their behavior since Stalin died in 1953 has been on the whole remarkably cautious. Their brutal crackdowns on Hungary and Czechoslovakia were from their point of view a matter of keeping what they already had rather than reaching out for new territory. They backed down on Berlin and Cuba. They have never used their own troops on any large scale in faraway places, as the United States has in Korea and Vietnam. That is not a tribute to their virtue. It is a tribute to their caution, which is consistent with a belief, up to now, that what they call the ''correlation of forces'' has not been clearly in their favor. Perhaps their perception is now changing; their behavior in the past is not conclusive evidence that they do not now feel stronger or will not in the next few years. What can be said now, therefore, is only that their behavior up to now *has not been inconsistent* with their words on this question.

The proposition stands: In all probability the Soviet decision-makers do not think they are decisively ahead or will be in the foreseeable future—except in the Middle East.

---

[2]Statement at a colloquium of the Institute for Sino-Soviet Studies in Washington, 1981. Cf. Garthoff (1978): ''The Soviet leadership accepts a strategic nuclear balance as a fact, and as the probable and desirable prospect for the foreseeable future.''

CHAPTER FOUR

Soviet Intentions

Their Great Fear: Another Big War

In Soviet minds there is an overwhelming emotional reason not to take any serious risk of starting a big war: the trauma of the Soviet experience in World War II.

The revulsion of Americans against war is great, but the revulsion of the Soviet peoples (and in all probability their government) is almost certainly greater. We sometimes forget: The United States in World War II lost a mere 300,000 lives on all fronts. The Soviet Union lost some 20 *million*. The war's devastation never touched our American homeland. It destroyed an enormous amount of the Soviet Union. The searing experience of the Soviet people in that war is a fact of which most of us are aware, but we often forget it when thinking of Soviet attitudes toward future wars. The Soviets do not forget it. One Western visitor (a guide at the major U.S. commercial exhibit in Moscow in 1959, at which there was a great deal of conversation between the guides and the Soviet people who attended) gave this account:

> They are not allowed to forget *their* war for a day. Their suffering was terrible. Perhaps they could not forget it even if allowed, but officially it is enforced so much that even the young, who didn't know it [at the time], are tremendously and emotionally aware of it. . . . Often it is strict party-line propaganda even to the words used, but very often it is fervently believed. There were many, many tearful eyes when this subject came up. (Private communication)

The men in the government suffered too; Khrushchev's son, for instance, was killed in the war.

That scarcely describes a country that would deliberately embark on another big war. For the most convincing of all reasons—self-preservation—it would seem that the Soviet Union wants peace.

The rest of this chapter will examine six possible Soviet intentions in the field of foreign policy, all of them aggressively warlike. In thinking about each one, this emotional background factor should be kept continually in mind.

A Nuclear First Strike?

Knowing, or at least believing, that we ourselves could never be the ones to let the nuclear genie out of the bottle, many of us have vaguely assumed that if either side were to precipitate the ultimate nightmare it would have to be the other side. That assumption is dubious on several grounds.

It is true that some considerations count on the side of that expectation. To begin with, let us distinguish two ways in which it could conceivably happen: (1) a nuclear first strike against the United States or (2) a first strike against Western Europe, along with an invasion of Western Europe and an explicit warning to the United States that any nuclear weapons launched on its part will bring total devastation upon itself.

The second option would be the more rational in four ways. It would be the only plausible way to neutralize the immense retaliatory power of the United States—immense even if it consisted only of a few surviving nuclear-armed submarines—and save the USSR from unthinkable devastation. They could believe that it would achieve almost immediately the geopolitical objective of adding Western Europe to the Soviet power sphere and giving the USSR decisive superiority in the world balance of power. They could believe that it would eliminate the fearsome land-based first-strike weapons, especially the quick-striking Pershing II, which by then would probably be present in large numbers in Western Europe. And finally, with the Kremlin's considerable superiority in conventional forces, now designed mainly for offensive action in the West, and its probable continuing superiority in theater nuclear forces, the Soviet decision-makers might hope to reach their objectives quickly. They could conceivably see in the taking of Western Europe a quick checkmate of the capitalist West.

If in some future crisis, possibly arising in the Middle East, the Soviet rulers were to become so afraid of a Western first strike that this strategy seemed to them the only alternative to annihilation, they might have an adequate incentive to do it, even with their horror of war, and even without being at all sure it would succeed.

(Note: we are now engaged in the chessplayer's type of empathy, which consists of an intellectual attempt to anticipate what the opponent might rationally do, purely in his own self-interest, in an attempt to capture one's own king while not greatly endangering his own. The Russians are good chessplayers. Along with understanding of an opponent's more human emotions, the chessplayer's type of understanding is essential.)

The other form of attack, a nuclear first strike directly on the United States, would be more reckless and much less rational. It would call forth enormous anger in the United States, far more than Pearl Harbor did, and an immediate unleashing of all the retaliatory power that America still possessed. It would be, and the Kremlin should expect it to be, literal mutual suicide.

How plausible is either of these scenarios?

Not plausible at all, *unless* the United States persists in emphasizing a destabilizing first-strike capability and continues its present dangerous policies in the Third World, especially the Middle East. That is precisely the chemical combination that could produce the great explosion, for it could give the Soviet decision-makers the feeling—mistaken but intense—that they must strike first or be annihilated.

Lacking such a feeling, the Soviet dread of war as such, especially nuclear war, would almost certainly prevail. For one thing, the horrors of World War II are still vivid in the decision-makers' minds. For another, their public statements are full of the dread of war. We should not forget that a propagandist is likely to become convinced by his own propaganda, especially if he starts out believing most of it (Janis and King, 1954). Witness:

Nikita Khrushchev: "In our time only a madman can start a war, and he himself will perish in its flames" (1960, p. xxxi).

Leonid Brezhnev: "Anyone who starts a nuclear war in the hope of winning it has thereby decided to commit suicide" (quoted by Gottlieb, 1982, p. 13).

Marshal Nikolai Ogarkov, chief of the Soviet General Staff: "In terms of the ferocity and the scale of mutual destruction [nuclear war] could be compared with no wars of the past. The very nature of modern weapons is such that, if they were put into play, the future of all mankind could be at stake" (*ibid.*).

Additional examples abound (see Cox, 1982, pp. 116–17). Western visitors to the Soviet Union testify that their private utterances show the same dread of war.

The Soviet government in October 1982 permitted a nationwide telecast of a panel of three American and three Soviet physicians, elaborating on the medical aspects of a nuclear disaster, organized by International Physicians for the Prevention of Nuclear War. They have faced those facts no less than we.

The second-strike capability of the United States, plus that of Britain and France, is now so great that it probably could be drastically and unilaterally cut back without losing its deterrent power. According to Bundy, Kennan, McNamara, and Smith (1982),

> What would be needed under no-first-use is a set of capabilities we already have *in overflowing measure*—capabilities for appropriate retaliation to any kind of Soviet nuclear attack which would leave the Soviet Union in no doubt that it too should adhere to a policy of no-first-use. The Soviet government is already aware of the awful risk inherent in any use of these weapons, and there is no current or prospective Soviet "superiority" that would tempt anyone in Moscow toward nuclear adventurism. (All four of us are wholly unpersuaded by the argument advanced in recent years that the Soviet Union would ever rationally expect to gain from such a wild effort as a massive first strike on land-based American strategic missiles). [p. 764; italics added; cf. Maxwell Taylor, 1981; McNamara, 1983]

A Conventional Invasion of Western Europe?

There are some reasons to think the Soviet Union might be tempted to invade Western Europe. Its conventional forces are now deployed as if in preparation for invasion, with their SS-20s pointed at Western Europe. The geopolitical importance of Western Europe could be described as a queen plus a rook or two in the great chess game. The Soviet hierarchy's traditional fear of a repetition of Hitler's onslaught by a combination of a newly aggressive America and a newly aggressive West Germany and their habit of focusing mainly on the West, especially Germany, when thinking of ultimate questions of power and security—facing west, so to speak, more than south or east—might make such a plan credible. Their present respect for the quality of the West German Army, in addition to being a deterrent, could give them an incentive to eliminate it if possible. A strategy that would seem more rational than a combined nuclear and conventional attack is a purely conventional attack with an explicit threat that if either Western Europe or the United States were to fire a single nuclear weapon Western Europe would be demolished by the SS-20s.

There are at least six cogent reasons, however, to believe that the Russians would not even seriously consider such an adventure, except perhaps in a crisis in which it seemed the only alternative to annihilation.

1. As we have pointed out before, they have an intense revulsion from any big war. It would surely be a big and costly war even if it remained conventional and they won it. Even the present level of conventional strength in Western Europe should be enough to ensure a big and costly war, though not a Western victory, if all the relevant factors are taken into account, including those mentioned in Chapter 3: the near-certainty of ultimate Soviet defeat if it should become a long war; the quality of Western weapons, including antitank weapons (and secret weapons they might reasonably suspect the West of having developed); the quality of the West German Army; the unreliability of East European troops; the real or imagined danger of a Chinese attack while the USSR was preoccupied in the West; the general advantage (3 to 1? 1.5 to 1?) of the defense over the offense after the first phase of a conventional war; logistic difficulties, including long lines of supply and communication going through disaffected East European countries and therefore vulnerable to sabotage; the near certainty that France would join the ranks of the NATO countries in self-defense if there were an actual invasion of Western Europe (Blaker and Hamilton, 1977; Cox, 1982, pp. 107–10).

2. They probably have a strong (and possibly realistic) suspicion that the United States or others might be mad enough to resort to first use of nuclear weapons if actually invaded (Cox, 1982, p. 107; M. Taylor, 1981).

The fact that battlefield nuclear weapons are now deployed in Western Europe and that NATO doctrine (amazingly) up to now has been to use them in case of an initially successful Soviet attack, even if the other side does not, would give much ground for that suspicion. From the Soviet military point of view, even more than from our own, that is a crazy idea. Soviet military writers deny the possibility of limited nuclear war and tend to take an all-or-none position; they say that if the West crosses the great divide between conventional and nuclear weapons, the Soviet Union should and will go all-out with its great nuclear destructive power (Cox, 1982, p. 117). Having committed themselves to that extent, they must be hoping against hope that no madman in the West will cross the line and force them to go all-out in mutual self-destruction. Their ideology tells them, though, that they must not trust us to be sane. It tells them that in its dying throes capitalism would lash out blindly in suicidal rage. In its current version it also tells them that one faction within the "ruling circles" of the West does consist of political "madmen" whose insensate hostility to socialism could lead them even to nuclear war rather than see the game won by the socialist camp (Khrushchev, 1960, pp. xx, xxxi).

That suspicion is fortunate for us, however mistaken it may be. It probably adds much to the many other factors deterring them from an invasion. And, fortunately, it would probably not be much diminished even if we were to proclaim a no-first-use policy, explicitly including no first use of battlefield nuclear weapons. It would be lucky for us if they refused to take our words at face value and, with their semiparanoid thinking, suspected a dark plot to lull them into a false sense of security so that we could, in case of war, catch them off guard. We could then have our cake and eat it too: the self-saving and world-saving value of an actual no-first-use policy and the deterrent value of a suspected first-use policy. (We could of course still *deploy* battlefield weapons, saying—and meaning it—that we would never use them unless the other side did so first.)

3. In their desire to expand their influence (which does not necessarily imply military conquest or control) the Soviet decision-makers for many years have turned their attention much more to the Third World than to Europe or the United States. They have learned the hard way that Soviet-oriented revolutions in the democratic welfare states of the West just do not occur. The significant leftist revolutions of the postwar period have all occurred in the Third World (China, Vietnam, Cuba, Nicaragua), and all the recent direct or indirect military actions of the Soviet Union (Angola, Ethiopia, Cambodia, Afghanistan) have been

there also. Their attention has been turned in that direction roughly since the time of the Bandung Conference of 1954, and the turn is enshrined now in their doctrine ("wars of liberation") as well as in their practice.

4. They have learned from bitter experience, especially in Hungary, Czechoslovakia, Poland, and Afghanistan, about the economic and political costs of domination. Even semidomination, as in Cuba, South Yemen, and Vietnam, has cost them more rubles than they like to think about. Would they want, in West Germany, France, or Britain, a bigger Poland (Barnet, 1981a, p. 25)?

5. Things are going fairly well for them now in Western Europe without war, conquest, or threats of conquest. Their trade relations, represented for instance by the gas pipeline, are profitable to both sides, and they have recently learned how useful the economic gains of Western Europe can be in driving a wedge between it and the United States, if the United States tries to restrict them as it did in the pipeline transaction. They know that any serious threats of military conquest, in an attempt to "Finlandize" Western Europe more than its economic interests have already "Finlandized" it, could ruin all that and drive the West Europeans back into the arms of "American imperialism."

6. The old men in the Kremlin, including Yuri Andropov, are also cautious men (Burns, 1983, p. 28; M. Taylor, 1981), and have been at least since the death of Stalin, who in a different way was very cautious too, in 1953. They have shown it many times. The Soviet decision-makers backed down on Berlin and Cuba; they used force in Hungary and Czechoslovakia only to keep what they already had; they swallowed their pride when we mined the harbor of Haiphong; they backed down immediately after our SAC-alert threat in 1973; and even in Afghanistan they probably thought beforehand that they were taking very little risk. We Americans should be aware that during the period since World War II we have fought two full-fledged wars on faraway foreign soil, and while one of them, Korea, was unequivocally defensive the other one, Vietnam, was not. We sometimes forget that during the same period the Soviet decision-makers have never done so. Their caution—not their virtue—has made such actions seem too risky. At least when they do not feel decisively stronger, they play a surprisingly cautious game of chess. One observer has described the Soviet leadership as "highly risk-

averse'' in its global comportment (Lambeth, 1982, p. 194; cf. Cox, 1982, p. 108).

It should be pointed out that not one of these six reasons rests on any assumption of Soviet virtue, goodwill, or trustworthiness. Not one rests on the words they say about themselves or on any evidence of democracy inside the USSR. All six reasons are strictly matters of Soviet national self-interest, as we have reason to think that the Soviet interest is perceived by the men in the Kremlin (cf. Barnet, 1981a). They are chessplayers' reasons.

''Finlandizing'' Western Europe?

When those who believe the Soviet decision-makers have a fixed determination to dominate Western Europe are confronted with the question, ''Do you really think they would risk a big *war* in order to dominate all of Europe?'' they often retreat to the Finlandization thesis and say something like this: Oh no: that's unlikely. What is likely is that the *perception* of greatly preponderant Soviet power would be enough to intimidate a Western Europe that is already somewhat intimidated, since it is now largely deprived of the reassurance that the American nuclear umbrella once gave it. An even more intimidated Europe would be a Europe subservient to the USSR, at least in its foreign and defense policies, as Finland now is; and the world balance of power, now resting on an anti-Communist Western Europe as its decisive component, would tip decisively in the Soviet Union's favor. All of the Free World, including the United States, would then be in danger (Lellouche, 1981, p. 829; Scheer, 1982, pp. 11–14).

Without doubt the Soviet decision-makers want to influence Western Europe to loosen its ties with the United States, and without doubt their influence is greater now that the USSR looks strong than it would be if the USSR looked weak. But how much intimidation can they hope for? Finland itself is a thriving democratic country, fairly independent in domestic affairs in spite of being a next-door neighbor to the Soviet Union and therefore subject to the Soviet Union's obsessive desire for buffer territory along its borders. Western Europe is much farther away, and different in many ways. As we have seen, the hope of the Soviet decision-makers to dominate Western Europe is probably relatively weak compared with their desire for expanded influence in the

Third World. Most of Western Europe's leaders, unlike most of America's, appear to have had for many years some understanding of the reasons why the USSR would not want or need to attack them in cold blood. If in addition Western Europe had what it felt to be a reasonably adequate conventional defense, with continued American cooperation, it is probably quite unlikely to let itself be intimidated (Barnet, 1981b, p. C5; Jervis, 1982, p. 168).

An Invasion of the Middle East?

When the Soviet Union intervened in Afghanistan, at a time when the West's anxiety about its long-term access to Middle East oil was becoming more and more acute, a great many of us wondered whether this unprecedented Soviet move might be the first step in a calculated plan to seize the oilfields. Is it, we wondered, the beginning of an attempt to put a thumb on the economic jugular vein of Western Europe and Japan, if not also the United States?

Our anxiety diminished as we watched Soviet troops getting bogged down in Afghanistan and as our domestic economic troubles occupied more of our attention. Perhaps it should not have diminished. Anxiety about possible aggressive Soviet moves in the Middle East is probably more realistic than anxiety about such moves anywhere else in the world. The West has much at stake there, not only access to oil but also concern for the survival of Israel and fear of a major shift in the world balance of power if the Soviet Union were to dominate the entire Middle East.

It is true that the relevance of the Soviet intervention in Afghanistan to the other countries of the region is doubtful. If the argument in Chapter 2 is valid, that intervention was adequately explained by long-term defensive considerations, from the distorted Soviet point of view. It is a mistake also to regard it as necessarily unprecedented, since in Soviet eyes it probably was, like their crackdowns on Hungary and Czechoslovakia, more a matter of keeping what they already had than of reaching out for something new. Moreover, a look at the map of Iran raises doubts as to whether Afghanistan made any sense as a way-station on the path to the Persian Gulf oilfields of either Iran or the Arab states of Iraq, Kuwait, and Saudi Arabia. They are on the western edge of Iran, while Afghanistan is on its far eastern edge, with much mountainous country in between. If the Soviet Union were determined to seize the oilfields it could, with its enormously superior land forces, strike directly southward along a far shorter path, not through Afghanistan but through Iranian Azerbaijan.

The danger of a Soviet invasion of the Middle East is relatively serious primarily because of the nearness of the area to the Soviet border and the area's exceptional vulnerability.

The proximity is important for two reasons. First, logistic problems are easy for the Soviet army but would be extremely difficult for the American army. Second, Soviet behavior historically has shown a great desire for buffer territory on the Soviet border, with relatively little willingness to use Soviet troops in faraway places. The three places where Soviet troops have been used decisively since 1945 are Hungary, Czechoslovakia, and Afghanistan. All three have probably been perceived by the Kremlin as in the category of buffer territory. Iran, at least, and to some extent all of the Middle East down to Suez and the Persian Gulf, could also be seen as buffer territory, so close to the USSR as to constitute part of its natural defensive sphere, as Cuba and Mexico are part of that of the United States. In chess terms, they surround the king.

The vulnerability to invasion involves several things. The logistic inequality just mentioned is one of them. Another is the absence of natural barriers such as seas or mountains, from the Caucasus mountains to the Indian Ocean. Another is the probable susceptibility of a number of states to revolutions, which the Soviet Union could exploit, and the antagonism between states, epitomized by the Iran–Iraq war, which it could also exploit. Still another is the anti-Western feeling of the Islamic fundamentalists, epitomized by Khomeini's calling America the "great Satan" and among the Arabs stemming from America's policy in favor of Israel. The Turks do not necessarily play a large role here, because they could be circumvented by going through northwest Iran, but even they, formerly pro-American, are now decidedly alienated by what they regard as America's pro-Greek policy on Cyprus. The Turkish army, by the way, is the only one in the area except for Israel's that has really earned much respect from the Russians or anyone else. Compared with the USSR's the others must look weak.

It is no wonder that Paul Nitze, probably the most experienced and respected of the outstanding hard-liners in the United States, is on this issue anything but hard-line. His statement, quoted in Chapter 2, bears repetition:

> I see no prospect, at least until there has been a substantial improvement in the military balance, for the successful use of American military force in that area except in circumstances where a majority of Muslim states as well as Israel, our European allies, Japan and China join in resisting the expansionist pressure of the Soviet Union. [1980, pp. 98–99]

Those are stiff requirements.

In judging Soviet intentions, though, it is as necessary to consider why they might want *not* to do something as to consider why they might want to do it. There are three important reasons why they would want not to invade: the danger of an American nuclear response, as seen by them; the prospect of intense Moslem resistance to atheist Communism; and their basic desire for peace.

Henry Trofimenko, another student of American affairs in Arbatov's Institute of U.S.A. and Canada Studies, is respected enough in the United States to be published in *Foreign Affairs*. It is safe to assume, of course, that he is, like Arbatov, a propagandist for the Soviet Union whose statements do not necessarily reflect what he really thinks. His statement on this question nevertheless deserves consideration: "All those who might plan such a 'thrust' [into the Middle East] realize full well that it would certainly lead to rapid escalation of a Soviet-American conflict in that region to a nuclear level. The price of Arab oil thus obtained could bear no comparison with the price (consequences) of a strategic nuclear war for this oil" (1981, p. 1036).

The word "certainly" in this statement is disturbing. In effect he attributes to us with certainty a degree of insanity, in the form of willingness to unleash nuclear war, that we can only fervently hope our government does not have. One wonders why he thinks so, if he really does. Of course, one reason is our stated policy of possible first use in case of Soviet nonnuclear aggression, but surely he is not naive enough to take at face value everything we officially say or even the apparent implications of our deploying battlefield nuclear weapons. Another probable reason is the so-called Carter Doctrine, enthusiastically applauded by Congress when President Carter announced it, according to which we would use force if necessary to repel a foreign threat to the oilfields, even though the only significant force we could use in that area would be nuclear force. Bold words. And, in view of the near certainty that the Soviet Union would be able and willing to reply in kind, probably with great escalation, with no net effect on the outcome of the land battle, they are dangerous and perhaps suicidal words. Or Mr. Trofimenko may assume that our need for oil is so imperative, or our identification with Israel so strong and unchangeable, that we would even risk nuclear war (in which Israel too would probably be destroyed) because of them. In any case he could well be sincere in attributing such insanity to us, and if so the Soviets, from their own point of view, would have a potent reason not to invade.

An expectation of intense Moslem resistance to atheist Communism (the other great Satan in Khomeini's psychological world) is also probably a potent factor. The Russians have always been aware of Islamic hatred of Communism, and their recent bitter experience in trying to quell the anti-Communist rebellion in Afghanistan has undoubtedly intensified their awareness of it. Trofimenko again has something to say, and in this case it makes good sense: "No strategic military considerations can force the Soviet Union to extend its borders 1,000 kilometers southward to such a highly explosive region" (1981, p. 1036). The Iranian and Iraqi armies, now battle-hardened, could be very troublesome even though not dangerous from a Soviet viewpoint.

Still another potent factor we should never forget is the basic Soviet revulsion from war as such and probable conviction that war should always be avoided except when the necessity of it seems great and/or when the risk of it seems small, as in the cases of Hungary, Czechoslovakia, and Afghanistan. If they do have that basic orientation, not radically different from our own, it may be that they have always defined their goals in the Middle East, somewhat opportunistically, as the extension of their own influence and diminishing of America's, as circumstances permit, but always staying within the limits necessitated by avoiding any big war. They know they have little to fear from that quarter, they don't need oil yet, and therefore they probably have their attention focused far more on Europe and on China than on the Middle East. The basic diabolical image of the Soviet rulers in American minds, in thinking about their foreign as well as their domestic policies, may be basically mistaken as applied to their foreign policy. Perhaps they are not continually itching to put their thumbs on the jugular of the West, even when they think the risk in doing so is only moderate. Perhaps to them peace matters much more than expansion.

Then what is the upshot? How anxious should we be?

One answer is that we should pay close attention to the area, since our stakes in peace there are so great, but in doing so we should scrupulously avoid exaggerating the Soviet danger or engaging in actions that would increase their incentive to invade. As Nitze implied, our position of power, realistically considered, is so weak in the Middle East that every effort should be made to avoid overcommitment.

A New Aggressiveness in the Third World?

It is a striking fact that in recent years the chief instances of aggressive Soviet behavior, as seen by the West, outside the more or less recognized Soviet power sphere—in Angola, Ethiopia, Yemen, Cambodia, and Afghanistan—have all been in the less developed Third World countries. There is unquestionably a new activism of the USSR in the Third World.

Whether most of that behavior should be called outright aggression is debatable, and so is the question whether the USSR has been more aggressive than the United States during the period since the Korean war. The actions of the United States in a considerable number of countries—Korea, the Philippines, Vietnam, Cambodia, Laos, Iran, Iraq, Jordan, Somalia, Zaire, Brazil, Argentina, Chile, Venezuela, Nicaragua, El Salvador, Guatemala, Cuba, and the Dominican Republic—should be examined too, and judged by the same standard.

Our present purpose, though, is not to sit in judgment on the relative degrees of guilt, or of imperialism, in the two superpowers. It is to judge present Soviet motives and intentions in the Third World with as much realistic empathy as possible. In doing so it is only fair to consider the historical context of Soviet behavior in each separate instance, as we have done in the most conspicuous case of Soviet aggression in the Third World, Afghanistan. All too briefly, their contexts can be described in this way:

Angola. The Soviet rulers could see their intervention as justified by a desire to help the Angolan people defend themselves against an actual invasion by South Africa, aided by Zaïre and by the CIA. That invasion did occur.

Ethiopia. They could consider their siding with Ethiopia justified by Somalia's armed aggression in an attempt to seize the Ogaden province.

Yemen. They could see their aid to South Yemen as on a par with American aid to North Yemen.[1]

Cambodia. They could see their client state, Vietnam, as liberating the Cambodian people from the unspeakable wholesale cruelty of Pol Pot, in a manner strictly comparable to the liberation of the Ugandan people from Idi Amin, which received no condemnation in the United States.[2]

Afghanistan. As we have seen (Chapter 2), the Soviet behavior in Afghanistan could have seemed as legitimate to Moscow as our behavior in Vietnam seemed (in the earlier part of the war) to us.

This is not to say that Soviet actions in the Third World have been less blameworthy in recent years than our own. Perhaps theirs have been worse. It is to say that if we want to understand why the Soviet government has done what it has done in Angola, Ethiopia, Cambodia, and Afghanistan we should look within ourselves. We should ask why we have done what we have done in Guatemala, Cuba, Iran, and Vietnam.

Most of us have not felt at all like aggressors in those countries; we have felt like defenders of the right side against the wrong. Perhaps they have too. We have given aid and arms to pro-American dictators and oligarchies, telling ourselves that, with all their faults, they were at least less evil and dangerous than the pro-Soviet rebels and would-be dictators who might follow them. They have given aid and arms to pro-Soviet rebels and would-be dictators, probably believing that, with all their faults, they were at least on the side of the underdogs and therefore less evil than the reactionary oppressors and lackeys of American imperialism whom they were trying to overthrow. Probably there has been a great deal of rationalization of their own sins and projection of those sins onto their image of the other side. Has there been a similar kind of rationalization-projection in us?

In any case we have to recognize the rising anger in Soviet minds at what they think is our arrogant refusal to allow them the

---

[1]On Angola, Ethiopia, and Yemen Barnet (1981a) is an especially useful source.

[2]For an incisive Soviet pointing up of this parallel see Arbatov (1982, p. 177).

same right to compete in the Third World that we claim for ourselves. An example is our total exclusion of them from the peacemaking process in the Middle East, though it is in their own sideyard and not in ours. In the past they have swallowed such affronts to their pride, probably with sullen anger but often with outward good grace. Now that they feel militarily at least equal to us, their anger is showing. As their Foreign Minister, Andrei Gromyko, put it: "There should be no international question of any significance which could be decided without the Soviet Union or in opposition to it" (quoted by Gottlieb, 1982, p. 33). That statement calls for study, word by word. It is an extraordinary assertion of global aspirations, and the final five words, "or in opposition to it" sound like an assertion of a Soviet right to veto what the majority of the other nations want on any significant international issue. We can hope he did not mean it in that way, or at least that he did not mean to give that impression. But his anger is understandable. If we were in his position, wouldn't we feel somewhat the same way? Isn't equality as legitimate an aspiration in our value system as it is in theirs?

World Domination?

Paul Nitze put a great deal of Western thinking into a nutshell when he said of the Soviet decision-makers, "They don't want war; they want the world" (1980 , p. 90).

He had the realism to grant that "they don't want war," though perhaps he greatly underestimates the intensity of their longing for peace. As for "they want the world" it would probably be more accurate to say: They probably would *like* to have the world (though they often deny it), but they know they can't get it for a long time to come, and their horror of war is so great that they are quite unlikely to take, knowingly, a serious risk of a big war in order to expand their power, even if they think they can win.

Robert Kaiser and Seweryn Bialer, two men who know the Soviet Union much more intimately than Paul Nitze does, would probably prefer that formulation to Nitze's. Kaiser (1981) says:

> As Seweryn Bialer has put it so aptly, the Soviet leaders dream of world domination *but do not expect to achieve it*. By discounting the likelihood of success themselves, the Soviets can easily for-

give the steps they take (subjugating Afghanistan, for instance) that arouse in Americans the fear that they are really bent on imminent world domination. In the minds of the old men who have risen to the top of the Communist Party of the Soviet Union, any step that enhances Soviet security is easy to justify. Equally, moves that enhance Soviet prestige and power without endangering national security are difficult for them to resist. [p. 517; italics Kaiser's]

CHAPTER FIVE

More Plausible Scenarios for the Outbreak of Nuclear War

The Great Danger: Defensively Motivated Aggression

In at least one way Western military men tend to be more rational than most of the rest of us: In their war games and contingency planning they cultivate the chessplayer's type of empathy. They consider not only the opponents' power and possible general strategies but also how we ourselves might react in case an opponent did such-and-such, how the opponent might then react to our reaction, and so on. In a word, they cultivate scenario thinking.

If there is a limitation to the way they go about it, that limitation probably consists in following too closely the analogy of a chess game—that is, postulating on each side a pure power calculus, with a total concentration on how to avoid losing and how to win. In the real world of international affairs that could mean not giving enough weight to emotional, nonrational (but not necessarily irrational) factors such as an intense longing for peace (which could lead to forgoing a power advantage or, less rationally, to a rejection of the entire chess game); intense anger, fear, or wounded pride (which might cause either side to do irrational things); and, most of all, the strategic advantage, in our nuclear age, of reducing tension on both sides and thereby making it more likely that both sides would willingly accept a stalemate.

This last point calls for recognition of the crucial importance of defensively motivated aggression. The central thesis of this book is that defensively motivated aggression is actually more frequent and more important than cold-blooded power-motivated aggression. In practical terms that means that if we in the West don't want the Soviet Union to attack we would be wise to reduce the Soviet decision-makers exaggerated, somewhat paranoid fear of what we might, in cold blood, do to them. That thesis will be examined in various ways throughout the book, especially in

53

Chapter 8 and in the systematic comparative history chapters, 13–16. At this point it should suffice to say that all of the following four scenarios embody what is almost certainly the most realistic assumption, namely, that in our nuclear era neither side would knowingly, in the absence of any kind of fear, precipitate nuclear war or even take a serious risk of nuclear war. Neither Yuri Andropov nor any American president is likely to have the kind of homicidal-suicidal personality that Hitler had.

In other words, these scenarios are direct attacks on the paradox of unwanted war. How could it happen?

Four Scenarios and a Query

Sudden Panic: Accidental War

The date is August 16, 1985.

Yuri Andropov, despite his iron nerves, is trembling. He has just heard from a source he has always regarded as reliable that "an undetermined number" of Pershing II missiles are apparently headed for Moscow from West Germany and likely to arrive within twelve minutes. Knowing that each warhead carries much more destructive power than was used against Hiroshima or Nagasaki, and knowing that the newest, most sophisticated defenses Moscow possesses cannot destroy more than a quarter or a third of the incoming weapons, he estimates at least a 90 percent probability that Moscow will be almost totally destroyed, along with most of the command and control system of the Soviet retaliatory force—and he with it. Incinerated. He knows the time is too short to seek verification of the not-quite-certain report he has received.

There is one obvious thing to do: He can press a certain button on his desk. It has been there, with its preprogrammed consequences, since March 1985. That was when he and his colleagues decided on what they felt was the only rational response to the recent deployment of large numbers of Pershing II missiles in Western Europe, those near the eastern border of West Germany being capable of reaching the western border of the USSR in only six minutes. Those Pershing IIs made it imperative that the Soviet Union compensate for the shortness of the time by maintaining and publicly announcing, for its deterrent value, the policy of launch-on-warning, which in a less hair-trigger form had already been established. (The process has not yet been automated, however.) The Western leaders' knowledge of that policy, it was hoped, would deter them from imagining that in one surprise attack they could succeed in a ''nuclear decapitation'' of the USSR, knocking out in one blow its much too vulnerable command, control, communication, and intelligence (C^3I) system (Steinbruner, 1981–82) and simultaneously all of its leaders stationed in Moscow. Such a blow would immediately destroy Andropov's ability to order the all-out, coordinated counterattack, which, if done before the Western missiles arrived, would at least destroy most of the West's land-based offensive power and keep the military balance of power from a total collapse. That is, it would destroy his ability to do so *unless* he could do it before the missiles arrived. As the Americans themselves were saying, ''Use 'em or lose 'em.''

Knowing that pressing the button cannot save himself or Moscow, but knowing too that it is the only rational and patriotic thing to do, he presses it.

The missiles do not arrive. Fifteen minutes later he learns that the warning was mistaken. There has been a human or a computer error somewhere.

This scenario is not a science fiction fantasy. It is an all too possible consequence of the present trend toward emphasizing first-strike, counterforce weapons on both sides, with shorter flight times for those weapons. This trend is epitomized by the deployment of long-range Pershing II missiles in Western Europe, which the United States, at this writing, is still urgently pushing.

Arthur Cox, an exceptionally hardheaded, well-informed expert on nuclear strategy and on the USSR, discusses the matter in some detail in the first chapter, ''Accidental Nuclear War,'' of his recent book, *Russian Roulette: The Superpower Game* (1982). According to Cox, ''there were 3,703 false alarms [in the United States] in the eighteen-month period from January 1979 to June 1980. Most of these were routinely assessed and dismissed, but 147 false alarms were serious enough to require evaluation of whether or not they represented a potential attack'' (p. 4). They may well be more frequent in the Soviet Union, since ''the Soviet C^3 [command, control, and communication] is even more vulnerable and more prone to error than the U.S. system'' (p. 10). ''The first U.S. strategic counterforce weapons are scheduled [tentatively, depending on the final decision of the West German government] for deployment in Germany in early 1984. Pershing II missiles, which will be deployed there, are very accurate and will be capable of blowing up Soviet command and control, and some Soviet missiles, within six minutes of being fired'' (p. 25). [Cox was writing in 1982. The deployment is now—October 1983—scheduled for December of this year.]

Cox is by no means the only expert who is disturbed by the danger of accidental war. One of the many others is Fred Iklé, now Undersecretary of Defense for Policy and (unlike Cox) a prominent member of the Reagan Administration. In June 1980 he wrote:

> The crux of the matter is that the more important it becomes to ''launch on warning'' the more dangerous it will be. The tightening noose around our neck is the requirement for speed. The more certain one wants to be that our missile forces could be launched within minutes and in all circumstances, the more one has to practice the system and to loosen the safeguards. And remember: As in June, 1980 [when there were two serious U.S. false alarms, both caused by the same faulty computer], there will be false alarms. [Quoted by Cox, 1982, p. 26]

A still more ominous possibility is that the process of launch-on-warning will be put on computers—automated—in the USSR, the United States, or both. No human source of restraint could then intervene to prevent a cataclysm if a serious computer error were to occur.

It seems likely that, with or without automation, this is *the* most possible way in which nuclear war could start.

How often has it been refuted, or even publicly discussed, by those who now favor placing Pershing IIs—with their extraordinary speed and accuracy—in Western Europe? Is the ignoring of it a case of deliberate, or subconscious, selective inattention?

Intervention by Both Superpowers in a Civil War

It is December, 1986, and the Islamic fundamentalist government of Iran is in trouble. During the six years since the seizure of the American hostages in November 1979, the economy has gone from bad to worse, and politically the country seems to be falling apart. National separatist movements have begun to flourish among three of the nationalities: the Arabs, the Kurds, and especially the Azerbaijanis in the northwest corner of Iran, next to th Soviet border and next to the Soviet Republic of Azerbaijan. Most of the Azerbaijanis on both sides of the border aspire to national unity and independence. Like the government of another multinational state on the borders of Russia—Austria-Hungary during the years before 1914—the Iranian government has been deeply and increasingly anxious about the danger that the country will literally fall apart and that the dismembered parts will be dominated, in fact if not in name, by the Russian colossus. Azerbaijan has become the equivalent of Serbia. Americans who think in geopolitical terms are similarly anxious. Total Soviet domination of most of the Middle East, including all of the important oilfields, seems a real possibility.

The first open rebellion has just occurred, and so far it has succeeded. The Ayatollah Maharashtri, known to be friendly to the Soviet Union but also a fervent Azerbaijani nationalist, has taken power in Tabriz, the capital of Iranian Azerbaijan, has declared complete independence, and has actually appealed to the Soviet Union for military aid to defend his infant nation against the expected Iranian onslaught. Crowds in the streets are shouting their approval.

The perceptions on the two sides differ radically. On the Azerbaijani and Soviet side the conflict is seen as a struggle for independence from the oppressive and irresponsible rule of Teheran, and the expected Iranian attack is seen as unequivocal aggression. On the Iranian side the conflict is seen as a struggle for survival, with dismemberment and Soviet domination as the only realistic alternative. Iranians cling to the thought that Maharashtri and his band of ''assassins'' (the takeover did involve a number of assassinations) represent only a minority and that the majority in Iranian Azerbaijan would actually welcome a reestablishment of the beneficent all-Iranian regime, in which, the Iranians believe, Azerbaijanis have fully shared. Both sides are now mobilizing militarily, the Azerbaijanis with much Soviet help. No one thinks of the possibility of nuclear war.

The Americans are at first divided. Since the hostage episode there has been no love for Iran, and only recently the Ayatollah Fathali (who had replaced Khomeini after the latter's assassination) has repeated Khomeini's denunciation of America as "the Great Satan." Now, though, Fathali is desperately pleading not only for American weapons but also for American troops. He is claiming that a Soviet-plus-Azerbaijani attack on Teheran (uncomfortably close to Tabriz) is imminent and that the next step after seizure of Teheran will be a seizure of the whole country, making it a Soviet satellite and enabling the Communist atheists to get a stranglehold on all the oilfields in the Persian Gulf area. He likens the situation to the Munich crisis in which Hitler first dismembered Czechoslovakia, then gobbled up the whole country, and soon went on to a career of world conquest that threatened even America.

These three themes—the threat of Soviet domination of the entire Middle East (including Israel), the threat to the oilfields, and the Munich analogy—have evoked a powerful response in the United States. The dominant mood is to stand firm in the face of Soviet aggression. On the other side are those who see a possible nuclear war in the offing. That fear too is potent in the minds of nearly everyone, but the interventionists win out when the new Democratic President argues eloquently that Andropov is another Hitler and that appeasement does not mean "peace in our time" but the shortest road to war.

An appearance of compromise is achieved, which most Americans on each side of the controversy can live with: Restrain Fathali from attacking Iranian Azerbaijan, but help him to hold the line, with great strength and determination, between Iranian Azerbaijan and the rest of Iran. Freeze the *status quo* and, to make it stick, send a tough message to Moscow saying that if the line is crossed America will use "whatever means are necessary, not excluding the use of force" to preserve the territorial integrity and independence of Iran.

In addition, to prove that those are no mere words, a contingent of American troops is sent to Teheran, armed with short-range battlefield nuclear weapons. The American military, though much more dubious and divided about the whole enterprise than most of the civilians, is nearly unanimous in the view that *if* there is to be effective deterrence the pitifully weak American contingent (weak, that is, when compared with the enormous Soviet superiority in ground forces and logistic advantages) will have to be supplemented by at least an ambiguous, implicit threat of a possible nuclear war. After all, they say, that ambiguous threat has successfully kept the peace in Europe for many years. And the ambiguity of the threat means that there will be no serious loss of credibility if, in the crunch, it is not carried out. Nothing official has to be said about the battlefield weapons even to the American public; their mere deployment should be enough to deter a Soviet advance.

In a way, that is how it turns out. There is no Soviet advance. Instead, a kind of unplanned escalation occurs in the fighting along the new border. Fathali's seasoned troops (seasoned in the war against Iraq), with his tacit approval, make a series of pin-prick raids across the border, comparable to those that Syngman Rhee tacitly approved across his northern border into Communist North Korea during the months just before the Korean war broke out. The newly recruited Azerbaijani troops, almost wholly unseasoned and undisciplined but handling some first-class Soviet tanks and thus made self-confident, carry out an unauthorized, fairly large-scale commando raid on the American contingent, hoping to capture its battlefield nuclear weapons. They fail, but in the process the American troops, caught by surprise, assuming that the big war has started, and imbued with the philosophy of "use 'em or lose 'em," use them.

The psychological firebreak between conventional and nuclear war has been crossed. The Soviet troops fighting with their Azerbaijani comrades also have short-range nuclear weapons, and are imbued with the orthodox Soviet doctrine that, once either side initiates use of nuclear weapons of any sort, there is necessarily an all-out nuclear war. They return the fire, doubling its intensity. Nuclear war has started.

While the details of this scenario seem unlikely to be duplicated in any country in the future, including Iran, the number of countries in which something like it *could* occur is large enough to justify the guess that this general pattern should be ranked second only to accidental war in probability.

The underlying pattern is a civil conflict in which the sympathies of one superpower are engaged on one side and the sympathies of the other on the other. That pattern has appeared many times in fairly recent history. The Spanish civil war, with the Soviet Union on one side and Hitler and Mussolini on the other, was a classic case. The Vietnam War was similar in this respect, and the Korean war (less accurately described as a civil war) was also. Still other possible examples include Greece, China, the Philippines, Iran (in 1953), Lebanon, Guatemala, Cuba, the Dominican Republic, Hungary, Czechoslovakia, Angola, Ethiopia, and Afghanistan.

Looking to the future, and noticing particularly other states, in addition to Iran, in which that pattern could emerge, close enough to the USSR to give it a relatively strong incentive to intervene, we probably should consider at least Yugoslavia, Turkey, Iraq, Saudi Arabia, Afghanistan, and Korea. Yugoslavia is a multinational state like Austria-Hungary and Iran. Turkey once looked solid but no longer does. Iraq has been unstable in the past and is, like Iran, a large oil producer. Saudi Arabia is the largest oil producer and could become unstable in the future.[1] Afghanistan has already been subject to Soviet intervention and, perhaps after an interval, could be again. Korea has two dictatorial governments, either of whose populations could rebel, with the superpowers taking opposite sides.

Even if the probability of a scenario resembling this one is not greater than one in ten in any single country, the possibilities add up.

Theoretically the same kind of intervention by both superpowers at the same time could occur in any international war— not just any civil war. A possibly relevant example is the implicit threat of nuclear war by Nixon and Kissinger in the form of their SAC-alert at the end of the 1973 Israeli–Egyptian war. There have been many wars between whole nations during the period since 1945, as well as between factions or regions within nations, and the superpowers have sometimes had clearly different preferences as to which nation should win.

Fortunately, however, not one of these has yet led to direct military intervention by the troops of *both* superpowers, let alone the use or threat of nuclear weapons. Each has presumably been aware of the great danger to itself if it did so, especially when the other has already clearly taken sides. In the 1973 war, for instance, Brezhnev quickly and wisely backed down in the face of the Nixon–Kissinger threat, humiliating though his backing down was. That is a reassuring augury for the future.

[1] Barry Blechman (1982, p. 417) speaks of triggering possibilities in ''civil strife in Yugoslavia, turmoil in Poland, or anarchy in Italy.'' Richard Burt (1982, p. 421) similarly mentions ''disintegration of existing rule in several countries including Iran, Turkey, Pakistan, and Saudi Arabia.''

The Losing Side Goes Nuclear

It is 1986, and Israel and the Arabs are at war for the seventh time.[2]

Israel has possessed nuclear weapons, or at least the ability to assemble them quickly, since the early 1970s, and fear of them has for many years been a major deterrent to an all-out Arab attack on tiny Israel. In the previous six wars Israel has never been on the losing side. This time things are different. They began to be different in 1973, when the Egyptians successfully moved back across the Suez Canal to what they felt was unequivocally their own land, stolen from them by Israel just six years earlier. During the thirteen years since then, in spite of America's lavishness in supplying Israel with the most sophisticated military equipment, the underlying military balance has shifted in favor of the Arabs, imperceptibly for some years but rapidly since the Israeli intervention in Lebanon in 1982.

The Arabs' growing strength has been the result of three factors: their numerical superiority (more than 30 to 1), the wealth of the oil-rich states in contrast with Israel's meager resources, and—an indispensable ingredient—the technical skill provided partly by the Russians and partly by a few highly educated Lebanese and Palestinians. They have worked together quietly to give the Arabs the ability, at long last, to equal or surpass the fighting strength of the Zionist monster, even in the nuclear dimension. The Arabs have caught up with Israel in the nuclear field, as the Soviet Union has caught up with the nuclear strength of the United States.

In the past four years the Arabs' prospects have also been mightily helped by the aggressive policies of Menachem Begin, Ariel Sharon, and their successors in Lebanon and on the West Bank. Those policies have brought the hitherto divided Arabs together as never before, and have greatly diminished the still predominant pro-Israel sentiment in the United States.

The 1976 war, like those of 1956 and 1967, began as a preventive war by Israel. Rising violence and organized terrorism on the West Bank and in Lebanon, sometimes spilling over into Israel itself, plus Jordan's increasingly pro-Arab policy, have finally led

[2]Yes, the seventh. The war of 1973 was the sixth, if we count, as we should, the Civil War of 1936–39 and the War of Attrition, 1968–69. For a more detailed psychological analysis of the Arab-Israeli conflict see White (1977).

the new Israeli government—in spite of its relatively peace-oriented policy as compared with that of Begin and Sharon—to express in action Israel's long-term siege mentality. In three lightning strokes it has seized the major Arab cities in its immediate neighborhood: Beirut (again), Damascus, and Amman. All three operations were brilliantly successful. As usually happens, the initiator of the war had the advantage of surprise—at first. Then, however, the psychological and logistic factors that usually favor the defense began to operate, as they did in World War I against Germany and in World War II against both Germany and Japan. The fact of clear Israeli aggression, however morally justifiable it may have been when seen in its full context, united Israel's enemies still more and further alienated its one strong friend, the United States. Egypt, Iraq, and Saudi Arabia, their latent stereotype of "Zionist expansionism" now vividly reinforced, joined with the submerged and temporarily intimidated populations of Syria, Lebanon, Jordon, the West Bank and Gaza to defend the Arab world against the spreading Zionist cancer that, in their eyes, Western "imperialism" had planted in their midst. The Soviet Union is cheering them on, and the American people, thoroughly shocked, are insisting that their government stay out of the war. Israel, with a thousandth of the world's population and an even smaller proportion of its land area and resources, is now isolated and knows it.

In this extremity a policy of sweet reasonableness and immediate total retreat to Israel's pre-1967 borders—a policy dramatically contrasting with what has gone before—might still save it. But that is now psychologically impossible. The psychological momentum of war itself is unstoppable and now carries everything before it. The long-latent "Masada complex" takes hold, and the feeling spreads that perhaps all Israelis will have to die, but all will die fighting.

First, of course, there is a threat. The Israelis hope against hope that it will remove the necessity of dying. Their government announces to the world that with their still unused nuclear weapons they will instantly destroy Cairo, Alexandria, Baghdad, and Riyadh, as well as Beirut, Damascus, and Amman, if the Arabs are unwilling to accept Israel's generous terms of peace. Those terms now include retreat from every piece of disputed territory except Israel's historic homeland, Judea and Samaria [which of course includes Arab East Jerusalem]. The Arabs, also in the grip of the psychological momentum of war itself, are in no mood to accept that last proviso. They offer to accept Israel's terms, all but the last one, and threaten to obliterate Israel totally with their own nuclear weapons if Israel dares to use its own.

Israel does use its own. Cairo, Alexandria, Baghdad, Riyadh, Beirut, Damascus, and Amman are destroyed, and Israel is totally obliterated.

The rest of the world heaves a great sigh of relief. It could have been so much worse if either Moscow or Washington had entered the game of threats from which it is psychologically impossible to back down.

War for the Oil Fields

It is 1989.

The dependence of Western Europe and Japan on Middle East oil is still great. Even now it has not been drastically reduced. The Soviet Union has continued to be self-sufficient in oil, but in order to supply the energy needs of Eastern Europe the Soviet leaders have begun to see some economic value in ensured access to the oil of the Gulf region.

Chiefly because of its own and its allies' need for oil, the one-sided concern of the United States with political "stability" in the area (stability being defined one-sidedly as the continuation of all established governments) has continued. It is the same concern that in the 1970s led to all-out support of the Shah, which had much to do with the Islamic fundamentalist, thoroughly anti-American revolution of 1979. Now a similar revolution (Islamic, not Communist) threatens in the six closely allied GCC (Gulf Cooperation Council) states: Saudi Arabia, Kuwait, Oman, the United Arab Emirates, Qatar, and Bahrein. Under the calm and seemingly stable surface, the pro-underdog and anti-Western forces of Islamic fundamentalism, Sunni as well as Shiite, have become more and more powerful.

Although nearly all of the revolutionary groups shun any contact with "atheistic Communism," there are exceptions. In one of the emirates, Abu Dhabi, the small Shiite faction has fairly close ties with the equally small Moscow-oriented Communist group. That fact has been uncovered and publicized in the West. The inveterate American tendency to explain all signs of instability as the result of a Moscow plot, without giving enough weight to local sources of discontent, comes strongly into play. That perception is also much reinforced by Moscow's own strong verbal support of what it calls "the upsurge of the Arab peoples against imperialism."

The new American President, elected in 1988 after a hard-hitting, hard-line anti-Communist campaign, feels sure that the entire revolutionary movement is Moscow-inspired and Moscow-controlled; his hand-picked advisers, not surprisingly, agree with him, though most of the lower-level Middle East specialists in the Department of State and the intelligence community do not.

Suddenly the revolution explodes in all six of the GCC countries, with many assassinations of Americans and of government officials. Vast mobs gather in the streets, shouting for an end to government by the rich and by the lackeys of American imperialism. The American President publicly describes the whole movement as Communist-controlled. The Defense Council of the six nations, seeing its opportunity, appeals to him with the utmost urgency to save them from Communist subversion and a Soviet invasion, which they say is imminent. Moscow as yet has taken no military steps and declares its official neutrality but says it is watching the situation closely and will move decisively to protect the Arab peoples if the imperialists embark, with military force, on "the export of counterrevolution."

Within the Politburo there has been for several years an increasing feeling that the United States has been "pushing us around" everywhere in the Third World, especially in the Middle East. Some say, "If we are realistic we must recognize that the President wants war. We must be ready for it."

The President alerts the Navy in the Arabian Sea, the Air Force and the Rapid Deployment Force, with its tactical, battlefield nuclear weapons. The Politburo alerts the Soviet troops near Yerevan and those near Baku for a possible move southward. It asks the Iranian and Iraqi governments for permission to move through their territory if the interests of Islam and circumstances in the Gulf require it. The request is granted.

The President asks for a joint session of Congress. He thinks he knows what he must say but is not sure he knows how to say it. What he is most sure of is that his mettle is being tested by the Communists and that he does not want to go down in history as another Chamberlain. (He assumes that human history will continue.) He knows the risk is serious but clings to the thought that on all previous occasions (the Cuban missile crisis, the SAC alert of 1973) Moscow has backed down rather than run any risk of nuclear war. He thinks, ''The firmer we are the more sure they are to back down.''

The next morning he addresses Congress. His somber, dignified address stresses two points: ''It is unthinkable that the Soviet thumb should be allowed to rest on the jugular vein of the Western world—our access to oil.'' And ''The future of liberty and of civilization is at stake. Our courage and our American principles face their most severe test since the darkest days of the Civil War.'' He announces that ''whatever force is necessary'' will be used. Congress responds with an ovation, as it did in response to President Carter's similar address, with a similar message, proposing the ''Carter Doctrine'' in 1980.

Soviet troops advance into Kuwait. Commanders of the American Rapid Deployment Force, knowing that they will be immediately overwhelmed if they do not use their battlefield nuclear weapons, proceed to do so. The Soviets respond in kind. Nuclear war has begun.

Cumulative Fear of Us, Leading to a Soviet Attack

What follows is not really a scenario but a question raised about the ultimate psychological effects on our opponents of the kinds and amounts of nuclear weapons the United States is now making and deploying.

In Chapter 4 six reasons were suggested for thinking that the Soviet Union has little or no desire to invade Western Europe, although a great many in the West believe it does.

That argument seems valid—for the present. There is one motive, though, that might at some time in the future cause such an attack: the unhealthy ''paranoid'' type of fear in Soviet minds, fueled largely by our American behavior in the meantime.

The existence of that kind of fear in the Soviet Union is hardly open to question. The obsessive concern of the USSR with the security of its borders, often called ''paranoid,'' was dramatically demonstrated once more by the recent downing of a Korean airliner. It should not have surprised anyone familiar with the history of Soviet behavior in that respect. As suggested in Chapter 2, Soviet behavior in Afghanistan was probably primarily a result of the same obsession. The Soviet ''siege mentality'' has deep roots in Russian history and is testified to by most if not all of the Western observers who know the Soviet Union intimately.

The danger inherent in that kind of fear and in the kind of conflict behavior that stimulates it will be discussed at some length in Chapters 7–10. It may be enough to say here that the West needs to consider whether its present defense plans and proposals are creating in the Soviet Union more of the healthy kind of fear that deterrence is designed to create or more of the unhealthy kind that promotes defensively motivated aggression.

An amount of weaponry in the West and a rate of increase in the West's weaponry that the Soviet decision-makers perceive as indicating a desire for decisive nuclear superiority, far beyond what the United States actually needs for its defense, can hardly fail to create and intensify in them the unhealthy kind of fear. If our weapons are primarily the kind that seem designed for a nuclear first strike (as is true especially of the ten-warhead MX, the Pershing II, and the ground-launched cruise missile), such fear is likely to be increased all the more. We are likely to look all the more as if we have the desire, and at some not-too-distant time will have the ability, to attack and destroy the USSR. If any motive in their minds could induce them to take the risks and pay the costs of attacking Western Europe, it could well be the desire to preempt or prevent that kind of attack on themselves.

CHAPTER SIX

Three Unpromising Approaches to Peace

In response to the question "How can war be prevented?" three answers are often given: military superiority, military equality (often called a "balance of power"), and arms reduction agreements. A plausible argument can be made for each of them, and is made here, but a skeptical analysis suggests that each of them is unlikely to achieve peace (or is unlikely to occur at all) unless there is also a drastic reduction of international tension.

Military Superiority Without Tension-reduction

For people who are caught in a conflict *and* who have a black-and-white conception of it (which includes most of us) there is an obvious answer: Be stronger than the Bad Guys. From that standpoint it is imperative to be *at least* as strong as the Bad Guys, since both peace and independence depend on it; and it is even better if we, the Good Guys, have a margin of superiority. *They* are the aggressors, the only possible aggressors, and the only language they understand is the language of force. Therefore armed deterrence is the one essential, and the more of it the better. There should be no chance that the enemy might miscalculate our strength or our resolve. He should know that if he attacks us, our allies, or our vital interests, he will be disastrously defeated.

It should be noticed that the basic premise underlying this train of thought is a diabolical enemy-image, and if that image were much mistaken or much exaggerated the whole line of thought could be wrong, and perhaps disastrously wrong. A different basic premise would result in a quite different conclusion. Suppose the enemy were actually somewhat like us, wanting peace as we do and fearful, as we are, of being attacked by other people perceived as Bad Guys (in their case, us) unless they are strong enough to deter us. The best the world could then hope for, from a policy on both sides of straining for military superiority, would be an unending arms race, exorbitantly straining the economy on each side, because neither side could feel satisfied with merely equal power. Both, driven mainly by fear, would continually strain for that small but supposedly unmistakable margin of superiority. And, all too possibly, the race would not be unending. It could end in a nuclear explosion, made more likely by all the suspicion and anger the race would generate, and probably destroying other countries in addition to the main combatants.

The evidence offered in Chapters 2 and 3 and elsewhere in this book supports that premise and that line of thought much more than the first one, especially as applied to the present arms race between the West and the Soviet Union. The evidence indicates that for us in the West to strain to be stronger than the USSR is the worst of all the alternatives. All of what has just been said, and more, applies to the men in the Kremlin. They are somewhat like us, at least in their thinking about matters of defense. They want to avoid any big war at least as much as we do, and they are afraid of being attacked by other people perceived as Bad Guys (us, especially if we deploy the Pershing II in Western Europe) unless they are strong enough to deter us. Like us, they see equality (or better still, superiority) as essential for security.

In addition, as Chapter 4 has indicated, there is reason to think that becoming or remaining equal to us in the eyes of the world has become almost an obsession with them. Their pride as well as their fear demands it. There is also a perceptual factor. Their military men, like ours, apparently tend to engage in worst-case thinking, which in this context means an overestimation of their opponents' military strength and a relative underestimation of their own (Chapter 3). If so, a situation actually approximating equality would appear to them as some degree of Soviet inferiority. A straining of the West to achieve a ''margin of safety'' would seem to them even more intolerable and more indicative of aggressive Western intentions.

Finally, there is right now a very great question as to whether decisive superiority of the West over the USSR is attainable, given the Soviet Union's conventional superiority, the meaninglessness of ''superiority'' in nuclear weapons, and the ability of the Soviet government to insist that its people concentrate on guns rather than butter. According to Barry Blechman (1982,

p. 412), "none but the most naive believe that such an end [strategic superiority] is attainable."

A Balance of Power—Defined as Military Parity—Without Tension-reduction

The case for rough parity in arms is much more plausible. The leaders of both the United States and the USSR now publicly proclaim it as their goal (even though probably both would prefer superiority), and even those who are skeptical of the simple Good Guys–Bad Guys picture of the world are usually strongly drawn to it under the name "balance of power." It sounds eminently fair, and terms like "balance" and "equilibrium" sound as if equality would provide a more stable basis for peace than any other strategy. Surely, it seems, a balance would not create excessive fear or wounded pride on either side, or a straining to catch up. The arms race might continue, perhaps, but surely not at the breakneck pace that would result from both sides' striving to be superior. Most of all, it should deter *both* sides from starting a war, since neither, presumably, could count on winning.

There is one trouble with that highly plausible case: it does not square with the historical facts. In our century at least, *major wars have occurred more often when there was a near approach to equality than when one side was clearly superior.*

That statement is so startling and so much at odds with what seems like common sense that it calls for a very careful examination of the evidence. If valid, it should lead to a basic revision of fundamental assumptions. Let us look at the record. Three principal facts support it:

World War I occurred when the balance was more nearly equal than during most of the peaceful period that preceded it or the peaceful period that followed it.

The relatively peaceful period that preceded World War I (peaceful between the great powers of Europe, that is; there were wars elsewhere, such as the Boer War and the Russo-Japanese War) lasted from the end of the Franco-Prussian War in 1871 to the outbreak of World War I in 1914—forty-three years. During most of that time, 1871 to 1904 (thirty-three years), Germany and its allies were quite clearly stronger than France and its allies. During the remaining ten years the balance was much more ambiguous. Germany remained the strongest military power on the Continent, but France, which already had Russia as an ally, developed a close relation with Great Britain, the dominant naval power, from 1904 on, and retained its alliance with the huge Russian Empire. By 1914 either side, by focusing on its own elements of strength, could persuade itself that it was stronger.

The relatively peaceful period that followed World War I showed no such ambiguity. France and its allies were unquestionably stronger than Germany, so much so that even Hitler, the great adventurer, did not dare to take a serious risk of war until 1938—twenty years after World War I ended.

World War II also occurred when the balance was more nearly equal than during the peaceful period that preceded it or the peaceful period that followed it.

During the period from 1918 to 1938 neither Hitler's predecessors nor Hitler himself dared to challenge the Versailles Treaty structure of power, though they certainly had major grievances. There was near unanimity in Germany as to the injustice of Versailles, but the disparity in power was too great to be challenged.

After 1945 Germany's power was much less than that of either the United States or the USSR. It could not have dared to make war on its own even if it had wanted to. The same was true of Japan.

It was only between 1938 and 1941, when Hitler's rearmament program had brought him into a situation of ambiguous near equality with his immediate and potential enemies, that he could dare to embark on his career of conquest; and he dared to do so only because, unlike his generals, he thought Britain and France were "little worms" who lacked the courage to oppose him effectively even though they could have done it.

The present period of the East–West conflict, since approximately 1975, has been one of controversial, ambiguous near equality, and tension has risen much higher than during the long period of clear inequality, let us say 1953–75, that preceded it.

If we look only at those years the rule holds: rough equality, not clear inequality, coincides with increased tension and potential war. What about the previous period, from 1944, when the USSR began its occupation of Poland, until 1953, when Stalin died and the Korean war ended? On the face of things that looks like an exception to the generalization. In both economic strength and in nuclear arms the West was then still incomparably stronger than the East, yet the East was much more aggressive. In Eastern Europe, in Iran, in China, in Berlin, in Southeast Asia, and finally, as a climax, in Korea, the Soviet Union and Communist China were the challengers of the *status quo.*

However, a more analytical approach suggests that that period too was one of ambiguous near equality. The United States, perhaps mistakenly (as Bertrand Russell believed), scarcely even considered using its vast nuclear superiority, which left the USSR and Communist China obviously superior in land forces on the Eurasian continent. They also had all the logistic advantage of local superiority in both Eastern Europe and, after the Chinese Communist victory in 1948–49, in East Asia. Secretary of State Acheson (with General MacArthur in agreement) gave them an ambiguous green light on Korea. North Korea, with its advantage of surprise, almost won the war when it advanced almost to Pusan. All things considered, therefore, it is legitimate to think of that period as one of ambiguous near equality, with some advantage, psychologically, on the Communist side. Each side, focusing on its own genuine elements of relative strength, could rationally contemplate taking the kinds of risks that were actually taken. And tension was very high on both sides, probably higher than it has been at any time since the end of the Korean war in 1953. Therefore the rule still holds: Equality, if combined with high tension, promotes war.

Why? Why has a "balance of power" (meaning in this case an ambiguous near equality of power without tension reduction) so often proved to be a breeding ground not of peace, as "common sense" suggests, but of war?

One reason has already been suggested. Deterrence, in the form of clear, unambiguous military superiority, usually does work—in the short run. And the "short run" can last as long as thirty-three years (1871–1904), twenty years (1918–38), or twenty-two years (1953–75). When the disparity in strength is clear and cannot be denied by wishfully focusing mainly on one's own genuine elements of strength, the weaker side does not dare to start a war; but when there is ambiguous near-equality, either side may do so.

A. F. K. Organski, the political scientist who first persuasively argued that inequality was more stable than equality

(1958), put that point succinctly when he said that in a situation of clear inequality "the stronger does not need to attack and the weaker does not dare to."

A related point is that the elements of military power, tangible and intangible, are so many and so varied that any approach to overall equality creates ambiguity and thereby makes wishful misperception easy. It becomes too easy for one side, or sometimes both, to overestimate the chance of a quick victory, at an acceptable cost, by focusing mainly on its own genuine elements of strength.

For instance, the Germans in 1914 could dare to be aggressive chiefly because, although they were probably unduly pessimistic about their long-term prospects, they were unduly optimistic about their short-term prospects. By focusing on their undoubtedly superior military strength and prowess they could reasonably hope that, if war had to come, they could gain a quick victory by crushing first the armies of France and then those of Russia. What the two most responsible individuals, the Kaiser and his Chancellor, Bethmann-Hollweg, tended to forget or underestimate was the likelihood that Britain, fearful of a collapse of the balance of power if both France and Russia were crushed, would then have a very strong incentive to join the ranks of Germany's enemies. That intangible element of power was not focused on (except by the top military men, who were more realistic), and there was horror in Germany when it became tangible.

Hitler, by focusing on the presumed cowardice of his potential enemies, made a similar error in 1939. North Korea and the USSR, probably led by the statements of Acheson and others to ignore or underestimate the danger of American involvement, made a similar error in 1950 (Khrushchev, 1970, pp. 367–73).

In all three instances tension was high at the time of decision-making and may well have contributed to selective inattention to the risks being run.

That is one reason, then, for the relation between a "balance" and war. A balance is necessarily ambiguous, and ambiguity opens the door to wishful thinking and military overconfidence on one side or both.

A quite different reason is that, in times of ambiguous near-equality, a nation's fears as well as its hopes may be unusually high. A loose intellectual structure gives freer play to emotions of all sorts, including fear, that can influence perception. Most particularly, there is likely to be fear of a *future* "collapse of the balance of power," and the nation's leaders may believe that such a danger can be warded off only by taking advantage of a relatively favorable present military situation.

There have been many historical instances of that kind of thinking just before a war. Richard Ned Lebow (1982), in his study of twenty-six international crises that could or did lead to war, generalizes that "the most common external catalyst of brinkmanship was the perception that decisive action was required to prevent a significant adverse shift in the strategic or political balance of power" (p. 334). Four examples will illustrate the point:

• Napoleon III, seeing the rapid rise of German power and unity under the leadership of Bismarck, thought he saw a future Germany overshadowing France (he was not far wrong); and, with a large measure of wishful overconfidence in the present strength of France, he went to war in 1870 to prevent it. (Bismarck's trickery contributed, but it was not the basic reason for the war. It was France that declared war.)

• The Germans and Austrians in 1914, looking at the future, thought they saw themselves encircled by an increasingly united Triple Entente, while Austria–Hungary disintegrated, leaving Germany isolated among enemies. Wishfully clinging to the assumption that Britain would not fight in "a Balkan quarrel," they saw their present chances of winning not necessarily as very good, but as certainly better than they would be in another three or four years, when the huge Russian Army would be modernized and much better.

• Japan in 1941 saw "Western imperialism" closing in and strangling its economy unless it could quickly consolidate its Greater East Asia Coprosperity Sphere. The result was Pearl Harbor.

• Americans today think they see a Soviet Union that is forging ahead militarily and has already at least caught up with the United States. Many Americans infer that unless the West strenuously arms, the Communists will become (or perhaps are already) strong enough to attack the West or intimidate Western Europe and Japan, isolating and in the long run endangering the United States. The United States has reacted, and tension at this writing is high.

All four of these instances have contained an ambiguous near-equality; fears of a future imbalance have flourished, and it has been possible for the *status-quo* country that felt threatened to think it could ward off the future danger by acting quickly, before it was too late. In three of the four instances war has occured. In all four there has probably been worst-case thinking about the future combined with, in the first three, perhaps, wishful thinking about the present balance of military strength.

Still another reason to challenge the fixation of most of the people in the United States and the USSR on a "balance" (meaning rough equality) of military strength is that in the sphere of nuclear weapons a great deal less than equality may be sufficient for deterrence.

That is one of the corollaries of the unthinkable horrendousness of nuclear weapons. The ratio between the harm they can do to the enemy and what they cost is so tremendous that each side can hardly make itself believe that with even five nuclear-armed submarines it could threaten "assured destruction" of two hundred enemy cities, which, for deterring the other side from starting a nuclear war, would in all probability be enough. (For a sophisticated argument on this point, see Jervis, 1982.) Fixated on the outmoded idea that equality or better is essential for deterrence (which still has a measure of validity when applied to conventional arms), the leaders and the public on both sides continue applying the old idea to new facts that it does not fit. The result is a wholly unnecessary and horribly dangerous nuclear arms race.

In sum, approximate equality without tension-reduction is dangerous. It was the situation at the outbreak of both world wars. It exists now.

One probable reason for its danger is that, because of its inevitable ambiguity, it makes wishful thinking about the present military situation too easy. Each side, by focusing on its own elements of military strength, can unrealistically expect victory at an acceptable price. Another is that perception of a strong opponent "coming up from behind" and now approximately equal often creates dire expectations of a future upset in the balance of power unless drastic action is taken now. Examples are Napoleon III, the Kaiser in 1914, Japan in 1941, and, perhaps, the United States in the 1980s.

In addition, the general fixation on equality as a goal is inappropriate when applied to nuclear weapons.

Arms Reduction Agreements Without Tension-reduction

For nearly a century the nations of the world have been trying, in their fashion, to eliminate war by agreeing to eliminate or at least reduce the weapons with which war is fought. The result has been continual, heartbreaking, almost total failure.

Barbara Tuchman recently (1982) reviewed that record in dismal detail from the First Hague Conference in 1899 through the Washington Naval Conference in 1922, the League of Nations Disarmament Conference of 1932–33, the Limited Test Ban Treaty of 1963 (which did stop some kinds of testing but not the arms race), and SALT I (which did head off an ABM race but, again, not the major arms race) to SALT II, which, after great labor, never even reached a vote in the U.S. Senate.

The extent to which we ever hopeful peaceniks have turned our minds away from that dismal record, or perhaps have not even studied it, is in itself something of a psychological puzzle. We should have been asking what has gone wrong. What has gone so continually wrong, especially in recent years when so much of the human race has been so obviously terrified by nuclear weapons? Surely it is now high time for all of us (with help from Barbara Tuchman) to take a long and honest look at the possible reasons for our eight-decade failure and to ask what can be done about those reasons.

Such a candid appraisal might well begin with a look inward, at ourselves and our own thought processes.

The simplest psychological process we may discover in ourselves is sheer association. Weapons remind us of war, instantly and inevitably, because they are parts of the same image. Any realistically vivid image of war—guns shooting, shells tearing human flesh, human bodies horribly burned by the astronomically intense heat of a warhead that fell miles away—includes weapons as an integral part. To think of war is to think of weapons, and to feel an intense emotional revulsion against war is to feel at least a moderate emotional revulsion against weapons. That is not an irrational response. It is rational, as far as it goes. It is a realistic recognition of the real danger that lies latent in every weapon.

Not to feel it would imply a kind of schizophrenic apathy, a "psychic numbing." But it is incomplete; if there is to be realistic action to ward off that latent danger, the initial association needs to be supplemented with more complex forms of thinking.

The next step toward realistic complexity involves making a distinction between two weapon images: the image of weapons-in-use that has just been described and an image of weapons not in use but standing quietly ready for use and perhaps serving effectively to deter the use of similar weapons by others. That raises the question of deterrence and the psychological effectiveness of armed deterrence. Whatever the answer given by a proponent of disarmament may be, he at least needs to come to grips with that question, with full honesty, if he wants to cope effectively with the deterrence-minded people who have always been the chief skeptics and often the chief opponents of disarmament, or if he simply wants to understand the central reason why disarmament and arms control negotiations have so often failed.

The typical deterrer's argument is straightforward and not irrational if its premises are granted. It has already been outlined in connection with the simplistic black-and-white thinker's argument for military superiority. In modified form it goes like this:

The enemy is inherently aggressive, and his word is never to be trusted. We must have arms at least equal to his to deter him from attacking us or our allies. We need a margin of superiority, because we don't know what arms he is preparing in secret. As for his signing a disarmament or arms control agreement, his signature would not be worth the paper it is written on. On that point we cannot afford to be naive. *And*, please notice, you disarmers, we deterrers care as much about peace as you do. We are simply more realistic about how to achieve it. We recognize the horrors of nuclear war as clearly as you do, but we live in the real world and understand better how to avoid them.

Perhaps the one-sided deterrers who neglect arms reduction and tension reduction are not as realistic as they think they are, and perhaps they do not picture vividly enough the full horrors of nuclear war, but they think they do. As long as they believe it, arms reduction on a meaningful scale will remain an uphill struggle. Jonathan Schell's (1982) most eloquent writing about incinerated bodies and about our obligation to unborn future generations will not budge them. They think they understand well enough the critical flaw in his thinking, which is, as they see it, that he ignores or belittles the diabolical nature of the enemy and the consequent imperative need for deterrence.

This is not the place to discuss in detail how that formidable psychological obstacle to arms reduction can be best coped with. (For a fuller discussion see Chapter 20.) What is most needed here is simply a recognition of how formidable the obstacle is.

It is all the more formidable when seen in the light of the unconscious or semiconscious psychological forces that sustain it. The one-sided deterrers, those who give little or no importance to arms control or tension-reduction, undoubtedly gain conscious satisfaction from feeling that they are less naive, more hardheaded, more realistic than their opponents, the one-sided disarmers, who give little or no importance to deterrence. "Naive" is one of the most devastating of political epithets, with the added psychological advantage of seeming to put the user of the word on a level of benign, tolerant sophistication rather than emotional denunciation. "You disarmers are not unpatriotic. You mean well, but you are naive, and you have allowed yourselves to become the dupes of our mortal enemies." Those who get a glow of satisfaction from such thoughts of their own hardheadedness and sophistication may on a less conscious level cling to and irrationally defend the beliefs that enable them to feel so superior and sophisticated. In any case they do feel genuinely superior, and the more simple-minded disarmers, who have never really come to grips with the problem of deterrence, make it easier for them to do so.

If the one-sided deterrers are to experience the wholesome jolt of realizing that they themselves may have been naive, their opponents need to begin by showing an understanding of, if not full agreement with, the case for deterrence. They must go beyond the simple tendency to associate weapons with war, based on images of mushroom clouds, horribly burned bodies, and the rest, and grant the legitimacy of the deterrers' image of weapons not in use and serving as a deterrent. Specifically, they need to take very seriously the case for an adequate second-strike capability (see Chapter 7) and, if they agree with it, say so to the deterrers, because in the deterrers' eyes anyone who does not accept even that much of the deterrence philosophy is palpably, unquestionably naive.

More broadly, partisans of each side in the arms-agreement controversy need to incorporate both the weapons-in-use image and the weapons-serving-as-a-deterrent image in a larger mental pattern that includes both images, along with whatever evidence is available, especially historical evidence, as to when the one image is appropriate and when the other is. There can be no true sophistication or hardheaded realism short of that kind of analysis.

That brings us again to Barbara Tuchman. After detailing what she calls the "always futile" and "dreary" record of disarmament efforts, she goes on:

> I think a change is possible because a new factor, terrible as it may be, has intervened. . . . Until now, the finality of the human race and its living space was not within the framework of expectation. Today it is, which gives the question of control an urgency it never had before. The new factor is fear.

At an earlier point she had quoted Salvador de Madariaga, a man with great experience as "the general manager of disarmament," who said, "Nations don't distrust each other because they are armed; they are armed because they distrust each other." She now says:

> I come back to the Madariaga theorem: The source of hostility must be eliminated or mitigated before nations will give up their weapons. . . . I will grant that it is very difficult, but not more so than disarmament, which has eluded our efforts so far. . . . Mistrust has to be tackled and that is the hardest task. [1982, pp. 95, 96, 100]

In other words, tension has to be reduced before arms reduction, on a significant scale, can be achieved.

Is a freeze possible? Yes, probably. But not significant arms reduction.

Does that mean that we in the West should not even try, should not even negotiate in good faith to achieve verifiable reductions that would give the two sides something like equality in nuclear arms?

Of course not. We should do it, even if only as one part of a broader program of tension-reduction (see Chapter 19). The act of negotiating with open minds and in good faith is an important part of such a program. And rather than waiting until other policies have reduced tension before starting such negotiation, we can start good-faith negotiation now, concurrently with our other tension-reducing actions and nonactions. The main point of this whole discussion, though, is that we should measure our success not in terms of major reductions or binding agreements arrived at but in terms of whether the process of negotiation itself seems to have succeeded, in some degree, in reducing tension.

CHAPTER SEVEN

The Case for Minimal Deterrence

What It Means

In the vastness of the earth's oceans five nuclear-armed submarines would be extremely hard to find and destroy. Experts tell us that no promising method of finding and destroying submarines has yet been devised, and none seems probable. Yet those five, even if reduced to two or three by methods of antisubmarine warfare not yet invented, pack enough destructive punch to reduce the two hundred largest Soviet cities to smoking, radioactive rubble. Or the two hundred largest American cities. Those are hard facts, presumably well known to the defense communities on both sides of the East–West conflict.

A first step in concretely defining minimal deterrence therefore consists of the proposal that each side should retain as many as ten submarines armed with SLBMs (submarine-launched ballistic missiles), with the best possible system of command, control, and communication, to ensure that the submarines remain in good touch with the decision-makers in the United States and the USSR.

A second step is the proposal that the defensive conventional forces in Western Europe should be kept as strong in quantity as they are now, and made stronger in quality, planning, and coordination (including France if possible), but not increased in quantity.

The essential argument against increasing them in quantity has been presented in Chapter 4. It consists of the six reasons, all of them in terms of hard, selfish Soviet self-interest, why the Soviet rulers would be foolish to attempt an invasion of Western Europe. It should be noticed, though, that the first and most emotionally potent of those reasons is the Soviet revulsion against any big war. It can be argued that the conventional forces in Western

80

Europe therefore need to be strong enough to make the Soviet rulers realize that an attack on Western Europe would mean a big and costly war even if it remained conventional and they won it.

The essential argument against increasing those conventional forces also includes the very strong case against burdening the West's economy with unnecessary military expenses at a time when its health is especially precarious, and the further case against unnecessarily increasing the vicious circle of mutual hostility when it has gone as far as it has already.

A third step—since deterrence involves maintaining an opponent's respect for one's own resolve as well as strength—consists of the proposal that clear international aggression (not ambiguous international aggression, or subversion, or civil war) should be resisted by the collective force of as many nations as possible, but without escalation or counterattack on the conventional level, and absolutely without escalation by first use of nuclear weapons.

Those three proposals will be elaborated in the remainder of this chapter and further elaborated, and added to, in Chapter 17.

Why It Is Needed

A key word covering all three of the proposals that have just been made—a much better term than parity, which as we have seen is based on a historically and psychologically unsound premise—is *sufficiency*. That was President Nixon's term during the period of détente, and properly interpreted it is precisely the term we need. To keep the peace we do not necessarily need arms equal to those of our opponent. We do unquestionably need arms that, taking into account the opponent's other reasons for wanting or not wanting to attack us, will be sufficient to keep him from doing so.

How much nuclear strength does the West need? Not necessarily a matching of Soviet strength, weapon for weapon, or anything near it. Perhaps ten fairly invulnerable submarines, almost certainly able to destroy the two hundred largest cities in the USSR, would be sufficient to keep the other side from starting a nuclear war. If so, we don't necessarily need anything else for that purpose—not ICBMs, not Pershing IIs, not land-based cruise missiles, perhaps not bombers, and not even a number of nuclear-armed submarines comparable to theirs. An invulnerable ability to strike terror into the hearts of the Soviet decision-makers should be enough.

How much defensive conventional strength in Western Europe does the West need? Again, not necessarily a matching of Soviet conventional weapons or anything close to that. If the Soviet rulers have several excellent reasons not to want to attack, even apart from the costs and risks of a major war, as was argued in Chapter 4, then perhaps a level of strength half or two-thirds of theirs would be enough to deter them. At least those are the terms in which the question should be put, not a blind, unthinking assumption that parity is the answer.

The psychologist Kurt Lewin has proposed a pair of terms that may help us to ask ourselves the right questions: "driving forces" and "restraining forces." As Lewin might put it, the goal of armed deterrence should be to make it highly probable that the psychological restraining forces in the opponents' minds will outweigh and more than counteract the psychological forces driving them toward aggression. That is not an answer, of course; it is only a description of the two questions that most need to be asked if we want to understand any piece of human behavior. Those questions are: What would make the person want to do that thing, and what would make him want not to do it?

Another advantage of Lewin's terms is that they fit so neatly the key terms of this book, deterrence and tension-reduction. Deterrence by the West is essentially a way of increasing the restraining forces in Soviet minds, while tension-reduction covers all the things we can do to reduce the driving forces, such as anger and "paranoid" fear, that might lead them to attack. The chief limitation in the thinking of the all-out deterrers is that they tend to focus only on the restraining forces they want to create, while that of the all-out tension-reducers is to focus mainly on the driving forces they want to reduce.

What are the restraining forces in Soviet minds? They include fear of defeat in war and fear of the costs (economic costs as well as human suffering and loss of life) of war itself; and they are based on such things as the actual strength of the West (perhaps magnified if the Soviet decision-makers engage in worst-case thinking), the West's resolve to resist clear Soviet aggression, and the clearness with which the West communicates its resolve to the men in the Kremlin. What the all-out deterrers often ignore or underestimate, on this side of the equation, is the Soviet decision-makers' revulsion against war itself, which we know would be strong even if they think they are fairly sure to win it. The deterrers' case is convincing to the extent that it requires the West to be strong enough to make a particular war a big one—big enough to mobilize in advance the Soviet fear of any big war as such (or, probably, even a medium-size war). It is not convincing when it asks for great economic sacrifices by the West, and the increased risk of war that an arms race might bring, in order to create in the adversary much more than the necessary amount of healthy fear.

That subject is important enough to call for separate discussion.

Why More Would Increase the Danger

In addition to the argument that arms beyond the necessary minimum are not needed and the obvious fact that they are exorbitantly expensive at a time when that is the last thing the economy of the West needs, there is another extremely strong positive argument against them. The West's nuclear arms, on their present level of overkill capability, are *increasing* the war-promoting kind of tension in Soviet minds, and, by way of the arms race and what Morton Deutsch calls the "malignant process of hostile interaction," they are also increasing the likelihood of an unnecessary, dangerous use of force by the West. At a time when the malignant spiral has reached a fairly high level and drastic tension-reduction is urgently needed, they are having just the opposite effect. They increase tension.

That argument does not apply to conventional arms. There is hardly any danger that a moderate increase in the West's conventional arms (which is all we could afford anyway) would create undue alarm in the Kremlin, as our nuclear arms do. In conventional arms the USSR is already so far ahead that it doesn't have to worry. Given the great Soviet superiority now in troops, tanks, and artillery, given the Soviet Union's continuing high rate of arms production, and given the traditional advantage (3 to 1?) of the defense over the offense, there is no rational reason why they should fear a Hitler-like or Napoleon-like conventional attack from the West. A successful conventional attack from the area of the Middle East is even less thinkable. It is only in the Far East that the specter of a possible future Chinese attack, using sophisticated arms supplied by the United States, might have some plausibility.

Primarily, then, what might increase the ''paranoid'' Soviet fear of a Western attack is only the continuing and now intensified nuclear buildup in the West, with its emphasis on fast, accurate counterforce weapons that could be used in a first strike and its innovative developments, including the Pershing II and wide use of cruise missiles. Given the worst-case thinking that apparently characterizes the Soviet military as well as the American military, that probably does create in Kremlin minds the exaggerated, unhealthy, ''paranoid'' type of fear and increases the spiral that could lead straight to war.

An additional psychological reason for that kind of fear, which very few on either side seem to have thought about, is what will be called here the injured-innocence mechanism. It could also be called the arms-against-an-innocent-self mechanism. It begins with the large amount of evidence that the great majority in the USSR, like the great majority in the United States, have a sense of innocence, a moral self-image. They do not think they are threatening anyone unduly. To Americans who take it for granted that the Bad Guys in the world must know they are Bad Guys, that may seem incredible, but the evidence indicates that it is true at least as far as the Soviet public is concerned. Western visitors (e.g. Feifer, 1981; Kaiser, 1976, pp. 206, 306, 502) often report that whatever their criticisms of their government may be—and those criticisms are now often very bitter—they tend to rally around it on questions of foreign policy and to believe its claim that its one great foreign policy objective is peaceful coexistence. Actions such as the intervention in Afghanistan are rationalized to an amazing degree. Given that innocent national self-image and the basic sense of insecurity described here in Chapter 2, they naturally interpret as unnecessary America's long-term insistence on remaining ahead in the nuclear arms race. Why, they wonder, are the Americans insisting on keeping ahead in the most terrifying weapons of modern war, against *us*, who have never threatened them and are one of the most peace-loving nations in the world? It cannot be for defense, since we have no desire to attack them. Their only purpose can be offense. Therefore we must at all costs defend ourselves.

The image of arms-against-an-innocent-self is a frequent one, there as well as here. Robert Kaiser puts it this way:

> Until the mid-1960s American nuclear strategy was based on America's capacity to deliver a devastating blow before the Soviets could take any military action, with confidence that this first strike would be so effective that the Soviets could not retaliate. This was no secret from the Russians: successive American Secretaries of Defense advertised it regularly—always with the disclaimer that America had no intention of using superior force, naturally. But what Soviet leader could allow himself to rely on that assurance? Why did the Americans build those weapons if they had no intention of using them? [1976, p. 502]

We in the West exhibit the same mechanism in our interpretations of the Soviet arms buildup, including the long-term Soviet superiority in conventional weapons, the apparently offensive deployment of Soviet land forces in Eastern Europe, and the large number of SS-20s pointed at Western Europe.

To us such things seem obviously offensive in purpose. Why, we wonder, are they threatening *us*, the West, when our purposes are so obviously peaceful? It does not occur to most of us that their image of us in the dimension of peacefulness might be much less favorable than ours and that they might really feel a need to balance our nuclear threat, as they perceive it, with a conventional threat of their own. The men in the Kremlin, like the Soviet public, could be saying to themselves and each other: "Our best way to be safe, while also holding our end up in our competition with imperialism in the Third World, is to hold Western Europe hostage. If we do that the imperialists won't dare to attack."

If they do think in those terms it would be psychologically comparable to our holding their homeland hostage for many years (and now again, if we deploy the Pershing II) with our nuclear superiority. The men in the Kremlin probably felt for many years that our ability to strike first and destroy the Soviet Union was in a sense holding their homeland hostage, while we worked our evil will in many other parts of the world—Korea, Iran, Vietnam, Indonesia, Jordan, Guatemala, the Dominican Republic—and held them, worldwide, in an inferior power position. Probably in some degree that was true. Our nuclear superiority probably was one main reason for the marked degree of Soviet caution during the years 1951–79.

That does not prove that the Kremlin's holding Western Europe hostage is free from any thought of future aggression against it. But their primary motive, like ours in clinging to our nuclear superiority, could be defensive. The Soviet rulers have not attacked Western Europe during all the years they have had the conventional strength to do so, just as we have not attacked the Soviet Union during all the years when we have had the nuclear strength to do so. They also have all the reasons described in Chapter 4 for not wanting to do it: revulsion against any big war, especially nuclear war; a main focus on the Third World; the costs of domination; a favorable situation without war; uncertainty of quick victory; inherent caution. It is therefore a reasonable hypothesis that Moscow's main reason for holding Western Europe hostage is defensive.

In any case it does seem likely that the injured-innocence line of thinking occurs in Soviet minds and that it is a main reason why they put the worst possible interpretation on our offensive first-strike weapons.

If that is true one can imagine their sense of relief from fear, and relief from the need to sacrifice economic progress for defense, if we were to adopt voluntarily a policy of minimal—but prudent and adequate—deterrence.

CHAPTER EIGHT

The Case for Drastic Tension-reduction

The concrete operational meaning of drastic tension-reduction, as proposed here, will be spelled out in some detail in Chapters 18 and 19. More fundamental, though, is the concept of tension itself in an international context. What does it mean psychologically?

The Psychological Meaning of Tension

Common parlance almost requires use of the word tension. Political leaders such as President Reagan (sometimes) and ordinary people of all sorts find themselves using it naturally and habitually. It seems natural to think and say such things as "the present level of tension in the world is alarming"; "East and West are caught in a vicious circle of rising tension"; "a summit conference at least offers hope of some reduction in tension even if it accomplishes nothing concrete." Social and political scientists often do the same, conspicuous among them being the psychologist Charles Osgood (1962), whose proposal of GRIT (Graduated and Reciprocated Initiatives in Tension-reduction) uses tension as its central concept, and the sociologist Amitai Etzioni, whose book *The Hard Way to Peace* (1962) was a pioneering systematic study of the problem. In it the "hard way" was tension-reduction.

But what *is* "tension"? How can we reduce it effectively without a clear idea of what it is? And is "tension" the best word for the thing or things it represents?

There have been few attempts to define it with any precision, and with good reason: The concept as commonly used has a number of aspects, and consequently a writer with even a moderate degree of semantic sophistication hesitates to pin it down too precisely. Hayakawa, in his *Modern Guide to Synonyms* (1968), says that "tension has come popularly to denote any state of strained relations like that caused by conflict or hostility between persons or groups of persons." *Webster's New Collegiate Dictionary* speaks of "nervous anxiety" and "a strained condition of relations, as between nations." It will be noticed that the first of these definitions contains the word "hostility" and the second contains the word "anxiety." Those words resemble rather closely two key terms in this book, which together represent most of what is meant here by tension—two shorter and blunter words, anger and fear. Tension as defined here includes both.

It will be noticed too that both definitions contain the inconspicuous preposition *between*, which implies a mutual, interactive process. It looks as if the common sense embodied in common usage implicitly recognizes here a familiar and important fact, which is that hostile words and actions on one side of a conflict tend to evoke hostile feelings, words, and actions on the other side, which in turn evoke hostile feelings on the first side, and so on around. That links the concept of tension with present-day "systems theory," which emphasizes circular processes of various kinds. The vicious circle represented here also seems equivalent to what Morton Deutsch calls the "malignant process" of hostile interaction.

Both the interactive concept of tension and Deutsch's concept suggest Charles Osgood's hopeful and extremely important idea (embodied also in Deutsch's concept of "constructive processes") that it may be possible to set up a *constructive* circular process that reverses the malignant process of hostile interaction and saves the human race from nuclear catastrophe. It cannot come quickly—it is, as Etzioni says, the "hard way"—but perhaps it is our last, best hope.

Coming back to the definitional problem: So far we have distinguished three elements that could be included in a useful definition of tension: anger, fear, and an interactive, vicious-circle relationship between groups that are angry, fearful, or both. So far the whole thing sounds purely emotional, with no cognitive, perceptual (or misperceptual) element in it. That element has to be added in the form of a distinctive type of perception: the black-and-white, good guys–bad guys picture, consisting of a diabolical enemy-image and a moral self-image, both of which usually contain large elements of misperception that can be remedied only if large amounts of realistic empathy (another cognitive process, but this time a very healthy one) are brought into the picture.

We are now prepared for a single-sentence definition of tension in the context of group conflict: *Tension is a blend of emotions in which anger and fear are usually prominent, which often grows through the vicious circle of hostile interaction, and which often involves a black-and-white picture that grossly distorts the psychological reality on both sides.*

That is at least the kind of tension that, it will be argued in this book, is most dangerous to peace. It is the kind that is meant when, in this book, various forms of tension reduction are urged.

There is one thing wrong with it, though. In its apparent implication that all kinds of fear are forms of tension and need to be reduced in order to prevent war, it ignores the role of healthy, realistic fear in the process of deterrence. There is such a thing as healthy, realistic, war-preventing fear, comprising both fear of defeat in war and fear of the consequences of war itself. Here is a real paradox that needs to be candidly faced up to. The next chapter attempts to do that.

Now, is "tension" the best single word for the blend or cluster of emotions and perceptual processes we are talking about?

A runner-up candidate is the word "hostility." It too can be defined broadly enough to include both fear and anger as well as the process of hostile interaction and the black-and-white picture. Dina Zinnes, in her recent mathematical treatment of war's causes, uses hostility as her central concept, and uses it apparently with roughly the same broad meaning that has been given here to the word "tension." If it is defined as broadly as that there can be little objection to it. To do so, however, probably violates common usage, in that hostility, in common usage, does not imply fear; one speaks naturally of fear *and* hostility, meaning by hostility something more active in the sense of wanting to do harm to the object of hostility. Since the historical analysis in this book leads to a strong emphasis on exaggerated fear and on defensively motivated aggression as causes of war, any exclusion of fear-reduction from the concept of tension-reduction would lead away from the core of our war-prevention problem. Therefore the broader term, tension, seems preferable.

It should be noticed, finally, that the definition of tension offered here leaves wide open the question of what other psychological factors may often be involved in the blend or cluster of processes we are talking about and also the question of how and why the components of the cluster are related to each other. There is ample room here for historical and other kinds of research. For instance, wounded pride (called ''narcissistic injury'' by some psychiatrists) may be, along with fear, one of the most frequent causes of anger; a *macho* type of pride (which some psychiatrists might call a special form of narcissism) may make a leader or a nation unduly susceptible to wounded pride and belligerent anger; a sense of bafflement at being unable to cope with the ills of one's own economy may be a factor facilitating both fear and anger; a fear of losing territory, an ally, or access to a natural resource such as oil may be another. Also, since by our definition tension is a blend or cluster, there can be much variation in the relative importance of its components. In one case fear of a future imbalance of power may be predominant (e.g. Austria, Germany, France, and Britain in World War I); in another, anger based on wounded pride (e.g. Russia in World War I).

Another reason to focus first on this whole cluster of psychological processes rather than on only one to two of them is that there are many close relationships between them that we know exist without yet knowing to what extent or just why they exist. Fear and anger, for instance, as psychiatrists know, strongly tend to go together; we seldom find much of one in an individual without finding some of the other, at least on an unconscious or semiconscious level. A frightened, anxious child is almost sure to be in some ways also a hostile child (Horney, 1937, pp. 60–77). That appears to be true also on the international level. Dina Zinnes shows a striking simultaneous rise in both ''perception of hostility'' [in an opponent] and ''expression of hostility,'' during the crisis of 1914, based on a content analysis of diplomatic correspondence and other documents representing all the major powers (1968). That makes sense, too. It would be hard not to experience anger at another person who was perceived, realistically or not, as both wanting to hurt oneself, for no good reason, and strong enough to hurt oneself; and if the initial impulse was one of hostility or anger it would be surprising if there were no tendency to project that hostility onto the other, as if saying ''I don't hate him; he hates me.'' Circular relations of that type, with the cause-and-effect relation going both ways, probably exist between several of the variables in the cluster that is here called ''tension.''

A close relation between fear and anger exists also on the level of animal behavior and on the physiological level in the human species. A frightened, cornered animal often turns and fights viciously. The bodily changes (e.g. the production of adrenalin) in intense excitement of any sort, including fear, rage, pain, and intense exertion, are so similar that they are difficult if not impossible to distinguish; from a physiological standpoint they can all be appropriately called simply ''the emergency reaction'' (Cannon, 1963).

That brings up, however, another distinction that does make a difference on the level of international behavior: the distinction between the ''hot'' emotions of fear and rage that are mobilized in times of crisis, and probably do often have bodily concomitants, and the ''cold'' beliefs and feelings that a person may have about an adversary during the years between crises. Between crises the central fact may be simply a firm conviction that the adversary is both hostile enough and strong enough to hurt one's own country badly, unless deterred by the strength and resolve of one's own country and its allies. While such a conviction necessarily carries with it much negative feeling and is ''affective'' in that sense, it is primarily cognitive. The label ''emotion'' is definitely not appropriate for it, and it probably does not imply any significant pumping of adrenalin into the blood. The evil and strength attributed to the adversary may be accepted, with a certain calmness (as long as one's own country is seen as adequately strong), as a basic fact of international life. Yet such a conviction certainly should be included in a term as inclusive as tension or hostility, since it can have great motivating power in promoting strenuous arming and other power-oriented policies.

That distinction has much importance in the analysis of what happens psychologically when a crisis comes and acute fear and anger are injected into the situation. There is then a change in the quality as well as the intensity of tension. Fear approaching panic may take hold, and because of it there is likely to be a new fear of fear, a stiffening of the spine, a concentration on macho pride, and a determination not to feel or show cowardice. Cold hostility becomes hot anger, sometimes described by observers as fury. Up to a certain point of no return there is typically an absorption in the search for peace on ''acceptable'' terms; after that point the hope of peace may be virtually given up, and there is immersion in the task of winning or preparing to win the war that seems to have practically started. The influence of military men may become decisive.

Perhaps the word tension is too mild for the extremely dangerous explosive forces that then come into play. Or perhaps we can retain the word tension and distinguish between two rather different kinds of tension, a peacetime blend in which relatively cold calculations of power and security predominate, and a war-crisis blend in which hot emotions predominate and rationality often takes a back seat. Tension has risen to the snapping point.

If that is true, a large part of war-prevention should consist in trying to keep the war-crisis type of psychological escalation from ever getting started.

How that can be done will be much discussed in later chapters. One aspect of it can be mentioned here: the need for an effort, in noncrisis periods, to promote realistic empathy with the opponent and to break down the prevailing black-and-white picture of the conflict. Once that picture is well established, any ambiguous action by the chief opponent (e.g. the assassination of the Archduke as seen by the Germans and Austrians in 1914, the Austrian reaction as seen by the Russians, the Soviet emplacement of offensive missiles in Cuba) is likely to be given the worst possible interpretation and the war-crisis type of psychological escalation may occur.

The Malignant Process of Hostile Interaction

The interactive nature of tension between persons or between groups has been the chief focus of attention, by way of controlled experimentation and systematic theoretical analysis, in the work of the psychologist Morton Deutsch (1973, 1983). He has recently made a major contribution to understanding of the vicious-circle type of hostile interaction both in his choice of the term ''malignant process'' and in his development of theory as to its nature. He finds that

> . . . sane and intelligent people, once they are enmeshed in a pathological social process, engage in actions which seem to them completely rational and necessary but which a detached, objective observer would readily identify as contributing to the perpetuation and intensification of a vicious cycle of interactions. We have all seen this happen in married couples or in par-

ent–adolescent relations where the individual people are otherwise decent and rational. They trap themselves into a vicious
social process which leads to outcomes—hostility, estrangement,
violence—which no one really wants. So this can happen with
nations: otherwise sane, intelligent leaders of the superpowers
have allowed their nations to become involved in a malignant
process which is driving them to engage in actions and reactions
that are steadily increasing the chances of nuclear war—an outcome no one wants. In such a process, both sides are right in
coming to believe that the other is hostile and malevolent: the
interactions and attitudes which develop in those involved in
such a process provide ample justification for such beliefs. [pp.
4–5]

Such a process, then, brings out the worst on both sides.
Among other things, this passage suggests that each side is realistic in feeling that *some* hard-nosed preparations to deter the other
from doing his worst are needed. More importantly, though, it
suggests that a reversal of the malignant process, if at all possible,
is urgently needed—in other words, tension-reduction.

Elsewhere (in an unpublished paper), Deutsch has other things
to say on the psychological effects of the process, relevant to the
nature of tension and the causes of war. For example:

"Communication between the conflicting parties is unreliable
and impoverished."

"The view is stimulated that the solution of the conflict can
only be imposed by one side or the other by means of superior
force, deception or cleverness."

"A suspicious, hostile attitude develops that increases the sensitivity to differences and threats while minimizing the awareness
of similarities."

Is there hope of reversing such a process, as Deutsch, Osgood, Etzioni, and others have urged? The familiar term "spiral" suggests that there is none, that it is like a snowball rolling
downhill in its inevitable self-reinforcing character. Actually the
record of twentieth-century history does not support that conclusion. Tension between nations has often gone down as well as up;
it can go down when statesmen and publics have become aware of
the danger and have deliberately tried to counteract and reverse
the upward tendency. During the three years between the fairly
acute second Morocco crisis, the Agadir affair in 1911, and the
crisis of 1914, the tension between the German-Austrian alliance
and the French-Russian-British Triple Entente diminished on the

whole; and during the few months just preceding the crisis of July 1914 the success of the British and Germans in resolving the problem of the Berlin-to-Baghdad railway was especially notable. More relevant to the present is the fact that from 1951, when the Korean war was at its height and many in the United States believed that World War III was about to start, until approximately 1975, when the two nations were really collaborating in space and reaching the Vladivostok agreement, the movement of the curve of tension was downward more often than upward. It had peaks—Hungary, Berlin, Cuba, Czechoslovakia, Vietnam—but none of them led to war, and the general trend was clearly toward relaxation.

Nevertheless, since 1975 or so there has been a classic, fairly steady upward spiral, and given the nuclear possibilities in the background we would be naive if we were not terrified. By now it has gone fairly far. In a greatly oversimplified form (which may help us to see the forest rather than the trees) it looks something like this:

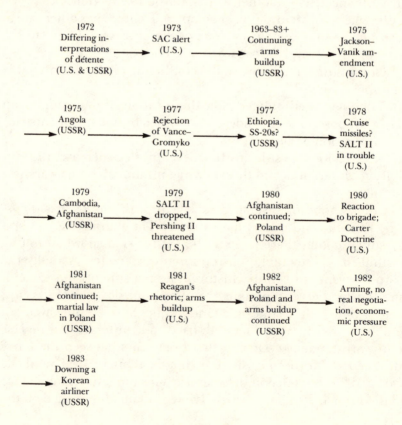

| 1972 | 1973 | 1963–83+ | 1975 |
| Differing in-terpretations of détente (U.S. & USSR) | SAC alert (U.S.) | Continuing arms buildup (USSR) | Jackson–Vanik amendment (U.S.) |

| 1975 | 1977 | 1977 | 1978 |
| Angola (USSR) | Rejection of Vance–Gromyko (U.S.) | Ethiopia, SS-20s? (USSR) | Cruise missiles? SALT II in trouble (U.S.) |

| 1979 | 1979 | 1980 | 1980 |
| Cambodia, Afghanistan (USSR) | SALT II dropped, Pershing II threatened (U.S.) | Afghanistan continued; Poland (USSR) | Reaction to brigade; Carter Doctrine (U.S.) |

| 1981 | 1981 | 1982 | 1982 |
| Afghanistan continued; martial law in Poland (USSR) | Reagan's rhetoric; arms buildup (U.S.) | Afghanistan, Poland and arms buildup continued (USSR) | Arming, no real negotiation, economic pressure (U.S.) |

| 1983 |
| Downing a Korean airliner (USSR) |

The oversimplification here takes several forms. The diagram suggests that each tension-increasing action is solely the result of the immediately preceding single action by the other side, which is far from true. Each was rather the result of the cumulative impression from all the previous actions by the other side, filtered through quite different perceptual processes. In the case of the Soviet strategic arms buildup, the marked acceleration of which began after the Soviet humiliation in the Cuban missile crisis of 1962, it would have been more accurate, if feasible, to show it as a continuous thing, with a cumulative impact. The introduction of new missiles or initial substantial public knowledge of them, such as the SS-20s, the cruise missiles, and the Pershing IIs, has been assigned somewhat arbitrarily to a single year, whereas it too was cumulative. Many items, such as South Yemen and the possible or probable arming of Nicaraguan revolutionaries on the Soviet side, and the Olympics and grain embargo on the American side, have been omitted. Some notable efforts to reduce tension, such as the initial Vance–Gromyko communiqué intended to initiate cooperation on the Arab–Israeli conflict, are not shown.

Certainly there is no implication here that the amount of guilt or the amount of tension increase attributable to the two sides is equal. That seems quite unlikely, since the items obviously should be given widely differing weights. The reader may find it interesting to assign his own weights to them, checking or double-checking the ones he thinks are important, in order to test or buttress his own present general conception of which side has been more responsible for the increase.

Three general conclusions, though, can perhaps be drawn:

• The record has been by no means wholly one-sided, as black-and-white thinkers on each side have often supposed. Even if given the benefit of every doubt, each has done some things that in retrospect should be reconsidered and perhaps regretted.

• By paying attention selectively to the sins that can be attributed to the other side, putting the worst interpretation on them and the best interpretation on the actions of his own side, a black-and-white thinker on either side can rather easily arrive at an honest impression that the other has been much more guilty.

• There is little or no doubt about the ominous increase of tension on both sides since about 1975.

The advanced state of that spiral justifies a very broad conclusion: The time has come to give much more emphasis to tension-reduction than to deterrence. The danger in letting the spiral go even higher is beginning to look critical.

Defensively Motivated Aggression in Recent History

A strong reason for stressing tension-reduction more than deterrence is that an arms buildup intended as deterrence, and not combined with tension-reduction, may instead be interpreted by the other side as preparation for deliberately planned aggression. It is then a source of the unhealthy, exaggerated kind of fear that promotes arms races and the malignant process of hostile interaction. In the end that process may bring about literal aggression by the other side that is, amazing as it may seem, literally motivated mainly by fear.

That has happened in our century much more often than is usually realized. Let us look briefly at the record.

• The German and Austrian attack on Serbia in 1914 was motivated largely by fear that Russia—with its huge and growing army, its alliance with France, its semialliance with Britain, and the disintegration of Austria–Hungary, which Austria wanted to stave off by taking a ''firm stand'' against Serbia—would in a few years be able to overwhelm the German–Austrian alliance (Fay, 1966, II: 550–54).

• The German attack on France through Belgium in 1914 was probably motivated mainly by fear that if France were not quickly defeated Germany would be overwhelmed by a two-front war, including a Russian invasion from the East (Tuchman, 1976, pp. 33–36, 93–95).

These two acts of aggression, as will be discussed in more detail in Chapter 13, were the climax of a period in which both sides pursued armed deterrence policies without real efforts to reduce tension. Both failed. The extent of the failure on both sides is well represented by Sidney Fay's summary (1966, II: 547): ''None of the Powers wanted a European War. Their governing rulers and ministers, with very few exceptions, all foresaw that it must be a frightful struggle, in which the loss of life, suffering and economic consequences were bound to be terrible.'' In spite of all this, the war came. The malignant process of hostile interaction (including two arms races, the naval race between Britain and Germany and the land army race between Germany on one side and France and Russia on the other) had gone too far. Each side was convinced, and remained convinced, that the other side was "the aggressor."

The resemblance between that story and what is happening now between the West and the Soviet Union is far too close for comfort. It is much closer than the resemblance between what is happening now and the one-sided series of Axis aggressions that preceded World War II.

• The treatment of Germany after the Treaty of Versailles was in a sense aggression and did pave the way for Hitler and World War II, but in the eyes of the French it was unquestionably defensively motivated. They felt that they had been invaded twice by Germany in less than fifty years, that Germany was much stronger in population, industry, and potential military power, and therefore France's very survival depended on making use of their present military power to hold Germany down (A.J.P. Taylor, 1961, pp. 28–29, 32).

• The large-scale Soviet takeover of most of Eastern Europe in 1944–48 was aggression by almost any clear definition of the term and (see Chapter 15) probably motivated mainly by a need to build a buttress against another attack from the capitalist West, after the enormous trauma of World War II (Shulman, 1963, pp. 20, 26).

• The reinstatement of the Shah on his throne in Iran in 1954, aided if not engineered by the American CIA, has often been called aggression. It was to a large extent unequivocally defensive in motivation; it followed a period, 1944–50, in which the Soviet Union had been more expansionist than in any other period before or since, including an episode in 1946 in which the Soviet Union kept its army (violating a wartime promise in doing so) in northwest Iran. Of all the countries on the periphery of the USSR, it looked then as if Iran might be the most vulnerable to renewed Soviet expansion unless a safely non-Communist government could be maintained there. (Oil probably had something to do with it too, but the security motive was probably much more potent.)

• In their 1948 attack on the fledgling state of Israel the Arabs clearly felt that the U.N.'s partition plan amounted to a barefaced seizure of Arab land against which they had every right to defend themselves (White, 1977; pp. 198–99, 206–8; Sachar, 1976, pp. 317-17).

• Israel's attack on Egypt in 1956, in collaboration with Britain and France, grew out of Israel's perennial fear of being attacked and overwhelmed by the Arabs, who outnumbered Israelis more than 30 to 1 and whose fedayeen raids seemed to demonstrate implacable hostility (White, 1977, pp. 200–201, 205, 208–9; Sachar, 1976, pp. 429–96).

• Israel's preemptive attack on Egypt and then Syria in 1967 was largely based on the same perennial fear, heightened by the fact that the Arabs then seemed to be on the verge of a concerted attack (White, 1977, pp. 209–10; Sachar, 1976, pp. 615–38).

• The Soviet Union's crackdowns on Hungary and Czechoslovakia in 1956 and 1968 could have been mainly based on fear of a domino process of defection from the "socialist camp" if either were allowed to succeed. (See Chapter 15.)

• The large-scale American intervention in Vietnam, now regarded by some Americans as an aggressive act comparable to the Soviet intervention in Afghanistan (see Chapter 2), was certainly mainly defensively motivated. Its essential purpose was to "stop Communism" and to prevent a domino process that might encompass all of Southeast Asia and impair America's credibility everywhere (White, 1970, pp. 182–240; *Pentagon Papers*, 1971, pp. xix, 492).

• Egypt's crossing the Suez Canal in 1973, although the Israelis saw it as aggression, was from an Egyptian standpoint a continuing defense of their own soil, which had been stolen from them as recently as 1967. (For more detailed treatment of all four of the major Arab–Israeli wars, in psychological terms, see White, 1977, pp. 205–12.)

• The Soviet intervention in Afghanistan has already been discussed in these terms (Chapter 2). The interpretation suggested in that chapter becomes still more acceptable when it is seen as one of a long list of instances of aggression motivated mainly by fear—not fear of an imminent Western attack in this case, of course, but fear of a significant loss in the East–West balance of power.

In addition to these instances in which fear has probably been the main reason for aggression, there have been in our century at least twelve other instances in which it seems to have been a minor, supplementary reason. For instance, the Japanese attack on

China, from 1931 to 1945, was not from the Japanese viewpoint a matter of sheer lust for conquest or macho pride, though an unbiased observer might well judge that that motive, thoroughly rationalized by the Japanese, was primary (Butow, 1961). From the Japanese conscious point of view the chief reason for it was to escape from the economic stranglehold that Western imperialism supposedly had over all the peoples of Asia, especially overpopulated Japan—to escape by building a Greater East Asia Coprosperity Sphere. Probably, therefore, it was at least a supplementary motive. Another example is the Israeli invasion of Lebanon in 1982. It is hard under the circumstances for an observer not to think that in the minds of Begin, Sharon, and most of the Sephardic Jews in Israel it was primarily a result of macho pride, glorying in Israel's newfound strength. However, there was still in the background Israel's perennial feeling that it had to be strong in order to fend off an ultimate concerted Arab attack, and on the conscious level there was the perennial combination of fear and anger engendered by PLO terrorism.

History suggests two sound principles: If you want to be attacked by your enemy (1) make him think you are an unmitigated devil and (2) make him think you are strong enough to do him great harm—or will be if he doesn't strike first.

If defensively motivated aggression has been so frequent, why haven't more people recognized that that is the case? Why do most people on both sides of the East–West conflict take it for granted that aggression is usually the act of a power-mad would-be conqueror, arrogantly self-confident, who "understands only the language of force" and would interpret efforts to be friendly only as signs of weakness?

Unfortunately there is much truth in that last proposition. By the time the malignant process is well established, both sides do have such an ingrained power orientation and such deep suspicion of trickery by the other side that there is a real likelihood of interpreting conciliatory efforts as weakness and trying to take advantage of them (cf. Jervis, 1976, pp. 90–94). That is a strong argument for at least prudent, minimal deterrence. The opponent should be given no rational basis for interpreting conciliation as due to weakness, fear, or trickery. However, taking the long view and recognizing how often the opponent is far more fearful than we think he is, efforts to reduce his exaggerated fear of one's own country seem likely to be more fundamentally effective than hardball politics and military threats.

The problem remains: *Why* do so many people fail to recognize the frequency of defensively motivated aggression?

One reason surely is that they have not studied enough history with an effort to avoid nationalistic and ideological preconceptions. Another probably is that there are subconscious satisfactions (see Chapter 10) in clinging to a black-and-white picture of whatever conflict the individual is caught in. Still another probably is that an atypical war, World War II, in which Hitler was *not* motivated mainly by fear but by an extraordinary lust for conquest, is so prominent in the experience and in the minds of most of us. Most people take seriously only the history that they themselves have lived through or that they have often heard about from their parents. For both Russians and the peoples of the West, that means primarily World War II. For them that is the model, the paradigm, of war itself. In the words of the psychologists Tversky and Kahneman (1973), images derived from that war are more ''available'' in our minds than images of any other; they come crowding into our minds whenever we think of any kind of war. Hitler, Munich, appeasement, Chamberlain, and Pearl Harbor are almost household words. Too often the frequency of a quite different kind of war never enters our consciousness, because our consciousness is already so filled with a war that is not typical.

Is Tension-reduction Feasible?

Tension-reduction is entirely feasible, if we really want it.

The universal longing for peace and the staggering expense of the arms race, at a time when the economies on both sides are staggering anyway, are potent psychological reasons for thinking it is feasible. There are also many fairly recent historical examples of tension-reduction between strong nations with adequate arms.

Two examples have already been cited (pp. 93–94): the lowering of tension in Europe between 1911 and 1914 and the lowering of tension in the Cold War between 1951 and 1975. There are many others. Gladstone and others achieved a rapproachement between Britain and the United States after the American Civil War during which tension was high. Bismarck achieved a lasting rapprochement with Austria–Hungary and a fairly lasting one with Russia after 1871. Edward VII and others accomplished a similar feat in the 1904 entente between Britain and France after several centuries of intermittent war and the Fashoda crisis of 1898. All the strong nations of the West, plus Japan, have maintained surprisingly cordial relations with each other since 1945; their coming together includes the achievement of Jean Monnet, Konrad Adenauer, and others in finally putting an end to the centuries-long conflict between the Germans and the French. Statesmen can sometimes do it.

It is true that, notably in the case of France and West Germany, such comings together have often been facilitated by a spirit of common defense against a real or partly real common enemy, but that factor should not be exaggerated. The Arabs have had surprising difficulty getting together in spite of having a common enemy in Israel. Britain and the United States had no clear common enemy after the Civil War, but they got together, obviously for other good reasons. In Bismarck's time, after 1871, France was not strong enough to threaten any strong neighbor, and the only country it wanted to threaten was Germany; yet Bismarck found willing allies. Germany did not yet look like a very threatening common enemy when France and Britain got together around 1904; in fact Britain had considered allying itself with Germany instead of France. The good relations among the Western powers after 1945, though certainly facilitated by the real or partly real Soviet enemy, were probably as strong as ever (and stronger than later) during the period roughly between 1963 and 1975, when the Soviet Union looked least threatening. The Soviet Union and the United States have had no common enemy since 1945 (except of course the horrendous common enemy of nuclear war), but there was a real prospect of détente, though on a partly illusory basis, between the late 1960s and about 1975.

Today the great common enemy is nuclear war. It still exists in an even more horrendous form. There is no good psychological reason to think it could not be a sufficient basis for a gradual, continuing reduction of tension between the United States and the USSR, providing that both sides show even a moderate amount of common sense.

Slippages in Deterrence

Tension-reduction is more feasible, then, than is commonly believed. Effective deterrence is less feasible.

Many of the examples of defensively motivated aggression mentioned previously in this chapter are also examples of failed attempts to achieve peace through armed deterrence that was not combined with tension-reduction. In most of them the armed deterrence was *too* successful in its purpose of inspiring fear in an opponent—since the fear it inspired turned out in the long run (though often not in the short run) to be the unhealthy fear of being attacked that promotes arms races and the malignant process of hostile interaction.

There are also many examples of armed deterrence not successful even in its short-term purpose of preventing violence by inspiring the healthy, war-preventing kind of fear. Alexander George and Richard Smoke (1974) have pointed out than an already hostile and determined opponent can often find ways (or think it has found ways) to circumvent it. It can "design around" the kinds of armed deterrence it confronts.

Such an adversary can sometimes achieve surprise, as Japan did at Pearl Harbor, as North Korea did, as Israel did in 1967, and as Egypt did when it crossed the Suez Canal in 1973. It can work through proxies, as the Soviet Union did in the Korean war, Angola, Ethiopia, the Vietnamese invasion of Cambodia, and the recent crackdown on the Polish people. It can supply weapons to one side in a civil war, as both superpowers have done on many occasions. It can support unpopular governments against popular rebellions, as the United States did in the early stages of the Vietnam war and in Iran, and as the Soviet Union is doing now in Afghanistan (though that method is not generally to be recommended). It can support guerrilla movements that are completely beyond the deterrent power of nuclear weapons. It can circumvent a fortified area by going around it, as Germany did in two World Wars by avoiding the main fortified French border and going through Begium. It can hope to exploit the logistic difficulties its opponent would have in effectively reaching the field of battle, as Germany did in 1914 when it hoped to crush France before either Britain or Russia could be fully mobilized and effective; as Germany did again when it hoped to isolate Britain by its submarine warfare before America could be fully mobilized and across the Atlantic; and as it did a third time when Hitler attacked Poland in full awareness of the difficulty both Britain and France would have in reaching the Polish front. Although the defender of territory often has the traditional three-to-one advantage in the long run, the attacker in the short run has the great advantage of choosing his own means of "designing around" the defender's defenses.

Without tension-reduction, which over a long period can greatly reduce the attacker's incentive to attack, all the forms of warfare described above are more likely to occur. When the fire is hot, steam finds ways to escape around the lid of the kettle. Tension-reduction reduces the fire.

Why the Reduction Should Be Drastic

The Western effort to reduce tension must be drastic, first because of the fairly advanced state of the malignant process it is designed to stop and reverse. Reversing a process of such magnitude and momentum on both sides of the East–West conflict necessarily calls for a massive investment of thought and effort along many different lines (Chapters 18, 19, 20). It also calls for courage—the courage to challenge a number of deeply ingrained assumptions still held by the majority in one's own country and the courage of stubborn individuals to face the inevitable charges, in some quarters, of being called "soft on Communism"—plus patience in explaining why that is not the issue.

It should be drastic, second, because of the inevitability that minor changes in Western policy will be ignored, belittled, or even denounced as window dressing or as trickery by the other side. There surely is immense bureaucratic and psychological inertia, there as here, sustaining established policies and assumptions and buttressed by all the defense mechanisms unconsciously employed by insecure individuals to maintain the cherished distortions and delusions in their minds. Psychiatrists know how, when a well-meaning friend or doctor tries to help a paranoid psychotic to understand the falsity of his delusions of persecution, the paranoid person is likely to turn against the friend, concluding that the friend also must be part of the plot that has been hatched against him and is now trying to deceive him by lulling him into a false sense of security. Since there is some genuine resemblance between the ingrained suspicions of a paranoid individual and those of a typical nation in conflict with another nation (Chapter 10), somewhat the same kind of suspicion and resistance is to be expected, unless the changes in policy on the initiating side are genuine, major, varied, well-explained, and sustained. Charles Osgood's discussion of how his GRIT proposal (Graduated and Reciprocated Initiatives in Tension-reduction) ought to be implemented is very relevant here (1962).

An important psychological principle, well established in experimental psychology, applies here: the principle of assimilation and contrast. It can be stated this way: When a new stimulus is only slightly different from what a person is used to in a given context, the change is likely to be underestimated or not noticed at all. The new stimulus is "assimilated" to previous experience. However, when a certain threshold of amount of change is reached or exceeded—that is, when the new stimulus is different enough from the old ones—the amount of change tends to be actually overestimated. There is a "contrast effect." It is doubtful that the contrast effect would be found in Soviet responses to Western initiatives in tension-reduction or vice versa; the paranoia-like defences on each side would tend to counteract it. The assimilation process, however, can be confidently predicted. Unless tension-reduction by one side is fairly drastic it is not likely to be fully noticed by the other side or taken seriously at all; the initiators are then likely to be disappointed and give up too readily, with no net result from the standpoint of preventing war.

How Deterrence and Tension-reduction Can Reinforce Each Other

The practical upshot of this book, packed into a single sentence, is this: To prevent nuclear war there should be on each side a *combination* of minimal deterrence and drastic tension-reduction.

It is a simplifying mental device, and therefore a tempting one, to neglect one or the other side of this combination because of a feeling that they are more or less incompatible and that the less important one should give way to the more important one. All-out deterrers are likely to belittle what they see as the well-meaning soft-headedness of the tension-reducers, while the all-out tension-reducers tend to belittle what they see as militarism or chauvinism on the part of the deterrers. The result is acrimony and disunity where there should be American, and Western, unity behind a program that combines both.

The acrimony and disunity are unnecessary, because each side should welcome the other's contribution to peace. That is partly because the right kind of deterrence does not conflict much, if at all, with the right kind of tension-reduction, and vice versa. It is also because, if properly defined, each reinforces the other. The all-out deterrers should welcome the help they get from the sensible tension-reducers and vice versa.

The clearest way in which one reinforces the other is well represented by a remarkable statement, already cited here (p. 6), by Winston Churchill: "Appeasement in itself may be good or bad according to circumstances. . . . Appeasement from strength is magnanimous and noble and might be the surest and perhaps the only path to world peace" (quoted by Fulbright, 1966, p. 103). In this statement Churchill seems to be using the word appeasement in its broader, pre-Munich sense of negotiating and seeking legitimate compromise, rather than in its post-Munich sense of rewarding outright aggression by failing to resist it. Nevertheless, since Churchill has become for us a symbol of stalwart courage and nonappeasement in the latter sense, his words can serve as a wholesome reminder that there are times when compromise with an enemy is an act of statesmanship rather than a dangerous rewarding of aggression, and this is particularly true when one's own strength is not open to question. Or, as Jervis has put it (1976, pp. 84–90), compromise by a person or nation perceived as weak is likely to be perceived by a tough opponent as a sign of weakness or even cowardice rather than as a sign of goodwill or magnanimity. It then does nothing to discourage, and may encourage, a policy of tough self-assertion by the opponent.

In other words, adequate armed deterrence could be a precondition for the success of a policy of drastic tension-reduction.

Is the reverse relationship also real—that the right kind of tension-reduction aids deterrence?

It is—not so certainly, but quite plausibly.

A united nation is essential in any war that is not catastrophically sudden, and in our day a nation is much more likely to be united in war if its people are convinced that, before asking them to fight, the government had done everything it honorably could to preserve the peace. Loyalty to the government and all-out condemnation of the enemy are both likely to depend on that conviction, which in the United States was strong in World War II but grew progressively weak in the Vietnam war. That probably applies to deterrence also. At Munich Chamberlain could not convincingly tell Hitler that his people would back him up in a war to keep Germany out of the Sudetenland; Hitler had good reason to think that was not so, and at the time it certainly was not. By the time of Hitler's attack on Poland Britain was far more united behind a tough policy, partly because the British people knew their government had done its best for peace, and Hitler had violated his promises. If Hitler had been capable of seeing the full extent of the shift in British attitudes, he might well have been deterred from attacking Poland, and World War II, conceivably, would not have occurred. He was not—but that is another story.

PART II

Political Psychology: Motives and Perceptions

CHAPTER NINE

War-promoting Motives

Limitations of Conventional Deterrence Theory

What could make a nation's decision-makers *want* to precipitate a nuclear war? Or a conventional war that might become nuclear?

That is the basic, baffling psychological question that conventional deterrence theorists have rarely attacked in a systematic, evidence-oriented way. It is nevertheless basic. It brings up immediately the paradox of unwanted war, which was the starting point of this book. The unwantedness of war is greater now than ever before, yet few would be so foolhardy as to predict that it could not be started, in a sense deliberately, by one superpower or the other. Why? Can conventional deterrence theory give us an answer?

Up to a point, yes.

The word "conventional" is applied here to three kinds of thinking about deterrence:

1. There is the ordinary, simple Good Guys–Bad Guys thinking that prevails among the majority of people, leaders as well as followers, in the USSR—in fact, especially in the USSR—and in the West. Its basic rule is: In time of peace prepare for war. Be at least as strong as the Bad Guys, and stronger if you can.

2. There is the "flexible response" doctrine of many Western

A Note on Political Psychology: Although the term "political psychology" is fairly new, the field of interest it represents is at least 2,400 years old. Plato and Aristotle, Machiavelli and Tocqueville were political psychologists. Most of the relevant research and writing, though, has occurred since Harold Lasswell's ground-breaking work, *Psychopathology and Politics* (1930). The term "political psychology" has come into use chiefly as a result of the *Handbook of Political Psychology*, edited by the late Jeanne Knutson (1973), and the vigorous new organization, the International Society of Political Psychology, initiated mainly by her. It is a highly interdisciplinary as well as international organization in which the chief single elements are the psychologically oriented political scientists and the politically oriented psychologists. This book owes much to the mutual stimulation provided by that group.

strategists who believe the Good Guys should if possible be at least as strong as the Bad Guys on every level of the escalation ladder (Kahn, 1965) to keep the Bad Guys from daring to escalate to that level (Nitze, 1976–77; Kissinger, 1961; Schlesinger, 1975).

3. And there is the theory of Mutual Assured Destruction (MAD), held by many other Western strategists (e.g. Brodie, 1946, 1959; Wohlstetter, 1959; Jervis, 1979–80; Keeny and Panovsky, 1981–82). It holds that the one essential for mutual nuclear deterrence is possession by each side of enough nuclear retaliatory power to cause unacceptable devastation on the other side, even after a possible first strike by the other side. In other words, the essence of nuclear security, for either side, is a relatively *invulnerable second-strike capability* of the kind that nuclear-armed submarines and well-warned bombers can provide.

As background for arms control negotiations it is of interest that in the writings of Soviet strategists the idea of assured destruction (of the enemy) is present, and an invulnerable second-strike capability, in the form of nuclear-armed submarines and hardened silos, is fully accepted in practice, but the idea of mutuality is missing. They accept AD—assured destruction—and have clearly achieved it, but not MAD—mutual assured destruction (Cf. Warner, 1982; Ermarth, 1982). The idea of strategic stability as a two-sided concept apparently hardly exists in their minds.

For a closely reasoned advocacy of MAD and comparison of it with the flexible-response theory, see Jervis (1979–80). For a critique of MAD, see Colin Gray (1979). Both are reprinted in Reichart and Sturm (1982).

The minimal deterrence strategy advocated here accepts the basic idea of mutual assured destruction and combines it with the proposition that, if bilateral or multilateral negotiations for deep cuts in nuclear weapons are unsuccessful, either side could, with increased safety and great profit, cut back its nuclear arsenal to a fraction of what it is now, provided only that the remaining fraction should consist of a relatively invulnerable second-strike capability.

Here is an appraisal of each of the three theories:

1. Some of the actions that follow from the Good Guys–Bad Guys picture make sense. It will be remembered that the kind of minimal deterrence advocated here includes a highly invulnerable nuclear second-strike capability, adequate conventional

strength in Western Europe, and collective action against clear aggression (see the opening of Chapter 7). On the other hand, the assumption that the conflict is essentially between Good Guys and Bad Guys is psychologically unsound; it creates the exaggerated, unrealistic kind of fear on our side; it is fatal to any realistic empathy with the opponent and any realistic thinking about tension-reduction. Therefore it is the straightest road to nuclear war.

2. Flexible response, as far as it goes, makes fairly good sense. Both conventional aggression and a nuclear first strike by either side have to be deterred, and, roughly speaking, those are the two "levels of the escalation ladder" that must be considered. It is important to preserve the psychological "firebreak" between conventional and nuclear war. The amount and kind of strength needed on each of those levels, though, need to be considered more skeptically than they usually have been by advocates of flexible response. Exaggerated fear inflates our conception of what is needed on every level.

3. Mutually assured destruction is by no means as insane as its easily lampooned acronym, MAD, suggests. The capability for it exists now in overflowing measure on each side and has probably been a main factor in keeping the rising tensions of the past several years from tempting either side to go to the brink of nuclear war. On the other hand, each side now has far more MAD capability than it could possibly need. As Kennan (1982) puts it, the "redundancy" in ability to inflict mutually assured destruction on both sides is "grotesque." It is literally true that if bilateral negotiations for deep cuts in nuclear arsenals are unsuccessful either side could, with reasonable safety, cut back to a fraction of what it has now, provided only that, chiefly by keeping an adequate number of nuclear-armed submarines, each side's second-strike capability continued to be highly invulnerable. And the gain in terms of tension-reduction could be immense. It is exaggerated fear that keeps us from doing it.

A more basic limitation of all three conventional theories is that most of the people who focus on them give little attention to the motives for aggression that their deterrence is designed to counteract.[1] Yet those motives certainly matter. It is as if the theo-

---

[1] The exceptions include the less conventional, more psychologically oriented deterrence theorists such as Robert Jervis (1976), Richard Ned Lebow (1981), Hedley Bull (1980), and Alexander George and Richard Smoke (1974). But even they have in general treated the problems of perception and misperception more thoroughly than the problems of motivation.

rists assume that the badness of the Bad Guys is in itself a sufficient reason for them to commit aggression whenever they dare
to. But badness alone is not a motive. There are always more specific reasons to attack or not to attack, and the balance between
them is what counts. On the negative, war-preventing side are
the motives the deterrer hopes to create in his opponent: fear of
war and fear of defeat in war. On the positive, war-promoting
side are—what?

Both historical evidence and psychological evidence suggest
that two motives stand out as frequent driving forces toward aggression: an exaggerated, misconceived, "paranoid" form of fear
and a macho type of pride.

That evidence will occupy us in the latter part of this chapter,
but first it is necessary to say something more about the war-preventing kind of fear—the realistic kind that deterrers can realistically hope to create in their opponents. The distinction between
realistic war-preventing fear and unrealistic war-promoting fear
is crucial. It is crucial in practice as well as in theory, since if we
want to prevent war we need to enhance the one and diminish the
other.

Realistic Fear and Deterrence

Sigmund Freud was aware of two different kinds of anxiety. He
called them "objective" and "neurotic" anxiety. As he put it,
objective anxiety is "a reaction to the perception of an external
danger"; it "may be regarded as an expression of the instinct of
self-preservation" (1953, p. 401). It is realistic and necessary as a
basis for coping with real danger. However, in the case of those
with neurotic anxiety,

> . . . we find a general apprehensiveness in them, a "free-float-
> ing" anxiety, as we call it, ready to attach itself to any thought
> which is at all appropriate, affecting judgments, inducing ex-
> pectations, lying in wait for any opportunity to find a justifica-
> tion for itself. We call this condition *"expectant dread"* or "anx-
> ious expectation." People who are tormented with this kind of
> anxiety always anticipate the worst of all possible outcomes, in-
> terpret every chance happening as an evil omen, and exploit
> every uncertainty to mean the worst. [p. 405]

A distinction resembling this one is as necessary in the world's
search for peace as Freud's distinction is in psychiatry and in the

lives of ordinary individuals. It will be called here the distinction between realistic fear and exaggerated fear. Realistic fear is healthy and necessary, both in oneself and in any opposing country that is caught, with one's own, in the malignant process of hostile interaction. It is necessary in oneself both in order to face with clear eyes the unprecedented danger of nuclear war and in order to recognize honestly the genuine hostility in the opponent, which may combine with defensive fear to produce actual aggression. It is prudent, up to a point, to promote realistic fear of one's own arms in the minds of opponents, as a motive counteracting whatever other reasons they may have for starting a war. Exaggerated fear, on the other hand, is probably the number-one psychological reason for war in the present-day world, since it not only fuels the arms race, with what Kennan calls the "grotesque redundancy" of the most lethal arms on both sides, but also increases greatly the danger of defensively motivated aggression by one side or the other.

Freud, by the way, would be one of the last to ignore the reality and intensity of aggressive impulses, especially subconscious, unacknowledged aggressive impulses, in opponents' minds as well as in one's own. His view of the human species is at the opposite pole from a Pollyanna optimism. He, much more than the majority of academic psychologists, has stressed the reality and intensity of aggressive impulses in human nature as such, the importance of acknowledging them honestly, and the importance of learning to cope with them in a constructive rather than a destructive way.

The distinction between the two kinds of fear becomes even clearer if we ask ourselves a simple question: In order to keep the peace should we ("we" in this case being either the West or the USSR) try to create fear of us in the minds of our adversaries? That question comes close to the heart of this book.

Those who stress deterrence much more than tension-reduction (for brevity, and without prejudice, we can call them the deterrers, while recognizing that most of them favor some kinds of tension-reduction also) are likely to have an unequivocal answer: Yes, of course we should. The danger of war comes only from *them. They* understand only the language of force. Of course we should create a healthy fear, in them, of the harm they would suffer if they attack us or our allies.

Those who stress tension-reduction much more than deterrence (for brevity, and without prejudice—which would be especially inappropriate since this writer is one of them—we can call them the tension-reducers)[2] are likely to have an equally unequivocal answer: No, of course we shouldn't. There is entirely too much fear in the world already. Fear is what fuels arms races and an exaggerated preoccupation with power in order to be safe. It is a major cause of war. We should cultivate trust and friendship, not fear, if we want peace.

What both sides usually fail to realize is that the familiar little word "fear" encompasses two quite different things, and the answer to the crucial question depends very much on which of those meanings the speaker has in mind. A more adequate answer than either of the above would be that, to keep the peace, we should encourage realistic fear on both sides and discourage exaggerated fear on both sides.

Exaggerated Fear and Freud's "Neurotic Anxiety"

Freud's "neurotic anxiety," or something like it, is illustrated by a surprisingly large number of instances of aggression that have probably been mainly defensive in motivation. In recent history most of them have turned out badly for the aggressor, which raises sharply the question of how realistic the fear was in the first place. Several of them were briefly described in the last chapter. In still briefer summary:

- The German–Austrian attack on Serbia in 1914, probably motivated mainly by fear that if a "firm stand" against Serbia were not taken Austria-Hungary would disintegrate.
- The German attack on France through Belgium, motivated in large part by fear of a Russian invasion in the East.
- The "dismemberment" of Germany between 1918 and 1938, motivated mainly by France's fear of a third German invasion.
- The takeover of Eastern Europe by the USSR in 1944–48,

[2]Real harm is done when deterrers and tension-reducers call each other names, rather than being courteous and listening to each other. Calling anyone a "hardliner" or a "hawk" is name-calling, since both terms suggest unpleasant things such as *machismo* and bellicosity. Calling anyone a "softliner" or a "dove" is name-calling, since both suggest weakness of will and lack of courage if not also softness of mind. Deterrer and tension-reducer are descriptive, not pejorative terms.

motivated largely by fear of another invasion coming from the "capitalist West," comparable to Hitler's onslaught in 1941–45.

- The American action to restore the Shah in 1954, motivated mainly by fear of a Soviet absorption of Iran and domination of the Middle East.
- The concerted Arab attack on Israel in 1948, motivated by the feeling that "imperialism" had just implanted an expanding alien body in the heart of the Arab world and that Arab manhood demanded its destruction.
- Israel's attack on Egypt in 1956, growing out of Israel's perennial fear of being destroyed by the encircling Arabs.
- Israel's preemptive attack on Egypt in 1967, stemming from the same fear.
- The Soviet Union's crackdowns on Hungary and Czechoslovakia in 1956 and 1968, based mainly on fear of a domino process in Eastern Europe and a crumbling of the bulwark it had built against another attack from the West.
- The American war in Vietnam, based mainly on fear of a similar domino process, first in Southeast Asia and perhaps later in many Third World countries.
- Egypt's armed crossing of the Suez Canal in 1973, based mainly on the conviction that the Sinai was still part of Egypt, torn away by a still-expanding Israel in 1967.
- The Soviet intervention in Afghanistan, probably motivated (see Chapter 2) mainly by fear that the Soviet position in the entire Middle East, already unfavorable, would be made worse if a hitherto friendly border state were allowed to fall under hostile "imperialist" plus Chinese control.

That list is repeated here because the generalization that emerges from it is both fundamental and seldom fully recognized. What emerges is the really startling importance of fear (sometimes realistic but usually exaggerated) as a cause of aggression and therefore of war. That generalization has great practical as well as theoretical importance, since it is the chief basis for the major practical upshot of this book: the primary importance of tension-reduction—meaning chiefly the importance of reducing exaggerated fear on both sides—as a way of avoiding nuclear war.

Several of the twelve interpretations in the list are of course controversial. The historically informed reader will almost certainly question some of them in the necessarily oversimplified form in which they are presented here. Such a reader will find the evidence for eight of them elaborated, to some extent, in Chapters 2 and 13–16 of this book (and the other four, dealing with the Arab–Israeli conflict, in White, 1977). The main point now, though, is that there are twelve of them and that they represent most of the acts of aggression in our century that are familiar to Americans (the chief ones not mentioned being Hitler's aggressions, Japan's, and North Korea's). If not enough to establish the proposition that exaggerated fear is the number-one motive underlying twentieth-century acts of aggression, they are probably enough to establish fairly solidly the more modest proposition that exaggerated fear is *often* a major factor.

That statement does not challenge any established consensus among either historians or political scientists. Historians rarely make any generalizations of that sort, since by nature and training the ones who study war's causes focus intensively on the causes of a single war, or two or three at most, rather than extensively on many wars. As for political scientists, they are much more prone to generalize, and when they do their emphasis is usually on national security and on power as a means to security. The difference between them and this psychological approach is mainly a difference of words, not substance, since fear is a word for wanting security and not having it. The psychohistorical viewpoint of this book differs from theirs not in any greater emphasis on fear but in its sharper focus on exaggerated fear as distinguished from realistic fear, on the question of why fear of other nations is so often exaggerated, and on the question of how exaggerated fear can be reduced.

Why is fear of other nations so often exaggerated? The thought that the problem could be basically psychological is suggested by a nonpsychologist, George Kennan:

> We have gone on piling weapon upon weapon, missile upon missile, new levels of destructiveness upon old ones. We have done this helplessly, almost involuntarily, like the victims of some sort of hypnotism, like men in a dream, like lemmings heading for the sea, like the children of Hamlin marching along behind their Pied Piper. And the result is that we have achieved, we and the Russians together, in the creation of these devices

and their means of delivery, levels of redundancy of such grotesque dimensions as to defy rational understanding.'' [1982,
p. 176]

Again Freud, a specialist in irrational behavior, can help us.
He interprets compulsive acts, such as the hand-washing compulsion, on the basis of their symbolic reassuring function; they
serve to keep the underlying neurotic anxiety from reaching the
surface of consciousness:

> [There are] patients whose symptoms take the form of obsessive
> acts, and who seem to be remarkably immune from anxiety.
> When we restrain them from carrying out their obsessive per-
> formances, their washing, their ceremonies, etc., or when they
> themselves venture an attempt to abandon one of their compul-
> sions, they are forced by an appalling dread to yield to the com-
> pulsion and to carry out the act.'' [1953, p. 411]

There are at least some similarities between this and the arms-
building compulsion that Kennan describes. In both cases there
is an underlying intense anxiety; in both the anxiety is less acute,
at least on the conscious level, when certain acts have been carried out; and in both there is much question as to whether in the
real world those acts, judged rationally, are fulfilling a rational
purpose. In both there is a kind of symbolic rationality if not an
evidence-based rationality: Handwashing presumably symbol-
izes getting rid of some kind of sin, the specific nature of which is
more or less completely excluded from consciousness, and the
piling up of redundant amounts of nuclear strength may symbol-
ize extra reassurance against being hit first by the diabolical enemy. (It should be remembered that what we are now talking
about is not all armed deterrence but the present redundancy of a
particular kind of armed deterrence. A main thesis of this book is
that, while an adequate second-strike capability and adequate
conventional strength in Western Europe are rational enough,
the redundancy—the excessiveness—of nuclear weapons, especially vulnerable nuclear weapons capable of a first strike, is not.)

Now, how can we, the peace-oriented people who constitute
the immense majority of the people in the world, cope with our
own compulsive tendency to build redundant nuclear arms?

At this point it is necessary to depart somewhat from Freud's
analogy of a compulsively hand-washing neurotic person and to
consider how the responsible foreign-policy-makers on both sides
probably differ from compulsive neurotic hand-washers.

One fairly obvious difference is that the national decision-makers are more rational than the hand-washers. Their fears have a more rational basis. Their positions in government show that they are at least somewhat intelligent and quite capable of coping with some aspects of the real world. Surely nothing so obviously irrational as washing their hands twenty times a day would come into their minds. Their minds would insist on some element of rationality even in their least rational public decisions. In this case at least one such element of rationality probably exists: the political value of seeming to be stronger, overall, in the eyes of potential opponents and of other countries who might be intimidated by the apparently stronger side. The side that other countries believe to be stronger would probably have a greater chance to prevail in tense controversies not only throughout the Third World but also in controversies involving Berlin, Yugoslavia, or Israel, and for those on each side who take it for granted that their side is always much more right than the other side that is an important consideration.

Those whose thinking is excessively anxiety-ridden may be prone to irrationality, though, in at least three other ways: (1) a failure to think candidly about whether the danger of nuclear war may be far greater than the danger of having a lower batting average in the many local controversies that crop up; (2) a failure to engage in the chessplayer's kind of empathy with the other reasons an opponent might have to refrain from starting either a nuclear or a large-scale conventional war; (3) an unwillingness to recognize the malignancy of the malignant process of hostile interaction and the likelihood that it is already making their own country, as well as its opponents, too belligerent and too ready to take serious risks of war.

What keeps so many intelligent people from thinking along those lines?

One answer is that their deeply ingrained diabolical enemy-image—deeply ingrained partly for psychological reasons that have not yet been discussed here—fills their minds so fully that other thoughts, not based on it, are crowded out. Another answer is that the thought of a monster-like enemy—an enemy who also has in his hands the most lethal weapons the world has ever seen—imperatively demands tangible reassurance, and the most tangible reassurance the present-day world offers is to have in one's own hands weapons as lethal and as numerous as his. (A more rational, more discriminating answer might be that one's own weapons should be as lethal as his but, because of overkill, could safely be much less numerous than his, with great profit from the standpoint of making him less of a monster.) Tangible symbols of reassurance are seized and clung to, with no effort to empathize with the enemy, partly because they are tangible—a kind of magic security blanket—and partly because the image of the opponent as a monster, with no human characteristics such as longing for peace or fear of oneself, precludes all empathy. How can anyone empathize with a monster?

If that is the case, it is obvious that there are great psychological obstacles to rational thinking about nuclear weapons. Strong unconscious or subconscious emotional needs block the path. Etzioni was right in calling tension-reduction "the hard way to peace." It will necessarily be long as well as hard.

The same analysis, though, suggests that a rational strategy for persuading the anxiety-ridden clingers to nuclear parity that they can relax their grip should contain two elements:

1. On the one hand, accepting their subconscious need for tangible symbols of safety and satisfying it, to a considerable extent, by agreeing that both a second-strike capability and adequate conventional strength are needed
2. On the other hand, patiently and factually discussing the case against nuclear redundancy and the nature and value of realistic empathy with one's own worst enemy

Macho Pride

The following statement was endorsed by a majority of those with opinions in Gallup national surveys conducted in 1964 and again in 1976:

> "The United States should maintain its dominant position as the world's most powerful nation at all costs, even going to the brink of war if necessary."

It goes without saying that there are healthy kinds of pride: self-confidence, for instance, and self-respect. According to the old Catholic theologians, though, pride is the first of the seven cardinal sins. Here again the apparent disagreement probably depends mainly on the varying meanings of a multimeaning word. Macho pride is a particular form of pride, distinguished from moral or intellectual pride, that will be defined here as undue satisfaction from, or an undue craving for, an image of oneself or one's own group as powerful, prestigious, tough, and courageous, usually with a strong underlying assumption that those are masculine attributes. ("Undue," of course, calls for further definition.) It will be suggested here that if the term is so defined the Catholic theologians have been right about at least this kind of pride, since it has probably been second only to exaggerated fear as a motive promoting aggression and therefore war (Cf. Niebuhr, 1960, pp. 178, 180).

Fighting in situations of clear self-defense, such as the situation faced by France in 1914 and by the USSR in 1941, is not considered here. It is too natural and inevitable in those circumstances and could stem entirely from the healthy kinds of pride, especially self-respect, although some macho pride may always be combined with it. The focus here is entirely on aggression, illustrated by the twelve instances listed at the beginning of the previous section, since without some kind of aggression—however justified the aggressor may believe it to be—there can be no war. Obviously this includes all the cases in which the more aggressive nation has exaggerated fear and believes it is fighting in long-run self-defense. Exaggerated fear and macho pride are not opposites. They often occur together and reinforce each other.

Historically, macho pride has been a major factor, if not *the* major factor, in several kinds of war-causing behavior: empire-building, empire-keeping, territory-regaining, protégé-protecting, and humiliation-avoiding. Some possible examples:

• *Empire-building*: Alexander, Caesar, Napoleon, the British and French empires, the United States in the Philippines, Czarist Russia's border aggressions, Hitler, Japan in China and Southeast Asia, the Soviet Union in Eastern Europe. It will be noted that nearly all of these were prenuclear. It seems likely that the coming of nuclear weapons has considerably discouraged the old-fashioned barefaced kind of national aggrandizement, at least by the major powers.

• *Empire-keeping*: Austria-Hungary in 1914, the stubborn resistance of both sides to Wilson's peacemaking efforts during World War I, Hitler's fighting after Stalingrad, the Soviet Union's crackdowns on Hungary, Czechoslovakia, and Afghanistan,

Israel's unwillingness to withdraw unilaterally from any of the Sinai between 1967 and 1973, France's fighting in Vietnam and Algeria after 1945.

- *Territory-regaining* (including wars of national independence and national unification—all fully justified from a national standpoint): Germany and Italy in the 1860s; the Arabs versus Israel; Israel and the biblical Judea-Samaria; the North in the American Civil War; North Korea in June 1950; South Korea in October 1950; North Vietnam throughout the war against France, 1945–54, and the war against the Saigon government, 1957–75; France and Alsace-Lorraine; Germany and the Polish Corridor; Argentina and "the Malvinas."

- *Protégé-protecting:* Russia for Serbia in 1914; Britain for Belgium in 1914; the United States for Britain, France, and Belgium in 1917; the United States for China and most of Europe in 1941 [probably balance-of-power considerations were predominant in such cases]; the United States for South Korea, South Vietnam, and Israel; Turkey for the Turks in Cyprus; Britain for the British in North Ireland and "the Falklands."

- *Humiliation-avoiding:* France at the outset of the Franco-Prussian war, Britain in the Agadir crisis of 1911, Russia in 1914, Britain and France in the Suez crisis of 1956, the United States in the Cuban missile crisis (note Kennedy's desire for choices other than "humiliation or surrender"), the United States after committing itself in Vietnam, the Soviet Union after committing itself in Afghanistan, Iran and Iraq after committing themselves to war, both Argentina and Britain in the Falklands-Malvinas dispute, the United States in the hostage dispute.

Again there is plenty of room for controversy and legitimate differences of interpretation, but the sheer bulk of the evidence makes it seem fully adequate to justify the modest generalization that macho pride is sometimes a primary factor, and more often an important secondary factor, in disputes that can lead to war.

It does not take a Freud to recognize that it is nearly always more important under the surface of consciousness than on the surface. Looked at with candor it is an ugly thing, with near-synonyms such as chauvinism, arrogance, domineering, bullying, power hunger, and imperialism. In the consciousness of those who have it, though, it is likely to appear as virility, courage, resolve, patriotism, honor, self-respect, self-defense, defense of what is obviously one's own, defense of allies, Manifest Destiny,

the White Man's Burden, vital economic interests, punishing assassins, maintaining stability, maintaining or achieving a balance
of power, avoiding appeasement, opposing aggression. In other
words, it is rationalized, projected, denied, or ignored, while attention is focused only on the other motives—often quite legitimate—that are usually combined with it. Its victims, though,
and relatively detached onlookers are likely to see it for what it is,
or even exaggerate it, while not seeing the legitimate motives with
which it is combined.

The statement at the beginning of this section, "The United
States should maintain its dominant position as the world's most
powerful nation at all costs, even going to the brink of war if necessary" (Watts and Free, 1976), is unusual in that macho pride
appears in it almost nakedly, in unadorned candor. It includes
the superlative expression "most powerful," the extreme phrase
"at all costs," and the ugly words "dominant" and "war." To a
nonmacho American it is shocking in what it shows about his
countrymen.[3] Among other things it casts great doubt on the assumption of many liberals that "the powers that be" or "the Establishment" are more chauvinistic than the "common people."
It could be the reverse. Yet even here a charitable observer might
speculate that those endorsing the statement were often thinking
that American power was a means to an end, the end being defense of the Free World and deterrence of Communist aggression.

Whether that eliminates the likelihood of considerable rationalization is dubious. A person could value American power both
as an end in itself and as a means to what he pictures as defense
of the Free World. If such a person consciously sees only the end
of defending the Free World and not the satisfaction he gets from
contemplating American power and prestige as ends in themselves, he is to some extent deceiving himself.

Freud with his concepts of repression, resistance, and projection and Harry Stack Sullivan with his concept of selective inat-

[3]The dates of the surveys cited, 1964 and 1976, should be noticed. It is not
clear whether the same preponderance of chauvinism would be shown today.
In 1976 the figures were 52 percent agreeing, 41 percent disagreeing, and 7
percent no opinion. The question has not been asked since then. Other evidence, including survey evidence, suggests that American chauvinism and
self-assertiveness rose considerably between 1976 and 1980 (Yankelovich and
Kaagan, 1981) and rose again as a result of the shooting down of the Korean
airline and other events in 1983.

tention (1953) are probably, along with Anna Freud (1946), the students of irrationality who have contributed most to understanding such forms of self-deception. More recent work on narcissism by analysts such as Kohut (1971) and Kernberg (1975), and on the narcissism of political leaders by Lloyd Etheredge (1979), is also relevant.

The person who has been most prominent for his emphasis on the superiority–inferiority dimension in human behavior, however, is undoubtedly Alfred Adler, to whom we owe the term "inferiority complex," He has been the chief source of the important proposition that what appears to be a superiority complex (including what is here called macho pride) is often a compensation for, or a cover-up of, an underlying inferiority complex. That proposition, well supported by Karen Horney in her chapter "The Quest for Power, Prestige and Possession" (1937, pp. 162–87), is perhaps as important on the national level, as a cause of war, as it is on the individual level. On the individual level, as Horney puts it, "the normal striving for power is born of strength, the neurotic of weakness" (p. 163).

That idea is supported also by the prevailing psychiatric interpretation of paranoia—the paranoid psychoses and paranoid personalities. The word "paranoid" is commonly defined in terms of two types of delusion—delusions of persecution, usually regarded as primary, and delusions of grandeur—which often occur together. The delusions of persecution have some resemblance to what is here called exaggerated fear, and the delusions of grandeur have some resemblance to what is here called macho pride. In an actually psychotic person it is often fairly clear that his delusions of persecution stem from a projection of his own inner hostilities (closely connected with anxiety) that he cannot consciously face and has to project onto the people around him. His delusions of grandeur, similarly, are based on dissatisfaction with himself. They are in part a derivative of the delusions of persecution ("If they persecute me they must think I am important") and in part a direct compensatory cover-up of the basic sense of weakness and unworthiness.

These ideas fit the personality of Hitler like a glove. His skid-row days in Vienna and his sexual abnormalities, plus much else, would have given him a basic sense of unworthiness (Heiden, 1944, pp. 52–76, 382–87); both his personal delusions of grandeur (partly true but exaggerated) and his national delusions of both grandeur and persecution (partly true, but greatly exaggerated after 1933) are well known. He as an individual and as a reflection-plus-exaggeration of the "paranoid" tendencies of the German people in his period of history support an emphasis on compensation for a sense of inferiority as an interpretation of the importance of macho pride and its role as a direct and indirect cause of war. (For an elaboration of these ideas see Chapter 14.)

Do the same ideas apply to the Soviet Union today? And the United States?

There is much informed testimony that they do apply to the USSR. At least since Peter the Great the "Westernizers" in Russia have been admiring the more advanced West and in some ways trying to imitate it, while the "Slavophiles" have been defensively insisting that Russia was better than the West. Now, with the Soviet GNP per capita still far below what is typical in Western Europe and only a little more than half that of the United States, the same two tendencies exist, often in the same person. Public morale is low (Feifer, 1981). The Soviet economy has mysteriously slowed, as that of the United States has slowed. Since 1960 there have been serious losses in the outside world: China, Indonesia, Egypt. The partly compensating gains in Angola, Ethiopia, Nicaragua and elsewhere have been meager and in out-of-the-way places. That story is familiar. Only in the military competition have there been striking gains. It is not surprising if Soviet minds turn in relief to their military achievements as a source of macho pride and of solace for their insufficient achievements in other ways. Their new aggressiveness in the Third World (Chapter 4) and their new demand for equality of status with the United States are understandable in those Adlerian terms. That does not mean they are more aggressive than we are. It does mean that we need to take their macho pride very much into account, including their demand for equality of status, if we want peace.

In his book *Russia: The People and the Power* Robert Kaiser wrote that Khrushchev's diplomacy "reflected the personality he revealed in his recollections: proud yet fearful, boastful but timid, desperate for respect and admiration" (1976, p. 503). "True equality with America on all counts must be the broad aim of all Soviet policies. Equality (if not superiority) is all that could satisfy Russian insecurity, Russian pride and Russian ambition" (p. 522). Among other things that implies sensitivity to the humiliation of being excluded from the affairs of areas near their border in which they have a natural interest. "Henry Kissinger's shuttle diplomacy humiliated the Russians. I was in Moscow when it began; several Soviet journalists and officials urged *me* 'not to cut us out of the Middle East'" (p. 523). (There is little evidence that the general Soviet public cares much about the Middle East, but "journalists and officials" apparently do.) This does not mean that the Soviet leadership's hunger for equality of status is comparable in intensity to its fear of a big war. Kaiser has also said, in interpretation of the Soviet move in Afghanistan, "In the minds of the old men who have risen to the top of the Communist Party of the Soviet Union, any step that enhances Soviet security is easy to justify. Equally, moves that enhance Soviet prestige and power without endangering national security are difficult for them to resist" (1981, p. 517).

Seweryn Bialer (1983), like Kaiser, stresses the pride as well as the fear in Soviet motivation. "In the great debate over nuclear weapons and how to control them, one key fact gets too little attention: The Soviet Union depends on its nuclear arsenal not only to protect itself and to threaten others, but for its very status as a great power. Without nuclear weapons the Soviet Union would not be a superpower."

There is additional, though somewhat outdated, evidence of Soviet macho pride in the work of Nathan Leites (1953), Gabriel Almond (1954), Joseph Novak (1960), and Bertram Wolfe (1962). At least the assumption that conflict is inevitable and that therefore winning is the one thing that matters most was central in official Soviet thinking in both the Lenin and the Stalin periods. Wolfe describes Marxism-Leninism as "a combative ideology. At the core of things it finds conflict" (1962, p. 161). He speaks of "what can only be described as a paranoiac vision of self and 'enemy' and reality that is not subject to rational refutation" (p. 166). "Paranoiac" presumably implies here delusions of grandeur, including macho pride, as well as delusions of persecution, implying exaggerated fear. The two tend to go together, in international affairs as well as in psychiatry. Somewhat similar characteristics also tend to go together in the "authoritarian personality" (Adorno, Frenkel-Brunswik, Levinson, and Sanford, 1950), e.g. fear of the unfamiliar, "intolerance of ambiguity," emphasis on power, authoritarian aggression, and authoritarian submission.

Robert C. Tucker, in *The Soviet Political Mind* (1963, pp. 39–44), similarly describes what he calls the "warfare personality" of some leading individuals and relates it to paranoia:

> Hitler and Stalin were examples who also happened to be, in their respective ways, men of outstanding leadership ability. The warfare personality shows paranoid characteristics as psychiatrically defined, but what is essential from the standpoint of this discussion is that it constitutes a *political* personality type. The characteristically paranoid perception of the world as an arena of deadly hostilities being conducted conspiratorially by an insidious and implacable enemy against the self finds highly systematized expression in terms of political and ideological symbols that are widely understood and accepted in the given social milieu. [p. 40]

It should be stressed again that use of the word "paranoid" in this book, and by others such as Wolfe and Tucker, does *not* imply psychosis, even though some leading individuals, such as Hitler and Stalin, were probably sometimes close to the border of psychosis. It does imply an interesting similarity between certain motives and delusions that are characteristic of many nations, including our own, and the exaggerated fear and macho pride that are found in borderline personalities such as Hitler and Stalin, who carry those characteristics to an almost psychotic extreme.

How about the United States?

Statement by our national leaders are in line with the opinion survey evidence that has already been cited. Lyndon Johnson, for instance, at the height of the Vietnam War, declared, "We are the number one nation and we are going to stay the number one nation" (cited by Barnet, 1972, p. 3). Vietnam was so far from our shores that fear for our own security, even when defined in long-term balance-of-power terms, does not seem plausible as our primary motive for fighting there. It is a tenable hypothesis that, under all the more high-minded and far-sighted reasons such as credibility, the domino theory, obligation to our Vietnamese allies, and so on, macho pride was the most important reason for our staying in the war, if not also for our getting into it. The others could have been primarily rationalizations.

Richard Barnet offers an acute psychological analysis of what he calls "the operational code of the national security managers" in Washington and other capitals:

The "name of the game" (a favorite expression in the national security world) is to avoid losing "influence" and if possible to gain more. . . . Power, as it is conceived in the national security bureaucracy and in the chanceries of all nations big enough to be contestants, is the capacity to dominate by using the technology of intimidation. It is a game in the exact sense because it is without higher purpose beyond winning (or, more accurately, avoiding loss). . . . Playing the game, even when you win, is an uneconomic, indeed very expensive activity. . . . There are only two principal rules. The first is that no rival nation or combination of rivals can be allowed to become powerful enough to threaten your own power. . . . That is the time-honored principle of balance of power. [Barnet is saying that in governmental practice "balance" of power means something other than equality.] The second rule is that all the world is the playing field. There are no spectators. Every nation, no matter how small, insular, or neutralist in outlook, is a potential member of somebody's team. [1972, pp. 96–97]

Is the word macho justified here? Barnet says yes. He speaks of "glory, *machismo*, and the excitement of winning" as the main goals of the national security managers (p. 237). A skeptical reader may be permitted to question the words "dominate" and "intimidation" in the above description, but "influence" and "power" seem quite acceptable.

The proposition that pride is second only to fear as a dominant motive in foreign affairs is expressed with similar psychological sensitivity by Robert Osgood:

It follows from the intangible and indefinite nature of national security and from its centrality among national interests that the motive of security is easily combined with other motives. Where does the search for self-defense stop and the pursuit of primacy for primacy's sake take over? What is real security and what is merely a sublimation of self-assertion or aggrandizement? When does maintaining the credibility of the nation's will to use force for the sake of deterrence give way to the pursuit of national pride and prestige? [1982, p. 380]

Another near-synonym of macho pride is self-assertion. Yankelovich and Kaagan, reviewing the mood of the American public in 1980 primarily on the basis of opinion polls, entitle their article "Assertive America" (1981).

The public had grown skeptical of détente and distressed by American impotence in countering the December 1979 Soviet invasion of Afghanistan. It felt bullied by OPEC, humiliated by the Ayatollah Khomeini, tricked by Castro, out-traded by Japan and out-gunned by the Russians. By the time of the 1980 presidential election, fearing that America was losing control over its foreign affairs, voters were more than ready to exorcise the ghost of Vietnam and replace it with a new posture of American assertiveness. . . . The national pride has been deeply wounded; Americans are fiercely determined to restore our honor and respect abroad. [p. 696]

How does all this relate to the prevention of nuclear war?

In two ways. One is that in some future crisis we or our opponents may be so driven by pride and fear of humiliation that we threaten the use of force and then, having threatened it, even more driven by pride to carry out our threat. The crisis of 1914 illustrates the reality of that danger.

The other point of relevance is that an unacknowledged need for power as such may be even comparable to exaggerated fear as a reason for the present irrational, even "grotesque" redundancy of nuclear weapons themselves. Whether the symbolism of male potency is involved here or not (Freud would surely say it is), there is in any case no other kind of imagery as dramatically, totally self-assertive as the image of clobbering an opponent with nuclear weapons.

Anger, Hate, and the Psychologists' Term "Aggression"

Political scientists, with their typical focus on power and security as the major goals behind international behavior in general, have seldom given much emphasis to such nonrational emotions as anger, hate, or what the psychologists call "aggression" as motives for war or for the kinds of behavior that lead to war. That is an unfortunate gap in their thinking, because many examples in recent history show how such emotions intrude on and distort what would otherwise be a much more rational and predictable process. It is a gap that this book especially must try to fill, since our focus is less on international behavior in general than on the causes of war, including especially the emotion-filled crises that usually precede and often directly lead to war. Such examples include:

- The mood of the French public (somewhat influenced by Bismarck's provocative and deceptive editing of the Ems telegram) when France declared war on Prussia in 1870
- The mood of the crowds in the streets of Vienna and Budapest when the crisis that began with the murder of the Archduke was coming to a head in late July 1914
- The mood of the British elite and public when the Kaiser's armies swept through neutral Belgium on their way to France
- The mood of Americans after the Zimmermann telegram and the German declaration of unrestricted submarine warfare in early 1917
- The mood of Americans after Pearl Harbor
- The feeling of Arabs about ''Zionist expansionism''
- The feeling of Israelis about ''PLO terrorism''
- Hitler's pathological hostility to the Jews
- The healthy, realistic feeling of hundreds of millions about both Hitler and Stalin
- The heady excitement of the Arabs and the grim feeling of the Israelis just before the Six Day War of 1967
- The feeling of the Russians about the Germans after World War II, and their feeling against the United States when they first felt it was ''arming the Germans against us''
- Brezhnev's reaction to the SAC alert crisis in 1973
- The reaction of most Americans to Soviet intervention in Afghanistan (as they perceived it) and to the long, steady Soviet arms buildup (as they perceived it) after about 1975

What can be said about such emotions, briefly, from a psychological standpoint?

In order to think clearly about them we must first try to define anger, hate, and what the psychologists and psychiatrists call aggression.

Their meanings overlap, and the boundaries between them are not clear. It is worthwhile, though, at least to try to distinguish between anger and hate. The word anger usually refers to a ''hot,'' short-term emotion that can and often does occur between friends and is felt to be a reaction to a particular piece of objectionable behavior on the part of the other. The word hate implies a colder, deeper, steadier negative emotion, lasting a long time, felt to be a reaction to a long accumulation of objectionable, hate-deserving acts by the other. Examples of hate among those cited above include the feelings of Arabs about Israelis, Israelis about Arabs, Hitler about Jews, millions of people about Hitler and Stalin, and Russians about Germans. The others could mainly be called simply anger, though in most of them there had been a previous accumulation of a good many grounds for hate.

The two have much in common, though. Hate might be well described as long-term anger. Both certainly include, while they last, an intensively negative image of the other and probably some desire to do the other harm, *as an end in itself* rather than as a means to some other end—some more "rational" end such as security, power, or economic welfare. It is in that sense that both can be called nonrational if not irrational. Neither leads to behavior that is a chosen "instrumental" means to ends that are usually seen as important for human happiness. Both usually lead to behavior that conflicts with those ends. Both often lead to behavior that, if its results are honestly evaluated, is in retrospect deeply regretted.

Yet both are natural, often inevitable, and sometimes realistic in that they do contribute to other ends, such as security or freedom. There is a strong consensus among psychologists, psychiatrists, and leaders of therapeutic groups such as encounter groups that becoming clearly conscious of one's own angers and hates is a wholesome process. If nothing else, honest recognition of them permits clear conscious thinking about the degree to which they are realistic or based on one's own unconscious needs. Becoming clearly conscious of them, though, is often a difficult process, since in our culture and many others the aggressive impulse is strenuously and indiscriminately condemned, and consequently denied, rationalized, ignored, or projected onto others. It then continues to operate on an unconscious or subconscious level, which usually means irrationally and destructively.

It is more difficult to define what is meant by the word "aggression" in its psychological sense, partly because various psychologists use it in various ways. Behaviorist psychologists who pride themselves on not using such "subjective" words as a negative image or a desire to hurt (e.g. Dollard, Doob, Miller, Mowrer, and Sears, 1939) have tried to define it only in terms of the behavior it leads to. Violent behavior or an "instigation" to violent behavior is then called aggression, whether it is obviously defensive or not, and whether it is a means to an end or an end in itself. Fortunately such a taboo-ridden type of psychology seems to be giving way to a commonsense willingness to use "subjective" terms if they are legitimately inferred from objective indications.

In any case there is now some consensus among psychiatrists, psychoanalysts, clinical psychologists, and many social psychologists on a meaning of the word "aggression" that is very close to what we have noted as common to anger and hate, namely *an intensely negative image and an impulse to hurt, as an end in itself.* "Sheer meanness" might be a near-synonym. "Destructiveness" is another (Fromm, 1973). That meaning, stemming probably more from Freud than from anyone else, leaves open the question of whether and to what extent such an impulse is innate—a question that will not be gone into in this book at all, since it is so clear that in any event circumstances have a great deal to do with the intensity and forms of expression of aggressive impulses.

It should also be especially noted that the psychologists' meaning of "aggression" is different from its common meaning in history, political science, and ordinary usage. There it means, roughly, an unprovoked, unjustified attack, almost always with strong condemnation implied. There is no such necessary condemnation in the psychologists' use of the term, not because they would be any less ready to condemn a clear case of international aggression such as Hitler's attack on Czechoslovakia or the Holocaust itself, but simply because to them, in their habitual contexts, the word *means* something different. It means an impulse—usually a subconscious or unconscious impulse—not an action, and the context is individual, not national. They are thinking of the word in the sense in which a person might say he was "getting rid of his aggressions" by cutting down trees or "getting to recognize his aggressions" by participating in an encounter group.

There is probably some consensus too on the proposition that bottled up aggression in the psychological sense has a free-floating character, somewhat like Freud's "free-floating anxiety." Like neurotic anxiety it can be, to use Freud's words, "ready to attach itself to any thought which is at all appropriate, affecting judgments, inducing expectations, lying in wait for any opportunity to find a justification for itself.''

''Displacement'' of aggression—the scapegoat phenomenon—is a case in point. A father who has been berated unfairly by his boss at the office and has bottled up his anger may come home and take it out on his wife or his ten-year-old son. It should be noticed, though, that some apparent external provocation is usually necessary even then. In his conscious thinking he is reacting to a real event in his environment. The son has perhaps failed to do an expected chore, and the father lashes out at him verbally in sudden anger. The father does not come home and immediately lash out with no such stimulus. Until he discovers the neglected chore he may be glowering, but his superego (conscience) and his ego (prudence) keep him from overt action. A new perception of evil attributable to someone else is needed to trigger the anger and provide a seemingly justifiable outlet for the bottled up anger. In the eyes of observers, though, including the wife as well as the son, he may have grossly overreacted to a trivial stimulus.

In international affairs the same kind of thing can happen. The Austrians in 1914 were frightened and humiliated by the real evidence of their approaching disintegration. Their great fear object was Russia, but they did not lash out at Russia. It was too strong. They lashed out at little Serbia, the triggering event being the truly atrocious murder of the Archduke and his wife. It was not wanton, unprovoked aggression. It was an overreaction.

How important are anger and hate (which together are roughly what the psychologists call aggression) as causes of war? And which of them,·anger or hate, is more important?

The answer to be given here is that both are important (though less, basically, than exaggerated fear and macho pride), and that hate is basically much more important than anger.

Psychologically oriented readers may be surprised to find their central concept, aggression, which they may have been thinking of as the primary cause of war, subordinated here to exaggerated fear and macho pride. The chief reason lies in the impressive body of historical and contemporary evidence, summarized above, as to the importance of exaggerated fear and macho pride. It lies also in the substantial body of recent historical research, chiefly by psychologically oriented political scientists, on

the nature of peace-endangering crises (e.g. Snyder and Diesing, 1977; Lebow, 1981; Allison, 1971; Hermann, 1973; Janis,
1973). A main upshot of that research is that national decision-
makers at a time of crisis usually do, according to their lights and
within the framework of their basic assumptions (which may be
very faulty), try to think rationally and responsibly. They are
quite aware of and probably exaggerate, the danger of being carried away by anger. Their decision process bears little resemblance, psychologically, to the emotion in the mind of an angry
ape, a child with a temper tantrum, or a glowering father coming
home from the office. Snyder and Diesing (1977, p. 291) find *no*
instance where war occurred because "tempers got out of control." We psychologists have given too little respect to the typical
intelligence and thoughtfulness of the responsible national leaders in times of crisis. In fact a major reason why our talk about
aggression has so often been ignored by historians, political scientists, and political practitioners may lie precisely here, in our
apparent unawareness of how genuinely national leaders usually
try to be rational.

The irrationality lies elsewhere: in the basic assumptions from which their reasoning starts. Their rationality is
"bounded" (Simon, 1957) by the nature of the assumptions they
bring to the decision and remember to use. Within the bounds of
the shared assumptions of the high-level group discussing what to
do in the crisis, it is fairly logical. Those assumptions, though,
are likely to include such things as the obvious innocence of the
national self, the obvious guilt of the enemy, the unchangeable-
ness of the enemy's evil nature, the efficacy of force in dealing
with such an opponent, and the inefficacy of anything but force.
Given those assumptions there can still be highly rational discussion of what kind of force and how much force to use, but probably no discussion of genuine efforts to compromise. The result
can easily be a war that could have been avoided.

In other words, what is called here the diabolical enemy-
image is at the heart of the irrationality that, in historical retrospect, is often displayed by decision-making groups in times of
crisis. And since a diabolical enemy-image is usually ingrained
over a period of many years, becoming the essential core of what
is commonly called hate, it is justifiable to say that hate is more
important than anger as a cause of war. Anger may indeed pro-

vide the final trigger, the spark that ignites the fuel. Even then, though, the hate-filled diabolical enemy-image is something more than passive fuel waiting to be ignited; it functions actively in facilitating the anger by predisposing the involved persons to put the worst possible interpretation on what the enemy (or someone associated with the enemy, as in the case of the murderer of the Archduke) has just done.

CHAPTER TEN

War-promoting Perceptions

How Motives and Perceptions Combine

If a person *wants* something and *believes* that a certain kind of behavior will help him to get it, he is likely to tend to engage in that kind of behavior. This is the obvious, everyday, commonsense proposition that describes roughly how motives (wants) and perceptions (beliefs) combine to produce behavior. It justifies this book's emphasis on motives and perceptions.

Which is more important, to understand the motives related to nuclear war, as we tried to do in the last chapter, or to understand the perceptions related to it?

In my judgment, understanding the perceptions is more important, if only because they are much more varied. Hawks and doves in the West both want peace. Both are, with rare exceptions, convinced of the horrors of nuclear war. Both also, with rare exceptions, want very much to preserve the independence of their country and its NATO allies. There are differences of emphasis on those two goals, but as a rule the differences are not great. Both hawks and doves want both. They differ greatly, though, in their beliefs as to what policies are most likely to preserve peace and independence at the same time, and those differences in turn depend greatly on widely different perceptions of the men in the Kremlin—their power, relative to ours, and their primary foreign policy goals and intentions. As the statisticians might put it, the variance of perceptions on this subject is considerably greater than the variance of motives and therefore contributes much more to the variance of attitudes and behavior.

How They Influence Each Other

Although motives and perceptions are different in their essence, they are so closely intertwined that as a rule neither can be understood without some reference to the other.

Consider for instance the deceptively simple little word, fear. As we have seen, fear is an extremely potent motive in international affairs and can be an extremely destructive one. It is probably the chief motive, surpassing even macho pride, that pushes forward the nuclear arms race, causing its grotesque redundancy on both sides; as history has shown, it also underlies a great many of the aggressive actions that directly cause war. Is it a motive or a perception? Obviously, it is both. It has a motivational side and a perceptual side. When we speak of exaggerated fear we are focusing on its perceptual side; we are calling it a misperception, or rather a partial misperception, which is what nearly all misperceptions are. The perception of danger naturally comes first, but almost simultaneously with it there is an urge to avoid the danger either by escape or by attack. The perception and the impulse to action are so intimately, inextricably bound together that we naturally speak of them together as fear. But if we want to diminish the exaggerated fear in ourselves or our opponents, we need to focus on its perceptual side and treat it as a problem in perception.

Or consider another deceptively simple and familiar word, anger. Ordinarily we focus on its motivational side, the desire a person has to hurt the object of his anger. But it, like fear, also has a perceptual side. The object of the anger is perceived as deserving to be hurt. In the word ''anger'' there is a strong connotation of reactiveness. A person who is angry is assumed to be angry because of something another person has done that is so hurtful or so wrong (as he perceives it) that it deserves retaliation or punishment.

That can be a mistake, or a partial mistake, and if so the retaliation or punishment that occurs can be called an overreaction. As a rule we do not speak of exaggerated anger, but we often should, because very often the perceptual side of it is exaggerated.

The father who comes home glowering because of a humiliation at his office and lashes out at his son because of a trivial misdeed really believes, at the moment, that the son's misdeed was not trivial but serious. His overreaction is the direct result of a misperception—not a cold, cognitive misperception but a hot misperception suffused with an emotional sense of the outrageousness of what his son has done. The Austrians and Hungarians who, with strong German backing, precipitated World War I by declaring war on Serbia had a similarly hot misperception that an atrocious murder, the murder of the Archduke and his wife, committed by one Serbian fanatic in the name of national independence, was necessarily the result of a diabolical plot against the beneficent Austro-Hungarian empire by the government of Serbia, probably backed by Russia. In their minds the attribution of evil, which was realistic enough when evil was attributed to one murderer, Pashitch, and his two accomplices, had spread to include, automatically and without evidence, the government of Serbia and the entire nation it represented. Austria, in their eyes, was being attacked by *Serbian* subversion and assassination. The danger represented by that attack had to be fought off, and the crime had to be punished. But what came first in their minds was their perception of the danger and their perception of the nature and source of the crime.

The psychologists (Dollard, Doob, Miller, Mowrer, and Sears, 1939) who have conceived of "aggression" or "instigation to aggression" as a direct response to an external stimulus or as a direct response to frustration have not seen all of the psychological picture. They have not clearly seen that, between the stimulus and the response, there is a necessary "intervening variable" consisting of perception of danger, of evil deserving punishment, or of both. Nor have they clearly seen how importantly those intervening variables can be influenced by factors within the person such as the "floating anxiety" Freud talks about or the floating anger and hostility that we ourselves should be talking about. Their term "frustration" covers some of those factors within the person but not all of them. As a minimum we need to recognize the great perception-determining importance of a long-term, deeply ingrained diabolical image of a national enemy. Among the many forms of what Jervis calls "preexisting beliefs" this is the one that most powerfully and directly influences the specific perceptions that directly mobilize the motives and cause the actions that cause war.

Jervis's Motivated and Unmotivated Errors

It is clear, then, that perceptions often influence motives. It is also clear that motives, including subconscious and unconscious motives, can influence perception.

In his book *Perception and Misperception in International Politics* (1976), now a classic, and in subsequent writings, Robert Jervis

makes a fundamental distinction between the subconscious motives that influence and often greatly distort perception, on the
one hand, and on the other hand the nonmotivational cognitive
factors, such as preexisting beliefs, that can also have major distorting effects.

The rest of this chapter deals with errors (that is, misperceptions) that seem to be due mainly to subconscious motives, while
Chapter 12 deals with those that seem to be mainly cognitive in
origin.

Subconsciously or unconsciously motivated misperception
has already been referred to at several points: the process of rationalization, presumably motivated by a need to think well of
oneself or one's own group (the extended self); the process of projection of blame, presumably motivated largely by a need, when
someone has to be blamed, to blame persons other than oneself
or one's own group; and the Adlerian process of compensation
for inferiority feelings by exaggerating the power or the toughness of the self, motivated largely, once again, by a need to think
well of the self. The importance of various kinds of self-deluding
pride in all of these is obvious. The distorting influence of
Freud's "free-floating anxiety" as a factor in the origin of exaggerated fear and of worst-case military thinking has also been
mentioned. In that case the unconscious motive presumably is
not a need for self-esteem but a need to find a tangible, specific
external resting place for an internally generated diffuse anxiety.
As Freud put it, the anxiety is "lying in wait for any opportunity
to find a justification for itself."

More systematically, we shall now consider five kinds of motivated misperceptions that are especially related to the causes of
war:

1. A diabolical enemy-image
2. A moral self-image
3. A "pro-us" illusion
4. Overconfidence and worst-case thinking
5. Overlapping territorial self-images

A Diabolical Enemy-image

People tend to assume that what is familiar is also understood. A
case in point is the black-and-white picture (or better, since black

is not bad, the Good Guys–Bad Guys picture). It is extremely familiar. Everyone who has read a cheap thriller or seen a cheap Western movie knows about it and is prepared to smile benignly about it, as if he understood it.

He probably does not. There is a mystery in it that very few people have thought much about but that lies close to the heart of the problem of how to prevent nuclear war. The mystery lies in the question: Why do intelligent people torment themselves by imagining a monster-like enemy, or at least imagining that their human enemies are more monster-like than they actually are? Why do they wantonly *increase* their own fear?

The Good Guys part of the picture seems immediately understandable as a form of wishful thinking. People would like to think they are good, and by various psychological devices, including trying to be really good in their behavior, manage to believe that they are. Rationalization helps too. The urge to think well of oneself is so obvious and universal that we feel we have explained a psychological process when we have attributed it to that urge. The mystery lies far more in the Bad Guys part of the picture. Is *that* wishful thinking? For instance, do people on both sides of the East–West conflict *want* to believe that their opponents, now armed with the most lethal weapons the world has ever seen, are also incurably evil in all respects, including foreign policy, and implacably aggressive? Do they want to believe it, when there is so much evidence that it is far from true?

The fact itself has been discussed on the descriptive level at several points in this book, under names such as exaggerated fear, worst-case thinking, and—most disturbing at all—defensively motivated aggression. Not only the nuclear arms race but also the possible actual outbreak of another major war, which could be or become nuclear, seem likely to be due to the diabolical enemy-image more than to any other single factor.

On a more explanatory level the thought has been advanced that there could be obscure unconscious or partly conscious satisfactions in creating and clinging to the monster image. Freud's concept of projection of guilt has been invoked, namely, that when blame has to be attributed to someone it is usually attributed to someone or something other than the self. Freud's concept of free-floating anxiety "lying in wait for any opportunity to find a justification for itself" has also been invoked. Are those explanations adequate?

Probably not. Both seem tenuous when compared with the anxiety we *create* for ourselves by picturing human opponents, who are probably as frightened of us as we are of them, as villains or monsters.

There is very little reason to think that most of us in the United States carry around with us a deep or unconscious sense of national guilt that has to be projected onto another nation. Why should we? Objectively speaking, it is true, our nation has done its share of bad things, but *we* didn't do them. Our government did. At the time they were done our government leaders probably seemed to have pretty good reasons for doing them. Perhaps we then felt a certain amount of vicarious guilt, semiconsciously if not consciously, because it was our country acting and we felt identified with it; but that could be handled either by the universal process of rationalization (which our leaders and the mass media helped us to perform satisfactorily) or by consciously blaming our leaders themselves, perhaps projecting what was left of our sense of guilt on them but not on the enemy. After that, very little would be left.

Floating anxiety seems like a somewhat more plausible explanation but not much more. Most of us *are* anxious a good deal of the time; sometimes we feel just generally anxious without knowing why. Few of us, though, have the kind of clearly neurotic anxiety on which Freud was focusing, and those of us who are not so neurotic usually have a fairly good idea of what we are anxious about—meeting next month's bills, for instance, what will happen to interest rates, an unfriendly remark by a friend, or the chance of nuclear war. It does not seem plausible that many of us have any great need to find a tangible justification for diffuse internally generated anxiety of the type Freud was talking about.

The mystery deepens when a puzzled psychologist notices how often intelligent people, many of them liberal on domestic issues and normally skeptical of the rightness of their government's foreign policies, relax their skepticism when it comes to accepting the conventional wisdom with regard to the implacable aggressiveness of the Soviet rulers. Worse, they often do not seem properly curious or thoughtful at that point. They make no effort to imagine how the world looks to the men in the Kremlin or what defensive reasons those men might have for actions such as Afghanistan or the big arms buildup. It seems not to occur to them that they themselves might be indulging in the kind of Bad Guys imagery that they smile about when they see their children drinking it in at a Western movie.

It may sound naive to a psychiatrist, but my own hunch is that our best single clue lies precisely there—in the pleasurable excitement that many people, especially children, get from drinking in an absorbing melodrama. For a good reason our films, television, comics, and video games are full of it. Conflict is always exciting. Football and basketball games are exciting, but they do not usually have the extra punch that is provided by a hero who is fighting for Good against Evil and with whom we as individuals can identify. The more evil and the more powerful and threatening the enemy can be made to seem, the better. It is only then that the righteousness and the virility of the hero and his inevitable ultimate triumph can fully stand out in contrast.

I would call this macho pride. We come back to macho pride, glorified by an intense sense of righteousness, on a semifantasy level. It is wonderfully satisfying to those who are psychologically able to give themselves up to it, unless it comes *too* close to home, as the danger of nuclear war now does.

Could we melodrama-lovers dramatize ourselves, with comparable satisfaction, as Good Guys fighting valiantly against nuclear war itself? Some are doing it now.

The other best clue, in my judgment, lies in the satisfaction of feeling more grimly ''realistic'' about an enemy than others are.

There is nothing wrong or conducive to misperception in getting satisfaction from feeling realistic. That is an appropriate reward and reinforcement for *being* realistic. There is often something conducive to misperception though (and akin to macho pride) in feeling more *grimly* realistic than other people. Realism actually calls for nothing but great respect for evidence and for orderly, honest thinking on the basis of evidence. Grimness and feeling superior to others should have nothing to do with it—any more than wanting to be benevolent and peaceful should have anything to do with it. For some reason, though, many people apparently assume that there is something hard, virile, and automatically realistic about totally condemning an outgroup that their own group condemns and putting the worst possible interpretation on anything it does. An American who thinks he sees anything good about the Soviet Union (or, formerly, Communist China) is dismissed as ''soft'' on Communism, and there is no more potent verbal weapon with which to handle heretics than the word "soft." (The opposite is more plausible. It takes more courage to disagree with one's own group than to agree with it.) Perhaps the line of association is that seeing an outgroup as diabolical connotes readiness for violent conflict, and readiness for violent conflict connotes virility. It is a fighting stance. In any case an association between a diabolical enemy-image and a macho self-image does seem to exist, and to distort realistic judgment.

In this way, again, we come back to macho pride. On a subconscious level it is hard to give it up.

Even those two reasons, however—macho melodrama and supposedly grim realism—do not seem fully adequate to explain the hold that the diabolical enemy-image has on our minds. Some of the mystery remains.

A Moral Self-image

The nearly universal tendency to a moral self-image is obvious. Probably no modern nation (including Germany and Japan) that was embarking on what its neighbors regarded as aggression has talked about it in those terms or even, apart from some lone dissenters, seemed to wonder whether that was what it was doing. The process of rationalization, when most of the members of a group join in reinforcing each other's rationalizations, is obvious and powerful in defending their collective Good Guys image.

There is also a fairly obvious reason for rationalization: a need to think well of one's own group, at least in comparison with others. Group pride is a gratifying thing, and by various psychological ego-serving devices (rationalization, projection, denial, selective inattention) groups usually succeed in achieving it.

There is one interesting and not yet answered question, though: What harm does it do? Does it make war more likely? Since nations serving their own self-interest will do what they want to do anyway (one might argue), why deny them the innocent satisfaction of believing that what they do is right? The war-promoting nature of the diabolical enemy-image is relatively clear: It fuels the arms race on both sides, and it increases the chances of defensively motivated aggression on both sides. Does the moral self-image do anything that bad?

Probably not, but bad enough. In the first place, the cynics who say that nations always act in a completely selfish, conscienceless way may be going too far. Although Niebuhr is probably right in his book *Moral Man and Immoral Society* (1960) to picture nations as morally worse in dealing with other nations than most individuals are in dealing with other individuals, that does not necessarily mean that they act with total disregard for the demands of conscience. Therefore, if a nation that has some conscience left narcotizes its conscience by rationalization and proceeds to aggression or other war-promoting actions that it would not have engaged in if it had honestly recognized how bad they were, the harm done is clear. Rationalization after an action has occurred may do no harm; it is then too late to reconsider. But rationalization when contemplating a future action that might not occur if its wrongness were recognized in time is a different story.

The Vietnam war is a case in point. A great many Americans came around eventually to thinking it was morally wrong as well as expensive in lives, money, and the future soundness of the American economy. Whether all of that was true or not, the great majority now wish they had never gone into it. From their standpoint, wouldn't they have been wiser to recognize all of the counts against it, including the moral ones, before rather than after getting thoroughly involved? We Americans were rationalizing in a highly efficient way during the early years of the war (as many of us in retrospect see it). Couldn't our rationalization then be regarded as a cause of the war? It supplied little if any of the motive power behind our fighting, but perhaps it took some of our brakes off when they should have been on.

How about the USSR? Do the Soviet people feel as innocent as we in the West do?

There is abundant evidence that the great majority do, even in the face of such seemingly obvious instances of Soviet aggression as the takeover of Eastern Europe and the invasion of Afghanistan, and even in the minds of people who are in other ways deeply discontented and disillusioned. Frederick Barghoorn reported as long ago as 1950 (when Stalin was still in power): "Unfortunately, particularly among the party and armed forces, it is possible that the Soviet government's monopoly of the instruments of communications may have persuaded the majority of the Soviet people that if there is war between Russia and America, America must inevitably be the aggressor'' (1950, p. 250). Bauer, Inkeles and Kluckhohn, reviewing several reports by Western visitors inside the USSR, wrote that ''in the majority of instances they indicated a complete acceptance of official propaganda with regard to foreign affairs'' (1956, p. 124). George Feifer, along with many detailed reports of discontent and disillusionment in recent years, says that

> . . . the threat to the world is all the greater because disillusionment in the Soviet system rarely carries over into opposition to Moscow's foreign policy. Even Russians brimming with discontent still tend, with their villagelike patriotism, to rally around the Motherland when it appears to be in trouble. . . . Most Russians are content to believe that their tanks went to the aid of an Afghan people menaced by imperialist interference, as they rescued the Czechoslovak people from a similar danger in 1968. [1981, p. 55]

As for Afghanistan, Robert Kaiser's description of Soviet perceptions is strikingly at variance with typical American perceptions of what happened:

> When the Soviets realized that they had caused an international furor much stronger than they had expected, they reacted bitterly, if also typically. Dr. Freud could have had the Russian nation in mind when he devised his theory of projection. Our fault? How could this be our fault? Clearly the Americans were to blame for the unhappy change in the international atmosphere brought on by the Soviet Union's fraternal help for the people of Afghanistan. This was the Party line, and because it so suited the national personality, a great many Russians obviously accepted it. Like people everywhere the Russians are gifted at presuming their own benevolence. [1981, p. 511]

It is obviously impossible to tell how fully the top Party people, as distinguished from the general public, believe their own propaganda about America's guilt and their own innocence, but there are psychological reasons (White, 1965, pp. 242-44, 269-74) for thinking that probably most of them do believe most of it.

Like our own, their rationalizations of outright aggression are truly frightening. The brakes are off when they should be most firmly on.

The "Pro-us" Illusion

Another war-promoting misperception, much less often recognized than the two that have just been discussed, can be called the "pro-us" illusion (White, 1969, pp. 34–38; 1970, pp. 29–30) and can be defined as the tendency to perceive others as more friendly to one's own country—*or less hostile*—than they actually are.

That is, or at least appears at first sight to be, the exact opposite of the diabolical enemy-image. That image normally includes the idea that another country is implacably, aggressively hostile to one's own country, while the "pro-us" illusion pictures others as more friendly or less hostile than they are. It is suggested here that both forms of perceptual distortion exist, that both promote war more often than not, and that to some extent they do conflict with each other, but that to a larger extent they apply to different things and can coexist without conflict as parts of a larger psychological pattern.

The following examples will give substance to the idea:

• Hitler in 1939 greatly underestimated the massive shift of British and French opinion against him which had just occurred as a result of his takeover of the Czech part of Czechoslovakia, breaking the promises he had made at Munich. He therefore imagined he could get away with his attack on Poland without having to fight a major war. He was wrong.

• The Japanese, in deciding to attack Pearl Harbor, underestimated the intensity of the wounded pride and the tenacity of the anger their action would create in the United States. They realized that America would fight but clung to the hope that after several initial defeats the fighting spirit of Americans would fade. It did not.

• President Kennedy and his chief advisers appear to have half-expected that a landing at the Bay of Pigs would touch off a popular pro-American rebellion in Cuba against Castro. It did not. And they should have known better. State Department intelligence, under Roger Hilsman, knew better, and the last honest opinion poll in Cuba (by Lloyd Free; see Cantril, 1967) had indicated a considerable majority favoring Castro at that time.

• For many years the United States fought in Vietnam, not really imagining that most of the people were on our side and against the Viet Cong but believing that the majority "couldn't care less" about the outcome of the war, and vaguely assuming that those who were strongly on our side were as numerous as those strongly against us. The outcome, and other evidence (White, 1970, pp. 37–103), suggest that on the latter point we were mistaken, and that if we had judged more realistically the actual state of Vietnamese opinion in 1962–65, we would not have fought in that war.

• For several years after 1917 the Bolshevik leaders, especially Trotsky, clung to the hope that the successes of the Red Army would touch off revolutions in border countries such as Finland and Poland, and that Europe as a whole, exhausted and disillusioned by World War I, was ripe for Communist revolution. With some exceptions they were mistaken.

• For many years a great many people in the West clung to the hope that the common people of the USSR were their "secret allies" (Lyons, 1954) against the men in the Kremlin. The evidence that that was never very true, and that it is emphatically not true now, will be discussed in Chapter 15.

The "pro-us" illusion evidently takes several forms: underestimating the chance that certain potential opponents will become actual opponents and therefore initiating a war in a spirit of overconfidence (Hitler in 1939); underestimating the tenacity and fighting spirit of an actual or expected opponent (Japan in 1941); believing that the people in an opposing country are more acutely discontented and in a more revolutionary mood than they are (the United States and Cuba in 1961, the Bolshevik leaders and the rest of Europe in 1917–20, the West and the USSR for many years thereafter); and believing that a rebellion in some other country—a rebellion opposed to one's own interests—is less formidable and has less popular support than it does (the United States in Vietnam and, it should be added immediately, the Soviets in Afghanistan). In all of these cases the warriors have not been too fearful. They have been *not fearful enough*.

The tendency for the "pro-us" illusion to promote war is obvious. Why does it occur?

One is tempted to explain it mainly as a simple case of wishful thinking, which is probably true to some extent, but wishful thinking is a dubious explanation of anything since overanxious, worst-case thinking is also common.

Probably the main factor is the moral self-image, combined with a tendency to assume that others see our behavior in as favorable a light as we ourselves do. To assume that others see things as we do is a very common tendency. John Foster Dulles, for instance, once said "Khrushchev does not need to be convinced of our good intentions. He knows we are not aggressors and do not threaten the security of the Soviet Union" (Jervis, 1976, p. 68). Another example: We Americans in Vietnam—most of us—had by 1965 rather thoroughly rationalized our intervention, glossing over the corruption and other sins of the military oligarchy and perhaps unduly demonizing the Viet Cong leaders on the village level, who then were doing their best to win over the peasants. We persuaded ourselves that we were really helping, not hurting, the peasants. We did not persuade ourselves totally by any means but probably enough to make us underestimate the peasants' hostility to us as invading foreigners and to our Saigon allies as corrupt city-based usurers and exploiting landowners. If we had had more empathy with their anger at us and fear of us, or less self-righteousness to start with, we might not have sent our troops there in the first place or kept them there for so long.

Is the "pro-us" illusion, then, a motivated or a cognitive error?

To the extent that wishful thinking accounts for it, it is motivated, and since the moral self-image is clearly motivated an explanation based on it puts the "pro-us" illusion again in that category. On the other hand, the tendency to assume that others see things as we do, with no special effort to empathize realistically or to explore differences between their perception and ours, seems more like what Jervis would call a cognitive factor. The conclusion therefore might be that the illusion is both motivated and cognitive, but primarily motivated.

Finally, can anything be said about situations in which the hostility of others tends to be overestimated and those in which it tends to be underestimated?

On the basis of the examples cited here and some others, these very tentative hypotheses are suggested:

• Nations tend to overestimate the aggressiveness and the unchangeability of the hostility of their chief opponents (e.g. the United States and the USSR in perceptions of each other; the USSR and China; Israel and the Arabs).

• Nations tend to overestimate the insurrectionary possibilities (with implied friendliness to themselves) in countries whose governments they strongly dislike (the United States looking at Cuba; the USSR looking at the capitalist world in 1917–20; the West looking at the USSR, 1920–53).

• Nations tend to underestimate the insurrectionary possibilities (with implied hostility to themselves) in countries whose governments they regard as allies (the United States and the Saigon government; the United States and the Shah; the USSR and the present Kabul government), at least when those protest movements see themselves as defending their homeland against foreign intervention and "puppet" governments.

• Nations tend to underestimate the anger at themselves and the fear of a future upset of the balance of power in the minds of allies or friends of countries against which they are waging aggressive war (Germany versus Britain in 1914; Germany versus France, Britain, and the United States in 1939–41; Japan versus the United States in 1941).

• Along with overestimating the aggressive and unchangeable character of the hostility of their own chief opponents, nations tend to underestimate the elements of real fear and understandable anger in those opponents' hostility (the United States and the USSR; the USSR and China; Israel and the Arabs).

Overconfidence and Worst-case Thinking

Military overconfidence has played a part in the origin of a great many wars. As John Stoessinger (1974) has pointed out, no large nation that has started a major war in the twentieth century has ended the winner. Not Germany or Austria in World War I, not Tsarist Russia in World War I (to the extent that Russia started it), not Germany in World War II, and not Japan in World War II. All of them were disastrously defeated. Hitler was, as it turned out, disastrously mistaken when he thought he could overwhelm the Soviet Union in a matter of months. France and the United States were both overconfident in thinking they could win or at least hold their own, at an acceptable price, in Vietnam. The United States was overconfident when it crossed the 38th Parallel and carried the war into North Korea. The same has tended to be true of smaller nations also. Iran and Iraq, for instance, at different times have been overconfident that they could win without paying an irrational price. Argentina was overconfident when it thought it could challenge the British position in the Malvinas/Falklands.

One is tempted to say, as this writer did in an earlier publication (White, 1970, p. 28), that overconfidence predominates over underconfidence, and "this is not surprising, since overconfidence is a form of the wishful thinking that is the rule, not the exception, in human affairs." Jervis (1976, p. 369) makes a valid criticism when he says, "There may be many instances where decision-makers did not go to war because they underestimated the chances of victory. These cases are much less dramatic and harder to sample than are cases of wars. It is therefore hard to compare the frequency of this error with that of the opposite one." Examples might include the unwillingness of the United States to risk actual war over Hungary, Czechoslovakia, the Berlin Wall, or Afghanistan, and the unwillingness of the Soviet Union to risk war with its own troops at any time from 1945 to 1979, a period that included Iran, Vietnam, and Soviet backing down on Berlin and Cuba.

In addition, a striking phenomenon Jervis did not mention at that point supports his case: the predominance of worst-case thinking—apparently the exact opposite of overconfidence—in many contexts, including especially the thinking of military men about their strength compared with that of their possible opponents. That tendency powerfully exacerbates an arms race. It is my impression that one cannot yet make even a good guess as to whether overconfidence or worst-case thinking predominates, but both frequently occur, both can do much harm, and it is therefore well worthwhile to examine each and to try to discover which predominates in various types of situation, and why.

One hypothesis may help the examination process: The military thinking of governments in times of crisis is not more often overconfident than underconfident with regard to the chances of victory, but when the costs of war itself are fully taken into account decision-makers are more often irrationally overconfident than irrationally underconfident. Jervis says, "There may be many instances where decision-makers did not go to war because they underestimated the chances of victory." That may well be true, but at the same time it could be that, taking the costs and nuclear risks of any future war into account, any government should now require far more than a fifty-fifty chance of victory before deliberately starting any war. If, for instance, a government estimated its chances of winning at 80–20 when in fact they were only 60–40, a decision to start a war would still be irrational and call for psychological interpretation.

Following this logic one step further, the historical record of the many times a government has started a war that turned out to be unsuccessful is persuasive evidence that in many cases governments have done it not "deliberately," with a well-calculated estimate of their probable success, but rather under strong pressure of fear. The Germans and Austrians certainly felt such pressure in 1914, and in a quite different way the Japanese felt it in 1941. (They felt that their "China policy" was vitally important and that America's growing strength and belligerence endangered it.) In other words, this evidence counts on the side of the proposition that defensively motivated aggression is frequent.

Another promising hypothesis is that, while military men in a government that starts a war are probably as a rule fairly realistic about the purely military factors involved and underestimate their relative strength at least as often as they overestimate it, both they and the civilian decision-makers are often so lacking in empathy that they underestimate the psychological factors, among both enemies and potential enemies, that will be mobilized against them *if* they appear as the aggressors. This is the "pro-us" illusion which has just been discussed. The Germans might have won both World Wars if they had not underestimated the reactive fighting spirit of the British and Americans, and Japan might have won in the Far Eastern part of World War II if it had not calculated, mistakenly, that America's fighting spirit would not outlast a series of initial defeats.

Overlapping Territorial Self-images

The surface of the earth is dotted with ulcerous spots that have been the source of an exorbitant amount of bad blood and, often, of war: Alsace-Lorraine, Macedonia, Bosnia-Herzegovina, the Polish Corridor, the Sudetenland, Danzig, the West Bank and Gaza, Israel itself, the Sinai, Lebanon, Cyprus, Kashmir, Bangladesh, South Korea, South Vietnam, Taiwan, Quemoy, Laos, Cambodia, the Sino-Indian border, the Maritime Provinces of Siberia, Berlin, Northern Ireland, the Ogaden, the Shatt el-Arab, the Falklands/Malvinas. Each of these ulcerous spots is a zone of overlap, where one country's or people's territorial image of itself overlaps with another country's or people's territorial image of *it*self.

Historians are quite familiar with this as a cause of war, since in their studies of specific wars, countries, or groups of countries they have encountered it so often, usually giving it names such as "irredentism" or "territorial disputes." As might be expected from their typical antigeneralization attitude, however, few have counted up the remarkably large number of such spots in the world or talked about why the number is so large. As for political scientists, who can usually be counted on to generalize, they have not given it much attention either. It does not rank among their favorite subjects, such as the struggle for power, the balance of power, the security dilemma, or international organization. It should. If we are talking about the causes of war, it matters.

Neither the competitive struggle for power, nor economic competition, nor even fear can fully account for the intensity of these disputes. Often those factors are involved in some degree, but not to an extent sufficient to account for the amount of bad blood that exists. There is of course a struggle for power in each case, but what calls for psychological explanation is the special intensity of the desire for power over a certain piece of territory when that territory is perceived as part of the national *self*, even though it may make little contribution to the overall power of the nation. Taiwan is a good case in point. No doubt its present prosperity compared with the Mainland gives the Chinese Communists an incentive to try to incorporate it, but their desire to do so exceeds its present economic desirability. The intensity of their desire seems, and has always seemed, disproportionate. They have been fanatically intent on driving those they regard as invaders out of power in Taiwan—the invaders being, at the outset, the United States and the Nationalist Chinese under Chiang Kai-shek. In their eyes (and, interestingly, in the eyes of the Nationalists also) it is simply a part of China and belongs there, even though it would not add much to China's power or security.

Psychologists too have seldom realized the importance of the problem as related to war. (Few of them have studied much history, and most are preoccupied with the psychology of individuals and small groups.) Their chief direct contribution, probably, is to notice the similarity between territoriality in nations and territoriality in animals. Lorenz (1966), Ardrey (1963), Carpenter (1934), and others have described how many species of animals will spring to the defense of territory with which the individual animal has identified and that it seems to regard as its own. Of course, we must be on our guard against overhasty parallels between subhuman animal behavior and the behavior of human animals on the national level, but at this point the parallel seems to have some validity, since in both cases the process of identification is involved. A piece of land becomes identified with the self-image and is defended as such.

Psychologists have probably made an indirect contribution too, in their present typical strong emphasis on the self-image and on how, by a process of identification, the self-image comes to include many things that were not originally part of it. A nation, for instance, is a collective self. Psychologists use a variety of names in referring to the self-image. Many would call it simply "the self"; Kurt Lewin called it "the person." He spoke, for instance, of how a person's clothes come to be part of the "person." If clothes are identified with to such an extent that they seem to be part of the person or part of the "self," then surely the territory that represents one's own nation on the map—and perhaps all forms of socially sanctioned property—can also be part of it.

It is a good guess, too, that macho pride has much to do with it. Pride leads each side, in its perception of a disputed piece of land, to expand its self-image by thinking of that land as part of its own natural and rightful self, with selective inattention to the fact that others regard it as part of themselves. Then, when others are found living on that land or even claiming, with guns in their hands, that it belongs to them, macho pride comes in again. It seems intolerable that invaders should be permitted to occupy one's own territory without permission. If we are men worthy of the name, it seems obvious, we will at least have the courage to fight in literal self-defense.

Menachem Begin went through those two stages in relation to the West Bank, occupied at first almost exclusively by Palestinian Arabs whose ancestors had lived there for at least 1,300 years. He set his heart on it, called it not Palestine but Judea and Samaria, thoroughly identified himself and his people with it, and persuaded himself that the Arabs living there really belonged somewhere else. Understandably, those Arabs had an even more firm and solid territorial self-image, including not only the West Bank but also all of the part of Palestine that they saw taken away from them and now named Israel, and certainly the West Bank as an absolute minimum. It seemed to them that if they were men worthy of the name they would have the courage to fight to defend, and if possible to regain, all of the land that was still, in their eyes, part of their national self. Their chief motive could therefore be called defensive, even if not fearful.

What is most relevant to the East–West conflict is that such territorial self-images are not merely national; they now often include large groups of nations, such as the Free World or the Socialist Community.

The United States, seeing itself with some justification as the leader and indispensable defender of the entire Free World, which admittedly has had some outposts that were not so free, has fought to defend two of those outposts, South Korea and South Vietnam. Surely the mere fact of incorporating them in an expanded territorial self-image was not the decisive factor in our doing so. Considerations of the world balance of power and long-term security were decisive. Probably, though, our mental picture of a Free World with clear boundaries at the 38th Parallel in Korea and the 17th Parallel in Vietnam added much to the sense of obvious rightness that our leaders and most of the American public had at the outset in both cases (with much reason in the case of Korea but less reason in the case of Vietnam). It confirmed our justified impression that North Korea, backed by the Soviet Union, had committed unequivocal aggression by invading the Free World, and it confirmed our much less justified impression that the North Vietnamese (who in their own eyes were defending their own homeland against foreign occupation in the South) had also invaded the Free World. What Stalin and the North Koreans overlooked (with much selective inattention) was that there was no strong indigenous revolt in South Korea that they could claim to be supporting. What most of us in America overlooked at the outset of the Vietnam war was that there was a very strong indigenous revolt in South Vietnam that the North Vietnamese saw themselves as supporting in a common defense of their homeland against a foreign occupier. That (and not Communist fanaticism) was probably the chief single reason for the extraordinary tenacity of the antiforeign Vietnamese against first the French and then the Americans (and their "puppets" in Saigon). In their eyes we had stepped over the border of their homeland, with guns in our hands. We were therefore the obvious aggressors.

Is there something similar in the imagery of the men in the Kremlin? Do they picture the Socialist Community in somewhat the same way that many of us picture the Free World, as a genuine entity that they are committed to defend, and on the "defense" of which their credibility, prestige, and power depend? Evidence that they do have such an image is provided by the striking fact that their willingness to use their own troops on any large scale outside the borders of the USSR itself has been limited during the period 1945–79 to countries within their so-called sphere, namely Hungary and Czechoslovakia. Even their aggression in Afghanistan may have been motivated largely by the perception that a nation that was supposed to have joined the Socialist Community in the April Revolution of 1978 (and had been a "friendly" semi-satellite for many years before that) was in danger of disintegration and ultimate foreign control. In other words, somewhat ambiguously, the expanded territorial self-image of the men in the Kremlin was endangered.

A similar overlapping of territorial self-images might occur in the future at a number of points on the long periphery of the USSR.

Selective Inattention

Psychiatrists know how common selective inattention—that is, the tendency to push certain things out of one's mind—is on the individual level of human behavior. They know too how much harm it does to realistic thinking on that level. It is probably just as frequent on the level of international behavior, and just as likely to interfere with hard, evidence-based thinking.

It is the chief process by which unconscious or subconscious forces within the human mind bring about the five types of motivated errors discussed above. It is not itself a motive or a type of error. It is a *process* whereby subconscious motives influence a person's thought process and consequently influence the person's entire picture of the world he lives in. Subconscious motives such as anxiety and macho pride influence a person's "reality world" chiefly by first influencing what he thinks about—that is, what he pays attention to—moment by moment.

An example: In 1914 the Kaiser and his Chancellor, Bethmann-Hollweg, believed that even if their drastic action against Serbia were to result in a big war, Britain would not take part in it. That was a disastrous misperception of the "pro-us" type. For reasons that will be discussed in more detail in Chapter 13, it had much to do with the fact that World War I occurred and much to do with Germany's ultimate defeat. The war might not have occurred, and even if it had Germany might have won it, if the Kaiser had listened carefully to what his ambassador in London, Lichnowsky, was urgently trying to tell him. Lichnowsky was saying that *if* Germany were to follow the Schlieffen Plan and invade France by way of Belgium, Britain would probably fight. Chiefly because the Kaiser thought Lichnowsky had been duped by the wily Englishmen, he scornfully brushed aside Lichnowsky's warning. At that point he was not fearful enough. The war occurred, and Germany was defeated.

Another possible example: President Reagan and his closest advisers are now fixated on the idea of strategic equality (or superiority), as the Kaiser and his closest advisers were fixated on the Schlieffen Plan. George Kennan, Seweryn Bialer, and some others who know the Soviet Union at least as well as Lichnowsky knew Britain, are urgently trying to tell the President that his strenuous pushing of the strategic arms race, especially the Pershing II, is increasing the danger of nuclear war. Perhaps chiefly because he thinks such people have been duped by the wily Communists, Reagan and most of his advisors are scornfully brushing aside their warning. His selective inattention could make World War III more likely, as the Kaiser's and Bethmann-Hollweg's selective inattention made World War I more likely.

It is therefore worthwhile to listen, briefly, to what some psychiatrists and psychologists have to say about two psychological processes, selective attention and selective inattention.

William James, in his extraordinary but now little-noticed chapter on "the stream of thought" (1890, pp. 224–90), led the way. He pointed out that the direction of the stream of thought, as it shifts moment by moment, is always "sensibly selective," meaning perceptibly selective. We are always at least vaguely aware of how our own needs and interests determine what we think about (that is, pay attention to) as the thought process goes on, though we may not be at all clear at the time, and certainly not in retrospect, as to what those needs and interests are.

Freud added the idea that unconscious or ''preconscious'' factors may cause certain things *not* to be paid attention to. A patient on the psychoanalytic couch, engaging in relatively free association and in a relaxed way following whatever chains of association come into his mind, often shows what Freud called resistance. That is, when a train of thought comes too close to certain embarrassing or somehow anxiety-arousing thoughts, the person's mind veers away or a new start is made, with the result that the dangerous subject is avoided. It is an unconscious or only partly conscious process; the person is not able to say what he has been avoiding until, perhaps, later in the analytic process.

Freud added also the term repression, which in its stricter sense means that certain memories have been pushed down into ''the unconscious'' so thoroughly that they are not accessible even when the person consciously wants to recover them. If they are recovered it is only later, after the forces that maintain the repression have begun to relax. What resistance and repression have in common is that certain thoughts are somehow pushed out of the person's mind, but in the case of repression more thoroughly.

They have the same thing in common with three other processes that we have discussed in this chapter: rationalization, projection, and Adlerian compensation. In all three, some embarrassing idea is pushed at least temporarily out of the mind, but the manner of pushing varies.

Rationalization is defined here as pushing out of one's mind the less socially acceptable motives underlying what the person or his group has done or contemplates doing by focusing on acceptable motives—which may be genuine—for doing that thing. The ''good'' motives tend to crowd the ''bad'' ones out of consciousness while the bad ones still influence behavior.

For instance, let us say, on the basis of a good deal of evidence, that there were at least three motives involved in the German–Austrian attack on Serbia in 1914: exaggerated fear of Austrian disintegration, anger at the murder of the Archduke and the increasingly ''insolent'' agitation of the Serbian nationalists, and macho pride associated with the idea that the area of German-and-Austrian control was about to be successfully expanded in the general direction represented by the projected Berlin-to-

Baghdad railway, which could mean economic as well as ego advantages. Probably fear was the strongest of the three. More certainly it was the most acceptable as a reason for risking a big war, since they could then say, and believe, that they had fought only in self-defense.

As for the anger and the pride, the documentary evidence suggests that both were present in consciousness some of the time, but probably not, to any great extent, as reasons for risking a big war. At the point when the decision-makers were thinking about whether they were right to risk a big war they probably focused almost entirely on the fear motive, since it was the only one compatible with the thought ''We are peace-lovers and would never wage war except in defence of ourselves or our allies.''

If so, we could say that in this case rationalization had been served by selective inattention, since the less worthy motives of anger and pride (and perhaps economic gain), whether they were in fact secondary in the decision process or not, were at critical moments crowded out of consciousness by the more acceptable motive of fear. From then on the Germans and Austrians could say to themselves and each other, with conscious sincerity, ''We fought only in self-defense.'' And since in the records of what they were saying to each other the idea that they might actually be committing aggression is completely absent, it may be that to a very large extent it was excluded also from the clear central focus of their thoughts. If present at all it was probably only lurking around the edges and immediately denied if it made its appearance.

Projection is defined here as a substitution, when it is felt that someone has to be blamed, of thoughts of others' guilt for unacknowledged thoughts of one's own possible guilt. If unverbalized thoughts were put into words the words might be: We are not to blame; *they* are. In effect, again, the thought of blame attached to the collective self is not only denied. Denial may not even be needed, since that thought is already crowded out of consciousness by the thought of others' guilt. Again, selective inattention is in the service of a subconscious goal.

In international affairs projection is the rule and self-blame is the rare exception. Almost always the opponents and only the opponents are blamed for the conflict itself and, if war results, for the war. For instance, the Germans in 1914 blamed at first the Serbians, their Russian backers, and the French backers of the

Russians. After the British intervened they were blamed with a quite special bitterness and violence, though in fact they had less direct responsibility for the war than Germany, Austria, Russia, or France and had done their best, according to their lights, to prevent it. In German eyes, nevertheless, it was the English (as the Germans called them), jealous of German successes, who had plotted the whole affair. "Gott straf England." Selective inattention is achieved where it is most needed, at the point where Germans might otherwise have to think about their own blunders or misdeeds.

Finally, there is macho pride, in those cases in which it can be regarded as Adlerian compensation for (or in Freud's terms a "reaction-formation" against) a sense of one's own weakness or inferiority. It is evidently another reason for selective inattention. In such cases thoughts of weakness or inferiority (or, even worse, femininity) are crowded out of consciousness by their direct opposites: thoughts of strength, superiority, courage, and tough, hard, unequivocal masculinity.

It is possible, then, to think of all five of these processes—resistance, repression, rationalization, projection, and Adlerian compensation—as having in common, and operating through the process of, selective inattention. In each case uncomfortable or repugnant thoughts are pushed at least temporarily out of consciousness, and perhaps, in all or most cases, it is done by focusing attention on something else. In a broad sense of the word "repression" we can say in all five cases that certain thoughts are repressed. To do so would avoid the need to use the barbarous term "selectivity inattended." That would depart, though, from Freud's usage, which in general reserves the word repression for cases in which repugnant memories are fully and lastingly excluded from awareness (possibly by developing "cover memories" that can always be inserted into consciousness to crowd out the repressed one when there is danger of its becoming fully conscious).

In any case much recognition should go to the American psychiatrist Harry Stack Sullivan, who introduced the term "selective inattention." When used as a noun it serves the very important function of representing what all of the processes described here have in common. (For a general description of his thought, see Sullivan, 1953. The term was apparently first applied to international affairs by the collator and editor of his writings, Helen Swick Perry, 1954.)

In any case, if words are to be carefully used, selective *in*attention should be distinguished from selective attention, a term that has sometimes been applied recently to some of the processes described here. Selective attention is the more natural term for what William James was talking about—the universal and continual tendency to pay attention to whatever touches one's own needs or interests, positively or negatively, which implies a tendency to let all less interesting things fall by the wayside. That is not what has been discussed here. Selective attention is motivated inclusion in the process of attentive, focused thought; selective inattention is subconsciously motivated exclusion.

CHAPTER ELEVEN

The Chief Corrective: Realistic Empathy

Empathy is the *great* corrective for all the forms of war-promoting misperception that have just been discussed.

It will be remembered that empathy is defined, at the opening of Chapter 2, as simply understanding the thoughts and feelings of others. It is distinguished from sympathy, which is defined as feeling with others. Empathy with opponents is therefore psychologically possible even when a conflict is so intense that sympathy is out of the question. It is true that, to the extent it is possible, warmhearted sympathy may contribute much to peace, perhaps even more than empathy contributes, but that is not what we are talking about now. We are not talking about warmth or approval, and certainly not about agreeing with or siding with, but only about realistic understanding.

How can empathy be achieved?

Of course, those who have studied an opposing nation intensively can do it much better than the rest of us can, but all of us can do it after a fashion and can supplement our own thinking by listening to others who have special knowledge. The essentials do not depend on special erudition or on any special gift of sensitive, imaginative intuition. They depend mainly on an ordinary newspaper-reader's knowledge, plus a continual honest effort to be fair and to ask oneself repeatedly such elementary questions as: How would I feel if I were faced with the situation the Soviet Union now faces? How might my feelings be influenced by past experiences, such as what I, if I were a Russian, went through in World War II? Or my Communist education? How would I interpret recent American behavior if I had a tendency to put the worst plausible interpretation on whatever the American government does?

What is needed is much more than the cold, calculating chess-player's type of empathy described and illustrated in Chapter 4. Although the needed kind of empathy does not by definition im-

ply feeling with, it does imply understanding or at least genuinely trying to understand the feelings of other people. It means
jumping in imagination into another person's skin, imagining
what it might be like to look out at his world through his eyes,
and imagining how you might feel about what you saw. It means
being the other person, at least for a while, and postponing skeptical analysis until later. It means trying to understand the other
from the inside looking out, not merely from the outside looking
in. Most of all, it means trying to look at one's own group's behavior honestly, as it might appear when seen through the other's
eyes, recognizing that his eyes are almost certainly jaundiced but
recognizing also that he has the advantage of not seeing our
group's behavior through the rose-colored glasses that we ourselves normally wear. He may have grounds for distrust, fear, and
anger that we have not permitted ourselves to see. That is the
point where honesty comes in. An honest look at the other implies an honest look at oneself.

Empathy so defined should go far to correct each of the five
motivated types of error described above:

• Most clearly it should counteract exaggerated fear based on
the diabolical enemy-image, since it immediately humanizes the
image of the enemy and makes it possible to recognize, for instance, the possible defensive motives behind his most aggressive
behavior.

• It should counteract the self-deceiving parts of the moral
self-image by cutting through the rationalizations that sustain it.

• It should counteract the ''pro-us'' illusion by exposing the
reasons the other might have for anger and for long-term fear.

• It should counteract overconfidence by bringing out the
weaknesses on one's own side that wishful thinking might have
led oneself to gloss over, and counteract worst-case thinking by
bringing out the strengths on one's own side that worst-case
thinking by the other might seek out and stress.

• It should counteract excessive territorial claims by bringing
out the reasons why another country or people might have claims
and psychological reasons for identifying with the disputed land
as valid and as genuine as one's own.

• In all of this it would counteract the process of selective inattention, because absence of realistic empathy is probably the
most inclusive, the most predictable, and the most war-promoting of all the forms of selective inattention. What is or may be in

the mind of an opponent is one of the most important things to think about if we want peace, but also one of the easiest to push out of our minds.

In a natural-history approach to the kinds of nonempathy that are most common and most harmful, one quickly discovers three that stand out:

1. *Not seeing an opponent's longing for peace.* An extreme example is the American tendency not to remember, when thinking about Soviet attitudes toward World War III, what the entire Soviet people went through in World War II. That is not repression in the Freudian sense. We remember well enough the 20 million dead, the innumerable villages destroyed, the besieged people in Leningrad who ate rats to stay alive—when someone reminds us. It is strictly selective inattention. Our minds somehow ignore what they know about that gigantic suffering, even at the moments when it would be most relevant, namely when thinking about whether the Soviet decision-makers might or might not attempt a nuclear first strike or might or might not deliberately attack Western Europe.

Another example is the small number of Americans who have ever stopped to think of the obvious fact that in the years since 1945 we have fought two wars with our own troops in faraway places while the USSR has not fought any. Of course that is not the whole story, but it is a significant part of the whole story, and we don't think about it. The Soviets do. Though it says nothing about Soviet virtue, it does say something about Soviet caution—and American lack of caution. And it makes more credible the otherwise hard-to-believe proposition that the Soviets might really mean it when they talk about us (or our "ruling circles") as more warlike than they are.

The horrors of war, especially nuclear war, are now almost universally known and feared. Therefore anyone on either side of any acute conflict who accuses the other side of actually wanting war without thinking about the universality of the longing for peace is indulging in selective inattention and is not making even an effort to empathize realistically.

2. *Not seeing an opponent's fear of being attacked.* Herbert Butterfield expressed it well:

It is the peculiar characteristic of the . . . Hobbesian fear . . . that you yourself may vividly feel the terrible fear you have of the other party, but you cannot enter into the other man's counter-fear, or even understand why he should be particularly nervous. For you know that you yourself mean him no harm, and that you want nothing from him save guarantees for your own safety; and it is never possible for you to realize or remember properly that he cannot see the inside of your mind, he can never have the same assurance of your intentions that you have. As this operates on both sides the Chinese puzzle is complete in all its interlockings and neither party can see the nature of the predicament he is in, for each only imagines that the other party is being hostile and unreasonable. [1951, pp. 19–20; quoted by Jervis, 1976, p. 69]

President Reagan pictures the Soviet decision-makers as grimly determined to conquer the world. He does not picture them as afraid of sudden destruction by Pershing IIs or afraid of a gathering, aggressive coalition consisting of the United States, Western Europe, China, and Japan. The fact that they might have plausible grounds for fear apparently escapes him, as does the likelihood that, in a semiparanoid way, their fears of us might go well beyond what we really have any intention of doing.

Similarly, the entire Soviet propaganda apparatus pictures the capitalist and militarist "ruling circles" of America as being only aggressive, without acknowledging even the possibility that fear of Soviet aggression, which has been the mainspring of American foreign policy since 1945 or 1946, might be genuine and shared by American leaders and public alike.

That blind spot is common on both sides of other conflicts also. The Arabs do not seem to realize how desperately tiny Israel fears being ultimately overwhelmed by the encircling and intensely hostile Arabs who outnumber it more than 30 to 1. Meanwhile most of the Israelis seem to have no conception of how their actual territorial expansion, most of all in their recent invasion of Lebanon, has given a plausible factual basis to Arab fears of "Zionist expansionism" and to an Arab conviction (exaggerated, in a semiparanoid way) that Israel's immediate neighbors are all in danger as long as Israel exists. The "Chinese puzzle" that Butterfield talks about, "complete in all its interlockings," is as apt a description of the Arab–Israeli as of the East–West conflict.

3. *Not seeing an opponent's understandable anger.* The importance of anger and hate in international conflict was discussed at some

length in Chapter 9. How often do people on either side of the East–West conflict realize, or even try to realize, the ways in which their own behavior has created anger and perhaps hate on the other side?

We Americans know well the many things the Soviets have done that have angered us. Just in the past three decades (which leaves out all of Stalin's crimes, including the Gulag Archipelago) they have brutally cracked down on Hungary, Czechoslovakia, and (indirectly) Poland, which wanted only to be free from their oppression; they have deceptively entered the Western Hemisphere, our own backyard, and tried to establish offensive nuclear weapons in Cuba, aimed at us, only ninety miles from our shores; they have tried to subjugate free Berlin; they have denied freedom-loving Jews the right to emigrate; they have threatened to send troops against Israel and have armed the Arabs who most threaten Israel's existence; they have put honest dissidents into mental hospitals; they have invaded Afghanistan and relentlessly continued to wage war against its people; they have made similar trouble in Angola, Ethiopia, Yemen, Cambodia, and recently Nicaragua and El Salvador, in ways that have violated the spirit of détente; they have steadily built up a military force that is far greater than they need for purposes of genuine self-defense, which has also violated the spirit of détente; they have waged a continual propaganda war against us, depicting us as "imperialists" when they are the real imperialists in the present-day world; they have covertly broken their promises not to use chemical or biological weapons; they have murdered 269 innocent people on a Korean airliner.

At least that is roughly the way in which a great many Americans, probably a large majority, have perceived their behavior, and in most if not all of the accusations against them there has probably been a sizable kernel of truth. It is of psychological interest also that in most of these cases—perhaps all except the Cuban missile crisis and the strategic military buildup—there has been little or no imminent threat to the security of America. The threat of the others, if any, has been long-term, not short-term. In other words, anger and intense moral condemnation have probably predominated over fear in our reaction to most of them.

In how many of these cases have the Soviet decision-makers or the Soviet public recognized the anger for which they were providing a tangible basis or the effect of that anger in intensifying the malignant spiral process that has greatly increased the danger of nuclear war?

The Soviets have a somewhat similar anger list. One of them might say: For about three decades the ruling circles in the United States relentlessly kept far ahead of us in the unthinkably destructive weapons of nuclear war; they have never joined us in renouncing first use of those weapons; they have implicitly threatened use of them and forced us to beat a humiliating retreat on four occasions: Korea, Quemoy, Cuba, and the SAC alert crisis of 1973; directly or indirectly they have literally invaded several countries: Guatemala, Cuba, the Dominican Republic, Vietnam, Angola, and, most recently, Nicaragua; they have supported reactionary dictators or oligarchies against the people (whom we always supported) in South Korea, the Philippines, Vietnam, Laos, Iran, Iraq, Jordan, Saudi Arabia, Oman, Greece, Spain, Zaïre, Brazil, Argentina, Chile, Cuba, and El Salvador; they supported Israel in most of its wars of aggression; they humiliated us again by excluding us from the peace process in the Middle East; they have colluded against us with China and now with Japan; they violated the spirit of détente by backing out of the SALT II agreement.

Unquestionably many of these accusations are distortions or exaggerations of the facts, but again many probably have a sizable kernel of truth. And here too all except the nuclear accusations probably aroused more anger than short-term fear.

In how many of these cases did we Americans—whatever it was that we actually did—take fully into account the anger for which we were providing some tangible basis or the contribution made by that anger to the spiral process that has greatly increased the danger of nuclear war?

Why? Why are these three specific forms of nonempathy—subconsciously refusing to think about the other side's longing for peace, its fears, and its angers—so pervasive on both sides of the East–West conflict, and perhaps on both sides of every acute international conflict?

One clue is completely obvious, once it has been recognized: Each of the three suppressed forms of empathy is a dangerous challenge to the melodramatic Good Guys–Bad Guys picture that people emotionally involved in a conflict hug so lovingly to their breasts. The Bad Guys image is challenged by any recognition that the hated enemy wants peace as fervently as we do. The Good Guys image is challenged by any recognition that we ourselves, by our own behavior as seen from the other's point of view, have done much to arouse in him not the healthy kind of fear that would deter him from attacking us but the unhealthy kind, involving fear of our attacking him, that leads him to arm excessively and perhaps to engage in defensively motivated aggression. Finally, the Good Guys image is mortally challenged by any honest recognition of the ways in which, without meaning to, we have managed to instill in our opponents anger and intense moral condemnation of us.

Two kinds of pride probably underlie the subconscious cherishing of the Good Guys–Bad Guys picture: macho pride and moral pride—*false* moral pride. If the analysis in Chapter 9 has any validity, the diabolical enemy-image is cherished partly because it enhances a tough, heroic image of the collective self battling valiantly against great evil, and also because it enhances an image of the individual self as grimly realistic in fully recognizing the extent of an external danger. In both of those processes, if they do exist, macho pride is operating. The role of false moral pride is clearer and more certain. Recognizing the other's unhealthy fear is subconsciously avoided because it comes too close to admitting that, by actions verging on aggression, we have given him some basis for that kind of fear; and recognizing the other's anger is subconsciously avoided because it comes too close to admitting that, by morally objectionable actions, we might have merited some of the anger and moral condemnation in the other's mind. That is not true moral pride of the kind that the word conscience better represents. It comes closer to what could be more accurately called self-righteousness or self-deceiving hypocrisy.

It begins to look as if certain kinds of humility are the primary qualities we need to cultivate in ourselves if we want to avoid war. Realistic empathy—the great corrective of all our subconsciously motivated delusions—depends on them.

Can realistic humility and the art of empathizing with an opponent be practiced in our educational system?

They certainly can, in many ways. Role-playing, including reversal of roles and playing the role of an opponent, is the outstanding way to do it (below, Chapter 21; see also White, 1983). Another is listening to genuine dialogue between relatively open-minded persons on both sides, such as the dialogue between Amos Elon and Sana Hassan on the Arab-Israeli conflict (1974).

CHAPTER TWELVE

Unmotivated, Cognitive Errors

The word "cognitive" is applied here to all forms of misperception that cannot readily be attributed to subconscious emotional or motivational factors such as macho pride or ego defense. There are many such forms, and some of the more important of them will now be discussed.

The Influence of Preexisting Beliefs on Present Perception

Under many other names the influence of preexisting beliefs is familiar to nonpsychologists as well as psychologists. Jervis, who calls it "the assimilation of information to pre-existing beliefs" (1976, pp. 117–315), stresses it more than any other form of cognitive error. It includes the effects on perception of all well-established images and stereotypes. Evidence that is "dissonant" (Festinger, 1957) or out of "balance" (Heider, 1958) with established images tends to be ignored or rejected.

Its most conflict-promoting form is an established Good Guys–Bad Guys picture of the political world, such as the prevailing Western assumption that Communists are automatically Bad Guys and anti-Communists Good Guys or, in the Soviet Union, the mirror-image reverse of that. Harkabi (1971), Heradstveit (1979), and Kaplowitz (1976) have studied it and related phenomena intensively in the context of the Arab–Israeli conflict. In every conflict it has predictably baleful effects on at least one side, including for instance a tendency to see the other side's arming as necessarily mainly aggressive in purpose while one's own arming is not, and a tendency not to see that what looks like cold-blooded aggression on the other side may have mainly defensive motives.

As we have seen, the origin of that world-picture (apart from the considerable elements of realism that it typically contains) is probably mainly subconsciously motivated. Over a period of many years it can be gradually built up—a little motivated exaggeration of the opponent's wickedness here, and a little motivated selective inattention to one's own wickedness there, but almost always in those same two directions. It can be likened to a great flywheel, too heavy to be set in rapid motion all at once by any ordinary amount of force but having much momentum once it is well started. It creates confident expectations that whatever the diabolical enemy does will have evil motives and harmful effects, while whatever the good self does will have good motives and good effects. Those expectations, in turn, influence the perception of any new situation, especially if that new situation is at all ambiguous—open to varying interpretations—as most new situations are. *That* process is mainly cognitive, since there is a vast amount of evidence, in everyday experience as well as experimental psychology, that expectations influence perception. Expecting evil, human minds tend to put the worst possible interpretation on whatever the enemy does; expecting good, they tend to put the best possible interpretation on whatever their own group does. It is even possible that the whole effect of subconscious motives on present perception is the result of this two-stage process. They affect expectations, and expectations, by a process that is perhaps purely cognitive, influence perceptions of a present situation and behavior in it.

Take for instance a Soviet decision-maker's perception of the introduction of Pershing II missiles into Western Europe. It is inherently ambiguous as far as the motives lying behind it are concerned. Therefore the majority of the interested people in the West can easily assume that its sole purpose is defense; the Good Guys, as they perceive themselves, could never use it for a first strike, although it is so fast, so accurate, and so powerful that it could be used for a first strike. They see it only as a much-needed deterrent weapon. To the Soviet decision-maker it must look quite different. Taking for granted the evil purposes of the "ruling circles" in the West and the innocence of his own—an image that is now deeply ingrained in his mind and has the momentum of a flywheel—he naturally interprets its introduction as further evidence of the aggressive purposes of his encircling adversaries. Perceiving it in that way, he may decide that he is "forced" to advocate countermeasures, expensive as they are and hard-pressed as the Soviet economy is, that will deter nuclear aggression by the

Bad Guys. Perhaps even subconsciously he does not now want to put that ominous interpretation on what the West has done, but since to him the evil nature of the West's rulers is by now an obvious, almost tangible fact—a given, unchallengeable fact—he feels that his interpretation is the only realistic one. If a colleague questions it, he probably decides that the colleague is naive and may ultimately vote for exclusion of that colleague from the Politburo.

That brings up the vitally important process of social reinforcement of beliefs. Once a clear majority in any group begins to take a certain belief for granted, the pressures of conformity, in both their subtle and their obvious forms, begin to operate. To challenge such a basic belief of the majority begins to require a good deal of courage, and even the more independent and courageous individuals may decide prudently to keep quiet about their heretical perceptions. This is a flywheel too.

Sociologists and social psychologists are fully aware of such facts. Sociologists also have the related concept of cultural lag, meaning that in a changing world some institutions and customs resist change and last too long. Perhaps we need to put alongside it a concept of perceptual lag, meaning that in a changing world perceptions also tend to resist change and last too long.

In the East–West conflict there are two striking examples of perceptual lag, one on each side.

There are many Communists who seem to be still somewhat stuck in the nineteenth century. When they look at the "capitalist" countries of the West (now better described as semisocialist welfare societies) they apparently see something almost as heartless and exploitive of the poor as the laissez-faire capitalism that Marx and Engels described, somewhat more realistically, in the Communist Manifesto. It is as if their minds have only partly taken in the fact of Roosevelt's New Deal and, more important, its earlier counterparts in Western Europe (cf. White, 1966).

There are also many in the West who seem to be still somewhat stuck in the first half of the twentieth century, before Stalin's death in 1953. When they look at the USSR they seem to see something closely resembling the extravagantly ruthless, even sadistic policies of Stalin and the Gulag Archipelago. (There is a resemblance but not a very close one.)

Actually both societies have evolved in many ways since the early years of the conflict, but neither can fully acknowledge how much the other has changed. Probably part of this is motivated selective inattention and part is a simple lack of knowledge and human contact, but in addition there is the fact that firm old beliefs always find it hard to die.

Stalin too showed the same tendency. His ruthless takeover of most of Eastern Europe during the period 1944–48, which was probably the chief single action on either side causing the Cold War, came at a time when the West was less hostile to his country, more grateful, more sympathetic, and more friendly than it had ever been before and more than it has ever been since. He could not see it, nor could he see that he himself was transforming that friendliness into fear and bitter hostility.

The Persistence of Prenuclear Beliefs

There are several ways in which what has just been said applies to nuclear affairs.

The most basic is that, as Jonathan Schell (1982) has so powerfully argued, the human race is far from having fully assimilated the implications of the nuclear era it is now living in. There has been, at least until recently, a great deal of what Robert Jay Lifton has called psychic numbing. It is not that people do not know about the horrors of nuclear war. Almost everyone now knows that much. It is rather that the horrors have been too overwhelming. There has been motivated selective inattention on a grand scale. Human minds, not yet seeing clear and clearly acceptable ways of preventing nuclear war, have recoiled from the entire subject, including its possible action implications and the thinking that should precede action. That has been a motivated error, but there are also cognitive reasons for it. Old patterns of belief and of underlying assumptions have persisted, with their usual tenacity, including old assumptions about the inevitability of almost complete national sovereignty and old assumptions about deterrence as the primary way to prevent war. (The psychological realism or unrealism of Schell's own prescription—the abolition of national sovereignty—will be examined at the end of Chapter 19.)

Other prenuclear beliefs that need to be reexamined include the belief that total security, in a world as anarchic and as full of proliferating nuclear weapons as ours, is still as conceivable for

the United States as it was, say, before 1957; the belief that nuclear peace can be achieved without a fairly high degree of communication and cooperation between the United States and the
USSR; and, most of all, the belief that strategic superiority or
even parity is essential for peace (see Chapters 4 and 6). Conventional parity or some approach to it still makes some sense from
the standpoint of deterrence, even if the Soviet Union's six reasons outlined in Chapter 4 for not invading Western Europe are
fully taken into account. Straining for nuclear parity does not
make sense. If our minds were not stuck in old ruts we would realize immediately that the present grotesque amount of nuclear
overkill on each side makes no sense at all and that deep cuts,
down to the level really needed for an adequate second-strike capability, could be made even unilaterally, with a fair amount of
safety and much profit, by either side that has the courage and
wisdom to do it.

Another outmoded nuclear idea is that first use or the threat
of first use—which made some sense in the 1950s when the Soviet
Union did not have its present enormous retaliatory capability—
is still a sensible policy. Rationally it is hard to believe that the
Soviet decision-makers could still attribute to us irrationality
great enough to permit us to carry out our present threat of first
use, even if only with tactical battlefield nuclear weapons. It is
also startling that many West Europeans think the Soviet decision-makers would attribute to us that much irrationality. The
only thing that now makes sense in this connection is that each
side would observe, and cherish, the psychological firebreak between any kind of conventional war and any kind of nuclear war.

As Einstein put it, ''The unleashed power of the atom has
changed everything except our way of thinking'' (quoted by Cox,
1982, p. 206).

Blurred Distinctions and the Spread of Attribution

''Attribution theory'' has been a major development within
American social psychology during the past fifteen years or so.
The discussion that follows leaves aside most of the theory but
draws something from the experiments and the thinking of
Edward Jones and Richard Nisbett (1971) about how a person

who acts and an observer of his action tend to differ as to why the action occurred.

The concepts that will be briefly suggested here owe more to the thinking of Kurt Lewin, under whom the writer worked for two years, 1937–39; Fritz Heider (1958); and Tamara Dembo, a colleague in 1945–46. They begin with the idea that an image consists of parts, separated from each other by lines of distinction. In A's mind B and B's actions are not quite the same, but they are intimately related. One can say metaphorically that the line of distinction between them in A's mind is not very clear or very thick. There is a strong tendency to assume a resemblance between them. If B is perceived by A as a thoroughly bad person, there is a strong tendency for A to assume that any action by B is also bad—the attributed badness spreads. Conversely, if the action is first perceived as bad, the perceived badness tends to spread and be attributed to B as a person also. The implicit assumption is that bad people do bad things, and if an action is bad it must have been done by a bad person.

We all know that that is not necessarily true. We all know that a person is a complicated creature, sometimes good (as judged by some others) and sometimes bad (as judged by some others), but very seldom all one or all the other. On the other hand, the tendency for attribution of badness to spread from person to actions or vice versa hardly needs proof; it is a matter of everyday observation. So is the spread of goodness; people tend to assume that good people do good things and vice versa.

What is not quite so obvious is that the tendency in question is strong or weak depending on the clearness (or thickness) of the line of distinction between the parts of the image. (It may help to make this concept clear if we draw an analogy with cellular biology. Cells in a tissue have membranes separating them from adjacent cells, and osmosis from one to the other depends on the permeability of those membranes.)

The relevance of all this to dichotomous thinking and to the Good Guys–Bad Guys picture is perhaps obvious by now. On the international level the basic hypothesis takes this form: When the political world is divided between Good Guys and Bad Guys, perceived distinctions within the Bad Guys part of the world tend to be blurred, and the attribution of evil therefore tends to spread throughout that part of the world. (There is also a less clear tendency for the attribution of goodness to spread throughout the Good Guys part of the world.) Within either of those two great dichotomous parts of the perceived world there is often a near-total blurring of distinctions, for instance between bad actors and their bad actions, between one bad actor and another, between the badness of their actions and the unsoundness of all their ideas, between the legitimacy of using force against one and the legitimacy of using force against another. Liberals and democratic socialists are perceptually merged with Communists (by conservatives on our side); Tito is called a stooge of Wall Street (by Stalin); Khrushchev is called a revisionist and therefore a "capitalist-roader" (by Mao); the image of Stalin is merged with the image of Hitler (by Americans); the image of American "imperialism" is partly merged with the image of Hitler (by Stalin); the image of present-day America is merged with the image of the capitalism that Marx hated (by Marxists); the image of present-day Russia is merged with the image of Stalin's Russia (by Solzhenitzyn and hard-line Americans); and cooperation with the USSR for mutual survival today is merged with Chamberlain's appeasement of Hitler (by hard-liners in the West).

There are also other blurrings, more indirectly related to the Good Guys–Bad Guys picture, that have been discussed earlier in this book and are dangerous to peace: blurring the distinction between empathy with Communists and sympathy or agreement with Communists; blurring the distinction between the ruthless domestic policies of the Soviet government and its present self-preserving peace-seeking foreign policy; blurring the distinction between our knowing we want peace and our sometimes assuming that the other side knows we do; blurring the distinction between behavior and motivation—e.g. between calling the Soviet intervention in Afghanistan aggression and calling it aggressively, not defensively, motivated; blurring the distinction between needing a second-strike capability and needing a first-strike capability; blurring the distinction between creating in the Soviet decision-makers a healthy fear of what will happen *if* they attack others and creating in them an unhealthy fear of being attacked themselves by encircling enemies.

One is tempted to say that in the business of preventing war the most vital kind of learning is to see the world in a more and more differentiated way, with more and clearer distinctions between its various parts and aspects. (That was essentially the way Kurt Lewin conceived of all learning. Probably he went too far, but it is certainly a major and not sufficiently recognized form of learning.)

Finally, there is the distinction made by Jones and Nisbett (1971) between dispositional and situational attribution. According to them, an "actor" tends to attribute his actions to the situation he is in. He feels that anyone faced with that situation would have done something like what he did or is now doing. An observer, on the other hand, especially if his interests are hurt by what the actor does, tends to attribute it to a lasting, inherent "disposition" in the actor. If the action hurts the observer, he tends to think the actor has a disposition to do bad, hurtful things. The actor is, in two words, a Bad Guy. Unless the observer can empathize with the actor, looking out through the actor's eyes at the situation the actor thinks he faces, the observer is likely to go far wrong and take a long step toward Good Guys–Bad Guys thinking.

That applies in a high degree to our American reaction to the shooting down of the Korean airliner. It hurt us intensely because we empathized and sympathized so intensely with the innocent shot-down passengers. Yet the chief motive behind it was clearly defensive—obsessive, even paranoid, fear of intrusion by encircling enemies. That was the crucial fact, and few of us could see it.

Universalization and the Injured-innocence Mechanism

A basic tenet of attribution theory, which is also ordinary common sense, is that the attribution of any characteristic to any person or group is likely to be much affected by the context in which their behavior is seen. If a person attempts a task that the observer thinks is difficult, and succeeds, the observer is likely to attribute to him strength or competence; if the task looks easy he does not. If a person hits another with no apparent provocation we think he is aggressive; if we have seen the other hit him first we do not.

That commonsense proposition applies to the arms race in a way that seems obvious once it is recognized but has seldom been explicitly recognized or given a name (cf. White, 1965, pp. 264–67). It will be called here the injured-innocence mechanism. It is this: *Because each nation believes it is obviously innocent of any aggressive intention, it tends to infer that any strenuous arming by its opponent must have an aggressive purpose.*

For instance, we innocent-feeling Americans, apprehensively looking at the Soviet arms buildup since the Cuban missile crisis of 1962, have often inferred that they must want to attack us or their nearer neighbors. Why else would they arm so strenuously and expensively? Surely (we think) not because of any real fear of *us*. But that could be, and probably is, quite wrong. It could well be that their arming, like ours, is primarily intended for deterrence or, if worse comes to worst, for defense. If so, our diabolical enemy-image and our felt need to arm have both received an unnecessary boost. Similarly, if they, feeling innocent, see us strenuously and expensively arming, they probably infer that our motives must be aggressive and arm more than they would have otherwise. The reciprocal, back-and-forth nature of the process, resembling the Chinese puzzle Butterfield described, makes it especially ominous. It contributes much to the unhealthy kind of fear on both sides.

Is it subconsciously motivated? In part, yes. The feeling of innocence from which it starts is another name for the moral self-image, and it probably is partly motivated. It is true that in this case that image surely has a sizable kernel of truth on both sides. On balance, taking all the costs and risks into account, we certainly do not want to attack the Soviet Union, and for the same self-preserving reasons they do not want to attack us. As Butterfield put it, "You know that you yourself mean him no harm." That is probably not an exaggeration of the innocence on both sides, if we are talking about an outright, unprovoked attack; neither side wants to commit aggression directly against the other. It *is* probably an exaggeration, though, if applied to the competition for power and influence in the Third World. Both sides *are* "guilty" of wanting to play a vigorous role in that competition, whether it harms the other or not. In that context, therefore, the motivated mechanisms of rationalization and projection have some work to do, and to that extent motivation does enter in.

From there on the process is apparently unmotivated. Given a sense of innocence the next step is to infer that the other side *knows* you are innocent. Given all the evidence we have of Soviet insecurity and of a diabolical enemy-image in their minds as well as ours, that is highly questionable. Dulles was almost certainly wrong when he said "Khrushchev does not need to be convinced of our good intentions." Certainly the majority of Americans do not feel they "know" the Soviet decision-makers are innocent. Finally, the third step seems logical enough. *If* we are innocent *and* the other side knows we are, it is not at all illogical to conclude that strenuous arming by them indicates an aggressive purpose.

The irrationality lies in the premises: first, the premise that we are wholly innocent, and second, the premise that they know we are.

Why do many people assume (probably implicitly in most cases) that the other side "knows" they are innocent?

That question brings us back to the "pro-us" illusion described in Chapter 10 and gives some further evidence for the validity of that concept. The word "projection" comes to mind, since in a broad sense of that word it is possible to say that we project our own sense of innocence into others' minds, or rather into our image of their image of us. It should be noticed, though, that the word "projection" normally refers to the subconsciously motivated process of avoiding a subconscious feeling of guilt by projecting blame onto others. This is different. Blame is not involved here at all (until the final step in the three-step process).

A different word is clearly needed. Is there a single word that would suggest the nature of the reality we want to describe? The reality appears to be this: When a person perceives something as real it *is* real for him. Unless he is sophisticated enough to know and remember that others often live in a "reality world" (Hadley Cantril's term) that differs from his own, he makes the easy, effortless assumption that what seems obvious to him is in their psychological world as well as his.

That is how children think. Jean Piaget, interpreting the results of his experiment with children, using models of mountains seen from different points of view (1937) says, "The littler ones do not understand that the observer sees the same mountains quite differently from different points of view, and hence they consider their own perspective absolute. But the older ones discover the relativity necessary to objectivity." Empathy with the perceptions of others, when their perceptions differ from one's own, is an acquired art, calling for some mental effort as well as sophistication.

Is there a single word that could suggest all of that, even approximately?

The word proposed here is *universalization*. True, it is long and cumbersome, but it does suggest the essence of what happens. People in general, especially children, universalize their own perceptions and their entire "reality worlds," in that they tend to assume that what they perceive is simply *there*, as visible to others as it is to them, and in the same way. It is not a motivated error. It is the simplest form of cognition.

Credulous Acceptance of Propaganda

It is a common idea on each side of the East-West conflict that evil and powerful men on the other side deliberately dupe the mass of the people on that side, inducing them to accept a thoroughly distorted world view that makes war and strenuous preparation for war possible.

We in the West often—and rightly—stress the power of the Communist Party of the Soviet Union to inculcate in the Soviet people the orthodox Communist Good Guys–Bad Guys picture of the world. They in turn depict the conflict as caused mainly by the propaganda of capitalist devils, operating behind the scenes in the West through their control of the mass media, education, and the political process. For instance, Georgy Arbatov, attempting to explain why the American people became so much more hostile to the USSR during the postdétente period, writes:

> Real responsibility for the current deterioration of the world situation lies not with the Soviet Union . . . but with those influential Americans who simply longed to be provoked and were desperately searching for a pretext. . . . All those events [Angola, Ethiopia, Afghanistan, and Cambodia] were resourcefully and aptly manipulated by the opponents of détente to deceive and brainwash the public, whip up the hysteria and chauvinism. . . . This is the heart of the matter. [1982, pp. 182–83]

Arbatov ignores here a key fact: The top members of the Communist Party of the Soviet Union have a near-monopoly of the mass media, education, agitation, and censorship. They can mold public opinion in the USSR and on foreign policy issues have apparently done so with much success. The American government has no such monopolistic power, and no cabal of arms-making capitalists and arms-hungry militarists in any democratic Western country could possibly wield such a thorough monopoly of access to information and expression of opinion. There are too many different points of view, and the voters are free to listen to all of them. It is possible here to have a real mass movement against a Vietnam war, an El Salvador policy, or a Reagan Administration. There is no comparable anti-Afghanistan-war movement in the USSR. In this respect the two sides are by no means symmetrical mirror-images of each other, as they are, to some extent, in many other respects. All Westerners who have been in the Soviet Union for any length of time realize that that is true.

The very considerable power of propaganda, especially when wielded monopolistically, is not in question. Nor is there any obvious difficulty in explaining why, when it has little or no competition, most people credulously accept it. There are obvious motivational as well as cognitive reasons. A strong motivational reason is to get along better with other people, usually including people in authority; a strong cognitive reason is that, when there is no clear reason to challenge the ideas presented (based on contrary personal experience, competing authorities, or peer-group skepticism), the natural tendency is to accept what is said. Like empathy with people who see things differently, challenging what others say takes a certain amount of mental activity, and, when people's interests are elsewhere, such activity is predictably in short supply.

Two more things have to be said, though, in response to Arbatov. One is to grant a sizable kernel of truth in what he said. There is such a thing as a military-industrial complex in the United States, with economic vested interests or professional military interests in preparation for war if not also in war itself (*only* if it remains conventional). Such people usually have more money to spend on political campaigns for those Congressmen and Presidents who vote their way than other people have. For the sake of democratic pluralism, rational government decision-making, *and* peace, the facts about such people's propaganda activities need to be discovered and publicized, if not also effectively limited in amount.

The other response to Arbotov that seems needed is a sharp challenge to the idea he expressed about the United States, one that a great many Americans take for granted in connection with the USSR—the idea that the people in power are *in general* both more evil and less interested in peace than those who have less power. This is what I have argued against in other publications (e.g. White, 1970, pp. 29–30, 257–61, 312–13), calling it the ''black-top enemy image.'' Because that violates the principle that the word ''black'' should not be used as if it meant bad, I now prefer the term ''evil-ruler enemy image.'' (There is also a fairly common tendency to have an evil-ruler image of one's own country.)

To challenge that image is not to say that the influential people in a country are any better than others, everything considered, nor is it to deny that some rulers (Hitler, Stalin) have been much worse than most of the people they ruled. It is to say that to assume a real contrast between the goodness of the leaders and that of the led is a form of Good Guys–Bad Guys thinking and as dangerous as any other form of it. Both the more powerful and the less powerful are human, both are extremely varied, and in our nuclear age both can be relied on, on both sides of the East–West conflict, to have a horror of nuclear war.

That is a large subject that can only be touched on here, but one important element in it should be mentioned: that the leaders of a nation or a community (political leaders, journalists, professionals of many sorts, successful businessmen) are usually better educated than others, and that education tends to broaden a person's international horizon and diminish his tendency to Good Guys–Bad Guys thinking. There is a kind of chauvinism among the less educated, consisting of very simple nationalistic Good Guys–Bad Guys thinking, that needs to be recognized and kept in mind.

Extrapolation of a Trend

Those who focus on changes in the stock market know how difficult it is to predict the general upward or downward trends. It has been said that ''a trend has no momentum,'' and certainly none can be predicted with any confidence unless there has been a shrewd analysis of why something has been going down or up and some basis for thinking that those causal factors are continuing.

This same principle is probably as true in predicting future trends in international affairs as in predicting economic changes. In both areas there appears to be a frequent tendency, often mistaken, to assume that trends will continue in the future as they have in the recent past—in other words, to extrapolate a trend. Some examples:

• When in 1979 the Soviet Union invaded Afghanistan, there were many predictions that it was the first step in a new Hitler-like career of conquest and that the oilfields would probably be the next target unless heroic measures of defense were undertaken. Heroic measures were not undertaken (they would probably have been unwise if not impossible), but instead of grabbing the oilfields the Soviet Union has not, during the four years from 1980 through 1983, shown more of the particular kind of aggressive behavior it had previously shown in Angola, Ethiopia, Cambodia, and, at the highest point so far, Afghanistan. Why? Hard-liners have a plausible explanation ready at hand: The world uproar that Afghanistan touched off, the difficulties of pacifying Afghanistan, and the long-term increase in defense undertaken by the Reagan Administration have deterred the Soviet decision-makers from further adventures of the same kind, at least for the time being. Another possible interpretation, though, is that, as suggested in Chapter 2, the reasons for the Kremlin's intervening in Afghanistan in the first place were primarily local, and predictions of a new career of conquest were mistaken from the outset. Our fear could have been greatly exaggerated.

• Similarly, the fact that the Soviet Union ''relentlessly'' built up its strategic arms between 1962 and the 1980s has been interpreted by many in the West as indicating a determination to achieve strategic superiority, with the purpose of destroying the American ICBMs or, as a minimum, intimidating Western Europe. It has seldom been maintained that the USSR had by 1982 or 1983 actually achieved such superiority. The focus was rather on the ''relentless'' buildup as if it were proof that the trend could be extrapolated beyond the level of approximate equality to the level of clear superiority. From a Soviet point of view that was a gratuitous assumption. They were, according to their statements, striving for equality and felt that they had only barely, precariously achieved it. Many Western military experts agree. The Reagan Administration has gone ahead in an arms program considerably exceeding, in its real percentage increase per year, what the Soviet Union has steadily done (about 3 percent a year) for many years.

Again there are two possible interpretations. One is that the Soviet decision-makers really were on the verge of being strategically superior and would have achieved real superiority if the Reagan Administration had not wisely prevented it by his much larger percentage increase. The other is that, given a real desire for strategic parity through arms control, and through only matching the Soviet rate of increase, the President could have safely rested content with the approximate strategic parity that already existed. If the latter interpretation is more valid, he and those who thought as he did were unduly extrapolating the rate of Soviet gaining on the United States that did exist between the late 1960s and the late 1970s. And, if that is true, his undue extrapolation had a baleful effect, by intensifying the arms race, on the chances of peace.

• In 1914, as we now know, the Germans saw a steadily deteriorating security situation. The huge Russian army, far greater than Russia needed for defense, was steadily growing; Britain had in effect joined the Franco-Russian alliance against Germany; Germany was increasingly encircled; Austria-Hungary was disintegrating. Although Germany had been in a sense predominant on the Continent, it saw not only its predominance but also its safety disappearing. It extrapolated the trend and resorted to drastic measures involving military force, first against Serbia, then against France by. way of Belgium. There surely would have been a better way to do it, but Germany's sense of urgency, based partly on its dubious extrapolation, made it hard to think of that better way.

• Judging by defense expenditures, the West is now rapidly gaining on the USSR, from a baseline that in Soviet eyes was, apparently, approximate equality. In other words, increasing strategic superiority. Will the men in the Kremlin extrapolate that new trend and become still more afraid, with the unhealthy type of fear? If so, what effect will it have on the arms race, and on peace?

When Parity Means Overkill

It is now generally recognized that the nuclear overkill capability on each side, in George Kennan's words, has reached "levels of redundancy of such grotesque dimensions as to defy rational understanding" (1982, p. 176). One of the common metaphors is that East–West arguments about relative nuclear strength are like those of two boys in a closed room with gasoline up to their ankles, squabbling because one has seven matches and the other only six. It doesn't really matter, some say, whether we kill every Russian fourteen times or only ten times.

Some military strategists answer that it does matter how many missiles would be left over after an all-out counterforce exchange, a nuclear war of attrition. Those answers do not touch the core of the question. The core is that the fear of what even one nuclear-armed enemy submarine could do to one's own cities should be great enough to deter any rational government from deliberately starting a nuclear war. As Khrushchev said, "In our time only a madman can start a war and he himself will perish in its flames" (1960, p. xxxi). Each side now has far, far more nuclear weapons than could be carried on one submarine.

There is a psychological problem here. If so many people see the present overkill situation clearly and realistically, why don't they go on to see the obvious corollary, which is that either side could afford to cut back its nuclear arsenal, unilaterally if necessary, to a single nuclear-armed submarine (or, to be very cautious and conservative, five)? Wouldn't that give quite adequate deterrent power, along with a great economic gain and, by eliminating the nuclear arms race, a great gain in the chances of peace? If we don't need more than one match, why have more? It is a kind of Emperor's New Clothes question, but—why not?

The Reagan Administration, in opposing a nuclear freeze by saying it would freeze us into a position of inferiority, did not either demonstrate that we are now strategically inferior or answer that childlike question. It can be argued that clear conventional inferiority would be (and in fact now is) dangerous. But *nuclear* inferiority? If we still have a practically invulnerable second-strike capability? How?

Polls do show that at the time of this writing a majority of the American people reject a freeze "if it would mean we would be behind the Russians.'' Evidently, although most people see the irrationality of overkill, less than a majority see, as yet, the implications of that proposition. One suspects that a kind of knee-jerk macho pride blocks the minds of a good many people at that point and prevents the additional elementary thinking that is needed, including the elementary distinction between conventional and nuclear weapons. ''Should we be *weaker* than the Russians? Of course not!'' The words ''inferiority'' and ''weaker'' are thought-stoppers. Probably they should be avoided, where possible, by all prudent peace activists. But if the question were put somewhat differently, with more discrimination, the response might be quite different. Suppose it were put in this way: ''I'm in favor of adequate deterrence—certainly enough conventional strength in Western Europe to keep the Russians from attacking. But what about nuclear weapons? I understand we have enough destructive force on one submarine to destroy all the major Soviet cities. Do you think we need much more than that? Suppose the Russians don't agree to deep cuts. Couldn't we do it on our own initiative, being sure to keep enough for a second strike?'' That is not the suggested wording for an opinion-poll question. Of course, such questions have to be balanced, with no implied point of view. It is only a suggestion for a line of thinking, in conversations and in public discussion, that might move a good many people one step forward—and it is an important step—on this key question.

Neither is it a question of what ought to be proposed in negotiations now with the Soviet Union. In view of the great numbers of people on both sides (especially on the Soviet side) who are still hung up on the supposed necessity to be equal in every sort of power in order to be safe, there is probably no chance yet for effective arms control agreements on any very different basis. Rather, the immediate practical value of raising the question in this way, not in negotiations but in conversations and public discussions here in the United States, lies in staking out a position well in advance of what is now politically possible—a position that would make it politically possible for our negotiators to show some real flexibility on the *definition* of parity. If they knew that in America there was a large and growing minority even willing to make deep nuclear cuts on our own initiative, and if some of the negotiators themselves could come to see the logic of it—perhaps only after the 1984 elections—their flexibility and reasonableness might be considerably increased.

In any case, the apparent fact that a great many Americans already fully accept the essential idiocy of overkill should be a source of great hope for those of us who favor a freeze, a no-first-use policy, and deep bilateral cuts in nuclear arsenals. It gives us much to build on in talking with other Americans.

PART III

Comparative History

CHAPTER THIRTEEN

The First World War

There are four excellent reasons to study with some care the causes of World War I:

1. The events of those years, especially between 1904 and 1914, have a remarkably close resemblance to what is happening now. Any "lessons" of history that may help us to avoid nuclear war are more likely to come from that period than from the background of World War II.

2. According to the British historian A. J. P. Taylor, the causes of World War I have been much more fully explored and are now more thoroughly understood than those of World War II (1961, pp. 13–22). Surprisingly, more is known about that far-away event than about the more recent one.

3. World War II cannot be well understood without understanding how Hitler thought and felt about World War I and how the people who allowed him to get supreme power felt about it. As Taylor says, "the first war explains the second and, in fact, caused it, in so far as one event causes another" (p. 23).

4. While the story of World War II has been lived through or read about by many millions who are still alive, including those who have read Herman Wouk's *The Winds of War* (1973) or seen the television version of it, World War I is far less familiar. Even if the second were a better source of "lessons" than the first (which it is not), it would be better to understand both than only one of the two gigantic conflicts in our century that a possible World War III might resemble.

The following "condensed history" may serve as a kind of historical first aid to those readers who either have never studied the background of that war or studied it so long ago that they want their knowledge of the elementary facts to be refreshed.

A Condensed History

Landmark Dates

1870–71: Decisive defeat of France in the Franco-Prussian war, Germany dominant on the continent of Europe. German empire united under Bismarck's leadership.

1890: The new Kaiser, Wilhelm II, replaced Bismarck at the helm of German foreign policy.

1904: Entente between Britain and France.

1914: Beginning of World War I.

1917: The United States entered World War I.

Events in More Detail

1806: First stirrings of all-German power-oriented nationalism and militarism, spreading from Prussia to the rest of a hitherto very disunited Germany, in response to Napoleon's conquests and Napoleon's threat.

1848: Revolutions in a number of European countries. Western-style liberalism strong in Germany, but defeated.

1864: Defeat of Denmark by Bismarck; the first of the three wars that led to the unification of Germany.

1866: Decisive defeat of Austria—a major power—by Bismarck's Prussia. That victory gave to most of the Germans great respect for Prussia's military prowess, great respect for Bismarck as the architect of the victory, very great pride in Germany and in the prospect of coming unification, diminished respect for the liberals whom Bismarck opposed, and a tendency to identify German patriotism with military prowess and military glory. Regarded by some as the decisive beginning of Germany's "ego trip" or "paranoid period," which lasted, with variations, at least until 1945.

*1870–71:[1] War between Prussia and the France of Napoleon III, France declared war and was regarded by many (including Karl Marx) as the aggressor. Other causes, however, included Bismarck's trickery (falsifying a telegram), Napoleon III's persistent effort to prevent the unification of Germany (which would then be stronger than France), and intense German anger at his effort to do so.

---

[1]Asterisks indicate landmark dates.

The war ended with the German unification that Napoleon feared and with his own downfall. Germany took and kept Alsace–Lorraine, which caused extreme resentment in France.

1871–90: Surprisingly, once Bismarck had attained his two great ends (German unification and a number-one position for Germany on the Continent), he became a "man of peace"—a hardboiled peace maintained by military and economic strength, nonaggressiveness, and skillful maintenance of good relations with Austria–Hungary, Russia, Italy, and Great Britain. Only France was left out, and it was far from strong enough to challenge Germany again.

1882: Italy was added to the well-established German–Austrian alliance to form the "Triple Alliance."

1890: The new Kaiser—vain, erratic, and with an intense desire for personal glory, but not the deliberate warmaker his enemies often assumed him to be—decided to take charge of his own foreign policy and let Bismarck go. It was a bad mistake, as the next twenty-eight years of German foreign policy would show.

1894: Russia and France formed the Dual Alliance. It was a strange alliance between republican France and autocratic Tsarist Russia, but intelligible as a means of common defense against what they believed to be a common enemy, Germany, and its allies Austria and Italy.

1898: The centuries-long opposition and colonial competition between Britain and France came to a surprising end with the bloodless British victory at Fashoda, leading to unchallenged British control of Egypt and the Sudan. Paradoxically, this led not to great French resentment but to an eventual agreement to share North Africa between them, Britain keeping Egypt and the Sudan and France gaining most of the rest of North Africa—and keeping Germany out.

1899–1902: The Boer War. Great Britain fought against the Boers (descended from early Dutch settlers) in South Africa. Like many other peoples fighting on their own soil against foreigners perceived as invaders, the Boers put up a magnificent fight and were defeated by the British only with embarrassing difficulty. The sympathy of much of the rest of the world, especially in Germany, was with the Boers.

1904: Britain formed an "Entente"—a loose informal friendship—with France. There might have been a British entente or even an alliance with Germany instead because of the British feeling that isolation was no longer possible and because of colonial rivalry with both France and Russia. However, the Kaiser's erratic behavior and German feeling agains the Boer War prevented it. Britain turned to France instead.

1904–05: The Russo-Japanese war, in which Russia was decisively defeated by the emerging oriental power, Japan.

1905–06: The first Morocco crisis. Perhaps emboldened by Russia's defeat and the consequent weakness of the Dual Alliance, the Kaiser dramatically visited Tangier, in Morocco, which the British and French interpreted as his bid to control Morocco. This was followed in 1906 by the Algeciras Conference, in which Germany, outnumbered by Britain and France, lost out. An angry Germany "bullied" France into dismissing its able foreign minister, Delcassé. France was further humiliated and embittered.

1907: Improved relations between Britain and Russia led to Britain's being added, loosely, to the Dual Alliance (Russia and France, who were very closely allied), and the combination of three began to be called the Triple Entente.

Meanwhile Italy more or less defected from the opposing Triple Alliance, leaving Germany with Austria-Hungary as its only reliable ally. The Germans began to feel that they were encircled and that the balance of power was tipping strongly against them. But the German Army was still the strongest in Europe.

1908: In a *fait accompli* that greatly antagonized both the Serbians and the Russians, Austria-Hungary unilaterally annexed Bosnia-Herzegovina, an area which Austria-Hungary had controlled for many years without annexing it. It was largely inhabited by Serbs and other future citizens of Yugoslavia. The German government, though dismayed by Austria's action, felt bound to support Austria and did so, successfully. Russia was in no position to fight, though the annexation threatened its role as protector of the Slavic peoples in the Balkans (Serbs, Croats, Slovenes, Bulgarians) and its hope to gain control of the straits between the Black Sea and the Mediterranean.

1911: The second Morocco crisis. The visit of a German warship to Agadir, on the coast of Morocco, was interpreted by France as a threat of war. Though Germany got some concessions of French-controlled territory in central Africa, it essentially lost out again. The British-French combination was too strong for it. French fear of Germany was heightened, and so was Germany's feeling of being humiliatingly frozen out of the colonial competition.

1912–13: In two small Balkan wars Serbia emerged the chief gainer, with new self-confidence and new hope of liberating, and joining with, its countrymen still under Austro-Hungarian rule.

By this time the danger of total dismemberment of the ramshackle Austro-Hungarian empire was clear. The German-speaking Austrians and the Hungarians were predominant in a conglomeration that included also Czechs, Slovaks, Poles, Rumanians, Serbs, Croats, and

Slovenes. The old and beloved emperor, Franz Josef, who was a unifying symbol, might die at any time, and disintegration would then accelerate. Therefore, in Austrian and Hungarian eyes, if the Serbian fanatics were allowed to continue their nationalist, "irredentist" agitation, there would be a great danger that the empire would simply break in pieces. That was "unthinkable." Their fear of it became strong.

To the Germans the prospective disappearance of Austria-Hungary as a Great Power meant not only losing their one more or less reliable ally in a Europe in which they were already encircled by a powerful and hostile coalition. It meant also losing their hope of establishing a pathway of predominant German influence throughout the Balkans and the still decaying Turkish Empire. Their dream of a Berlin-to-Bagdad railway would go glimmering.

1904–1914: Naval competition between Britain and Germany, which in 1908 became intense. Britain was and remained by far the stronger in warships, but the British believed that, as an island country, their very life depended on control of the seas, while Germany, a land power with a short coastline, did not really need a navy at all. Besides, the British had a farflung empire to defend, and Germany did not. To the Germans this seemed like arrogant nonsense; since their own overseas commerce was expanding rapidly, it needed protection as much as Britain's did, and as for Britain's empire, it had no more right to a farflung empire than Germany did, but Germany had, as yet, hardly any. The Germans intensely wanted the status of a "world power"—at least on a par with Great Britain, the United States, and Russia—but felt that, encircled as they were, they had little chance to achieve it. (This was not fear; it was pride.)

1914: The coming of the Great War.

June 28: Assassination of the Austrian Archduke Franz Ferdinand, the heir to the throne, by a young Serbian fanatic who thought he was helping to liberate his countrymen from Austro-Hungarian rule. Intense anger in both Germany and Austria-Hungary, not only against the assassin but also against the "nest of assassins in Belgrade," condoned by the Serbian government, that they believed to be really responsible.

July 5: The German Kaiser and his Chancellor, Bethmann-Hollweg, with much popular support, gave Austria a "blank check," which virtually promised German support in any strong action, including military action, Austria might take against Serbia. In both countries the feeling was very strong that Austria's existence was in danger if such nationalist agitation and assassination were allowed to continue. Many saw little risk of war if Germany stood firmly by Austria's side as it had in 1908; many others saw a serious risk of a much larger war, but a risk that had to be taken if the beneficent Austro-Hungarian empire were to survive and if neither country were to "sink to the status of a second-rate Power." Serbia *had* to be punished.

July 23: Austria-Hungary sent Serbia an extremely stiff ultimatum. Its terms startled and shocked the other governments of Europe, which had been misled by the Germans and Austrians to believe that nothing so dangerous to peace was in prospect. Germany strongly supported Austria throughout six crucial days, July 23–29.

July 25: Serbia replied, accepting most of the terms of the ultimatum but rejecting the one that most clearly infringed on its sovereignty and hedging on others. In the eyes of the Serbians, Russians, French, and British, Serbia had gone far to placate Austria, but in the Austrians' eyes the reply was evasive. They immediately broke relations with Serbia.

July 28: Austria declared war on Serbia. Was this a "point of no return"? Had things gone so far that no further diplomatic action could succeed in preventing a much greater war?

July 29: Russia began to mobilize its immense but slow-moving military machine. (The advantages of quick mobilization and of a strike-first policy were so generally recognized by military men throughout Europe that it was generally assumed that "mobilization means war.")

For the first time, the British Foreign Secretary, Lord Grey, was able to give the Germans the impression that British intervention, in case Germany attacked France, was a real, imminent probability. In this new situation of suddenly mounting danger of war, not against two major enemies (Russia and France) but against three (Russia, France, and England), the Kaiser and Bethmann-Hollweg became frightened and genuinely, though not decisively, tried to restrain Austria.

France had done nothing to restrain Russia from premature mobilization and was ready to come into the war, apparently almost automatically, on Russia's side.

July 31: German ultimatum to Russia saying that unless Russia stopped mobilization Germany would fight.

August 1: Its ultimatum unanswered, Germany declared war on Russia.

August 3: Convinced that France would support Russia and afraid to allow time for full Russian mobilization, Germany began to strike at France through Belgium, following the Schlieffen Plan, which called for a quick victory over France before turning to the east against Russia. Going through Belgium, however, violated the neutrality of Belgium, which had been guaranteed by the European powers, including Germany.

Midnight, August 4–5: Britain at war. Fearing a collapse of the European balance of power if Germany crushed France, Lord Grey and many others would probably have favored war even if Germany had not gone through Belgium, but the invasion of Belgium clinched the matter.

August–September 1914: Spectacular German success at the outset—the Germans quickly went through Belgium and invaded northern France—was followed by stiff French resistance in the Battle of the Marne and a stabilizing of the front.

Russia invaded Germany but was pushed back. From then on the war was not fought on German soil.

September 1914: Encouraged by their great initial success, the Germans—most of the people as well as the government—agreed to demand very stiff terms of peace: German control over Belgium and its great colony, the Congo; cession of some French territory to Germany, especially the valuable orefield of Longwy-Briey; German hegemony over Central and Eastern Europe, especially Poland; a long-term weakening of Russia by annexations and of France by imposing heavy indemnities.

1914–18: These war aims remained fairly constant throughout the war, in fact right up to the turning of the tide against Germany in August 1918. From the standpoint of most of the German people these aims were justified chiefly as insurance against being "attacked again" and having to fight, again, a grueling and terrible war.

The Allies too refused to compromise and held out for stiff peace terms designed to keep Germany from ever "attacking again." (Most of their terms were actually imposed on Germany by the Treaty of Versailles, 1919.)

1915: The sympathies of most of the American people had been on the side of the Allies from the beginning. Hostility to Germany was further inflamed by the German sinking of the *Lusitania* in May 1915.

January 1917: In an effort to break the stalemate and end the war, Germany announced unrestricted submarine warfare.

*April 6, 1917: The United States declared war. It was probably just in time to prevent a German victory, since Russia collapsed in the fall of 1917.

In summary:

The imperialistic competition that preceded the war was conducted mainly by Britain and France, which got together in 1904 and more or less excluded Germany, the latecomer, from that competition.

Other important background factors were the resentment of France at Germany's seizure of Alsace-Lorraine (which led to its alliance with Russia in 1894), the naval competition between Britain and Germany, the Balkan competition between Germany and Austria on one side and Russia on the other, and German fear and resentment stemming from its "encirclement" by Russia, France, and Britain. Austria-Hungary was beginning to disintegrate. In spite of its outstanding army Germany had some reason to be afraid and exaggerated the danger.

In 1914, paradoxically, the military balance was equal enough so that both sides had some reasons for overconfidence and some reasons for exaggerated fear.

In the crisis of 1914 there is now some consensus that the two most aggressive actions were the German–Austrian declaration of war against Serbia and the German attack on France through neutral Belgium, but there is also some consensus that a main reason for those actions, if not *the* main reason, was fear. Both Germany and Austria-Hungary feared Austria's disintegration if it did not take a firm stand and punish Serbia for the assassination of the Archduke; both also feared that Russian mobilization meant an imminent attack if Germany did not get the jump on its "two assailants" by attacking France—a preemptive first strike—and then repelling the expected Russian invasion.

Recognition of German fear is the chief solid result of the "revisionist" movement among historians that occurred especially in the 1920s.

Psychological Parallels with the East–West Conflict

There are a number of parallels to be drawn between World War I and the East–West conflict, including the following:

A Dangerously Equal Balance of Power

As is usually true when there is an approach to equality in overall power, each side felt inferior in some dimensions of power and superior in others. Germany felt much superior in the quality of its army in 1914; inferior in the size of its army compared with Russia's and France's, inferior to Britain in naval power, and much inferior overall *in the future* if Austria were to disintegrate. There was ambiguity also as to who would be against whom. There was some expectation in Germany that Russia was not ready for war and would not support Serbia. It did. There was also much expectation that Britain would not actually go to war to defend Belgium and France. It did.

There is a similar ambiguous equality today between the West and the USSR (Chapter 6), and in both cases it coincides with much tension, competition, and fear on both sides. The USSR is rather clearly ahead in conventional strength; there is great controversy as to which, if either, is ahead in nuclear strength. There is also much uncertainty as to the future and as to who would be against whom if war should come. The Soviets fear an offensive coalition of Western Europe, the United States, China, and Japan; Western Europe tends to fear that the United States would not fully come to its aid if the Soviet Union should attack.

In a long-term perspective many in the West feel that the Soviet Union is "coming up from behind" and may surpass the West in military strength if it has not done so already. In a long-term perspective many felt in 1914 that Germany, since 1866, had been "coming up from behind" and might succeed in its great aspiration to share a place in the sun with the British Empire by dominating all of the Continent of Europe.

Fear on Both Sides

There is little doubt that in 1914 there was much fear on both sides. There is much on both sides today (Chapters 2, 4, 5, 9). Defensively motivated aggression (*mainly* defensive) was what started the war in 1914. If war comes now or in the next decade, the same would probably be true.

The evidence of this in 1914 is strong. The Germans felt that the balance of power had already tipped against them (Holborn, 1969, p. 418). There was urgent fear of Austrian disintegration (Holborn, 1962, p. 415; Fay, 1966, II: 552). "Dread of the Slavs at their back haunted the Germans" (Tuchman, 1962, p. 75). "In Berlin, on August 1, the crowds milling in the streets and massed in thousands in front of the palace were tense and heavy with anxiety. Socialism, which most of Berlin's workers professed, did not run so deep as their instinctive fear and hatred of the Slavic hordes'' (Tuchman, 1962, p. 94). The Kaiser's personal fear of being assassinated, as the Archduke had been, along with other European monarchs including the Tsar, was intense (Fay, 1966, II: 208-9). The political scientists who have studied the documents of 1914 most intensively and quantitatively agree with historians such as Fay and Tuchman that German fear (''perceptions of hostility'' in an opponent) mounted rapidly on both sides in the last days of July (Zinnes, 1968, p. 108; Holsti, North, and Brody, 1968, pp. 136-38). The conclusions of the latter group are especially striking:

> Perceptions of its inferior capability did not deter a nation such as Germany from going to war. The Kaiser's desperate reaction to the events which were engulfing him—perhaps best characterized by his assertion, ''If we are to bleed to death, England shall at least lose India'' . . . is the reaction of a decision-maker under such severe stress that any action is preferable to the burden of the sustained tension. This reaction in the face of an adversary's greater capabilities—a reaction strikingly similar to instances in the Peloponnesian Wars, the wars between Spain and England during the sixteenth century, and the Japanese decision to strike at Pearl Harbor . . . are not unrelated to the dilemmas of our own age of missiles and nuclear warheads. These findings underscore our need for re-examining the ''common sense'' and almost irresistible ''conventional wisdom'' which argues that deterrence is merely a matter of piling up more and/ or better weapons than the opponent can amass. [Holsti, North, and Brody, 1968, pp. 137-38]

Macho Pride on Both Sides

Let us consider the German side, though there is much evidence of macho pride on both sides, especially among the political élite of Tsarist Russia.

There is little doubt that in 1914 the German leaders and most of the German people cared a great deal about national power, national prestige, and their picture of themselves as a tough, virile people.

In brief summary, the evidence includes these things: (1) the great satisfaction they gained from Bismarck's triumphs; (2) their talk about being ''heroes'' (''Händler und Helden''); (3) their looking at the map and envying the power of Britain, Russia, and the United States; (4) their talk about having to become "a world power"; (5) their taking of Alsace-Lorraine, forcing the fall of Delcassé, challenging Britain's naval power, and supporting Austria after its annexation of Bosnia-Herzegovina; (6) their eager participation in the game of imperialist competition (irrational as it probably was in economic terms), especially during the two Morocco crises; (7) their identification with Austria's fear of dismemberment, which could be interpreted as actually a fear of losing a position of domination in Central Europe; (8) their fear of isolation if Austria disappeared, which could be interpreted as actually a fear of losing, or not regaining, their own predominant power in Europe; (9) their willingness to risk a big war, in July 1914, partly in order to achieve a resounding diplomatic triumph over the Entente; (10) their willingness to risk a big war, perhaps partly also because they felt that if war came they could probably crush quickly the armies of France and then Russia and leap into the coveted role of a world power, at least equal to Great Britain; (11) the stiff German terms of peace, emphasized by Fritz Fischer (1961), including expanded power in several ways, which were rigidly held to from September 1914 to approximately September 1918.

According to Tuchman the Kaiser and his people had "a terrible need for recognition." " 'All the long years of my reign,' he told the King of Italy, 'my colleagues, the monarchs of Europe, have paid no attention to what I have to say. Soon, with my great Navy to endorse my words, they will be more respectful.' The same sentiments ran through his whole nation, which suffered, like their emperor, from a terrible need for recognition" (1962, p. 21). Speaking more generally about the nations of Europe at that time, Fay says: "It is not so much questions of economic rivalry as those of prestige, boundaries, armies and navies, the Balance of Power, and possible shiftings in the systems of alliances, which provoke reams of diplomatic corespondence and raise the temperature in Foreign Offices to the danger point" (1928, I:46). It will be noticed that Fay puts the word prestige first.

There are many parallels on both sides today (Chapter 9), including the very similar Soviet feeling of coming up from behind, and not yet getting the recognition as an equal by the other superpower that its military power justifies, and the American assumption that America's rightful place in the world is Number One and anything less than that is abnormal.

Perhaps it needs to be repeated that none of this indicates any wanting of war by either Germany in 1914 or the Soviet Union or the United States today. The two men at the center of German policy-making were the Kaiser and his Chancellor, Bethmann-Hollweg. Bethmann-Hollweg is generally regarded by historians as a somewhat weak and limited but undoubtedly peace-loving man. As for the Kaiser, the relatively harsh judgment of Barbara Tuchman is that "he had never actually wanted a general war. He wanted greater power, greater prestige, above all more authority in the world's affairs for Germany but he preferred to obtain them by frightening rather by fighting other nations. He wanted the gladiator's rewards without the battle" (1962, p. 95). In other words, macho pride.

Anger and "Aggression" on Both Sides

Was the war entirely a matter of coldly calculated power and security considerations on either side? Hardly. The political scientists who stress such calculations sometimes underestimate the large amount of historical evidence of nonrational emotion, especially anger, at a time of crisis.

There are many indications that both the leaders and the general public were aroused and angry as well as fearful during the crisis of 1914, at least in Austria-Hungary, Germany, and Russia (the three countries where the public mattered least). In no country do we find evidence for the theory, later very popular, that diabolical leaders foisted the war upon a good but gullible public. Both leaders and public surely wanted peace, but both were nationalistic, both saw the enemy as forcing a war upon them, and both were carried along on a wave of anger. Bernadotte Schmitt (1930) speaks of the "wild enthusiasm for war manifested in Vienna and Budapest" (II:1). Bunsen, the British ambassador in Vienna, reported that "postponement or prevention of war with Serbia would undoubtedly be a great disappointment in this country, which has gone wild with joy at the prospect of war (Schmitt, 1930, II:77). The German ambassador reported that the Austrian Foreign Minister, Count Berchtold, "is in very good spirits and is proud of the countless telegrams of congratulation that are coming to him from all parts of *Germany* (II:77; emphasis added).

The Kaiser, whose rage at Edward VII is well known, was perhaps the angriest of the national leaders, to judge by his many exclamations (''Liars!'' ''Slippery eels!'') on the margins of telegrams, but most of the German public and nearly all of the German press seemed to be with him in his desire to ''punish'' Serbia. J. F. Scott, in a little-noticed but psychologically important book, *Five Weeks: A Study of the Surge of Public Opinion on the Eve of the Great War* (1927), has documented in some detail the positions taken by the press in all of the major countries and finds a high degree of agreement with the policies of the governments. (Partly, of course, this was a result of government influence on the press, but, as Fay has pointed out [1928, I:47–49], the press had often been more chauvinistic than governments.) In Germany, for instance, only the press of the socialist left (*Vorwärts*) and the extreme right (the Berlin *Post* and the *Rheinisch-Westfälische Zeitung*) denounced Austria's policy (Scott, 1927, 117–23). (The extreme right, surprisingly, protested against the German Empire's being drawn into an *Austrian* war of conquest.) But, as Schmitt (1930) puts it, ''these were lonely voices. The German press as a whole expressed complete approval of the Austro-Hungarian note, argued for the localization of the conflict, and advocated unflinching support of the Dual Monarchy [Austria-Hungary] by the German Empire'' (I:510–20).

Clausewitz (1968) expressed well the importance of both emotion and reason:

> War is . . . a trinity, composed of the original violence of its elements, hatred and animosity, which may be looked upon as blind instinct; of the play of probabilities and chance, which make it a free activity of the soul [what does he mean here?]; and of the subordinate nature of a political instrument, by which it belongs purely to the reason. [p. 121]

Clausewitz adds, ''The passions which break forth in War must have a latent existence in the peoples'' (p. 121).

There is a real psychological question here as to the relative importance at such times of anger or aggression in the strict psychological sense of the word (an impulse to hurt or destroy as an end in itself) and the pleasurable excitement, at the very outset of a war, of war itself. When Bunsen speaks of the Austrians as ''wild with joy at the prospect of war,'' is this in contradiction to what has been said here about the unwantedness of war? Or is it primarily a testimony to the long-accumulating anger of the Austrians at the Serbian threat to their empire and, as they thought of it, their "very existence,"—a threat which they now suddenly believed would be warded off by their own effort and their own courage, with the mighty German Empire fighting, if necessary, by their side?

Those of us who remember, as I do, the pleasurable excitement of an American child when America entered World War I—an excitement largely unmixed with genuine anger but consisting rather of the thrill of living in a momentous time, with the spice of danger added and a sense of belonging to a great country that was now doing a courageous thing—will hardly be prepared to rule out the attraction, at that critical moment, of war itself. There is no macho melodrama on film or television that can equal the thrill of, for once, actually living through such an experience. Those who remember, immediately after Pearl Harbor, the voice of Roosevelt talking about "a day that will live in infamy" can testify to a similar feeling. It is not primarily anger or hate. It is more like what people mean when they speak of wanting to "live dangerously." And it can be very strong.

Those of us who now want not to be swept into even a small war that could later become nuclear would be wise to be aware, and wary, of that feeling and along with it the desire to hurt for the sake of hurting. They are, or may be, closely related. After months or years of anger and a feeling of impotence at not being able to express the anger there is, as many people have testified, a welcome feeling of relief and release when the anger can finally be expressed in action.

A somewhat similar anger clearly exists on both sides of the East–West conflict today (Chapter 9), especially since the Korean airliner incident and the American response to it.

A Diabolical Enemy-image on Both Sides

The importance of the enemy-image in the East–West conflict, and its psychological roots, were discussed at some length in Chapter 12. It underlies both exaggerated fear and exaggerated anger.

Americans who have lived through both world wars know how totally evil our conception of the Germans (or at least of their leaders) was in both cases. Less familiar is the fact that a similarly diabolical image of the Allies was prevalent on the German side. It was peculiarly intense with regard to the British, and quite irrationally so in view of the fact that Lord Grey, more than any other national leader, had striven to prevent the war and had been opposed in doing it chiefly by the Germans. Two quotations, one from each of the two most important German decision-makers, may suffice to indicate its nature:

When the Chancellor, Bethmann-Hollweg, received Britain's final ultimatum he burst out in anger, saying that it was like "striking a man from behind when he was fighting for his life against two assailants" (Tuchman, 1962, p. 153).

Even before that the Kaiser had written on the margin of a diplomatic note: "The net has been suddenly thrown over our head, and England sneeringly reaps the most brilliant success of her persistently prosecuted, purely *anti-German world policy*, against which we have proved ourselves helpless, while she twists the noose of our political and economic destruction out of our fidelity to Austria, as we squirm *isolated* in the net" (North, 1967, p. 115; italics in the original). Though the Kaiser could hardly be called psychotic, this passage has the ring of pure paranoia. It contains both the typical paranoid delusions of persecution ("The net has been suddenly thrown over our head") and the typical paranoid delusions of grandeur—moral grandeur in this case ("our fidelity to Austria").

A Perception in One Country that It Is "Encircled" by Enemies

Georgy Arbatov's picture (1982) of a Soviet Union encircled by both capitalist and Communist enemies—the United States (which in his mind plays the central role the Kaiser attributed to Britain), Western Europe, China, and now Japan—has been presented here in his words (Chapter 3). The German picture of *Einkreisung* (encirclement), which grew greatly as Britain joined first France and then Russia in what the Germans saw as a conspiracy against Germany, was strikingly similar.

Psychologically there was an element of "breaking out of the encirclement" when Germany and Austria cracked down on Serbia. There may well have been a similar feeling in the Soviet Union when it cracked down on Afghanistan.

Almost No Empathy on Either Side with Opponent's Fear

All of the Allies, including the United States, had almost no empathy, during the war, with the very important element of fear in both Germans and Austrians at the start of the war. They did not begin to appreciate it until the historians' revisionist movement in the 1920s.

On the part of scholars there is something of that type of empathy now, at least on the Western side, but it is hardly shared at all by the general public or by our political leaders. In fact, a broader statement is justified both then and now: *The Germans and their opponents lived in radically different "psychological worlds"; so do the West and the USSR.*

The main psychological processes building up those different worlds, in the background of World War I, were probably selective attention and selective inattention (Chapter 12).

The Germans paid much attention to: France's declaration of war in 1870; the success of Delcassé and others in encircling Germany with enemies; the great and expanding British, French, and Russian empires; the great and expanding British Navy and Russian Army; the squeezing out of Germany in the two Morocco crises; the defection of Italy from the Triple Alliance; the impending disintegration of Austria-Hungary; the Russian mobilization in 1914; and the unexpected British intervention. The Allies much less often and only partially paid attention to those things, or to the German perception of them.

The Allies paid much attention to: the German invasion of France in 1870; Germany's taking and keeping Alsace-Lorraine; the German challenge to the British Navy; the German demand that Delcassé be dismissed; the Kaiser's blustering; the Austrian annexation of Bosnia-Herzegovina; the ultimatum to Serbia; and of course, above all, the wickedness of the German invasion of France and the German violation of Belgian neutrality. The Germans much less often and only partially paid attention to those things or to the Allies' perception of them.

It is interesting to notice how "true" both pictures were. The beliefs focused on by each side were, with few exceptions, based on facts—exaggerated in many cases but also, in most cases, more true than false. Almost all of them are in the condensed history at the beginning of this chapter. Some of the obvious distortion comes from slanted interpretation of genuine facts, especially the tendency to attribute the worst possible motives to an action by opponents, but most of the distortion comes from selection—not seeing at all the facts emphasized most on the other side. Sins of omission (if perceptual distortion can be called a "sin") outweigh sins of commission.

Much the same (Chapters 2 through 4) can be said about the pictures of the East–West conflict held by the protagonists on each side. Rightly or wrongly, the pictures in the heads of people on both sides tend to resemble mirror-images of each other.

Now, leaving psychology aside, what can be said about the relevance of World War I to our present problem of avoiding nuclear war, compared with the relevance of World War II?

Anticipating to some extent what will be discussed in the next two chapters, two hypotheses can be formulated immediately:

• World War I and the East–West conflict have been relatively two-sided conflicts, with much provocation and some aggression (not necessarily in equal amounts) on each side, over a long period of time. World War II, after Hitler came to power in 1933, was extremely *one-sided*; there was aggression on one side and not aggression but appeasement on the other.

• World War II, unlike both World War I and the post-Stalin part of the East–West conflict, was to a large extent a *one-man* war, the one man, in the European part of the conflict, being Hitler. Hitler had a docile nation behind him, but the impetus toward war and the actual decisions were his. That was not true in Germany in 1914. The German elite and the German people then were solidly, even enthusiastically, behind the Kaiser. They were frightened and macho and angry, as he was. It was a many-man war on each side.

Could the War Have Been Prevented? When and How?

Almost certainly World War I could have been prevented at any time up to perhaps July 29, 1914, if human beings had had the realism to do it. The motivation was there; the realistic perception of means to ends was not.

As for the motivation, Sidney Fay's (1930) summarizing sentences, already quoted, deserve repetition:

> None of the Powers wanted a European War. Their governing rulers and ministers, with very few exceptions, all foresaw that it must be a frightful struggle, in which the political results were not absolutely certain, but in which the loss of life, suffering and economic consequences were bound to be terrible. [II:547]

With that motivation it should have been possible for either side to stop the "malignant process of hostile interaction" at some point before July 29.

That was indeed a "point of no return"—a point that apparently is reached at some time before the actual outbreak of almost any war. It may have come earlier than July 29, but it is hard to imagine the vicious circle stopping after that (including the takeover of decision-making by the military), since by then the chance that Germany would decisively restrain Austria from going ahead with its war was just about to disappear. If Germany had done it on July 29, and done it decisively instead of half-heartedly—as its new realization that Britain probably would enter the war against it made it plain that it should—the entire colossal destruction of the war and perhaps World War II might have been prevented.

It follows that restraining an ally from committing aggression may be one of the most important ways to prevent a great war. (The United States in relation to Israel could be a case in point. See Chapter 5 under "The Loser Goes Nuclear.")

Our analysis also suggests many other things that could have been done or left undone to prevent World War I. Suppose for instance that Germany, perhaps as early as 1880, had permitted a plebiscite in Alsace-Lorraine to determine whether it would be French, German, or independent. Suppose that in 1914 Germany had urged Austria to adopt more stringent police measures within its empire and to present a fairly stiff ultimatum to Serbia but not to confront Serbia with unacceptable demands or reject a conciliatory reply. Suppose that Russia had not mobilized prematurely. Suppose that Moltke had known the truth, and told it to the Kaiser, about the German Army's ability to move only against Russia and not invade Belgium or France (Tuchman,

1962, pp. 99–103). Suppose, more generally, that most—not necessarily all—of the actions and nonactions on each side that caused the most fear and anger on the other side had been done differently and more wisely. Surely the war would not have occured—at least not in 1914.

Or, on a more fundamental psychological level, suppose the motives and perceptions that led to these actions had been more conducive to peace: less fear based on an unrealistically diabolical enemy-image, more restraint based on realistic empathy with the fear and anger that one's own contemplated actions would create in others, less insistence on keeping an existing level of national power and prestige even if it meant risking war, less assuming that colonies are economically important, more continual awareness of the chanciness of war itself and the catastrophic consequences of a long war. Surely, if these differences in motives and perceptions had been great enough, the actions resulting from them would have been much wiser and the war would not have occurred.

Most fundamentally, suppose either side had seriously adopted the basic strategy of combining deterrence with tension-reduction, but with greater emphasis on tension-reduction, as advocated here in Chapters 7 and 8. Wouldn't the malignant process probably have been stopped and reversed? As it was, only deterrence was attempted. In the absence of any serious policy of tension-reduction at the same time, it plainly did not work.

And now specifically, what could each country have done, or left undone, to reduce tension? What could each have done with dignity, without appeasement, and without letting down its guard, to reduce the war-promoting kind of fear in its opponents?

On the German and Austrian side five possibilities stand out. If its pride had allowed it, Austria-Hungary could have permitted much more rapidly increasing autonomy for its subject nationalities and could have refrained from annexing Bosnia-Herzegovina. If its pride had allowed it, Germany could have sponsored a plebiscite in Alsace-Lorraine to determine whether it should be returned to France. Germany could have refrained from demanding the removal of Delcassé. It could have refrained from challenging the two central elements in Britain's pride, its empire and its navy.

If their pride had permitted it, the Entente powers also could have behaved differently in several ways in order to reduce tension, probably without loss of real dignity, without appeasement, and without letting down their guard.

Russia could have been content with a slowly growing army, perhaps only one and a half times as big as Germany's. It could have actively discouraged the use of violence by its Slavic cousins within the Austro-Hungarian empire while at the same time urging Austria to grant them rapidly increasing autonomy. It could have refrained from an expansionist policy in the Far East against Japan and strictly limited its demands on the Straits. It could have postponed by a few days the mobilization in 1914—a blunder stressed by Albertini (1952–57).

While insisting on an open door for its commerce in Morocco, France could have refrained from its deceptive policy of taking over the country and from ganging up with Britain against Germany in the two Morocco crises. France and Britain together could have either begun to relinquish their own colonial holdings, as both did after World War II, or helped Germany to get colonies in central Africa comparable with their own in the rest of Africa. A more fantastic possibility: the French could have decided to be tolerant of the Kaiser's childish, neurotic vanity and, with formal diplomatic courtesy, could have invited him to visit Paris. According to Tuchman, "Paris, the center of all that was beautiful, all that was desirable, all that Berlin was not, remained closed to him. . . . No invitation ever came. . . . It is perhaps the saddest story of the fate of kings that the Kaiser lived to be eighty-two and died without seeing Paris" (1962, pp. 20–21).

Suppose Britain had not ganged up with France to squeeze out Germany in the Morocco crises, or fought the expansionist Boer War, or obstructed Germany's quite legitimate Berlin-to-Bagdad railway project for several years, or insisted on a navy far larger than Germany's. Suppose it had not teamed up with both France and Russia, thereby abandoning its traditional balance-of-power policy and making the Germans feel surrounded by a ring of strong and hostile powers.

Does it seem likely that in that case Germany would have felt it was imperative not to lose Austria in 1914? And if Germany had not supported Austria and had not actually egged it on (until July 29), would the war have occurred?

Or, looking at both sides, suppose both had been farsighted enough to work together cooperatively in establishing the right sort of international organization—partly to reduce tensions and partly to supplement unilateral alliance-deterrence with genuine collective deterrence?

The case for a combined strategy, including both deterrence and tension-reduction but with more emphasis on tension-reduction, seems at this point very strong.

It will not seem so strong when we look at World War II.

CHAPTER FOURTEEN

The Second World War

The background of World War II is very familiar to many readers. A discussion of World War II is included, however, for a number of reasons:

• World War II has some things to tell us about how to prevent nuclear war that did not emerge from our study of World War I. Those points of present relevance will be developed in Chapter 16, but as background for that integration many readers may want to refresh their present knowledge of most of the major events in the background of World War II, each in its proper sequence and historical context. (The really well-informed reader will probably want to skip or skim the "Condensed History," but not the last part of the chapter dealing with how the war might have been prevented.)

• Needless to say, World War II was a major war, and, as a basis for generalizing about the psychological causes of major wars (to be done in Chapter 16), three case-studies are better than two.

• Just as World War II cannot be fully understood without some understanding of World War I, so the East–West conflict cannot be fully understood without some understanding of World War II. For instance, the image of the enemy on each side of the East–West conflict is determined to a considerable extent by a previous image of Nazi Germany.

A Condensed History

Landmark Dates

1919: The Versailles Treaty.

1933: Hitler came to power.

1938: Munich. Hitler dismembered Czechoslovakia.

1939: World War II began. Hitler attacked Poland.

1941: Hitler attacked Russia. The United States entered the war.

Events in More Detail

August 1918: Germany came closer than ever before to winning World War I. Russia had collapsed as an effective enemy with the success of the Bolshevik Revolution in November 1917; German troops in large numbers had been released by the Russian collapse from service on the Eastern front to service on the Western front; and although America had entered the war in April 1917 its troops were only just beginning to fight in considerable numbers in France. The Germans in July finally broke the ghastly stalemate of trench warfare; in a major offensive they got closer to Paris than at any time since the first two months of the war.

November 1918: The Armistice; the end of the war. The tide had turned in August, and the Germans were retreating from then until November, almost but not quite to the borders of Germany. To the West it looked like a decisive victory.

To most of the German people it did not. Ludendorff and the other German generals knew the truth, but they told only some of it to the people. As most of the people saw it, neither side had won. Germany had held its own against a world of aggressive enemies, had knocked one of them out, and, with none of its own soil occupied, was still "unconquered in battle." It had, however, wisely decided to accept the relatively fair and honorable terms, the "peace without victory," that President Wilson had offered in his famous Fourteen Points.

1919:[1] *The Versailles Treaty* (always called a *Diktat* rather than a treaty by the Germans, because they had no part in framing it and were forced to sign it at gunpoint). To the Allies it seemed fair enough, since in their eyes Germany had started the war and should pay for its crime, at least partly. An aggressive nation that had proved so formidable in war should also have its power limited, where possible.

To nearly all of the Germans it seemed anything but fair; it seemed like a naked, obvious betrayal of the trust they had placed in President Wilson and the terms on which they had laid down their arms. They felt their enemies were taking full advantage of their helplessness (and of the "stab in the back" consisting of revolutionary disorder inside Germany) to inflict on them a truly Carthaginian peace. The aggressors who started the war but had never won it fairly in battle were now winning it by trickery and the breaking of promises.

[1]Asterisks indicate landmark dates.

The terms of the Treaty included:

- Requiring Germany to accept sole responsibility for the war (which the Germans saw as an obvious lie)
- Drastically limiting German arms (with vague expressions of an Allied intent to disarm—which never occurred)
- Demanding large sums over many years as reparations for the physical damage Germany had done, and including war pensions in the bill (which definitely went beyond what was in the Fourteen Points or in a later clarifying American statement)
- Giving Germany's colonies as ''mandates'' to Britain and France
- Diminishing or limiting Germany's territory in these ways:

  1. Most emotionally objectionable to the Germans (but fully justifiable on the basis of national independence for the new state of Poland), permitting Poland access to the Baltic Sea by way of a ''Polish Corridor.'' The people in the Corridor were overwhelmingly Polish, but the Germans felt that they were being ''dismembered'' by the separation of the province of East Prussia from the main body of Germany.
  2. Similarly, giving Poland the industrially most important part of Upper Silesia (inhabited mainly by Poles)
  3. Giving Alsace-Lorraine to France (without a vote of its mainly German-speaking inhabitants—though quite probably they would have voted for the return to France)
  4. Internationalizing the German city of Danzig in order to give Poland immediate and full access to a good port on the Baltic
  5. Letting France control the small but productive Saar area for fifteen years.

- Demilitarizing the Rhineland (the part of Germany west of the Rhine)
- Forbidding an *Anschluss* (unification) of German-speaking Austria with the German nation (though before the coming of Hitler most of the Austrians probably would have welcomed such a unification)
- Including in the new state of Czechoslovakia some three million Sudeten Germans (without consulting them). They had not been part of Germany before the war but did live just next to Germany and presumably would have voted to be part of it if given the chance.

The one requirement in the Treaty that kept German passions most inflamed during the 1920s was the requirement of reparations. The great majority of Germans assumed that their undeniable economic troubles, especially between 1920 and 1925, were mainly due to reparations. But that was far from true. "Germany borrowed far more from American investors (and failed to pay back) than she paid in reparations" (Taylor, 1961, p. 48).

1918–20: The end of the monarchy and the setting up of the Weimar Republic in Germany were accompanied and followed by much disorder, which was capitalized on by Communists who hoped to duplicate in Germany and Central Europe Lenin's 1917 Bolshevik revolution in Russia. Although the Communists were a small minority in Germany, other Germans, including most of the strong, moderate Social Democratic party, had much fear that the Communists might succeed.

The moderate socialist government put down rebellions of both the extreme right and the extreme left, but there were short-lived Communist governments in Bavaria and in Hungary. Many Germans, including Hitler, noticed that most of the Communist leaders were Jews— Eisner, Toller, Leviné, Bela Kun, Rosa Luxemburg—and inferred a Jewish Bolshevik conspiracy to control or destroy Germany.

1920: The United States refused to join the League of Nations, which President Wilson had taken the lead in creating.

1919–23: Inflation in Germany grew between these years and became uncontrollable and catastrophic in 1923. In November 1923 the mark was quoted at a trillionth of the value it had had in 1914.

1923: France occupied the Ruhr, the industrial heart of Germany, in an effort to collect reparations. (From the French standpoint reparations were only fair, even apart from Germany's war guilt, since the physical destruction the Germans had caused in France was very great, and France had caused no such destruction in Germany.) The French military occupation of the Ruhr, however, was only partly successful as a way of forcing the Germans to pay, and it brought to a climax German anger and hatred of the French.

Hitler's "beer-hall *putsch*"—his only attempt to seize power by force—occurred at the height of this feeling. It failed, and he was imprisoned. He wrote much of *Mein Kampf* while in prison, in 1924 (Hitler, 1925, 1927).

1919–33: Although the United States was relatively unharmed by the war (in some ways it had gained from it economically), and although Europe suffered enormously from the war and its aftermath, American help was not on anything like the scale of its help after World War II. There was no equivalent of the Marshall Plan, which helped Europe get on its feet in the late 1940s; America's refusal to cancel the Allies' war debts made it look actually miserly in British and French eyes. They were willing to forgo reparations from Germany if the

United States would cancel their debts to it, but the United States would not. The United States also put up tariff barriers in 1930 that made it still harder for Europe to pay its "debts."

1925–29: Good years for the German economy. A relatively prosperous Germany gave Hitler comparatively little attention, and his following declined.

1929–33: The Depression years. Hitler capitalized on them to foment internal disorder. Much street fighting between his Brown Shirts and the Communists, who also became more powerful. This gave plausibility to his claim in 1933 that he was saving Germany not only from the Depression, from the weakness of the Weimar Republic which could not cope with the Depression, and from the humiliation and helplessness of Germany in international affairs, but also from the threat of aggressive "Jewish" Communism. (This is the point where he appealed to fear, whether he himself felt it or not.)

1930: Hitler abandoned his highly chauvinistic propaganda line, which sometimes actually glorified war, and adopted the "peace line" ("I want peace; only my enemies want war."), which he continued until his death in 1945. (He also began to soft-pedal his anti-Semitism.) The results were spectacular: a massive increase in his appeal to the German people and in his opportunity to gain power by technically legal, apparently democratic methods. (Hitler, 1941; White, 1949.)

1931: Japan (not yet allied with Hitler) took Manchuria, the anarchic but industrially very valuable northeast corner of China. The rest of the world did nothing to stop Japan's aggression, and Japan gained in industrial strength and self-confidence.

*1933: Hitler came to power, not primarily on the basis of foreign policy chauvinism but primarily because so many Germans saw him as their savior from economic depression and parliamentary impotence. He was appointed Chancellor by the democratically elected President, General Hindenburg.

Like the inauguration of President Roosevelt, also in 1933, his totalitarian regime marked the beginning of economic revival for his country; by 1936 unemployment in Germany was virtually eliminated.

1935: German rearmament, hitherto secret, was openly proclaimed.

In a free election, 90 percent of the inhabitants of the Saar voted to return to Germany—one of many indications of Hitler's great and genuine popularity during this period (1933–39) in Germany.

Mussolini, the Italian dictator who was now more or less aligned with Hitler, attacked and conquered Ethiopia. The League of Nations tried half-heartedly to stop him, and failed.

1936: Germany reoccupied the Rhineland. It was a daring move that the French Army could have easily stopped; but France, mindful of the strong British feeling that the Rhineland was German and belonged to Germany, did not resort to force to stop it. Hitler's confidence in his ability to take international risks got its first big boost.

1936–38: The Spanish civil war. Franco, the winner, rebelled against the relatively democratic Spanish Republic. He was helped substantially by Hitler and Mussolini, while the Republic (the Loyalists) was not helped by Britain or France. Sentiment there was strongly pro-Loyalist, as it was in the United States, but, like the Americans, the British and French were preoccupied by fear of entanglement in another great war.

Russia did help the Loyalists with arms; as a result the Communists in Spain, who were by no means dominant at the outset, became dominant on the Loyalist side before the war ended. This gave some color to Hitler's claim that in fighting against Communism in Spain he was defending all of Europe against the overhanging Communist menace. Again, an appeal to fear.

1937: Japan, heartened by its easy conquest of Manchuria in 1931, began all-out war to conquer all of China.

March 1938: Without war, Hitler marched into German-speaking Austria, acclaimed by what seemed to be a majority of the Austrian people. His bluster had intimidated Schuschnigg, the not-very-democratic leader of Austria. Hitler's confidence in his ability to expand German power got its second big boost.

*September 1938: Munich. "Appeasement" of Hitler by Chamberlain, the umbrella-carrying British Prime Minister, and Daladier, the French Premier.

Hitler had fomented unrest among the Sudeten Germans on the borders of Czechoslovakia and, with actual encouragement by Chamberlain, had begun to demand incorporation of the Sudetenland into his German Reich. He got it.

A great many people in Czechoslovakia and elsewhere felt that Chamberlain and Daladier had missed Europe's best opportunity either to prevent World War II or to reduce it greatly in scope. Czechoslovakia's border fortifications (mainly in the Sudetenland) were excellent; its well-trained army was about three-quarters as large as Germany's; and if it had had the help of Britain and France alone (not to mention the United States and the Soviet Union—which at that time seemed much more ready to fight than Britain or France), the prospect of deterring or quickly defeating Hitler was probably excellent. At least that was the judgment of Hitler's own generals, some of whom were actually ready to rebel and try to overthrow Hitler if he went to war and if, as they expected, Britain and France were ready to fight. They assumed Germany would lose such a war.

But psychologically Britain and France were emphatically not ready to fight, and the United States was even less ready. There was an extremely widespread assumption that "the next war will be the end of civilization" and that nothing should be left undone that might stave it off. An overwhelming majority of the British acclaimed Chamberlain when he returned, and Roosevelt sent him a two-word telegram: "Good man." The result: Hitler won, and his self-confidence got a third big boost.

One reason was that, as usual, Hitler declared that the Sudetenland was his "last territorial demand in Europe," and a great many people were willing to take a chance on his really meaning it. Also, he was not asking (yet) for land inhabited by non-Germans. It seemed right for the Sudeten Germans to be in Germany if they wanted to.

November 9–10, 1938: Crystal Night. The first large-scale violence against Jews in Germany. It consisted mainly of Nazi-instigated window-breaking. (The actual gas chamber Holocaust did not begin until January 1942.)

March 1939: Prague. Seizing non-German territory for the first time, Hitler's troops marched into Prague, the Czech capital. It was the end of Czech independence.

Prague was followed by a remarkable revulsion in British and French feeling, especially British. It was now generally felt that appeasement at Munich had been a mistake, since Hitler was now clearly on the warpath and none of his promises could be trusted. Hoping to deter further Nazi conquests before it was too late to do so, Britain extended a unilateral promise of support to Poland in case Germany attacked it, although the Poles were far less capable of effective self-defense than Czechoslovakia had been, and without Soviet help there was no effective way for Britain or France to come to Poland's relief.

August 23, 1939: The Nazi–Soviet Pact, a bombshell. Although the terrible Soviet purges of 1936–38 were a recent memory, liberals and democratic socialists everywhere had at least looked to Stalin's Russia as the one strong, solid, antiappeasement country opposed to Hitler. Now he had made a pact with the devil. Hitler was jubilant; he felt he had split wide open the potential anti-Nazi coalition and could now concentrate on conquering a Poland that would be isolated because the West would not dare to fight alone without Soviet support.

In retrospect the Pact has seemed more understandable. Stalin had reasons for his anger at the West. He had been excluded from the Munich conference (Mussolini was included), and Western efforts to get his active cooperation in defense of Poland had been less than half-hearted. The Poles and Rumanians flatly refused to consider allowing Soviet troops on their soil even if Hitler attacked them, and there was no other way in which Soviet troops could be effective in their defense.

Since opposition was futile, Stalin obviously felt he could gain more by direct dealing with Hitler. In the short run he gained a good deal. Quite legitimately from a national standpoint, he gained the largely Russian-populated but Polish-controlled area east of the Curzon Line. Less legitimately, he gained a free hand to absorb the three Baltic states (Lithuania, Latvia, Estonia) and to make war on Finland, which he proceeded to do (not very successfully) in the winter of 1939–40. As he put it in a speech in March 1939, which should have served as a warning to the West of his later deal with Hitler, he was not willing to "pull the chestnuts out of the fire" for the capitalist West.

September 1, 1939: The beginning of World War II. Hitler attacked Poland.

Shrewdly keeping the approval of his own people by making his first demands moderate, Hitler at first demanded only a return of Danzig to Germany and either a return of the Polish Corridor itself or a German corridor through it to East Prussia. (He sometimes said one and then the other.) To most of the rest of the world also the return of Danzig and a corridor through the Corridor seemed like a fully acceptable compromise, though a return of the Corridor itself—overwhelmingly populated by Poles—did not.

The Poles, however, were not thinking in terms of compromise. They were unwilling even to talk seriously about the return of Danzig or a corridor through the Corridor.

That was understandable. The Polish Foreign Minister, Jozef Beck, had seen how Hitler had bullied and browbeaten the Austrian Schuschnigg and the Czechs Beneš and Hacha when they agreed to "negotiate," and how he upped his demands when his first moderate demands were granted. Beck did not want to undergo the same treatment. (He was right in his suspicions. As we now know, as early as April 3 Hitler had told his generals that he was determined to attack Poland.)

However, Beck's rigidity probably played into Hitler's hands, at least from the standpoint of his keeping the German people's approval of his actions. In what he told his own people his only demands were Danzig and a corridor through the Corridor. The fighting spirit and tenacity of the German people in the war that followed were probably due in part to his success, at the outset, in picturing Germany's enemies as denying even the most elementary national rights of Germans.

As in the cases of Austria and Czechoslovakia, Hitler's propaganda machine supported him with vicious accusations (probably largely trumped-up) of atrocities against Germans in the country he was about to attack or take over.

The British and French favored direct negotiation between Hitler and the Poles. Probably they hoped that in such negotiation the Poles would concede at least Danzig, depriving Hitler of that potent talking point with his own people. However, they put no pressure on the Poles to engage in genuine negotiation or to concede even Danzig. Their own mood—at least that of the British—was now one of grim determination to stop Hitler's career of conquest, even at great cost and risk. They felt that his word could not be trusted and that no "negotiation" with him could be genuine. The alternative to war, as they saw it, was a collapse of the European balance of power and ultimate domination of the democratic West by the Nazi-fascist-Soviet-Japanese coalition of aggressive, antidemocratic states.

Hitler's generals were more than dubious about the war, and the German people, though accepting it, were very far from the kind of unity and determination (and in a sense exhilaration) that had characterized them in 1914. The horrors of World War I were still in their minds, with the new great fear of airborne destruction in addition. Except among the Nazi faithful, there was no war enthusiasm. On September 1, while Hitler was announcing war in the Berlin opera house, "in startling contrast to the wild cheers of *Sieg Heil* in the opera house, the streets outside were almost deathly quiet" (Toland, 1976, p. 781).

The Armed Conflict

The military course of the war will be summarized here very briefly, since it has little to do with the war's causes (except for the participation of the Soviet Union and the United States).

September 1939: Hitler's *Blitzkrieg* (lightning war) quickly conquered all of Poland up to the old Curzon Line, and Stalin took the remainder.

Britain and France declared war but were prevented by geography from giving Poland any effective help. A "phony war" of several months resulted.

For the fourth time Hitler's overweening self-confidence got a big boost.

May 1940: Attack on the West. With Denmark and Norway already taken, Hitler's attack on Holland, Belgium, and France began on May 10 and had achieved spectacular success by May 19. His *Blitzkrieg* seemed invincible, in striking contrast with the stalemate of trench warfare in 1914–18, and his self-confidence got its fifth big boost.

Why he did it is something of a puzzle, since earlier and later evidence indicated that his empire-building ambitions were mainly in the

East, not the West. The chief reason probably was to secure his rear for a later attack on Russia.

With the fall of France the balance of power on the Continent of Europe was already shattered. The prospect that Britain as well as France might go down the drain began to have a great effect on American attitudes, which had previously been overwhelmingly in favor of staying out of the war. Both because of identification with Britain and because of fear of a collapse of the *world* balance of power, with ultimate danger to the United States itself, American sentiment moved first to "all aid short of war" and then to a state of ambivalence about entering the war itself.

June 1941: Attack on Russia. Hitler's most obvious blunder, perhaps his greatest.

Why did he do it? There was little or no provocation, since Stalin had scrupulously fulfilled the deliveries of raw materials agreed upon in the Nazi–Soviet Pact.

One reason certainly was his long-term, obsessive ambition to gain land for Germany in the East, but that in turn calls for explanation. Another was his now enormous self-confidence, in which one ingredient was his long-term scorn for the fighting abilities of the Slavs—but that too calls for explanation. At this point he surely had too little fear, not too much.

October 1941: Hitler's troops were stopped before reaching Moscow, his first major military setback. It meant having to dig in for the Russian winter, and Hitler had been so sure of quick victory that his army had not even been provided with winter clothes.

In the war that followed, Russia suffered colossal losses but sustained them with amazing tenacity. At the beginning many Russians accepted Hitler as preferable to Stalin, but the brutality and arrogance of his rule turned them back to a tenacious defense of their homeland.

December 1941: Pearl Harbor. Japan attacked and destroyed a large part of the American fleet in the Pacific. Hitler had already promised to help Japan if it fought the United States, and he now followed through with a declaration of war. It was an extremely foolish move, since it immediately enabled Roosevelt to put America's main fighting effort into Europe instead of the Far East.

1942–43: Nazi defeat at Stalingrad. At its point of greatest extension Hitler's army suffered an epoch-making defeat. One reason for it was his no-retreat policy, which led to the surrounding and surrender of a large part of the army. From here on, everything was downhill for the Nazis in Russia and Eastern Europe.

June 1944: The landing of American and British troops in Normandy. From the Russian point of view the setting up of a "second front'' in the West was far too long delayed; as they saw it they had borne the main brunt of the war and had actually virtually won it before the British and Americans appeared on the scene. But the successful landing and the fighting that followed did clinch the Allied victory.

May 1945: Total defeat of Germany on both fronts.

Could the War Have Been Prevented? When and How?

Hitler could have prevented World War II, if he had been a wiser, more realistic, and quite different man, at any time before September 1, 1939, when he declared war on Poland. He was not being pushed forward by German public opinion or by any frightening international crisis comparable to that of 1914 or the Cuban missile crisis. It was his war and his decision at that point. Simply by committing no more clear acts of aggression comparable to those he had committed against Spain and against the Czech part of Czechoslovakia, he could have done it.

If Hitler had stopped before 1939, Danzig would not yet have been united with Germany, and some small German-speaking parts of the Polish Corridor would still have been in Polish hands. He could argue that his duty as a German patriot was still to unite all German lands, even at the risk of war. But if that were his real goal he could, with his immensely superior German armed forces, have moved into the Corridor, taken Danzig back, and then stood his ground. He did not need to do what he actually did: continue the war until all of Poland was subjugated. That was the obvious, simple, direct cause of the cataclysm.

For us there is far more interest in whether Hitler's eventual opponents, including the USSR and above all the United States, could have prevented the cataclysm by acting more wisely earlier. With hindsight, what can we learn that might be relevant to the future?

A simple list of things that might have been done differently, some under the heading of tension-reduction and some under the heading of more effective deterrence, will at least provide food for thought. Certain forms of deterrence will be listed first, because in the background of World War II, quite unlike the background of World War I, the failures of adequate deterrence seem much more important than the failures of adequate tension-reduction—at least after the one-sided Axis aggressions began in 1935.

There are necessarily many speculative elements in any attempt to reconstruct history "as it might have been" if people had acted differently. The exercise is wholesome, though, since something can be gained by noticing the results that certain actions seem to have had. *Something* can be learned from experience, and when it could help in preventing nuclear war it is worth doing.

Deterrence

Suppose that instead of making peace in November 1918 the Allies had insisted on continuing the war until a large slice of German territory had been occupied and the German public itself could see that they had been decisively defeated. "Unconditional surrender" is not what is suggested here, but only a decisive unmistakable defeat that Ludendorff and the other German generals could not have concealed from the public and that would not have lent itself to the "stab in the back" myth that Hitler capitalized on. The results of the way the Allies handled German defeat in 1945 have been far better than the results of the way they handled it in 1918–19. The combination of decisive defeat with fairly magnanimous treatment after defeat worked far better than the combination of seemingly indecisive defeat and then harsh handling after World War I, which looked like a betrayal of Germany's trust. Perhaps one reason was that the Hegelian myth of a Germany "destined" to dominate an epoch (Wouk, 1973, p. 712) was so thoroughly knocked out of German minds, chiefly by the Soviet victories in 1942–45.

Suppose that Britain, France, the other members of the League of Nations, *and the United States* had joined in a boycott of Italy when it attacked Ethiopia, for no good reason, in 1935. That was the first of the Axis aggressions in Europe that were rewarded by appeasement and would probably have been the easiest to defeat by nonmilitary means if the League had hung together (with the United States in it by then).

Suppose the French had used force to prevent the German reoccupation of the Rhineland, also in 1935. It would have been easy to prevent, since, as we know now, Hitler's troops had orders to withdraw if any force was used against them. The French could then have magnanimously turned around and *invited* the

German to reoccupy it, in somewhat the way that China, in the Sino-Indian border dispute, proved strength and then withdrew. There is a principle here that nations find hard to learn: If there are real wrongs to be righted it is better not to right them at the point of a gun (that is, appeasement) but to do it before that or after—preferably before. The best might have been to invite German reoccupation immediately after the Allied forces withdrew in 1930. The next best might have been to repel the German troops by force in 1935 and then right the wrong.

Suppose Britain, France, *and the United States* had given military aid to the republican government of Spain, on at least the scale of Hitler's and Mussolini's help to Franco's rebellion. According to A. J. P. Taylor (1961, pp. 119–20; cf. Taylor, 1967, p. 226), ''one of the few well-documented facts of this time is that both Hitler and Mussolini were determined not to risk war over Spain. If challenged they would have withdrawn.''

Suppose that, when Japan in 1937 went far beyond its taking of Manchuria and started open war with China, the United States had at least been ready to stop sending arms to Japan. The British were ready to cooperate, but the United States, sunk in extreme isolationism, did nothing (Taylor, 1961, pp. 125–26). Japan would at least have been put on notice that in the future America might do something more serious to obstruct its conquest of all of China.

Above all, suppose that the United States had been willing at the time of Munich to play its part, along with Britain, France, and the Soviet Union (which at that time was strong for collective security) in insisting on an orderly democratic process in dealing with the Sudeten question.

It is true that Hitler's basic demand for the Sudetenland was not unreasonable, and it would have been psychologically impossible at that time for Chamberlain, Daladier, or Roosevelt to rally their respective countries to go to war to prevent such a reasonable and essentially democratic policy from being carried out. The negotiation process had not yet been tried. The same considerations had applied with greater force against going to war to keep him out of German-speaking Austria, where the evidence is strong that a majority wanted to join Germany (Taylor, 1961, p. 145). Neither Austria nor the Sudetenland was the place to resist the flowing tide of German nationalism.

What would have been entirely legitimate, however, would have been to insist on democratic procedures, such as a plebiscite in the Sudetenland under international auspices, partly to determine with precision the boundaries of the area that really wanted to be part of Germany, and also a reasonable transition period, perhaps two years, to give Czechoslovakia some chance to rebuild its fortifications, with help from the great powers, on unambiguously Czech rather than German land.

That was the crux of the problem, and a substantial crux it was, because the fine, strong Czech fortifications, located in the mountainous border zone of Czechoslovakia, were an important part of the defensive strength Czechoslovakia possessed. That strength was much greater than Chamberlain or even Hitler realized. Hitler was overconfident and Chamberlain underconfident. Together with even just the French Army, which then was still stronger than Hitler's, not to mention the British, the Americans, or the Russians, the surprisingly strong Czech army (thirty divisions, as against Hitler's forty) could in all probability have won. The German generals knew it, and some were even ready to revolt rather than be forced to fight a war they thought they could not win (Shirer, 1960, pp. 372–83, 404–14).

In the light of what happened during the following year, it now seems clear that a strong stand on behalf of orderly and democratic procedures should have been taken and that the United States would have been wise to play an important role in the process. That might well have stiffened the spines of both Britain and France. Hitler's bluff would have been called; he would have been forced to choose between a war he was still far from ready to fight and a not-too-humiliating let-up in his demands. Either choice would have been better for the world, including Germany, than what did happen, since his already burgeoning megalomania would have had a considerable setback. As it was, the German people were, as Shirer said, "rapturous" about his great bloodless victory; his self-confidence got a major boost, and the psychological stage was set for both the march into Prague and World War II (Taylor, 1967, p. 283).

This tough but reasonable course of action would have been both morally legitimate and politically wise, from the standpoint of both *Realpolitik* and war-prevention—which is not to say that it would have been politically possible. It clearly was not. It is unfair to pin the blame personally on either Chamberlain or Daladier, as is commonly done, rather than on the obsession of the British and French people with avoiding even a small war (to prevent a much larger one) and the self-righteous and aloof attitude of the American people during that period. Even Roosevelt, who showed in his "quarantine" speech in 1937 that he knew something about what was going on, retreated immediately when he discovered the political hot water it was getting him into; and the acclaim the British people gave Chamberlain when he returned, claiming "peace in our time," was enough evidence that he did what at that time was the only politically possible thing.

In the game of historical hindsight it is important to keep in mind the constraints placed on political leaders in democratic countries and to distinguish between the "guilt" (or misperception) of the leaders and the "guilt" (or misperception) of the public. In 1938 both leaders and public were still hoping, as the present-day American public surely would have, that a reasonable solution could be arrived at through negotiation rather than through war. They had not yet fully understood that Hitler's promise to stay within the limits of what was German could not be trusted. They learned better in March 1939, when his army marched into Prague.

Finally, suppose that all three, including the United States, had made a serious effort to enlist the support of the USSR against the menace of Nazi Germany. They never really tried. The Soviet Union was excluded from the Munich negotiation, and from then until the war started the treatment of the Soviet Union by England, France, and the United States was humiliatingly casual. They had some excuse, in that Stalin was insisting on the right to move his troops into both Poland and Rumania in case of a German invasion, and the Allies legitimately suspected that the result would be the kind of Soviet domination that occurred in 1944–45. But, in the light of what happened, that excuse was not good enough. Hitler had too little of the healthy kind of fear, and the direct result was war.

Tension-reduction

Those who have a simplistic picture of World War II as caused simply by Hitler's villainy and Chamberlain's weak appeasement have a large blind spot: Their historical perspective, when thinking about the causes of the war, begins in 1933, when Hitler came to power. They forget what they surely know about the *Diktat* of Versailles.

It is true that the Germans greatly exaggerated the iniquity of that *Diktat*. They failed to empathize with France's conviction that Germany, much stronger than France, was the sole aggressor in 1914 and that France's safety depended on limiting German strength in the future. They greatly exaggerated the extent to which German economic troubles in the 1920s were due to reparations rather than to the war itself (Taylor, 1961, pp. 46–50). They deeply resented loss of their colonies and loss of the Polish Corridor, although the colonies were not profitable and most of the Polish Corridor was rightfully Polish. It is true too that it would be unrealistic to blame the French and the British for carrying over into 1919 the passions of the enormous bloodletting from which they had just emerged. The *Diktat* was probably as fair and as good as was psychologically possible at that time.

Nevertheless, the psychological mistakes of 1919, which went far to create the emotional climate in Germany that made Hitler and World War II possible, call for a careful reexamination, with all the benefit of hindsight. The remedial actions that were psychologically impossible for the Allies in 1919 could possibly have been accomplished during the 1920s, some of them as early as 1922, *if* the United States had interested itself in joining with the British—over the certain opposition of the still-traumatized French—in order to achieve them.

A number of tactics could have been at least attempted:

- Retracting the war-guilt clause in the *Diktat*, which had saddled Germany with the sole guilt for the war
- Making real progress in Allied disarmament, which had been vaguely promised as a counterpart to the drastic disarmament of Germany but did not occur
- Eliminating the demand for German reparations, with the United States picking up the tab. That would have been only fair to the French, who had, like the Germans, suffered far, far more in the common tragedy than America had. It would have been in the spirit of the Marshall Plan, which the United States *was* psychologically capable of doing after World War II and which was highly successful in putting Europe economically back on its feet. It would also have made the occupation of the Ruhr unnecessary.

- Giving independence or international control to Germany's former colonies rather than keeping them as British and French "mandates"
- Letting Danzig fully return to Germany and permitting a corridor through the Corridor
- Letting Germany fully reoccupy the Rhineland and the Saar valley, much sooner than was originally agreed
- Permitting eventual plebiscites under international auspices (perhaps after ten years, and depending on German good behavior) in Austria and the Sudetenland, to determine whether they wanted to be part of the new democratic Germany

It will be noticed that French fears of another German invasion are fully accepted in all of these suggestions. The Allies would have been keeping up their guard and their military superiority to Germany. The narrow restrictions on German rearmament imposed by the *Diktat* are not challenged in this list, though perhaps after ten or fifteen years they could have been relaxed and a well-policed equality between Germany's arms and those of France could have been established.

Such revisions, made during the democratic Weimar Republic period of German history, would have had the great additional advantage of taking the ground from under Hitler's accusations that democratic leaders were futile in obtaining justice for Germany, and that only the Fuehrer principle would give Germany the strength and the backbone to demand justice. The psychological principle of positive reinforcement is relevant here. If the German people had felt rewarded by the results of allowing democracy to be established in their country, rather than punished by those results, they might have been far more resistant to Hitler's antidemocratic eloquence.

Finally, with a view to preventing World War III, it is noteworthy that France's opposition to the tension-reducing actions that have been considered here was caused primarily by the nearly total inability of the French to empathize with Germany. They had no idea of how innocent the Germans felt (mistakenly, to be sure) in 1914, or how betrayed they felt after 1919, or how great was the reservoir of partly justified anger on which Hitler capitalized in his climb to power and in his actions after getting power. Therefore, they had no understanding of how to combine tension-reduction with firm deterrence.

CHAPTER FIFTEEN

The East–West Conflict

The length of this chapter needs no explanation. Even though many of the events covered are much more familiar than those in the background of World Wars I and II, and even though many of them have been referred to in previous chapters, the subject matter is so immediately relevant to the causes of a possible World War III that a quick condensed history, reviewing the events in their historical sequence and context, may be useful to all except exceptionally well-informed readers.

A Condensed History[1]

Landmark Dates

1917: Lenin's Bolshevik Revolution.

1924: Lenin dies; Stalin more or less in charge.

1941–45: Nazi invasion; Soviet victory.

1945: Cold War begins in earnest.

1950: Korean war; climax of Cold War.

1953: Stalin dies.

1956: Hungary.

1965–73: United States in Vietnam war.

1968: Czechoslovakia.

1972: Nixon in Moscow; détente.

1979: Afghanistan.

[1]*Soviet sources consulted:* Khrushchev (1960, 1970); Ponomaryov, Gromyko, and Khvostov (1973); Zamoshkin and Batalov (1980); Nikhonov, quoted by Marder (1981); Trofimenko (1981); Arbatov (1982).
    Chief Western sources: Pares (1947); Shulman (1963); Halle (1967); Acheson (1969); Fontaine (1969); Ulam (1971); Kennan (1972, 1982); Tucker (1973); Kaiser (1976, 1981); Yergin (1977); Snyder and Diesing (1977); Lebow (1981); Smoke (1982); Cox (1982).

Events in More Detail

1848: The *Communist Manifesto* by Karl Marx and Friedrich Engels: "Let the ruling classes tremble at a Communist revolution. The proletarians have nothing to lose but their chains. They have a world to win. Working men of all countries, unite!"

1903: The Bolshevik (Communist) faction under Lenin separated from the Menshevik faction within what had been the united Social Democratic Party. That marked the decisive separation of those who after 1917 became known as Communists from those who continued to be known as Social Democrats or democratic socialists.

*1917:[2] The "February Revolution" in Russia, mainly by parties favoring a Western parliamentary type of democracy.

The "October Revolution" by the small Bolshevik Party led by Lenin and Trotsky. Effective withdrawal from World War I.

1918: Lenin, knowing that his own followers were a small minority in the country, used force to dissolve the Constituent Assembly that was to have set up a democratic constitution for Russia. The end of hope for a more Western type of democracy.

Exhausted by the great war and longing for peace, Russia signed the humiliating Treaty of Brest-Litovsk imposed by Germany.

1918–21: Civil war. Some Western (including American) intervention on the anti-Communist side, but final Communist victory in Russia. Communist efforts to touch off a world revolution, especially in Germany and Central Europe, all failed. "Red scare" in the United States.

*1924: Lenin, a towering figure in twentieth-century history, revered by good Communists throughout the world, died. Stalin, already entrenched within the Party, a calculating, vengeful, extravagantly ruthless bureaucrat, had the inside track for the position of all-powerful dictator, even when compared with the brilliant and popular intellectual Trotsky, who had played a far more important part in the Revolution. He played his cards cautiously, however, not clinching his victory over Trotsky until 1927 and not really establishing the cult of Stalin-worship, later called the "cult of personality," until the 1930s.

Stalin's doctrine of "socialism in one country" meant, in practice, a considerable soft-pedaling of efforts to revolutionize the world.

1929–34: A relatively militant period in foreign policy coincided with militance at home. Stalin proceeded to his program of forced collectivization of the Soviet peasant farms, with extravagant ruthlessness against the not-so-poor peasants, the "kulaks." One result was famine

---

[2]Asterisks indicate landmark dates.

(covered up by the authorities); another was low agricultural productivity from then on and smoldering discontent among the peasants. A series of many Five-Year Plans began, concentrated on building up Soviet industry, especially the industries basic to war. They stood the Soviet Union in good stead when it was attacked by Hitler in 1941.

1933: American nonrecognition of the USSR (it was now the USSR, not "Russia") ended. In the depth of the world Depression the new American President, Roosevelt, hoped to gain economic advantages from increased trade with the USSR. (It never materialized on any large scale.)

1936–39: The "Popular Front" period. One of several periods of relatively good relations with the West. Frightened by Hitler's militant anti-Communism and avowed desire to take Russia's borderlands, including the Ukraine, Stalin made common cause with democratic socialists in the West, achieved some respectability by joining the League of Nations, and did his best to forge a collective security Front to deter or defeat Nazi aggression. Alone among the great powers the USSR gave substantial help to the Loyalists in the Spanish civil war (though in the process it ruthlessly seized control of the Loyalist movement). The governments of Britain and France were lukewarm, to say the least.

1936–38: Stalin's Great Purge in the USSR, decimating the ranks of Old Bolshevik comrades and even the generals in the Red Army. From then on, the Gulag Archipelago was in full swing, with torture, forced confessions, and perhaps 20 million deaths. The labor-camp system was much reduced but not eliminated after Stalin's death in 1953.

August 1939: The Nazi–Soviet Pact. In an astonishing reversal, Stalin came to terms with his arch-enemy, Hitler. Apparently fed up with the lukewarmness of the West and its unwillingness to do its share against Hitler, and wanting at least to postpone Hitler's attack on the USSR, Stalin agreed to divide up the countries that separated them. At least that is what happened after Hitler declared war on Poland on September 1. Hitler took all of the Polish-populated part of Poland; Stalin took the Baltic states and the eastern, mainly Russian-populated, part of Poland.

The pact precipitated World War II. Having, as he believed, eliminated the danger of a two-front war, Hitler went ahead with his career of conquest.

1939–40: War with Finland. The dogged resistance of the Finns thrilled the Western world, which by now was almost unanimously anti-Stalin, but Stalin persisted and gained some territory that the Russians felt was important for the defense of Leningrad. Probably because of its dogged resistance Finland retained its essential independence even after 1945, when most of the East European nations became Soviet satellites.

June 1941: With almost no Soviet provocation Hitler attacked the USSR. In the light of the outcome it appears an act of near-madness. He had the rest of the European Continent at his feet but was frustrated by the nonsuccess of his air war against Britain. Perhaps he felt he must "secure his rear" against an attack by Stalin while he, Hitler, was trying to finish off Great Britain. Almost certainly he felt that this was a propitious time to fulfill his lifelong dream of realizing Germany's "destiny" to gain land in the East.

The Red Army stopped him in October before he got to Moscow, though he had boasted that the war was already virtually won. Again the world was thrilled by the dogged resistance of an underdog, this time the USSR. By now it seemed clear that Hitler and only Hitler (and his ally Japan) threatened to dominate the entire Eastern Hemisphere.

December 1941: Pearl Harbor and Hitler's declaration of war on the United States. We Americans were now "in it all the way," the courageous Soviet soldiers were now "our gallant allies," and for three and a half years there was a warmer feeling toward the USSR than at any time before or since. All of the anti-Nazi world was thrilled again when, in the winter of 1942–43, in the battle of Stalingrad, the Red Army turned the tide of the war and proceeded to a steady rollback of Hitler's arrogant forces. (His arrogance helped to do him in. Millions of anti-Stalin Russians and Ukrainians at first wondered whether Hitler might be their deliverer. His brutal treatment of them taught them otherwise.)

Although the United States gave much help through Lend-Lease (which later Soviet propaganda has tended to ignore or deny), there is little doubt that the Soviet Union continued to bear the brunt of the war and to deserve most of the credit for winning it, even after the landing of British and American troops in Normandy in June 1944. Soviet citizens are still immensely and justly proud of their war record and sometimes puzzled that many Americans seem to have almost forgotten it.

The war also caused colossal devastation and loss of life in the USSR, which people in the West sometimes forget when they compare Soviet living standards with those of the West and attribute the difference mainly to a superiority of the Western economic system. The Soviet economy has had at least two strikes against it: its far lower starting point (let us say in 1921, at the end of the civil war) and the devastation of World War II.

June 1944: Like Hitler when he began to take non-German land in March 1939, the USSR began to take non-Soviet land in June 1944, when it crossed the old Curzon Line into Poland proper. It set up the puppet Lublin government as the nucleus of what later became the Soviet-controlled government of Poland and proceeded to spread over essentially the same East European territory that it has since continued to occupy or control.

In the same month the British and Americans landed on the Normandy beaches, establishing the Second Front for which the Soviet people had been longing since 1942, with much impatience when it was so long delayed.

1945: The great turning point year in several ways:

The Yalta conference in February, at which the United States and Britain, Roosevelt and Churchill, agreed to temporary Soviet responsibility for most of Eastern Europe on the understanding that "democratic" governments would be set up.

The death of Roosevelt, who by then was something of a hero in the USSR, and the inauguration of Truman, who in Soviet eyes was the villain mainly responsible for starting the Cold War.

The establishment of the U.N.

The final victory over Nazi Germany and the establishment, at Potsdam, of British, French, American, and Soviet zones of occupation in Berlin and also in Germany as a whole.

Hiroshima, Nagasaki, and the capitulation of Japan, for which the USSR claimed some credit since in the last weeks of the war it had declared war on Japan and had overrun Manchuria. Thereafter the United States, through General MacArthur, assumed full control of Japan. Considering also the primary Soviet role in the victory in Europe, there has been some understandable Soviet resentment of America's monopolizing control of Japan.

The beginning of intense anti-Soviet feeling in the West, at least among the well-informed people who knew that in Poland and elsewhere the governments set up represented Soviet-style, not Western-style, "democracy." The fact that tightly closed borders cut the West off from full knowledge of what was happening added much to Western suspicions.

To many Soviet people the process seemed more or less legitimate, since the Soviet Union was felt to need a bulwark of "friendly" countries against the danger of another attack from the capitalist West. To well-informed Westerners, however, it seemed a gross betrayal of the promises of "democracy" that Stalin had given at Yalta, and totally unnecessary, since there was still a feeling of great warmth toward our wartime allies. "How could Stalin honestly suspect *us* of wanting to attack the USSR?" Many inferred that his motive must be aggressive, not defensive.

That was the real beginning of the Cold War.

1946: The anti-Soviet Cold War spirit developed rapidly in the West, spreading from the well-informed to the general public. Churchill's "Iron Curtain speech" at Fulton, Missouri, was a landmark in that spreading. So was the Soviet Union's refusal to fulfill its promise to withdraw its troops from northwestern Iran. Much effort through the U.N. was required to get the troops out.

1947: The Truman Doctrine. Against the background of the Soviet takeover of Eastern Europe, Soviet behavior in Iran, Soviet threats to Turkey, and suspicions (though apparently not valid) of Soviet activity behind the threatening situation in Greece, President Truman proposed aid to Greece and Turkey, saying it should be a principle of U.S. policy "to support free peoples who are resisting attempted subjugation by armed minorities or by outside pressures."

It was followed by the Marshall Plan, a really farsighted program designed to help Europe get back on its feet economically after the devastation of World War II. It had the added purpose of keeping the Communists, strong in France and Italy, from taking advantage of economic dislocation to gain control of any country. The plan was offered also to Eastern Europe, and Czechoslovakia wanted to accept, but the Soviet Union, suspecting "imperialist" designs, refused to let Czechoslovakia take part.

1948: The Czech coup. Czechoslovakia, the last of the East European countries to succumb to the "salami" (piecemeal) process of Soviet takeover, was finally taken over.

Tito's Yugoslavia, however, successfully asserted its independence.

1948–49: The Berlin blockade. From the standpoint of the Soviet and East German governments, their blockade of the Western sectors of Berlin was a defensive response to a currency reform in West Germany and to the challenge of a Western outpost, deep in socialist territory, which was a center for dangerous antisocialist espionage and propaganda. It was responded to, without violence, by the American airlift, which preserved the economic viability of West Berlin. The blockade was finally ended, and its ending marked a major propaganda victory for the West.

1949: NATO. In response to what was felt to be a great and increasing Soviet threat, several West European countries and the United States came together in the North Atlantic Treaty Organization.

Mao's Communists, after a long civil war and with much popular support, finally gained control of all of Mainland China. Chiang Kai-shek retreated to the island of Taiwan (Formosa).

A good deal sooner than expected, the Soviet Union exploded a nuclear device.

*1950: The Korean war. It actually ended in 1953, but all of its more dramatic events occurred in 1950. Coming at the end of six years (1944–50) of closely packed acts of self-assertion on both sides, but much more on the Communist side, it can be fairly regarded as the cli-

max of the Cold War. For the first time since 1945 an actual war was fought by Communist troops invading territory hitherto regarded as definitely not within the Communist power sphere. It was not to happen again until 1979, in Afghanistan, and then, in some ways, with much more ambiguity.

All of our evidence indicates that in June 1950 there was an attack by Soviet-oriented North Korea across the 38th Parallel into Western-oriented South Korea, though Communist historians still maintain it was the other way around. Whether the attack was provoked by actions of Syngman Rhee, the South Korean strongman, is still controversial. In any case it is agreed that after the first day of fighting North Korean troops advanced deeper and deeper into the South. The United States, with U.N. support, entered the war on South Korea's side. In September Gen. MacArthur's risky but brilliant landing at Inchon turned the tide of battle completely. In October he crossed the 38th Parallel going north and advanced to the Yalu River, the border of China.

It was a rash, ill-informed action. The Chinese Communists, fearful of an ''imperialist'' attack on Manchuria, the most industrialized part of China, intervened and pushed the humiliated Americans and South Koreans all the way back to the 38th Parallel.

The war ended in an essential stalemate, but that result was probably salutary for both sides. Each had crossed the line that was increasingly recognized as separating the Communist from the non-Communist world, and each had burned its fingers. From then until at least 1979 neither attempted it again. Deterrence had worked, on both sides.

*1953: Stalin died—a truly major event. His baleful presence no longer hung over the Soviet Union and no longer poisoned the international atmosphere. In many ways, domestic as well as foreign, his successors (Malenkov, Khrushchev, Brezhnev) have pursued much less aggressive and less ''paranoid'' policies. The twenty-nine years between 1950 and 1979, as we have just seen, though punctuated by several crises, saw no clear crossing of the emerging line. The Soviet policy was apparently to hold tight to the land it already had, using force if necessary, and regardless of the wishes of the people on that land, but not to use force to reach out for more.

1955: ''The spirit of Geneva.'' The first of several summit meetings at which smiles prevailed.

*1956: The Hungarian uprising. The first and so far the only major instance of an actual uprising against Soviet power within the Soviet Union's more or less recognized power sphere.

Encouraged by Yugoslavia's success in 1948 and Poland's partial success earlier in 1956 in asserting independence without war, and encouraged also by the relatively lenient and somewhat vacillating policies of the post-Stalin Soviet leadership, the anti-Russian majority of the Hungarian people evidently backed the active uprising centered in Budapest. It was crushed by Soviet tanks.

The "Suez crisis" occurred about the same time. A coalition of Britain, France, and Israel, responding to much Arab provocation, attacked Egypt. Israel quickly seized the Sinai and seemed likely to get the Suez Canal, which for France and Britain was the chief bone of contention with Nasser, Egypt's strongman. For once the United States and the Soviet Union found themselves on the same side. President Eisenhower stood by the principle that aggression was aggression even if committed by one's friends; the U.N. mobilized itself behind the same principle, and Khrushchev darkly hinted that Soviet rockets would fall on London and Paris if foreign troops were not withdrawn from Egypt. They were withdrawn.

1957: Sputnik, and the first successful testing of a Soviet intercontinental ballistic missile (ICBM). Americans began to wonder whether their superiority in nuclear weapons, hitherto relied on to balance the Soviet superiority in troops and conventional arms, would long continue to be meaningful in view of the emerging Soviet ability to retaliate with devastating thermonuclear destruction.

1958: The unprecedented nature of the nuclear threat led to an unprecedented output of creative thinking about how that threat should be met, especially in the United States (Wohlstetter, 1959; Kissinger, 1961, Brodie, 1959; Kahn, 1965; Schelling, 1963). One of the most influential writings was Wohlstetter's 1958 article, "The Delicate Balance of Terror," in *Foreign Affairs*. It pointed to the vulnerability of America's land-based missiles and the consequent temptation of an enemy to destroy those missile sites before they could be used against it. It was the argument, already made by Brodie and others, for a relatively invulnerable second-strike capability as an essential aspect of the stability of mutual nuclear deterrence. Three years later the incoming team of Kennedy and McNamara moved strongly in the direction of relatively invulnerable submarine-launched missiles.

1958-62: The second Berlin crisis—a long one that came and went intermittently. The Soviet leaders still felt they had a valid case for making Berlin a "free city" rather than an enclave of the West deep in East German territory and protected by the Potsdam agreement from being absorbed by the Communist-controlled East German government. The West disagreed and stood its ground. President Kennedy in 1961 reinforced the American troop contingent in West Berlin, and in the end, after the Cuban missile crisis, the Soviet government quietly abandoned its claims.

In the meantime, in 1961, a steady and increasing flow of East Germans leaving for the West by way of Berlin was forcibly stopped by the Communists' erection of the Berlin Wall.

1959: In spite of the Berlin crisis, which was temporarily in abeyance, 1959 was a year of exceptionally good Soviet–American relations. Cultural exchanges had already been established; the American National Exhibition in Moscow drew millions of Soviet visitors; Khrushchev was welcomed in the United States.

1960: The U-2 fiasco. A high-flying U.S. aerial-photography plane, the U-2, was brought down deep in Soviet territory. The Soviet government insisted that the United States apologize for violating Soviet air space. President Eisenhower refused, and the result was cancellation of a promising summit meeting and of President Eisenhower's expected visit to the USSR in return for Khrushchev's visit to the United States. Eisenhower, very popular until then in the USSR, might have done much to improve U.S.–USSR relations.

1961: The Bay of Pigs fiasco. Anti-Castro Cubans, trained and equipped by the CIA, landed at the Bay of Pigs in Cuba, apparently hoping that large elements of the Cuban people would rally to their banner and overthrow Castro. (It was a foolish hope; Lloyd Free's poll had shown that Castro then had strong popular support. See Cantril, 1967, pp. 1–5.) Castro disposed of the invaders almost immediately, and the United States looked inept and foolish as well as aggressive.

1962: The Cuban missile crisis. Perhaps testing President Kennedy's toughness and expecting him to be irresolute, but also hoping for a quick major gain in its overall power position, the Soviet government worked hard and secretly to establish intermediate-range missiles in Cuba, comparable to those the United States had in Turkey and elsewhere around the USSR perimeter.

Kennedy and his advisers, after an exceptionally thoughtful period of high-pressure group discussion, decided to react strongly, with a blockade and an implicit threat of possible nuclear war, but leaving Khrushchev a face-saving "out." It worked; the missiles were withdrawn.

After Kennedy proved his mettle in this risky way (some think too risky), there was a marked reduction of tension on both sides of the Cold War. A test-ban agreement in 1963 was one indication of it.

1962–?: After the missile crisis the Soviet Union began a steady, strenuous buildup of its strategic nuclear strength, which it could ill afford, and which still continues. One explanation is that the humiliation of being bested by Kennedy gave the Soviet leaders the feeling, "Never again!"

1965–73: Direct U.S. participation in the Vietnam war. A long story which by now is so familiar that it will not be even summarized here, except to say that it probably set back, by perhaps seven years (1965–72), the progress toward better Soviet–American relations that seemed to be in prospect in 1963–64. (For the psychological aspects of the war, including the evidence that probably at the outset a considerable majority of the emotionally involved South Vietnamese were more against the Saigon government than against the Viet Cong, see White, 1970, esp. pp. 37–103.)

1967: The Six-Day War and Resolution 242, accepted by the USSR.

1968: Czechoslovakia. There was no forcible uprising as there had been in Hungary in 1956; there was only a strong movement, even within the Czechoslovak Communist Party itself, toward free speech and a pluralist political system somewhat on Western lines. To the Soviet leaders this was an abandonment of "the leading role of the Party" and, apparently, unthinkable. With its Warsaw Pact allies it cracked down, quickly and totally.

1970: Brandt's *Ostpolitik*. Finally, after many years of uncertainty about an ultimate reunification of the two Germans and about the permanence of the Oder-Neisse line between East Germany and Poland, the West German Chancellor Willy Brandt negotiated a settlement in which both the division of Germany and the Oder-Neisse line were fully accepted. In return the Soviet and East German governments apparently accepted fully the *status quo* in Berlin, ending many years of tension and some danger of war on that score. Détente was an accomplished fact as far as Germany was concerned. The German people welcomed it, and during the next decade trade and travel between the two Germanys considerably increased.

1971: President Nixon's visit to Peking, ending twenty-two years of hostility and noncommunication between the United States and Communist China. (Since 1960 there had been a great and open breach between China and the USSR. Belatedly the United States was taking advantage of that breach and following the rule, "Divide and be safe.")

1972: President Nixon's visit to Moscow, keeping a balance between ties to China and ties to the USSR.

The first Strategic Arms Limitation Talks (SALT I) agreement, which limited antiballistic missiles (ABM) and, in an interim accord, limited offensive nuclear weapons.

1972–75: Those were probably the best years of "détente," but the two sides understood it differently, and the difference later caused trouble. To many Americans, encouraged by Nixon's talk about a "structure of peace,'' it apparently meant that the USSR had agreed not to disturb the *status quo* in the Third World and not to continue its strenuous strategic arms buildup. To the Soviet leaders it apparently meant that the United States had accepted the USSR on a basis of equality in every respect, including an equal right to maneuver for power and influence in the Third World, and including the use of proxy troops such as the Cubans. As it turned out, both were mistaken.

1973: The SAC alert. At the end of the 1973 Arab–Israeli war, Brezhnev felt that Israel had violated the cease-fire that he and Kissinger had worked out and Golda Meir had agreed to. He proposed that the United States and the USSR pressure Israel to pull its troops back to where they had been, and said that if the United States did not agree, the USSR would consider doing it alone. Alarmed by the prospect of Soviet troops in the Middle East, Nixon and Kissinger put the Strategic Air Command (SAC) on alert status, which implied a possible use of nuclear weapons. Brezhnev backed down immediately.

1975–79: The fading of détente. During those years each side did several things that the other side regarded as violating the spirit of détente.

The USSR used proxy troops in Angola, Ethiopia, Yemen, Cambodia; it refused to permit Jewish emigration on the scale the United States wanted; it continued to repress dissidence at home, which many saw as a violation of the Helsinki agreement; it continued its strenuous buildup of strategic arms to such a degree that some Americans thought it was aiming for a first-strike capability; it apparently encouraged a coup in Afghanistan in 1978, establishing a pro-Soviet government there that provoked a formidable rebellion, which had made great headway by the time of the Soviet invasion in December 1979.

The United States refused to grant the USSR trade status equal to that of other countries; it criticized Soviet violations of human rights; it developed super-accurate cruise missiles; it established closer relations with China; it excluded the USSR from the peacemaking process in the Middle East; Congress looked unlikely to accept SALT II in the form that, after long and strenuous negotiation, Brezhnev and the Carter Administration had finally agreed to. All of this before Afghanistan.

*December 1979: Soviet invasion of Afghanistan. (For full discussion see Chapter 2. The great question is: Was it primarily a step toward further conquests, or primarily defensive in motivation?)

1981: Martial law in Poland.

1982: Brezhnev died; replaced by Andropov.

1983: Soviet shooting down of a Korean airliner.

Which Side Has Been More Aggressive?

When we look back over the historical record since 1917, the first question we naturally ask ourselves is: Which side has committed aggression more often and on a larger scale? Which is more to blame for the predicament the world is now in?

To a typical Good Guys–Bad Guys thinker on either side that is an outrageous question, since it seems to imply that the guilt has been relative, not absolute, and that there has been at least some of it on each side. To a True Believer, such relativism is intolerable.

It does imply exactly that—or at least that a fresh look at the evidence is needed as a basis for judging whether either side's Good Guys–Bad Guys picture of the conflict is fully valid, and how each side may have contributed to, or mitigated, our predicament. What is now needed is a concentration on the historical evidence, with as much objectivity as we can muster, and with an awareness of how each side's preconceptions tend to distort its perception of the evidence (Chapter 10).

There is also a more basic question, rooted in philosophy and psychology as well as in semantics: What do we mean by "blame" or "guilt"? If a frightened animal lashes out in what it feels is self-defense, is it "to blame"? If two nations are caught in the malignant process of hostile interaction, each full of partly realistic and partly unrealistic fear and anger, is it realistic or useful to talk about blame at all? Shouldn't we all accept the wisdom of Spinoza when he said, "I have labored carefully not to mock, execrate or lament but to understand human actions"?

The answer offered here is similar, but not very similar, to Spinoza's. Of course, it includes the central theme of this book, that the main motive on each side of the East–West conflict (and of most of the other wars of the twentieth century) is exaggerated fear. Of course too, it includes a stress on misperception, rather than cold-blooded aggression, as the chief reason why fear is so often channeled into the actions that cause war rather than into the actions that promote peace. The concept of defensively motivated aggression is central, as is the concept of an arms race that is defensively motivated on both sides. But none of these ideas rules out the proposition that in any particular confrontation one side is usually more aggressive than the other (sometimes much more) or the proposition that one's own actions should depend, in a high degree, on the amount of aggressiveness being shown at a given time by the opponent.

For instance, between 1871 and 1913, the British, French, and Russian imperialists could be fairly described as much more aggressive than the Germans or the Austrians, while in the crisis of 1914 itself it was the Germans and Austrians who were decidedly more aggressive. Between 1919 and 1932 the French were clearly more aggressive than the Germans, while from 1935 to 1941 the Axis powers were unequivocally more aggressive than their victims.

The fact of aggression needs to be distinguished from the motives that lie back of it. Even if we have good reason to believe that the chief motive behind the German and Austrian aggression in 1914 was long-term self-defense, that does not wash out the fact that at that time they *were* aggressive and that, at that point, creating in them a healthy fear of an immediate war and of being defeated in such a war would probably have helped to restrain their aggression. It would have been appropriate to create one kind of fear in them in order to counteract another kind.

As for the basic philosophical and psychological question of whether blame is ever appropriate, the answer offered here is the same as Reinhold Niebuhr's: evil is real. Neither fear nor anger, whether realistic or not, is inherently evil, and neither is misperception, but some other things are. Ruthless disregard of the needs of others and active pleasure in hurting others—both of which are closely related to macho pride—are in a sense inherently evil. To recognize such evil for what it is, in oneself as well as in others, and to hate it, is a necessary result of elementary realism and healthy human sympathy. In this sense, guilt is real and blaming is appropriate. Some mocking, some execration, and some lamenting are appropriate.

Both Hitler and Stalin were inherently, inwardly evil in this sense. It was not just that the wars and injustices that resulted partly from their actions did enormous harm to others; the men themselves were rotten at the core and could be legitimately hated. To understand all is *not* to forgive all.

In any case, aggressive actions—defined somehow—are so clearly the chief direct cause of war that it is worthwhile in studying any conflict to consider whether one side has been *more* aggressive than the other.

In the case of the East–West conflict, my own answer is that since the United States became heavily involved in 1945, and by one particular definition of aggression—not the only possible definition by any means, but a relatively clear "operational" definition—neither side has clearly committed aggression more often than the other. The United States has done it at least six times and the Soviet Union has done it at least six times.

The question of definition is of critical importance. Dictionary definitions such as "initiating the use of force" or "an unprovoked attack" are too simple to be of much use. The definition used here is unfortunately more complex, but necessarily so. It is that aggression consists of *the use or threat of force, directly or indirectly through client governments, without adequate provocation, on land that is not clearly one's own, and without clear evidence that most of the emotionally involved people in the affected area want that kind of intervention.*

The pages to follow will be devoted to a relatively thorough discussion of my definition of aggression and will test out its appropriateness on a number of recent concrete examples, including some American and Soviet ones. Readers may be interested in this somewhat unusual form of semantic analysis from a legal, psychological, or ethical standpoint. The U.N. has struggled much with the problem of defining aggression from the standpoint of international law, since some key sections in the U.N. Charter depend crucially on what the word is understood to mean. Its psychological interest lies in the conspicuous tendency of all nations to evade defining the term or to define it in ways that make possible their most outrageous rationalizations, when they need to justify their own most aggressive actions (such as ours in Vietnam or that of the Soviet Union in Afghanistan) or their own projection of guilt onto the enemy. And its ethical interest lies in the question of what actions *should* be most strenuously condemned, when one's own country considers doing them or when another has done them. "Aggression," Michael Walzer says, "is the name we give to the crime of war. [Victims of aggression] are always justified in fighting" (1977, p. 51). The word is always so loaded with emotional condemnation that it should not be defined so broadly as to include misdeeds by an opponent that are not heinous enough to necessitate fighting as a response; but it should be defined broadly enough and clearly enough to include, without self-justifying evasion or rationalization, the actions by our own country that people in other countries, onlookers as well as victims, perceive as evil enough to justify applying that word to us.

These parts of the definition call for discussion:

1. "The use or threat of force." Hitler's bloodless conquests, in which no shot was fired, come to mind. When he marched his troops into Prague, what was left of Czechoslovakia had been abandoned by its friends, and the Czechs knew that armed resistance would be suicidal. Hitler boasted that he had not "made war." The non-German world knew better.

2. ". . . directly or indirectly through client governments." When the Communist-controlled governments of several Warsaw Pact countries joined in the crackdown on Czechoslovakia in 1968, wasn't the Moscow government that gave them their marching orders more responsible than they were? If Menachem Begin uses force in support of expanding Jewish settlements in the West Bank and the United States does nothing effective to stop him, but continues its military aid to Israel on a large scale, isn't it partly responsible?

3. ". . . without adequate provocation." Undefinable as it is, that proviso is crucial. Who is to judge whether provocation is "adequate"? Yet the common sense of the world makes such judgments all time time.

When Israel started the Six-Day War in 1967, the Arab provocation (even though some top-level Israelis reconsidered it later) seemed at the time to be wholly adequate. It looked to most of the world as if the Arab states were ganging up on Israel with an apparent intention to attack or to goad it into war. They had announced their intention to strangle its trade through the Gulf of Aquaba. Therefore millions in other countries were jubilant when Israel jumped first and little David overcame Goliath in a mere six days (Sachar, 1976, pp. 660–61; White, 1977, pp. 205–12).

On the other hand, the provocation was clearly inadequate in all of Hitler's conquests after Munich, in most of those of the Soviet Union when it took over Eastern Europe, and in a number of American actions including (in my judgment) the Bay of Pigs and the Vietnam war.

4. ". . . on land that is not clearly one's own." This too is hard to define, since there are so many ulcerous spots in the world (Chapter 10) in which two or more nations feel that a certain piece of territory is unquestionably theirs. The West Bank,

Quemoy, the Shatt el-Arab, Ogaden province, Kashmir, and Taiwan are only a few of those that still remain. Was the Sudetenland part of Czechoslovakia because it was "legally" Czechoslovakian and had never been part of modern Germany? Or was it German because nearly all its inhabitants spoke German and most of them wanted to be in Germany? Who is to say? The point of the present proposition, though, is that neither side has a right to enforce its own interpretation of what land belongs to whom at the point of a gun, when it is obviously a controversial issue. The danger of a larger war that could become nuclear is so great that the side that does so, instead of resorting to a plebiscite, arbitration, or simply the pressure of world public opinion, should be pilloried as "the aggressor."

5. ". . . without clear evidence that most of the emotionally involved people in the affected area want that kind of intervention." Vietnam and Afghanistan are both test cases, and both have been discussed here (Chapter 2). By the definition proposed, both were acts of aggression, since there was in neither case "clear evidence that most of the emotionally involved people in the affected area wanted that kind of intervention." There was ambiguity or uncertainty, and in cases of uncertainty either side that first resorts to force, in the absence of clear evidence that most of the emotionally involved people in the affected area want that kind of intervention, should be called the aggressor.

An important part of this proviso lies in the words "the emotionally involved people." That is the meaningful way in which democratic majority rule should be defined. In every country, and especially in the less developed countries, it can be taken for granted that on many issues great numbers of people are nonpolitical and have no firm opinion. To expect scientific evidence on what they want is ridiculous in any case. What matters in practice is the balance of feeling among the emotionally involved people who do care about the issue, even if the pros and the cons together are no more than a minority. In Vietnam in 1965, when the United States went in in force, there is now much evidence that among those who cared emotionally about the outcome of the war many more favored the Viet Cong side than the Saigon side (White, 1970, pp. 37–103). Something similar apparently holds true in Afghanistan. In both cases the guilt of the aggressor lay in resorting to a move as morally dubious and as dangerous as armed intervention in the absence of clear evidence that the people who counted wanted that kind of "help."

By those criteria the following Soviet actions since 1945 seem to justify the word "aggression":

1. The takeover of most of Eastern Europe
2. Attempts to take over West Berlin, 1948–49 and 1958–62
3. The Korean war
4. Hungary, 1956
5. Czechoslovakia, 1968
6. Afghanistan

1. *The takeover of most of Eastern Europe.* Perhaps this should be regarded as eleven acts of aggression, since it included eleven countries: Estonia, Latvia, and Lithuania (in 1940); Poland, East Germany, Czechoslovakia, Hungary, Rumania, Bulgaria, and, less fully, Yugoslavia and Albania.

It was achieved not by the use but by the threat of force, with the Red Army always in the background. Probably that threat was unnecessary only in Bulgaria and, because of Tito's own strength, in Yugoslavia. It was not provoked by the capitalist West, which had fought at the USSR's side in the war that was just finished and at that time felt more friendly toward the USSR than, probably, at any other time before or since. Although some form of socialism was apparently favored by most of the people in the countries concerned, alien Soviet control violated their nationalist feelings; there is little doubt that in their hearts the great majority, in most of the countries, opposed the takeover.

Probably more than any other action on either side, this Soviet action caused the Cold War. Combined with the image of Stalinist Communism that Stalin's own domestic policies had created, it built up an image of a thoroughly evil USSR boldly and inexorably expanding. That alone made it a blunder from the standpoint of the USSR's longterm interests; in addition, it created many specific headaches for the Soviet leaders, as events in Poland, East Germany, Hungary, Czechoslovakia, Rumania, Yugoslavia, and Albania were later to show.

2. *Attempts to take over West Berlin, 1948–49 and 1958–62.* Though both were unsuccessful, both can be called acts of attempted aggression, by our definition. They involved threats of starvation or of use of force by East Germany; provocation,

though it existed, was dubiously adequate; and both were clearly against the nearly unanimous desire of the West Berliners.

They were blunders, since both failed and both served to exacerbate the Cold War.

3. *The Korean war.* As Khrushchev's memoirs make clear, it was approved if not initiated by the Soviet Union, and it was an unequivocal breaking out of the sphere of predominant Soviet influence that had been established as early as 1945. It was an invasion, an attack, across a border. There was real provocation, in the form of raids across the border by Syngman Rhee, but nothing comparable to the North Korean attack in June 1950. There is some question about what the South Korean people wanted, since Syngman Rhee was not generally loved and American influence was heavy-handed and resented, but neither of those facts implies a preference for the kind of Communist rule represented by Kim Il Sung in North Korea. Certainly there was no overt indigenous rebellion comparable to what developed later in South Vietnam.

It was clearly a major blunder. Nothing was gained; North Korea suffered greatly, and the Cold War was exacerbated more than by any other Soviet action except the takeover of Eastern Europe.

4. *Hungary, 1956.* Direct use of force by the Red Army, crushing an uprising by unarmed civilians in the streets of Budapest. Provoked, in a sense, by the unprecedented overtness of the uprising, and by an understandable Soviet anxiety about a domino process in Eastern Europe, although little Hungary was certainly no direct threat to the big USSR. Clearly opposed by a majority of the Hungarians; even the Communist leader, Nagy, had gone along with the majority.

Very bad for the USSR in its international repercussions, since it shattered the myth that the Peoples' Democracies were independent and also the myth that the USSR was necessarily on the side of the working class, since most of the uprisers were workers or students. But apparently the Soviet leaders were willing to pay that price for the integrity of the outer zone of their territorial self-image.

5. *Czechoslovakia, 1968.* Worse than Hungary, in the judgment of a great many non-Communist observers. There had been less provocation, since the people did not "uprise"; all they wanted was free speech and perhaps a multiparty system.

6. *Afghanistan.* Direct use of force; not provoked by any real threat to the USSR; apparently against the wishes of a considerable majority in Afghanistan.

By creating fears of Soviet aggression outside the traditional Soviet sphere of influence—fears that had not been created to the same extent since the Korean war—it was counterproductive.

The following American actions seem to fit the definition:

1. Supporting Chiang Kai-shek in China
2. Crossing the 38th Parallel in Korea
3. Threatening first use of nuclear weapons
4. Imposing the Shah's rule on Iran
5. The Bay of Pigs
6. The Vietnam war

1. *Supporting Chiang Kai-shek in China.* It was an indirect use of force, through a government that depended on us, without adequate provocation, and against the fairly clear wishes of most of the involved Chinese people (Tuchman, 1970, pp. 158, 187, 261, 322, 461, 466; Kennan, 1972, p. 54). Toward the end Chiang lost the support of even a majority of the businessmen in China. (He did better in that way later, in Taiwan.)

U.S. support of Chiang was actually half-hearted, but at first it was "a vital factor in inducing Chiang to overextend himself" (Ulam, 1971, p. 158).

It was also a blunder, since it greatly increased the element of basic hostility in the ambivalent attitude of most of the Mainland Chinese toward the United States. Their present official friendliness toward us probably does not run deep.

2. *Crossing the 38th Parallel in Korea.* That was a direct use of force without adequate provocation since the danger to the independence of the South had been decisively overcome. Although we may guess that most of the people in the North wanted to be "liberated" from Communist rule, there was no clear evidence that that was true.

It too was evidently a blunder, considerably increasing the hostility to us in China that had been built up by our support of Chiang (Fairbank, 1958, pp. 288–89; Hinton, 1966, pp. 212–15; Kennan, 1972, pp. 23–27). By coming so close to China's boundary, the Yalu, we gave the Chinese a tangible reason to fear us, with the unhealthy, war-promoting kind of fear. And it did no good from a power standpoint; they retrieved North Korea.

3. *Not explicitly renouncing first use of nuclear weapons, and implicitly or explicitly threatening their first use four times: in connection with Korea, Quemoy, Cuba, and the SAC alert of 1973.* These were threats to use incalculably destructive force. It is true that they had much provocation in the form of Soviet aggressions before 1951 and in what we felt to be a Soviet threat of nonnuclear aggression against Western Europe, on which the world balance of power depended. However, they now seem justified only if strictly temporary and combined with a rapid buildup of conventional forces in Western Europe to a level that would reliably deter a Soviet attack. That was not done.

Our threats also set a dangerous precedent for possible future use of nuclear threats by both sides and gave the USSR a strong incentive, since 1962, to build up its own strategic strength. In both ways they were probably a blunder. (Note: in none of these cases was our aggression justified by practical considerations that might possibly outweigh the moral evil of aggression itself.)

4. *Restoring the Shah to power in 1953 and helping to keep him in power until 1979.* That was indirect use of force against the Iranian people, through a client government, with little provocation. A majority of the emotionally involved Iranians were apparently against him in 1953; and later the opposition to him became, chiefly because of the atrocities of SAVAK, both much more widespread and much more intense.

Perhaps our support of him bought time, in terms of postponing any Soviet incursions into the Middle East. However, events in 1979–81 have made it look like another blunder. Our alienating the less Westernized people of Iran led to the crumbling of our supposed ''bastion'' in the northern tier of Middle Eastern countries.

5. *The Bay of Pigs.* It was an indirect (through anti-Castro Cubans) use of force, with some direct American support. It was not adequately provoked, since Castro's offensive strength was far less than ours; and it was done in ignorance of the State Department's intelligence information about the general support of Castro in Cuba at that time, reinforced by Lloyd Free's poll data, which showed a strong majority feeling in favor of Castro in Cuba (Cantril, 1967, pp. 1–5).

Not a mere blunder—a fiasco.

6. *The Vietnam war.* It was an indirect and then direct use of force. It was not adequately provoked, since Vietnam was small

and on the opposite side of the earth from us. In retrospect we can see that we were going against what a majority of the involved South Vietnamese wanted (White, 1970, pp. 37–103).

In retrospect it too was clearly a blunder.

The Soviet list excludes a number of possible candidates for inclusion: an oversized army; troops in Iran in 1946; threats to Turkey; sending arms to Arbenz in Guatemala; attempted Communist coups in many places such as Indonesia; the Cuban missile crisis; the recent nuclear arms buildup; martial law in Poland; recent activities in Angola; Ethiopia; Yemen; and Cambodia; and the shooting down of the Korean airliner. So does the American list: America's insistence on remaining ahead in the nuclear arms race (MIRV, cruise missiles, the Pershing II, the MX); the U-2 incident; support of anti-Communist dictators and oligarchies in many places besides China, Vietnam and Iran; provocative—but not aggressive—actions during the 1975–79 period of mounting tension; support of Israel in spite of its aggressive behavior, especially under Begin; and belligerent rhetoric, especially since 1979.

The length of both lists gives support to two generalizations made earlier in this book: that the diabolical enemy-image on each side has much (not just some) factual basis and that the moral self-image on each side, involving rationalization and projection of many of one's own country's sins, is a gross distortion of reality. Insofar as the sins on one's own side are glossed over and ignored rather than rationalized, it is also a testimony to the commonness of selective inattention on both sides.

Another interesting outcome of the exercise is the astonishing number of times, on each side, aggression has turned out in the long run to be a blunder as well as a cardinal sin. Enlightened self-interest, based on realistic empathy with victims and onlookers, would have led in nearly every case to an avoidance of aggression.

Whether the same was true in previous centuries is an interesting historical question, but with enough instances on both sides to make the answer uncertain. Rome apparently gained from most of its conquests, including the total destruction of Carthage, and Bismarck gave Germans enormous satisfaction with his three successful wars against Denmark, Austria, and France. On the other hand, the unprovoked Athenian attack on Syracuse in the Peloponnesian War led to disaster; the Spanish Armada failed; Louis XIV gained little if anything, on balance; and Napoleon's wars after 1805, which were much more aggressive than his earlier ones, bled France and ended with no gain.

In the twentieth century, though, the examples have been nearly all on one side. It is astonishing that that fact has not been widely recognized and discussed. As far as I know, John Stoessinger, in his little gem of a book, *Why Nations Go to War* (1974), was the first to recognize that, as he put it, "No nation that started a major war in this century emerged a winner" (pp. 223–24). Obvious examples, covered earlier in this book, include:

- Germany and Austria, the chief aggressors in World War I, suffered greatly, lost, and were dismembered.
- Tsarist Russia, whose premature mobilization contributed much to the outbreak of that war, also suffered greatly and was decisively defeated, which led to disaster for the Tsar himself and the ruling group he represented.
- France's treatment of Germany after World War I had much to do with the coming of Hitler and World War II, in which France was ignominiously defeated.
- Hitler's aggressions after Munich directly caused World War II in Europe, and he lost disastrously.
- Japan's aggressions directly caused World War II in Asia and it lost decisively. More specifically, Pearl Harbor brought the United States in, which was decisive in causing Japan's defeat.

One reason for this is familiar to balance of power theorists: onlooker nations such as Britain and the United States, not immediately affected by a conflict, often enter it to prevent a *future* adverse balance of power. What the balance of power theorists do not always see clearly is that the fear engendered by perception of aggression as such, and the anger created by aggression as such, are at least as important in bringing new nations into the conflict as the power possessed by the aggressor. A strong country that is perceived as nonaggressive, such as the United States during most of its twentieth-century history, is not likely to be ganged up on by jealous others. But a less inherently strong nation, such as Germany or Japan, is ganged up on if its aggressive behavior creates an image of a cumulative, snowballing process of aggression that has to be stopped before it goes too far.

Another reason for it, probably, which is not so familiar to balance of power theorists, is psychological: a failure to empathize with the great increase of fighting spirit that is likely to occur in the immediate victims of aggression when they see their own homeland being attacked. Hitler underestimated the tough defensive nationalism of the Yugoslavs, the Poles, the British, and the Russians; Japan underestimated the long-term defensive fighting spirit of the Chinese and the mobilization of national pride and anger that its attack on Pearl Harbor would evoke in the American people. We Americans underestimated the extremely tough defensive fighting spirit of the North Vietnamese and the Viet Cong when they perceived that their homeland was "invaded" by Americans.

That in turn is partly due to the diabolical enemy-image; the enemy is pictured as a devil who is always implacably evil and hostile, rather than as a peace-loving human being who can be turned into a devil if sufficiently provoked. And it is partly due to the moral self-image; nations are so good at rationalizing their own behavior that they do not see their own behavior as aggression even when it is, and therefore find it hard to believe that others will see it as aggression.

The analysis in this chapter adds many other examples to those that Stoessinger discusses, and all of them are either in support of his proposition or ambiguous. The six American actions counted as aggression are all now to be regretted, even from the standpoint of *Realpolitik*, and so are the six most aggressive Soviet actions, with the possible exception of the crackdowns on Hungary and Czechoslovakia, neither of which was a conquest of new land that the USSR did not already control.

That is strong empirical support for some of the psychological concepts stressed here, especially military overconfidence and absence of empathy as a reason for military overconfidence.

Could the Conflict Have Been Mitigated?

Obviously the Soviet government could have greatly mitigated the long-term conflict if it had fully seen the need and had known how to do it. Could we have done so?

Yes, in many ways.

Hindsight is never actually 20/20 and usually nowhere near it. Speculating about what would have happened if we had done things differently is always an uncertain business. It is a worthwhile business, though, if we can learn anything at all from the abundant historical evidence of what came after what—which might or might not mean what caused what.

In that spirit let us do some supposing.

Suppose we, the Americans, whose suffering in the war against Hitler had been minimal compared with that of the Russians and whose economy was very strong when theirs was bled white, had had more empathy and sympathy with the Russians from the very beginning of the Cold War—let us say when their army first touched Poland in June 1944. That was a time when most of us were still full of sympathy with their suffering, admiration for their toughness and final success, and gratitude for their having borne the brunt of the war when we felt unable to do our share. With the right leadership couldn't the generous impulses of Americans, which three years later led to the Marshall Plan, have been translated into a truly grand-scale program of help to the Russians in economic reconstruction? Wouldn't that have transformed the atmosphere of all our relations with them from then on? It might even have softened to some extent the hard heart of Josef Stalin himself, whose first impulse would surely have been to see in it an extraordinarily clever plot to subordinate the economy of the USSR to that of the United States, or to save the United States from a postwar depression, and who would probably have done his best to keep full knowledge of it from the Russian people. But not all Russians were Josef Stalin.

A large part of it could have gone to the long-suffering Poles, and it would have been difficult in that case for Stalin to keep Poland hermetically sealed against Western visitors and Western firsthand knowledge, as he did during the next two years or so, enormously increasing Western suspicion and hostility.

The easiest time to stop a malignant process of hostile interaction is before it gets well started. The most difficult time is when it is far advanced.

Suppose that, even without such a major form of tension-reduction, the following forms of it had occurred:

- No abrupt ending of Lend-Lease; a tapering off

- Early development of trade in everything but weapons
- Cooperation in the Middle East to prevent war between the Arabs and Israel; *early* adoption of the policy represented by the Vance-Gromyko communiqué in 1977
- More stress on rewards for "good" Soviet behavior than on punishment for "bad," in keeping with the psychological principle of positive reinforcement. (There was a great change for the better in Soviet behavior after the death of Stalin in 1953, but Dulles, on principle, refused to reward or encourage it.)

Suppose we had always striven for good communication with the government and people of the USSR, in these ways:

- Establishing the principle that we communicate with everyone, regardless of approval or disapproval, and in that context beginning to communicate with the Soviet government as soon as it was firmly established, with full diplomatic recognition in 1920, say, rather than waiting until 1933
- Similarly, recognizing Communist China as early as 1949–50 if it agreed to treat our diplomats with normal courtesy and respect (which it did not do with the British), and lived up to its agreement
- Welcoming all sorts of exchanges, including those that would enable Soviet citizens to learn about our technology in civilian industries. (To them that would have been extremely meaningful and a real sign of goodwill.)

Suppose we had exercised restraint in our armaments in these ways:

- Aiming at rough equivalence rather than an intimidating superiority in nuclear arms—after achieving rough equivalence in conventional forces
- Emphatically renouncing first use of nuclear weapons
- Never threatening first use
- Accepting the Rapacki Plan for a nuclear-free zone in Central Europe including Poland, Czechoslovakia, and both Germanys
- Congressional approval of SALT II in 1979

Suppose we had exercised restraint in our interventions in these ways:

- Not intervening in Russia in a way that seemed to threaten the new Bolshevik government in 1918–20
- Not crossing the 38th Parallel in Korea
- Not helping Chiang Kai-shek on the mainland, even as much as we did, and not at all on Quemoy
- Not helping France to reconquer Vietnam, and not helping Diem after 1956
- Not restoring the Shah to power and, later, not arming him heavily
- No Bay of Pigs, and no harassment of Castro thereafter
- Restraining allies when necessary; for instance, putting real pressure on Chiang to withdraw from Quemoy and on Begin to withdraw from the West Bank, provided that effective demilitarization and security measures could be established
- No intervention in Laos on the side of a right-wing military ruler, or in the Dominican Republic, Guatemala, Chile, El Salvador, and so on

Suppose that, along with all these kinds of ''softness'' we had been ''hard,'' effective deterrers in these ways:

- Encouraging and helping the West Europeans (starting as early as 1949) to build up their conventional arms, to whatever extent the Soviet arms program seemed to necessitate, while keeping in mind the best military estimates of the advantage of the defense over the offense in conventional war. (The ratio aimed at might have been two West European soldiers for every three Soviet soldiers, and two West European tanks for every three Soviet tanks. This would not have looked aggressive to the Soviets, since in their own defense they would have had much more than enough.)
- Developing the deterrent strength of the U.N.
- Signaling clearly, beforehand, the West's willingness to fight in defense of South Korea
- Maintaining economic and financial strength, e.g. by not resorting to deficit financing in the Vietnam war and by strenuous oil conservation after 1973
- Developing the ability of the West to signal strong collective disapproval by methods short of war, which could have in-

cluded greater development of trade, so that cutting off trade in specific products, such as grain, could have a more tangible effect. (We learned to think in those terms in 1980.)

- Taking the lead, with as much support as possible from other maritime nations, in keeping the Strait of Tiran open in 1967, using naval force if necessary
- Doing what Kennedy did in the Berlin crisis and in the Cuban missile crisis, which in a less tense atmosphere would have been less risky

Suppose we had maintained continuity and consistency in ways such as these:

- Immediate acceptance by Carter of the kind of SALT II agreement hammered out during the Nixon and Ford administrations, which did not demand of the Soviet government the psychologically difficult requirement that it destroy existing weapons
- Acceptance by Congress of the SALT II agreement hammered out by the Soviet government and the Carter Administration
- Not abandoning the hopeful start on Middle East peace represented by the Vance–Gromyko communiqué
- Not making empty, unenforceable threats such as Carter's declaration that the Soviet brigade in Cuba was unacceptable

It is not suggested here that all or perhaps any of these things would have been politically possible at the time in the context of American domestic politics. That is a separate question. It is suggested only that *if* public opinion in the United States had supported them, most of them would have contributed in the long run to peace.

Nor is this list intended to imply that the United States has been less wise or good than any other government would have been in its place. We did a number of things that in retrospect seem statesmanlike: refraining from any actual aggression until the Soviet Union had committed aggression several times; offering Marshall Plan aid to all of Europe including even the USSR itself; using supply planes instead of violence in counteracting the Berlin blockade; willingness to fight against clear aggression in

Korea; Kennedy's conciliatory behavior after the missile crisis; Nixon's détente; Kissinger's extraordinary skill in making peace between Egypt and Israel; our fairly consistent support of the United Nations. Our mistakes, though, do seem more numerous.

CHAPTER SIXTEEN

The Three Conflicts Compared

Two Patterns of War Causation

Those who stress only deterrence and not tension-reduction often accuse their opponents of not having learned "the lesson of history," namely, that if you appease an aggressor, as Chamberlain did at Munich, the result will be not peace but war. History has shown, they say, that strength and resolve, not conciliation, are the important ways to seek peace.

As we have seen (Chapter 7), the right kind of deterrence *is* important as one of the two main ingredients in a rational strategy for peace, and analysis of the events leading to World War II (Chapter 14) does give strong support to that idea. But history teaches more than one lesson. The other main lesson it teaches, based partly but by no means entirely on the events leading to World War I (Chapter 13) and the years between 1918 and 1933 (Chapter 14), is that a policy of primary reliance on deterrence, with no strong efforts to reduce tension, doesn't work either. History and commonsense psychology teach that we need both.

To put it differently, two kinds of circular processes are conspicuous in recent history. One is the aggression-and-appeasement process, with aggression on one side and appeasement on the other. Appeasement feeds the self-confidence of the aggressor; it takes off the brakes that might otherwise deter further aggression. It predominated between 1935 and 1939. The other is the malignant process of hostile interaction (Chapter 8). It feeds exaggerated fear, anger, and a macho type of competition on both sides, defensively motivated aggression on both sides, and ultimately war. It predominated before World War I, especially from 1904 to 1914; it predominated between 1918 and 1933, when the emotions that gave us a Hitler were being built up in Germany; it has predominated in most of the other wars of our century, including the Arab–Israeli conflict. It has predominated in the

East–West conflict, especially since the death of Stalin in 1953. History taught us, in one striking four-year period, to avoid the aggression-and-appeasement cycle. It has taught us, in a much larger number of instances, to avoid the malignant process of hostile interaction and to reverse it if possible. There are times when deterrence should be the primary emphasis, but there are many more times when tension-reduction needs to be emphasized.

Which of these times are we living in now? Should deterrence or tension-reduction now get our primary emphasis? There is very little doubt about the answer: Tension-reduction should. What is going on now, and has been going on since about 1975, is the malignant process in its classical spiral form. The existence of super-fast, super-accurate, super-dangerous first-strike thermonuclear weapons has accentuated, not mitigated, that process. We are now in an advanced stage of what happened between 1904 and 1914—not an advanced stage of what happened between 1935 and 1939. The unhealthy kind of fear now predominates on both sides. Has either side appeased the other, in a manner reminiscent of Chamberlain at Munich? Is there any such prospect?

Our nation's primary strategy for peace with freedom should depend mainly on the nature of the adversary. When faced with an aberrant personality such as Hitler (or Stalin) wielding supreme power in a strong nation, and in a sense paranoid, our strategy should be primarily deterrence. When faced with more ordinary human beings such as Khrushchev, Brezhnev, or Andropov, acting as first among equals in a "collegial" oligarchic group with a long record of caution in foreign affairs, our strategy should be primarily tension-reduction. A paranoid individual, obsessed with suspicion and firmly believing his enemies are implacably hostile, tends to focus on power and power alone. He looks intently for "weakness of will" in his opponent and takes advantage of it. His macho delusions of grandeur, like his delusions of persecution, preclude empathy and preclude any frame of reference other than a competitive one. But Khrushchev was not that type, Brezhnev was not that type, and Andropov is not that type. (His successor conceivably could be, but the collegial organization of the Politburo makes it very unlikely.)

An analyst of twentieth-century history is tempted to generalize that there have been two types of major war. One is a mirror-image type in which, during the prewar period, each side resembles the other in aggressiveness and in the primarily defensive motivation of its aggressiveness, but with a large dash of macho motivation supplementing its exaggerated fears. That is the prevailing type, represented by World War I, the East–West conflict, the Arab–Israeli conflict, and various others. Then there is the one-sided-aggression type, represented at least by the behavior of all three Axis powers between 1935 and 1941, in which the behavior of the other side was far from too aggressive but, rather, too appeasing. It is a striking and arresting fact that both Hitler and Mussolini were one-man dictators, and also aberrant personalities of an extremely macho and narcissistic if not also paranoid type. Both, in contrast with the majority of their people, apparently relished war as such, but the people were helpless and befuddled by effective one-man propaganda which, in Hitler's case, successfully pictured offensive war as defensive in purpose. (Japanese aggression is a special case and not treated here. There was much machismo among the military leaders of Japan, but it was not a one-man dictatorship.) In the mirror-image conflicts, on the other hand, the nature of the governments on both sides has typically been either oligarchic or fairly democratic.

While that typology seems essentially valid, it needs refinement, chiefly by recognizing a distinction, in the background of the Cold War, between the Stalin period and the post-Stalin period. It is not a simple matter of two mirror-image conflicts and one non–mirror-image conflict. The East–West conflict was first one and then the other.

That reinforces, however, the importance of the distinction between the aggression associated with one-man rule by an aberrant personality and the much lesser degree of aggression associated with oligarchic rule by more normal personalities. Stalin, like Hitler, was unquestionably abnormal and, like Hitler, unquestionably a one-man dictator. The word paranoid is appropriate in both cases. On Stalin's abnormality and his relation to his colleagues, see Khrushchev (1970, esp. pp. 165–82, 245–320) and Robert C. Tucker (1973 and forthcoming volumes of his three-volume biography of Stalin; also 1971). Stalin's morbid suspicion of the West, resembling his morbid suspicion of even his most faithful colleagues, affected the future peace of the world most disastrously during the last seventeen years of his life and rule, 1936–53, which included the Great Purges, the heyday of the Gulag Archipelago, the Nazi–Soviet Pact, the Finnish war, the takeover of the Baltic states, Stalin's temporary breakdown when attacked by Hitler, the takeover of most of Eastern Europe between 1944 and 1948, the vicious campaign of propaganda against the West and especially the United States which began rather abruptly in October 1946, the Zhdanov period, the Berlin blockade, and as a climax, the Korean war (see especially Shulman, 1965, pp. 13–79). The most important and unnecessary step toward eventual war was probably the takeover of Eastern Europe at precisely the time when the West was more ready for friendly cooperation than it had ever been since 1917. It is unfair to attribute those crimes and blunders primarily to Russia or to Communism. They were attributable mainly to the trauma of World War II (which also led Russians other than Stalin to feel that a bulwark against another invasion from the West was needed) and, more importantly, to the paranoid personality and the one-man power of Stalin.

This approach is relevant to the prevention of an East–West war in two ways. First, it means that the fair comparison between present-day America and the present-day USSR is their record of aggression only since Stalin died in 1953—by no means unequivocally in favor of the United States (see Chapter 15). Second, it means that one way to prevent war is to keep anyone, and above all a person with paranoid or strong macho tendencies, from getting supreme power on either side. Democracy, or at least a genuine oligarchy, is a bulwark against war.

What All Three Conflicts Have in Common

More important than these differences, though, is a long list of characteristics common to the prewar periods in all three cases. Most of them are evident in many other conflicts also. If we want broad answers to the long-term question of what causes wars and how to prevent them, it will be worthwhile to review quickly at this point these apparently nearly universal war-causing factors.

First, four nonpsychological background factors should be outlined, all of them in the realm of *power relationships* rather than political psychology.

1. *National sovereignty*. Jonathan Schell's impassioned plea for an end to national sovereignty as the only fundamental way to

prevent nuclear war has much to support it, and in the present predicament of the human species it deserves some fresh thinking on the part of those who have been pushing it out of their minds as totally impractical (Chapter 20). Obviously, all three of the conflicts described here have occurred in an era when national sovereignty was rampant.

2. *An ambiguous equality of military power.* It is rather clearly a danger when combined with intense military competition and only feeble efforts to reduce tension (Chapter 6).

3. *A strong power surrounded by weaker ones.* A geopolitical perspective is appropriate in all three cases. In the two world wars the strong centrally located country, surrounded by many weaker neighbors, was Germany. In the East–West conflict it has been the USSR.

There are probably two reasons why that is an inherently unstable situation. One is that the strong centrally located power almost necessarily arouses fear among the others that they may be picked off and conquered one by one. Pursuing the normal balance of power inclination, they tend to combine for the sake of safety. The other is that their doing so makes the central power feel encircled by hostile neighbors who could, in combination, do it in. The stage is set for the malignant process of hostile interaction. A ''balancer'' (Britain at first in both world wars, the United States later, and the United States in the East–West conflict), wanting both security and power in relation to the central power, has a natural tendency to side with the weaker peripheral states. It may or may not, in doing so, play a constructive deterrent and tension-reducing role. In any case, there is usually fear on both sides.

4. *A central nation that is not yet accepted as an equal.* That was true of Germany before each World War. Barbara Tuchman's description of the Germans who ''suffered, like their emperor, from a terrible need for recognition'' will be remembered. It is true of the USSR now. We Americans, with the lack of empathy that we share with many other nations, are seldom aware of it. We would do a good turn for peace if, without letting our guard down, we were to satisfy their need for recognition in every legitimate way. We do not do that when, for instance, we exclude them from the peacemaking process in the Middle East, which is on their doorstep.

This is partly a psychological factor, since the feeling of being excluded or unrecognized is psychological. It should be understood, though, that what matters here is a ratio between a tangible fact, power, and an intangible one, respect as an equal. If the discrepancy between power and respect is large, trouble is brewing. Before the Soviet Union could claim military parity with the United States it did not seem so unnatural, in Soviet minds, to be denied equality of respect. Now it does.

Each of the three war-promoting *motives* emphasized in Chapter 9 has been present, though not necessarily prominent, on the more aggressive side in each of the three conflicts:

1. *Exaggerated fear.* The examples include German fear of being left alone if Austria disintegrated; Hitler's paranoid fear of "world Jewry" and less paranoid fear of a return of the Communist threat that had existed in 1919; mutual fears of the United States and the USSR, both supported by some tangible facts that can be plausibly interpreted as justifying them.

2. *Macho pride.* German national pride since Bismarck and Austrian pride in power over several subject nationalities were factors, as were extreme macho pride in Hitler and the Nazis, America's determination to remain Number One, and the USSR's belief that history itself is on its side.

3. *Anger.* The Kaiser reacted with fear and fury at the murder of the Archduke. Germans were angry at the *Diktat* of Versailles. There has been mutual anger on the part of the USSR and the United States at a long list of genuine grievances on each side.

Each of the subconsciously *motivated errors of perception* described in Chapter 10 has been present:

1. *A diabolical enemy-image.* Germany believed that Russia would be strong enough and aggressive enough to force the dissolution of Austria-Hungary or go to war in 1917; the Germans expressed paranoid rage against Britain when it intervened. Hitler scapegoated the Jews and "internationalism." The Americans harbor an image of Soviet aggression, and the Soviet image of Americans stresses imperialism. Note that the diabolical enemy-image is the perceptual aspect of both exaggerated fear and intense anger.

2. *A moral self-image.* The German myth of complete innocence in 1914 made possible Germany's intense anger at the war guilt clause of the Versailles *Diktat* at the end of the war. Hitler's heroic and guiltless image (at least publicly) of Germany in

World War II was in keeping with his constant "peace propaganda" from 1930 to 1945. America identifies itself with democracy and freedom, and the USSR identifies with socialism and national independence in the Third World.

3. *A "pro-us" illusion.* The Kaiser was confident that Britain would not fight against Germany. Hitler was confident that neither Britain nor France, neither Russia nor the United States would fight effectively against him. America underestimated the likelihood that China would intervene when the United States crossed the 38th Parallel in Korea and underestimated the tenacity of the anti-American Vietnamese. The USSR was surprised at the resistance in Afghanistan.

4. *Overconfidence.* Both sides believed in 1914 that it would be a short war. Hitler attacked the USSR. The United States supported the Bay of Pigs invasion. The Soviet Union intervened in Afghanistan.

5. *Worst-case thinking.* The Germans expected in 1914 that Russia would be immensely strong by 1917. Some German generals were too confident that Hitler would be unable to bluff the British and French in 1938. Many Americans believe that Soviet nuclear arms are now superior, and apparently the Soviets believe they are only approximately equal.

6. *Overlapping territorial self-images:* Serbia's self-image overlapped Austria-Hungary's in the Bosnia-Herzegovina area; Germany's overlapped Czechoslovkia's in the Sudetenland and Poland's in the Polish Corridor; the Free World's overlaps with the Socialist Community's in many border areas including Korea, Afghanistan, and Berlin.

Since *selective inattention* is a process by which all of the motivated errors are maintained, it does not belong in the present list, but some outstanding examples can be mentioned: the Kaiser's not listening to what his ambassador in London was telling him; Hitler's not listening to his own generals in Russia; Americans not thinking of what they know about the sufferings of the Russians in World War II.

Three forms of *non-empathy:*

1. Not seeing an opponent's *desire for peace.* The Germans did not see how earnestly Lord Grey was seeking peace in late July 1914. Americans did not see how completely Hitler gave up trying to make his people want war. Americans do not realize how

intensely the Soviet decision-makers now want peace, and how relevant that is to such questions as their aiming for a first strike or wanting to invade Western Europe.

2. Not seeing an opponent's *fear*. The Allies did not realize, all through World War I, that a main German motive at the outset was fear. Americans never realized that a basic Japanese fear was that "imperialism" might strangle them economically. Soviets and Americans do not realize how much fear, of the war-promoting type, some of their own actions are creating in their opponents' minds.

3. Not seeing an opponent's *anger*: The Germans did not realize how deeply the attack on Serbia would humiliate, and therefore anger, the Russians. Hitler did not realize how much anger, as well as fear, his breaking his Munich promises was creating in Britain. The Soviets did not realize how much anger as well as fear their takeover of Eastern Europe would create in Western Europe.

Five forms of *unmotivated, cognitive errors:*

1. *Preexisting beliefs*. The Germans and Austrians believed, on the basis of the Russians' retreating in 1908, that they would do it again in 1914. Hitler believed, on the basis of all the appeasing the British and French had done, that they would do it again when he attacked Poland. Both sides of the East–West conflict act as if they still lived in a nonnuclear world.

2. *Blurred distinctions and the spread of attribution*. The Germans and Austrians blurred the distinction between the assassin who killed the Archduke and the government of Serbia. Hitler managed an extraordinary blurring of the contrast between the "plutocrats" in the West and the "Bolsheviks" in the East, connecting them by way of the idea that both were dominated by Jews. American conservatives blur the distinctions among liberals, socialists, and Communists. Stalin called Tito a tool of Wall Street.

3. *The injured-innocence mechanism*. The Germans assumed in 1914 that, since they meant no harm to Britain, British intervention must have had a diabolically aggressive motive. The Americans assumed that, because we meant Japan no harm, Pearl Harbor must have had a diabolically aggressive motive.

4. *Credulous acceptance of propaganda*. The Americans tended in 1914–17 to accept British propaganda unthinkingly while totally rejecting the German. The German people gave credulous ac-

ceptance to Hitler's and Goebbels's propaganda. Most of the Soviet people apparently accept their government's version of what happened in Afghanistan.

5. *Extrapolation of a trend.* The Germans in 1914 tended to assume that three trends would continue unless forcibly stopped, the disintegration of Austria-Hungary, the increasing size and efficiency of the Russian army, and the consolidation of the British-French-Russian Entente. Hitler, according to Norman Rich (1973, p. 5) saw "time working against Germany" because Russia was increasingly able to combine its unlimited numbers with Western technology. Many Americans, seeing the USSR catching up with them and now roughly equalling them in nuclear strength, have become greatly concerned, and, in the judgment of many other Americans (including this one), proceeded to pile up far more nuclear arms than are really necessary.

Ideology?

Two negative generalizations also emerge from our comparative study. Not one of the three great conflicts seems to have been primarily based on ideological motives, and not one seems to have been based primarily, or even importantly, on economic motives. The primary motives on each side in all three were apparently some combination of fear, pride, and anger—not ideology and not economics.

Such a downgrading of ideology will necessarily sound strange and perhaps unbelievable to a great many on each side of the present East–West conflict, since on each side the primary official definition of the problem is ideological. Communists speak of it as a gigantic, world-wide, inevitable conflict between "socialism" and "capitalism"—that is, roughly speaking and from their point of view, between economic justice and economic injustice. A great many people in the West think of it as a gigantic, world-wide, and probably inevitable conflict between "democracy" and "Communism"—that is, roughly speaking and from our point of view, between freedom and an aggressive dictatorship.

Yet there is much reason to think that these ideologies which are so prominent in consciousness and in official speeches are mainly rationalizations of nationalist fear, nationalist pride, and nationalist anger. The robes of social justice on one side and of freedom on the other cover realities that are less idealistic. Free enterprise in the West has, fortunately, evolved into an ideologically inconsistent but fairly workable mixture of capitalism and socialism, with a fair amount of attention to social and economic justice; however, much still remains to be done along that line (see White, 1966, 219–21, 226–27). Communism in the USSR, perhaps fortunately, has become similarly inconsistent and similarly different from the radically egalitarian economic democracy that the earlier Marxists aspired to. Both sides, in mirror-image fashion, proclaim with apparent sincerity their willingness to settle for a live-and-let-live philosphy (the Communists call it "peaceful co-existence") if the other side will only cease its aggression and let them and all weaker countries alone. Most startling of all, two totalitarian Communist countries, the USSR and Communist China, actually seem more hostile to each other than either is to the relatively democratic and semicapitalist West. Meanwhile, the majority of Americans now (1983) seem somewhat friendly to a totalitarian Communist China and ready to cooperate with it against the great devil, the USSR. The ideologies are scrambled and what is left is mainly nations playing the old game of competition for power, motivated by nationalist fear, nationalist pride, and nationalist anger.

Is the same true of the other two great conflicts? To a surprising degree it is.

No nation called itself socialist in 1914 but some did talk about democracy. The lineup in 1914 was therefore surprising. It included a highly autocratic country, Tsarist Russia, incongruously allied with a relatively democratic France and a relatively democratic Britain against two somewhat autocratic countries, Germany and Austria-Hungary. It seems clear that, whatever the motives of the Germans and Austrians were, those motives involved German nationalism and Austro-Hungarian nationalism far more than any desire to defend autocracy as such or to attack democracy as such. It was essentially a nationalist war rather than an ideological war, and Lenin failed in his great ambition to transform it from a nationalist war into a class war.

In World War II there was somewhat more reason, but not much more, to define the conflict as ideological. Hitler did defend the "Führer principle" against the supposed corruption and weakness of parliamentary democracy, and Roosevelt and many others in the West did think of it as a struggle between "peaceloving democracies" and "warmaking dictators." Fascist-minded people in both Britain and France did condone the methods of Mussolini and Hitler and oppose war against them. Soviet leaders did (before August 1939 and after June 1941) define the Nazi regime as the archenemy of both democracy and socialism, while Hitler defined his Führer principle as a Germanic form of "true democracy" and called it National Socialism. Leaders everywhere are understandably ready to wrap themselves and their actions in the robes of whatever they think their followers want or admire. (On Hitler's ways of doing it, see White, 1949, 160–64.) But the nature of the ideological robes does not explain the actions. Deeper forces, and especially national interest as conceived by fearful, prideful, and angry people, are always at work.

Shifts in alignment are especially relevant here. Stalin, a Communist, suddenly formed an alliance with Hitler, who was supposedly his ideological archenemy. Hitler accepted the alliance, which was supposedly with *his* ideological archenemy, but later attacked the USSR. That attack probably stemmed more from his personal delusions of grandeur and of persecution, from his deeply ingrained nationalistic hatred of the Russians, and from his lifelong ambition to lead Germany in getting "land in the East," than from any ideological opposition to socialism or communism as such; and certainly it did not stem from any opposition to democracy, since Stalin was at least as autocratic as he was. The ideologies in that war were about as scrambled as they are now in the East–West conflict. Fear, pride, and anger (with fear relatively unimportant and pride extremely important in Hitler's mind) were probably the dominant motives.

Economic Motives?

The case for economic self-interest as a primary war-causing motive is weak in all three conflicts.

In the present East–West conflict, it is weak for two main reasons: (1) Each of the two superpowers covers a vast territory, lavishly endowed with natural resources. Neither needs resources that are possessed only by the other or unavailable by purchase from others. Unlike most of the countries in the world, both are comparatively self-sufficient economically. The talking-points of

Hitler and of Japan, that they needed "Lebensraum" or an outlet for surplus population, are nonexistent in both cases. (2) In
our nuclear era, the economic advantages of peace enormously
outweigh any conceivable economic advantages of war. Industries
and cities as well as people would be incinerated on a colossal
scale if an all-out nuclear exchange occurred. The threatened
groups include the political and economic elite in both societies.

There are three economic factors that might perhaps favor
actions that would make war more likely (such as an arms race or
armed intervention in Third World countries), but in each case
there are reasons to think the factor in question is not of vital importance:

1. *Oil.* The oil fields of the Middle East are highly vulnerable
to a determined Soviet attack and are regarded by many in the
West as vital to their economies. More than any other commodi-
ties in the past, oil looks as if it could be so desired by both sides
that they might fight to get or keep access to it.

On the other hand, the Soviet Union itself is so well endowed
with oil that its need for it will probably never be great in the
foreseeable future. There is also no reason why it should not be
able to buy from the Middle East whatever oil it might need. It is
true that for reasons of fear it might at some future time want to
seize the Middle East's oil, in order to put economic pressure on
Western Europe and Japan, but if that occurred it would probably be because the conflict had become, for other than economic
reasons, much more acute than it is now.

2. *The profits of arms makers.* There is such a thing as a military-industrial complex in the United States and elsewhere.
There is no reason to think it would favor war or serious risks of a
big war, since businessmen now have as much to lose from a big
war as anyone else. However, the coalition of arms-makers and
the Pentagon undoubtedly tends to favor large-scale production of
weapons, rationalizing its profit-making and its arms-getting as
"a guarantee of peace." When that means a grotesque amount
of nuclear overkill, there is every reason to think they are mistaken and that they are actually bringing nuclear war closer.

On the other hand, arms-makers are only a part of the business community, and the community as a whole suffers from the
economic stagnation that comes when interest rates and inflation
are unduly high because of heavy arms spending. That is now a
critically important factor. Therefore, businessmen must be of

two minds about heavy spending on weapons. When they favor it, without directly profiting from it, they probably do so mainly for the reasons that most of the rest of the people in the West favor it: exaggerated fear of the Soviet Union and unrealistic ideas about how to cope with that danger.

3. *Concern about the stability of the Third World and the safety of capitalist interests in it.* The Vietnam war is an example of how wrong Lenin was in thinking that a capitalist state, in its advanced "monopoly" stage, would necessarily fight with other capitalist states to get or keep markets, access to raw materials, and investment opportunities. In little Vietnam itself, there were no capitalist gains to be hoped for that could possibly match the great and many-sided costs of the war for the United States; and the war was not fought against a rival capitalist state but against North Vietnam and the Viet Cong. We did not fight to take plantations away from French landowners. We fought primarily to hold the line against an expansion of Communism that we believed would encourage future Communist takeovers in many other vulnerable Third World countries—perhaps in Nicaragua, Brazil, Nigeria, or the Congo as well as in nearby Thailand and Indonesia. Given the importance of the domino theory (broadly defined) in the minds of American decision-makers, as attested by the Pentagon Papers, that fear seemed to make sense.

To what extent is our government's fear of Communist takeovers now motivated by economic considerations? The general anti-Communism of the American public on all class levels is probably the main reason for it, including all of the realistic recognition of Communist evils, all of the nationalist feelings of fear, pride, and anger, and all of the possible misperceptions that have entered into American anti-Communism. Politicians who want to be elected or re-elected necessarily care about the strong anti-Communist feelings of their constituents, whether they fully share them or not. There are also long-term balance-of-power considerations that probably matter more among the educated elite in the West than among the rank and file. The question is, then, to what extent is our basic emotional anti-Communism supplemented by the economic self-interest of "big businessmen" who have interests in the Third World (such as fear of expropriation) that they want their government to defend? It is a plausible hypothesis that such self-interest—rationalized, naturally, in terms of more idealistic goals—is considerable, and that its political effect is considerable. In these days of expensive television the more well-to-do businessmen are in a position to contribute mightily to election campaigns.

In the light of such considerations, it seems to this writer that some economic motives do promote war today and should by all means be fully taken into account but that their importance should not be exaggerated. They probably rank only fourth, and a poor fourth at that, behind the primary war-promoting motives: nationalist fear, often based largely on misinterpreted dangers, macho pride, and anger based partly on misinterpreted misdeeds of national opponents. Also, insofar as human beings are rational, the economic reasons for peace should now enormously outweigh the economic reasons for war.

Could the economic motives in World Wars I and II be analyzed in similar ways? They could, and with a similar outcome.

For instance, the Leninist interpretation of World War I now seems largely mistaken. It is true that colonial rivalry was strong during the years before 1914, especially in the two Moroccan crises, but economic gain was by no means the only reason for that rivalry. Macho pride, rationalized in terms of economic gain, was probably more important, especially in view of the fact, now well established, that the economic gains of empire were often uncertain or negative. Also, it is doubtful that the colonial rivalry had much direct importance during the crisis of 1914. The chief motives that mattered then were probably exaggerated fear of a future imbalance of power, macho pride (fear of ''sinking to the status of a second-class power''), and anger.

The case for economic motives behind World War II is even weaker. Hitler was not an economic man; he was a seeker of power and martial glory, for his nation and above all for himself. His talk of Germany's needs for *Lebensraum* can be best interpreted as a rationalization of his hostilities and his hunger for glory, because he did not settle Germans on the land he conquered and because of the fact that a still more thickly populated Germany has prospered since he lost the war. Rivalry for colonies was not a factor on either side; the great age of competition for colonies had ended by 1920 and the great retreat from them began in the late 1940s. Japan had a stronger case for claiming an economic need to expand, but Japan also prospered greatly after the losses of the war (and of preparation for war) ended, without expanding onto Chinese land or controlling it by force. As for the enemies of the Axis, their essential motive was short-term or long-term independence, not economic gain. (It should be remembered that the trio of fear, macho pride, and anger is suggested here only as a rough description of the motives of the more aggressive side in any particular war, or of both sides when aggression is not clear. A self-respecting desire for independence is a sufficient explanation for the fighting on the defending side whenever aggression is clear and one-sided, as it was in World War II.)

The conclusion therefore stands: As far as the three great conflicts are concerned, the economic reasons for war in the twentieth century have in general been fallacious or nonexistent, while the net economic losses from war—and often from preparation for war—have nearly always been great.

The chief reason why economic motives are relatively weak in this context can be stated with surprising simplicity: human beings are seldom willing to die for material things that will be of no use to them when they are dead. They will willingly die only for a cause that to them seems to transcend their individual selves—a cause such as the survival or the independence, or sometimes only the urgent welfare, of their nation. (Hitler knew that principle and stated it in *Mein Kampf.*)

Nor will many knowingly send others to their death for less than what they feel is a transcendent reason. Many are evil and selfish in some ways, but few are *that* evil.

This chapter comes closer than any other to being a general analysis of the causes of war. Readers who want to pursue the subject on that level of generality will surely want to be familiar with Quincy Wright's early classic *A Study of War* (1942, 1964); James Schellenberg's *The Science of Conflict* (1982), which covers other kinds of conflict also; and Geoffrey Blainey's excellent study, *The Causes of War* (1973).

PART IV

Prevention

CHAPTER SEVENTEEN

Forms of Minimal Deterrence

Strength and Resolve

We have come to the practical part of this book. How, specifically, can nuclear war—and other wars that might become nuclear—be prevented?

Two broad answers have been given: minimal deterrence and drastic tension-reduction.

There is fairly general agreement that effective deterrence involves two necessary ingredients: adequate armed strength and the courage, or resolve, to use armed strength when necessary. Disagreement exists mainly with regard to how much and what kinds of strength are adequate in a given situation and with regard to what situations make the use of that strength necessary.

In the chapter on the case for minimal deterrence that term was defined, briefly and incompletely, in terms of two forms of armed strength (an adequate nuclear second-strike capability and adequate conventional strength) and one way of demonstrating resolve (collective defense against clear international agression). The meaning of "adequate" as applied to both nuclear and conventional arms has already been discussed at some length and will be further elaborated below. Something more should be said immediately, though, about what is variously called courage, firmness, or resolve.

World War II is of course now almost universally regarded as an example of what can happen when the second ingredient, resolve, is lacking. Both Japan and Hitler's Germany went from one relatively quick, cost-effective victory to another without being stopped. There was appeasement (that is, allowing clear aggression to be rewarded by cheap success) in response to at least four instances of Axis aggression that can be called clear: those against Ethiopia, Spain, China, and the Czech part of Czechoslovakia. (There was no lack of resolve—no appeasement—when

Hitler attacked Poland.) As a result of the democracies' failure to resist those four instances of clear aggression and some that were much less clearly aggression, by force if necessary, Hitler's already extraordinary propensity to delusions of grandeur and to outright calculated aggression was increased, and a great war occurred.

There is nevertheless a problem here: Is what *one* side perceives as aggression by the other side a sufficient reason to fight? The universal tendency toward black-and-white thinking, in any acute group conflict, is likely to produce major misperceptions on precisely this point. World War II was probably exceptional in the clearness and one-sidedness of the acts of aggression that preceded it. In a number of other conflicts in this century, including at least the period preceding World War I, most of the East–West conflict up to this point, the Arab–Israeli series of wars, the Greek-Turkish conflict, the India-Pakistan conflict, the Iran–Iraq conflict, the Vietnam war, and the Falklands/Malvinas conflict, each side has seen certain actions by the other as unequivocal aggression. Were both sides then justified in fighting? In our nuclear age, in which small wars can escalate and become big ones and conventional wars can become nuclear, an insistence that "resolve" must always be shown could become a prescription for catastrophe. It is necessary therefore to do some thinking beforehand about what kinds of behavior by an opponent justify all-out war as a response. We need to consider what are the right kinds of strength and what are the right kinds of resolve.

Strength of the Right Sort

Strict parity in every kind of armed strength, defined by numbers of troops, tanks, ships, planes, missiles, warheads and so on, is clearly not the answer. General Maxwell Taylor, whose credentials as former Chairman of the Joint Chiefs of Staff are impeccable, has argued ably in favor of concentrating on the missions we want our weapons to perform and the means necessary to perform those missions, rather than on some mythical parity with the Soviet Union. In any numerical comparison there are too many intangibles left out and too many tangibles that are difficult or impossible to measure: the quality as distinguished from the number of a given type of weapon, the skill and training of those who use them, the geopolitical factors of proximity that make some things more difficult for the Soviet Union and other things easier, and the willingness of friends and allies to fight for something other than literal self-defense. Much depends also on where the contemplated fighting might occur; for example, would it be in West Europe or East Asia, where the United States would presumably have strong allies ready to fight in self-defense, or in the Middle East, where the United States might well have to go it almost alone, with hostile Arabs and Iranians to contend with, and with all the logistic advantages on the Soviet side?

There is also the question of perception of what the relative strengths will be in a given situation, with worst-case thinking or overconfidence possible on both sides. As we have seen, worst-case thinking is apparently common on both sides of the East–West conflict, and if so each side is already deterring the other more effectively than it thinks it is. For instance, it may be that the Soviet Union is already deterred from all but the safest of military undertakings by its own troops, such as Afghanistan, or those regarded as most urgent and also fairly safe, such as the crackdowns on Hungary and Czechoslovakia. (On the other hand, worst-case thinking on both sides would make arms control much more difficult, since neither side would be likely to accept what the other regards as parity.)

The case against strict insistence on one's own conception of parity has been presented at some length in Chapters 6 and 12. The case for at least some flexibility of interpretation has been accepted by President Reagan and by the Pentagon in its use of the term "substantial equivalence." There is also the very strong case, when what is being discussed is nuclear strength, for either side to be willing to cut back drastically, unilaterally if necessary, to no more than is needed for a practically invulnerable second-strike capability (Chapters 6, 7, and 12). That would be consistent with Maxwell Taylor's plea for considering only the mission that a particular type of force needs to perform. In this case the mission of nuclear weapons would be regarded as solely to deter any use of nuclear weapons by the other side, and if an invulnerable ability to destroy the opponent's two hundred largest cities in retaliation was thought adequate to accomplish that mission it would be regarded as an ample amount—not parity but sufficiency.

In the negotiation that should precede any such unilateral action, however, a reasonable and flexible interpretation of over-all parity is probably the only feasible objective for the negotiators on either side to adopt. It is apparently the only psychologically possible basis for negotiation. Peter Jay, the wise British ambassador who served in Washington from 1977 to 1979, said as much when he remarked that because of their power the two superpowers are "doomed to watch one another like hawks, to negotiate constantly by day for strategic parity and to plot ceaselessly by night for strategic advantage" (Jay, 1980, p. 485). No negotiator could face his opposite number and say, "I insist on our having at least one and a quarter times as much strength as you have." His opposite number would walk out immediately. There must be at least a pretense of equality—a balancing of different kinds of strength which one side can with a straight face claim to be substantially equivalent even though the other side does not fully believe it—if negotiation is to proceed at all. The value that human beings almost inevitably place on some kind of "distributive justice" requires it, and the value that human pride places on the *right* to be equal, even if that right is not exercised, also requires it.

It is with that rough criterion in mind that we in the West should, in our negotiations, honestly aim at being substantially on a par with the Soviet Union in overall strength, making an honest effort to balance some kinds of superiority on one side against some on the other.

For instance, that could imply that we and our allies should undertake a strenuous beefing up of our conventional strength, at least in quality, while relaxing our effort (as many see it) to regain superiority to the Soviets in nuclear strength.

Some, of course, are saying that the nuclear superiority on which we have relied for so long no longer exists, has been reversed, or is about to be reversed. There is no doubt at all, though, that if an overall Soviet superiority exists it is much greater on the conventional than on the strategic nuclear side. Doesn't it seem likely, then, that in an actual war they would hope to fight it with the weapons that give them the greater advantage and, in the bargain, save their cities (and ours) from horrible destruction? Might they not assume that our apparent readiness to use at least theater nuclear weapons was a bluff and that we were not really insane enough to do it—uncorking the genie that could well go on to devastate our cities as well as theirs? A plausible guess is that it *must* be a bluff and that we are not actually insane enough to cross the firebreak between nonnuclear and nuclear warfare. If we are not, and if they are not similarly insane, then what we really need on the nuclear side is a reasonably safe second-strike capability and not much more. We could spend on conventional strength much of the money we are now spending on chasing the will-'o-the-wisp of nuclear parity.

If that were done there would be substantial psychological advantages both in rapport with our allies and in reducing the danger of war. We would be increasing our power to deter the one kind of war that is likely to be fought, and doing so without looking aggressive in the eyes of either our allies or our potential opponents. No one could plausibly say that we were "pushing the arms race" or preparing for aggressive war if we were concentrating on raising the West's conventional strength from, let us say, half to three quarters of that of the Soviet Union. The USSR would still be totally safe from any land offensive by us or by us and our allies.

Such a major shift of emphasis would be expensive. Conventional forces, properly trained and equipped, have always been expensive. One of the seductive advantages of nuclear superiority in the Eisenhower era was that it offered "more bang for a buck," and in those days, before the retaliatory power of the USSR had risen to its present level, that made some sense. It no longer does. Also, if a shift of emphasis to conventional strength significantly reduced the chance of war, especially if it significantly reduced the chance of nuclear war, it would be an incomparably good bargain.

Resolve of the Right Sort

What is the right sort of resolve to maintain?

Not dark threats of massive retaliation. The Soviet Union can now retaliate at least as massively as we can. Western Europe and Japan would probably be the great losers.

Not "tripwires," designed to give the probably dishonest impression that we ourselves might even now be willing to resort to first use of nuclear weapons. (One can only hope that it would be dishonest.)

Not empty threats of any sort that we do not have the strength or the will to follow up with action. When any bluff is called and proved to be a bluff the impression it creates is the opposite of firmness. President Carter's declaration that the Soviet brigade in Cuba was "unacceptable"—an implied threat—was a case in point.

Not shrill or grim polemics of the sort that the Soviet Union continually indulged in during the last years of the Stalin era. Speaking softly, or at least moderately, does not give an impression of weakness if the stick that is carried is big enough to deter.

Not cutting off or threatening to cut off communication. Communication is so valuable in so many ways, in terms of peace and our own self-interest, that cutting it off or reducing it is unlikely to be anything but a blunder in the long run.

Not intervening with force in the domestic affairs of other countries, except under rare, unusual circumstances (see Chapter 22).

And certainly not aggression of the kind that the United States has committed several times in the past, without ever calling it by its right name (see Chapter 12). The striking historical record of how often aggression has been counterproductive (partially covered in Chapter 12) is evidence enough that that is not the way to be "firm," although aggressors have often applied that word to it.

None of these responses provide the kind of firmness that will deter Soviet aggression. Some better ways to show resolve are: living up to promises; following through on threats; making public statements that are consistent, truthful, and credible; continuity in pursuing policies once they are announced; saying the same thing to different people or interest groups; being calm in voice and manner. When combined with real competence and strength, this kind of consistent and credible behavior will deter aggressive actions.

Most crucially, there must be the courage to fight on the rare occasions when fighting is really necessary. Military force itself does not deter if others believe that it will not under any circumstances be used (Clausewitz, 1968, p. 104; Payne, 1970, pp. 153–65). The classical case is Munich, with the series of unopposed aggressions by Hitler, Mussolini, and Japan that preceded it. Though Britain and France were arguably still stronger than Nazi Germany at the time of Munich, Hitler felt that their will was weak and that he could probably, by bluff and bravado, achieve his purpose without war. Their behavior before Munich gave him much reason to think so; and their behavior at Munich, though probably based more on misperception than on basic weakness of will, was as disastrous for peace as if it had been what he thought it was.

Other Components of Deterrence

Many people on both sides think of deterrence almost wholly in terms of weapons and armed forces. That is a gross misplacement of emphasis. If we define deterrence as all of the sources of healthy fear that would work in our opponents' minds against attacking us or our allies, the sources other than armed force may even be more important. Among those sources three stand out: economic strength, close relations of the United States with its allies, and good rapport between the United States and its friends in the Third World.

Economic Strength

Marxists, with their economic interpretation of history, pay much attention to economic strength. It includes the ability of the West to survive if necessary without Middle Eastern oil, and much more besides. As a deterrent economic strength matters in several ways: as a major element in the Soviet leaders' overall feeling that we are still vigorous, competent, and not to be lightly antagonized; as a safeguard against their getting the impression that by taking the Middle East's oil they could at one stroke get power over all of the Western world; as an assurance to our allies that in the long run, if they work well with us and we with them, the defensive strength of the West will be adequate and the peace will be secure; as a demonstration to the Third World that the West's combination of democracy and semisocialism is at least as vigorous and successful, and therefore at least as attractive a model, as the Soviet Union's combination of oligarchy and drastic socialism.

The many questions involved in achieving greater economic strength and oil independence fall outside the scope of this book, but it is within the scope of the book to underline, and double underline, the importance of those questions for deterrence.

Close Relations with Allies

The people of the United States constitute less than 6 percent of the world's population, and those the the USSR about 6 percent. The remaining 88 percent or so—the enormous majority—hold the balance of power. In the long run, and perhaps even in the short run, our fate depends on how they feel about us. That is a hard fact that our egotism seldom allows us to accept fully enough or to remember often enough, but it is a fact.

Those 88 percent can be divided for war-preventing purposes into two major groups that shade into each other but are useful to consider separately: (1) actual or potential allies and (2) actual or potential friends. Allies are defined here not necessarily as unconditional allies but as those whose sense of common purpose would probably lead them to fight on our side in an actual war, even if they themselves were not directly attacked, if the war was clearly defensive and was fought in their general part of the world—e.g. Western Europe or the Far East. Friends are defined here as those others whose ambivalent feelings are at least somewhat more pro-Western than pro-Soviet and who therefore would, in case of a defensive war, be somewhat more likely to help us than to help the USSR.

Our allies, actual or potential, now constitute a fairly well-defined group comprising the economically and educationally advanced, relatively democratic countries that in this book have been loosely referred to as "the West." They include at least Britain, West Germany, France, Italy, the Low Countries, Denmark, Norway, Canada, Australia, New Zealand, Japan, Israel, and—*if* it can be brought to move rapidly toward a settlement of its racial problems somewhat similar to what has been more or less achieved in Rhodesia (which is very unlikely)—South Africa.

It would be difficult to overestimate the importance of these allies in the world balance of power. Although in numbers they add only some 15 percent to our 6 percent, their economic, industrial, educational, and scientific advancement gives them a potential for military power, in this age of technological warfare, much greater than ours and probably much greater than that of all the Third World countries put together. According to Paul Nitze the aggregate gross national product of the Organization for Economic Cooperation and Development (the OECD, which is essentially the same as the group discussed here, plus the United States) is four times that of the USSR and its associates (Nitze, 1980, p. 84). That is an immensely encouraging fact that, if tempted to despair, we would do well to remember. For example, if they and we knew we had to, we could certainly build a combined conventional force much larger than that of the Warsaw Pact countries, including the USSR.

They are also our natural allies, in more ways than one. Their kind of democracy is like ours, their values are similar to ours, and if the USSR were foolish enough to let itself be perceived as the common aggressive enemy of all of us, as Hitler did, there would be the cement of a common enemy binding us more closely together than we are bound now. (That seems unlikely, however. The USSR, fully aware of its relative weakness if its potential enemies were united, apparently has as a first priority the task of dividing Western Europe from the United States.) All of them have had what Walt Rostow would call their economic take-off period and, partly because of New Deal–style and social democratic policies, are probably immune to the kind of Communist revolution that he calls "the disease of the transition of modernity" (Rostow, 1960), which still threatens many of the Third World countries. None of them have the basic animus against Western "imperialism"—that is, the tendency to identify "imperialism" with the West—that is still characteristic of most of the Third World. All of them are in fact more directly threatened by possible Soviet aggression or domination than we are. Each of them needs us at least as much as we need it. In short, they are our natural allies.

How can we keep them as allies?

We can do these things:

• *Consultation, listening, compromise.* Many West Europeans are perhaps even unreasonably sensitive to whether they are consulted, listened to, and compromised with, but it would be a foolish kind of pride if we were not sensitive to the sensitivity of their pride and not responsive to it. In their position of relative subordination, with another country arrogantly claiming its right to be "number one" and the "leader" of the Free World, we would be sensitive too.

• *Scrupulous nonaggression everywhere—especially in the Middle East.* After the Vietnam war it is understandable that many of our actual and potential allies might be afraid that we could drag them into an unnecessary and disastrous war with the Soviet Union. That is a fear that our entire policy in the Middle East needs to allay if we want them to have confidence in our cool good judgment.

Secretary Vance and his Middle East specialists in the State Department were apparently almost unanimous in feeling that cool good judgment implies, above all, not being the first to use force against Moslems in the Middle East, before the Soviet Union does; they opposed even the hostage-rescue mission on that ground, more than on the ground that it was likely to fail. They saw clearly the danger that if we were the first to use force *against Moslems*, and kill Moslems, the Moslem world would be confirmed in its incipient image of us as "the Great Satan," leaving the door wide open for the Soviet Union to appear as the protector of Arabs and/or Iranians against American "imperialism." (Fortunately it did not happen.) Probably from the standpoint of most of the American public President Carter was, if anything, not "tough" enough in responding to the hostage outrage, but from the standpoint of many in Western Europe Carter overreacted—as many Europeans apparently thought he did to the Soviet invasion of Afghanistan (Fontaine, 1981, p. 579).

• *Strong and genuine efforts to reduce tension between the West and the USSR.* Chapters 18 and 19 discuss in some detail what such efforts might include. Two examples here may suffice: rapid progress in negotiating an equivalent of SALT II, and a forthcoming attitude toward an early, satisfactory summit conference between President Reagan and Andropov. According to Seweryn Bialer, "The West European countries regard progress in negotiations on arms control as their first priority and the very precondition for the introduction of Theater Nuclear Forces (TNF) into Europe. They have tied their consent for the deployment of TNF specifically to ratification of SALT II" (1981, p. 535). That suggests that they are of two minds about TNF, but of one mind about SALT II. They know what war is like; they know they would be in the middle of it if "obsessive anti-Communism" in the United States, combined with Soviet power policies (which Europeans, more than Americans, tend to see as partly a reaction to American policies), were to bring about World War III; and they want none of it.

• *A fair settlement of the Palestine problem.* Whatever the rights and wrongs of that issue may be, there is no doubt about the prevailing feeling among Western Europe's intellectuals and government leaders: They are on the whole highly critical of what they see as a one-sidedly anti-Palestinian policy of the United States. For instance, Peter Jay deplores what he regards as the failure of the United States to satisfy even the minimum felt needs of the more moderate Arabs and the loss of rapport even with Saudi Arabia that he thinks has resulted from that failure (Jay, 1980, pp. 503–7). Michael Howard, an eminent British military historian, speaks of "an apparently unconditional American support for Israeli policy, determined rather by the pressures of domestic public opinion than by any clear calculation of American global interests" (Howard, 1981, p. 461). André Fontaine, editor-in-chief of *Le Monde*, goes farther:

> Paris did not approve the Camp David agreements between Egypt and Israel and has long thought that the way to peace is through an accord between Israel and the Palestine Liberation Organization (PLO). The sole means of attaining that, however, is to exert enough pressure on the Jewish state to make it accept such an accord. It was largely at the behest of Giscard d'Estaing that the European Council . . . adopted a resolution approving self-determination for Palestine. [1981, p. 590]

Given the present temper of the Israeli people, any such dealing with the PLO seems out of the question. However, there is little doubt that respect for the wisdom of American policies would increase markedly in Western Europe if the United Stated induced Israel to accept some other measures that are high on George Ball's (1980, pp. 251–54) priority list: "insisting that Israel cease its settlement policy," and providing for "genuine Palestinian participation in the major governing functions of the area"—two measures he thinks would not actually endanger the security of Israel, and "an unqualified acceptance of ultimate self-determination," which he thinks would not endanger Israeli security if accompanied by "demilitarization of a new Palestinian state for at least an agreed term of years while peaceful relationships develop, elaborate technical arrangements for surveillance that will assure Israel against the possibility of surprise attack, and even the possible establishment of an American military presence in the area.'' (For a much fuller analysis of the psychological aspects of the Arab–Israeli conflict, see White, 1977.)

• *Consistency, continuity, and credibility.* In that respect President Carter, with all his good intentions, failed. He created an image of himself, among our allies, as inconsistent, unwilling to pursue respectfully enough the successful policies of his predecessors, and in some ways not fully credible. He attempted too much in improving on the Vladivostok agreement and then abandoned the attempt; in the Vance–Gromyko communiqué he began a most promising cooperation with the USSR on a settlement of the Arab–Israeli issue, and then abandoned it; he flattered the Shah and then seemed to leave him in the lurch. Most of his reversals were probably wise, but it would have been better, in that case, not to start out so boldly on a course that might have to be reversed.

The result was to alienate, unnecessarily, opponents as well as allies. Vacillation was a frequent Soviet charge against Carter, and his reversals undoubtedly sustained and increased their paradoxical feeling that in this respect they would rather deal with a conservative President such as Nixon, because with a conservative ''we at least know where he stands.''

Rapport with Actual and Potential Friends in the Third World

There are at least three hard-nosed reasons why our own national self-interest makes it important to have many friends in the Third World: access to oil; feasible logistics in case of war; and reducing the number of inflamed trouble spots, in which anti-Americanism is one component, that might be starting points for a small war or a big one. The Middle East illustrates all three. It is by far the world's chief source of oil, which is urgently needed especially for the industrial economies of Western Europe and Japan. It can permit or deny staging areas for our armed forces and way stations for keeping them supplied in case of a small or big war in that area, which for us is most difficult (and impossible in any case if the Soviet Union is fully involved). And, with present American policies tending to alienate even Saudi Arabia, there is a growing danger that moderate Arab regimes will change their moderate policies or be overthrown, and that a Soviet-aided Moslem coalition will emerge, intensely hostile to Israel as well as the United States, and quite possibly with enough *hubris* to start a small war that will become World War III. Or we ourselves, feeling panicky about losing access to oil and about the danger to Israel, and committed by the Carter Doctrine to use force if necessary, may inadvertently light the match that starts a conflagration.

Some of us in the West, faced with such dangers—remembering Vietnam, knowing that we have fared badly with Arabs and Iranians, seeing the upraised fists and contorted faces of anti-American demonstrators in Teheran and Islamabad, and focusing selectively on Soviet gains in Angola, Ethiopia, Yemen, and Cambodia have almost despaired of gaining or keeping rapport with the Third World. Those things make some of us wonder whether an effort to do so is worthwhile. That is an extremely one-sided picture. Certainly we have lost influence there, at least between 1961 and 1983, but there has been no net gain for the Communist world during the past two decades or so.

The bitter, almost paranoid feelings on both sides of the conflict between the USSR and Communist China; the increasing alignment of Japan with Communist China; the apprehensions generated everywhere, including the Moslem world, by the Soviet crackdowns on Czechoslovakia and Afghanistan; the independent spirit of Eurocommunism; the reversal of the tide of anti-American feeling in Black Africa, which in 1975, when Cuban troops tipped the balance in Angola, seemed ominous—these are all parts of the diminishing of Soviet influence. Peter Jay speaks of

> . . . U.N. Ambassador Andrew Young's astute perception of the appeal to Africa of mature political and economic relations with the West. Andrew Young's personal credibility in representing a new and different American attitude to Africa undoubtedly contributed importantly to the speed with which good regionalism in Africa succeeded in fostering America's geopolitical interests there. [Jay, 1980, p. 501; cf. Young, 1981, pp. 649, 652, 656, 663]

Haven't there been Soviet gains in Angola, Ethiopia, South Yemen, and Cambodia? Yes, but those are all out-of-the-way places, and even those gains are not certain. Soviet and Communist gains anywhere, even on the edge of the central Soviet empire, have tended to be precarious, as has been shown in Yugoslavia, Poland, China, Iraq, Algeria, Ghana, Guinea, Somalia, Guyana, Jamaica, Afghanistan, and possibly even Vietnam (Scalapino, 1981, p. 692). We live in an age of burgeoning nationalism, and the spirit of national independence counts against Soviet as well as Western imperialism. Socialism of some kind may be the wave of the future, but, judging by developments since 1960, neither Soviet nor American domination constitutes any such wave. If we in the West succeed in identifying ourselves with the spirit of national independence everywhere, while the Soviet Union does not, we will have gone a long way toward assuring our future.

The economic record of Communist countries has been bad enough, and that of some non-Communist countries good enough, to deflate completely, among the well-informed, the myth that Communism is the way for the less developed economies to advance most rapidly.

The comparative stagnation and slowdown of the Soviet Union's own economy in recent years (which offers a curious parallel to our own former vigor and present stagnation) has been documented by many observers. Its built-in inefficiencies are familiar to all who have experienced Soviet life at first hand. It is true that there was marked progress during the 1950s and 1960s. Robert Kaiser, describing the psychology of the younger Soviet adults, speaks of their having "lived through an extended period of peace and prosperity" and having "personally experienced a revolution (albeit now a stalled revolution)" in living standards (Kaiser, 1981, p. 504). But "during the 1970's all the important graphs charting Soviet economic progress flattened out or turned downward. . . . Most significantly, agriculture failed to develop to meet the country's growing needs (p. 506). Bialer expects "far more severe" economic pressures in the 1980s (1981, p. 533).

In Asia the picture is similar. Although in many other ways Communist China has progressed, its economic growth has been irregular and far from spectacular. According to Robert Scalapino, China's real growth rate in 1979 was about 5 percent (1980, pp. 694–95). That is a little better than India's, which was less than 4 percent, but below Japan's 6 percent and definitely below those of South Korea, Taiwan, Malaya, and Singapore (all 7 to 8 percent). Through the years Japan's economic growth has of course been far greater than China's. "The Vietnamese economy remains in a shambles" (Scalapino, 1980, p. 697), while Indonesia's has been growing at a healthy average rate of 7.5 percent (Nagorski, 1981, p. 682).

Elsewhere too the picture is similar. Poland's economy is in terrible shape, and the only East European states where there has been really notable progress are East Germany and Hungary (Kaiser, 1981, pp. 505, 513). Cuba, reportedly subsidized by the USSR at a rate of ten million dollars a day, is a headache to the USSR and no economic magnet to the rest of Latin America.

In the world as a whole the Communist economic magnet has disappeared.

A related source of attraction is the ability to extend economic aid, and here too the Western record (with other Western countries outdoing the United States in aid as a percentage of GNP) is better than the Soviet record. According to Andrew Young, "Africa's economic partners and patrons continue to be virtually exclusively Western, since the Soviet Union remains unwilling or unable to invest in Africa, or give economic aid, on any significant scale" (Young, 1981, p. 656). Saudi Arabia and Sadat's Egypt have especially valued their present and anticipated economic ties with the United States, and even China has similar felt needs. According to Andrew Nagorski the Chinese leadership "fully intends to push new programs that will require increasingly heavy doses of foreign technology, capital and management skills" (1981, p. 687).

Largely as a result of its role in two world wars, America built up a reservoir of goodwill throughout most of the world. It appeared in both wars as a nation most reluctant to fight but powerful, determined, and victorious—and on the right side—when finally aroused.

Since then there have been many grounds for ambivalence, but opinion polls in many countries have shown a surprising continuance of the old good image of the United States, even during the Vietnam war and well into the 1970s.

Related to that image is the fact that even in the Soviet Union, and even in countries that are now as overtly hostile as most of the Arab countries are, Western visitors (including this one) have often gained the impression that there was an undercurrent of goodwill toward the West in general and toward the United States in particular (White, 1965, pp. 256–58; 1966, pp. 225–26). There is often, apparently, a sense of bafflement, as if people were saying to themselves, "Why are those *good* guys, the Americans, behaving like *that*?" "Behaving like *that*" usually refers to specific current actions such as the Vietnam war, our support of the Shah, our seeming support of Israeli expansionism, or our seeming support of South Africa. Presumably even then the old good image persists in the back of many minds and could quickly come forth if our current behavior seemed to warrant it. (In Egypt the undercurrent surfaced in the form of President Sadat's surprising turn toward an American alignment, even without any clear change in our behavior, and in the popularity of that policy among the Egyptian people.)

In short, the upraised fists and contorted faces in Teheran and Islamabad were not typical of feelings in most of the Third World and may not even have represented all of what was, or could be, in the minds of those whose fists were raised.

Another psychological asset is the almost universal human desire (at least on the conscious level) for democracy as contrasted with dictatorship, together with the fairly general identification of the United States with democracy and the fairly general identification of the Soviet Union with dictatorship. Here again impressionistic evidence is supported by opinion surveys (White, 1966, pp. 221–26). The commonest political philosophy in the Third World is some variety of democratic socialism, with disapproval of the capitalism attributed to the United States and stronger disapproval of the dictatorship attributed to the USSR.

Another asset is the English language, which is now studied and understood in the Third World far more widely than Russian. (Two other Western languages, French and Spanish, are also much more widely used in the Third World than Russian.) This language asset may be far more important in the Cold War than is usually realized, since it often promotes exposure to Western-language writing, Western scholarship, and the Western mass media. For instance, it has been estimated that three American magazines, *Time, Newsweek,* and the *Reader's Digest,* together have been more important than all the official output of the U.S. Information Agency in carrying Western interpretations of current events and of the Cold War to the Third World.

Still another asset is the superiority of the West in most of the sciences, in objective scholarship, and in most of the arts. We would be leaning over backward to be modest if we did not candidly recognize that superiority. It is no reflection on the basic abilities of the Soviet peoples; it reflects rather the decimation of the old, often brilliant Russian intelligentsia by the Revolution and by Stalin and the deadening effect of the lack of intellectual and cultural freedom. It is real however, and as a result a far greater number of Third World students go to Western universities than go to Soviet universities. (That is not an unmixed blessing, since the simplistic brand of Marxism preached at the Sorbonne and at many other universities outside the United States is emphatically not pro-Western, but that does not necessarily mean it is pro-Soviet.)

Finally, and probably most important: the cautious "salami" method of expansion characteristic of the Soviet leaders seems almost sure (if in fact Afghanistan is followed by several similar actions) to evoke a great increase in fear of Soviet domination throughout the Third World. Either our own fears of such forcible Soviet expansion have been greatly exaggerated, in which case we don't need to be too much concerned, or Soviet expansion will in that way be highly counterproductive for the USSR. That is the point at which the typical counterproductiveness of aggression in general, emphasized by Stoessinger (1974) and illustrated throughout this book (see especially Chapter 12), is most relevant. If they turn out to be the aggressors that most of us now believe them to be, they will hang themselves in the minds of most of the Third World. That is, they will hang themselves if we do not make the same mistake and allow the burgeoning nationalism of this century to be mobilized against *us*.

Those are probably our most important psychological assets in the process of making and keeping friends in the Third World. Against them, of course, must be placed certain liabilities, such as the curiously persistent Third World habit of referring to us, and not to the Soviet Union, as "imperialists" (or even as "imperialism"), their underestimation of our progress toward social justice (White, 1966, pp. 217–18, 226–27), realistic perceptions of the "obsessive anti-Communism" that is now resurgent in the United States, and their realistic or exaggerated perceptions of our real sins (in Vietnam, in Iran, in the West Bank, and elsewhere). On balance, though, it seems clear that our assets are greater.

That is not only a reassuring thought; it is a thought we would do well to keep in mind for the sake of peace. Our participation in the Vietnam war was to a considerable extent based on the domino theory—the idea that if we did not save South Vietnam from falling to Communism, Communism would spread like a row of falling dominoes, or like a fire or an epidemic, in the rest of Southeast Asia and probably elsewhere. Events have shown that there wás some truth in that idea, but not much; the North Vietnamese Communists did take over Laos and Cambodia, but at this writing they have not gone farther. The anxious Western image of the Third World as a tinderbox soaked in kerosene that would burst into flame if a spark from one successful Communist takeover touched it now seems greatly exaggerated. It now looks as if we would have been wiser to let indigenous forces in Vietnam take their course without interference by us and to rely on our many nonmilitary assets, rather than on force, to keep the spread from going much farther. Perhaps the same applies to future occasions on which we might be over-fearful of a spread of Communism and actually hasten its spread by casting ourselves in the role of the villain who uses force to oppose it. We need both a broad perspective that recognizes how relatively unimportant in the power balance the Third World itself is (except for oil) in comparison with Western Europe and Japan and a realistic appreciation of the psychological danger in using force to coerce any Third World country.

Then what can we do to make and keep Third World friends? There are a number of principles that seem fairly obvious:

Respect their independence. We should share, in words as well as actions, the Third World countries' opposition to every form of imperialism, including, of course, Soviet imperialism. We might remind them of our own War of Independence. We must not only refrain from actions that might even look like coercion of the majority in any country (e.g. El Salvador) but do what we can to restrain others from doing the same thing (e.g. in Namibia and the West Bank). It is wiser to wait for the Soviet Union to make that psychological mistake and then to capitalize on it.

Define aggression clearly, and be honest enough to see that some contemplated action by us is aggression. The very suggestion that we ourselves ever have committed or ever could commit aggression is so distasteful to some of us that we reject it out of hand as unpatriotic nonsense. That is the moral self-image in its most virulent, most dangerously self-deceiving form. We have done it, and we probably will do it again and again unless we learn to recognize a contemplated act of aggression for what it is, to call it by its right name, and to anticipate the probable perception of it by the rest of the world, before we do it.

That is not just a matter of morality—the fundamental virtue of being honest with ourselves. As we have seen, it also underlies the extremely practical virtue of empathy. Denying, ignoring, or rationalizing an aggressive act by oneself leads to not realizing that many others will see the act clearly, will not put it in the defensive context that we put it in, and because of their own inner needs will probably greatly exaggerate the heinous nature of what we are doing. It is chiefly for that reason that, as Stoessinger has said and as this book has illustrated many times (the evidence is summarized in Chapter 12), in the long run there is probably no other form of international behavior as counterproductive as aggression.

As an aid to self-honesty some clear definition of aggression, which can then be applied as stringently to our own behavior as to that of our opponents, is needed. It is our first line of defense against inadvertently using a double standard that automatically puts the best interpretation on what we do and the worst on what our opponents do. One such definition is presented and discussed in Chapter 13. Briefly stated, it is that aggression consists of using force, or threatening to use force, against the majority in any other country. There are other definitions of course, but the nature of the definition is less important than the requirement that it should be clear, so that if we apply it to our opponents' actions we will apply it with equal rigor to our own.

Pull away from any dictatorship or oligarchy that has lost the willing support of a majority of its own people. This is not a counsel of perfection. It is not equivalent to the utopian proposition that we should never give any kind of aid to a dictator or oligarchy. Some dictators are popular; Hitler was until at least 1939, and Lloyd Free's survey showed that Castro was at the time of our Bay of Pigs fiasco (Cantril, 1967, pp. 1–5). Some have domestic and foreign policies that, on balance, deserve approval. In any case, since most of the Third World countries are much less democratic than the West—democracy being a plant of slow growth, nurtured by prosperity, education, and long practice (Almond and Coleman, 1960)—a policy of aiding only democracies would doom us to ineffectiveness in most of the Third World. That does not mean we should condone the ugliest manifestations of dictatorship, such as the use of torture. It does mean we should not make our kind of democracy the first or only criterion of our willingness to help, especially when we have good evidence that the real alternative is a worse kind of dictatorship.

On the other hand, the harebrained enterprise of trying to shore up a dictator who has begun to be rejected by most of his own people is quite a different matter. That is the stupidest of all ways to combat Communism, as our experience with Chiang, Diem, the Shah, and others should have taught us. My own guess is that we would have been wise to pull away from Chiang by 1945 at the latest, from Diem by 1957 at the latest, and from the Shah by 1969 at the latest. We learn slowly.

Sometimes, help the non-Communist Left. When an authoritarian government, confusing land reform and other democratic measures with Communism, has decimated the ranks and discouraged the initiatives of liberals and democratic socialists, it is difficult to come to the aid of the left. In such cases (El Salvador may well be one of them), an evil less dangerous than intervention may be to leave well enough alone and do nothing to help either side. On the other hand, given the predominant approval of democratic socialism in most of the Third World, we would probably be wise to express publicly and often our preference for that kind of socialism when the alternatives are either reaction or Communism, and sometimes, when there is a viable middle group, we might back up our preference with action in support of it.

Show empathy with the felt needs and interests of every country. This means recognizing that for most of them the East–West conflict is subordinate to more immediate national concerns. As Kissinger (1968) once put it, "The problem of political legitimacy is the key to political stability in regions containing two-thirds of the world's population. . . . Nor should we define the problem as how to prevent the spread of communism. Our goal should be to build a moral consensus which can make a pluralistic world creative rather than destructive" (pp. 603–6). Peter Jay (1980), heartily endorsing those words, goes on to criticize especially American policy in the era of John Foster Dulles.

> In his thinking, preventing the spread of communism was identified overwhelmingly with the support of shaky alliance structures. . . . The underlying aspirations of peoples and areas were put to one side in the effort to create a fictitious "free world" that would hold off the Soviet Union—and for a long time "Red

China'' as well—by military force and often by political repression. [p. 488]

In milder ways we have often done the same since the days of Dulles. Andrew Young (1981) sees his own work in Africa as moving away from that tendency: ''To keep what we have gained, however, we must avoid a return to East–West analysis of events in Africa: that would return us to the days—only four short years ago—when American influence on the continent was lowest (p. 666).

Continue and expand economic aid, judiciously but generously given. Since the Third World is overwhelmingly concerned with overcoming its economic problems and achieving rapid economic progress, empathy and sympathy with it mean addressing ourselves, with some generosity, to that concern.

We are not generous now. Our economic aid is now a mere 0.19 percent of our enormous gross national product. In a world divided between rich nations, among which we are one of the richest, and other nations, in many of which poverty is pervasive and desperate, that is shamefully, embarrassingly niggardly. Even though there has often been some truth in the idea that giving to the less developed nations was ''pouring money down a rathole,'' the symbolic importance alone of something much more than 0.19 percent, as a legitimate way to gain rapport with the Third World, is surely great enough to justify it.

Induce both Israel and South Africa (if possible) to abandon the policies that most of the Third World perceives, with some reason, as imperialistic. The similarities between the two cases are interesting. Both are highly democratic (within the dominant majority or minority), highly competent, self-disciplined, economically and educationally advanced nations that in many ways we would be wise and proud to count as firm allies. Yet both are at the same time, chiefly because of fear, dominating over subjects and neighbors whom they regard, with much realism, as less advanced than themselves. Those policies are in each case, as the majority of relatively detached observers perceive them, endangering the long-term survival of the nation itself by alienating neighbors who outnumber them enormously. And those policies are perhaps the chief obstacles to rapport between the United States and two large areas of the world that are important for our own long-term survival: black Africa and the world of Islam.

Israel's fear is obvious, and South Africa's has recently become obvious (Young, 1981, pp. 658–59). It follows that a psychologically sophisticated approach would in each case necessarily include realistic and tangible ways to reduce the fear. This is not the place to discuss that at any length, but one part of the answer seems indispensable: effective demilitarization of the West Bank and the Gaza strip, chiefly in order to reduce the element of realism in the fear which Arab hostility, combined with Israel's tiny size and grotesquely vulnerable shape (within pre-1967 borders), has created. White South Africa too, outnumbered as it is, needs reassurance.

At the same time, something decisive has to be done to make Moslems and black Africans sure that there has been a major and genuine change in the present "imperialist" policies of Israel and South Africa, apparently backed by the United States. Given the momentum of those policies themselves and of the ingrained assumptions underlying them, it is hard to see any alternative to some drastic, unmistakable form of legitimate pressure by the United States—along with the needed forms of reassurance—to get those two countries to change their policies substantially. The denial of military aid that would otherwise be given is surely, under the circumstances, a legitimate form of pressure.

In sum, we in the West *do not need to use force* in ways that directly or indirectly increase the danger of nuclear war, in order to hold our own in the Third World and, in that respect, keep the Soviet Union from becoming overconfident.

CHAPTER EIGHTEEN

Forms of Tension-reduction: Arms Control

How Far Can We Trust the Russians?

"Is arms control really worth while? Sure, it would be wonderful if we could agree to reverse the arms race, and know that the Russians would live up to the agreement. But can we? When have they ever lived up to an agreement?"

For most of us in the West that is the first and greatest sticking point when we think about arms control. Those who speak in public for such things as a nuclear freeze report that the question their audiences most often ask is, "What about the Russians? How far can we trust them?"

There is a similar question on the other side. Alexei Nihkonov, described by Murrey Marder of the *Washington Post* as a "distinguished" member of Moscow's Institute of World Economy and International Affairs, said to Marder that to average Soviet citizens it would appear that "Americans are unreliable people, with whom you cannot do business and should *not* do business." According to Marder (1977, p.A2; 1981, p. A14), a great many Russians believe that President Carter deliberately trumped up the furor that was raised in the United States about the Soviet "combat brigade" in Cuba as an excuse for defaulting on the SALT II agreement that Brezhnev had signed, with Carter, after several years of strenuous negotiation with three American administrations. In their eyes Carter either did it deliberately or weakly succumbed, in order to be reelected President, to the war hysteria whipped up by the American hawks, headed by Ronald Reagan. What is the use of struggling for peace through arms control when that is the way it is going to end? How can you do business with people like that?

These are of course the normal diabolical enemy-images, expectable on both sides of any acute group conflict. Expectably, each tends to put the worst possible interpretation on the other's behavior. But that does not exclude a sizable kernel of truth in each image. An "image," as that term is used here, does not mean a delusion; it can have any degree of validity, from none at all to complete correspondence with reality, though nearly always it is somewhere between. In this case, given the exaggerated fear, the macho pride, and the anger generated by the long, malignant process of hostile interaction, it is almost a foregone conclusion that there would be a good deal of truth in the diabolical images on both sides. There is also plenty of specific evidence that in the past each side in this conflict has been largely if not wholly concerned with its own national self-interest (as perceived) and on occasion has been capable of deliberate straight-faced deception. As we have seen in Chapter 15, the Soviet decision-makers must have deliberately tried to deceive at the outset of the Korean war, in the Cuban missile crisis, and in their treatment of Amin at the outset of their intervention in Afghanistan. We Americans have done it, at least in the U-2 and Bay of Pigs affairs. That kind of thing must be recognized as, however regretably, par for the course in international affairs. Perhaps they have done it much more than we have; perhaps not.

Fortunately, we Americans have a clear answer to our unduly skeptical question, "When have they [the Russians] ever lived up to an agreement?" That question, put in that way, can only be the result of sheer ignorance, with the knowledge gap filled in by our own tendency to suspect the worst. The answer is that they have lived up to their agreements—at least the *letter* of their agreements—many times, including SALT I and up to now (though neither side has ratified the agreement) SALT II.

On that point there seems to be a consensus among well-informed American observers, Robert Einhorn, as a senior associate of the Carnegie Endowment, went into the question in some detail in an article in *Foreign Policy* (1981–82). His major conclusion with regard to SALT I (pp. 30–31):

> Officials involved in monitoring SALT compliance in the Nixon, Ford and Carter administrations acknowledge that the Soviets have tried to exploit ambiguities and have disregarded U.S. views on the spirit of the accords. But they argue that little basis exists for the charge that actual violations have occurred. They also maintain that they promptly raised questionable activities with Moscow and that in all such cases U.S. concerns were allayed.

Strobe Talbott, *Time* correspondent in Moscow, says that

> . . .the prevailing view of experts on verification is that, thanks to recent technical advances in the United States's ability to monitor Soviet actions from space and around the periphery of the USSR, those remote means need be supplemented by only the sort of limited ''cooperative measures'' that the USSR now seems willing to consider. . . . The Soviet Union has been at least as careful to abide by the letter [of its agreements] as the United States. . . . Limited on-site inspection should be enough, and they seem willing to consider it now. [1983, p. 27]

In the case of SALT II the record is more impressive since (as President Reagan's willingness to abide by its provisions indicates) those provisions probably favored both sides, and certainly the American side. In Adam Yarmolinsky's judgment (1982) ''the weight of concessions'' was on the Soviet side in the negotiation of SALT II, and Talbott (p. 19) declares that SALT II slowed down the ''juggernaut'' of Soviet production of MIRVs. On the same point Leslie Gelb, the *New York Times* Washington correspondent on national security affairs, judges that SALT II favors the United States because without it the Soviet Union, with its ''open production lines'' and heavy missiles capable of carrying many warheads, could have added more nuclear weapons far more quickly than we could.

The same cannot be said about compliance with the Biological Weapons Convention (BWC). Both in the case of the suspected production of anthrax-producing materials in Sverdlovsk and in the case of the strongly suspected provision of lethal mycotoxins to Vietnamese troops, the Soviet Union has not been forthcoming in providing the evidence that was sought (Iklé, 1982; Einhorn, 1981–82, p. 32). There is reason therefore to infer that in these cases it has something to hide and perhaps that it is likely to attempt deception when methods of sure detection do not exist and it thinks it can get away with it.

There is a clear lesson to be drawn. As Einhorn puts it (p. 38), we should in general try to ''make treaty obligations as detailed, quantifiable, and unambiguous as possible,'' although ''sometimes U.S. negotiators will insist on imprecise formulations to preserve U.S. flexibility. In SALT II the United States preferred not to define precisely the key term 'launcher' largely because of the risk that a specific definition might limit future basing options for the MX missile'' (pp. 38–39). (We too, like the Soviets, are evidently vigilant to make sure our own power interests are not ignored in any negotiation—and that is probably good, but it does not exclude a number of mutual-benefit, "positive-sum games.")

What if they do cheat, as they apparently have in the case of biological weapons such as "yellow rain" (Iklé, 1982, p. A17)? That is serious, but there are things to do, such as bringing them before an international supervisory group, publicizing what they have done internationally, and, as a last resort, renouncing the treaty they have violated—which, if it is based on mutual self-interest, experience has shown they would try to avoid. Experience has shown too that militarily significant violations hardly ever occur (Einhorn, 1981–82, pp. 33–34).

More basically, what we can build on is our knowledge that the Soviet negotiators urgently, emotionally want peace. For that and other reasons, such as wanting to look effectively peaceful in the eyes of their own people, we can hope for their agreement on what we believe would most effectively promote peace, if our case is sound and we present it well.

One answer to our initial question is, then, this: We *can* trust the Russians to do what they think is in their self-interest, as they perceive it, and there are several things—above all, the avoidance of nuclear war—that are overwhelmingly in their interest as well as ours.

Six Myths and a Blind Spot—a Review

What results of negotiation are both most desirable, from the standpoint of peace, and most possible?

Before trying to answer that question it will be worthwhile to gather up all that is most relevant in previous chapters of this book and relate it to arms control negotiation. Six misperceptions stand out:

1. *The nearly universal myth of diabolical, cold-blooded aggression by "the enemy."* Kennan talks about lemmings rushing blindly to suicide in the sea. A more accurate image is Matthew Arnold's "ignorant armies clashing by night"—armies believing that they are innocent and have been attacked by diabolical enemies. Each is driven by fear. Usually each is partly right, but usually too there is much misperception on each side, both about its own inno-

cence and about the diabolical nature of its enemies. There are Hitlers, but they are rare.

We have met the myth many, many times in this book: on both sides in World War I (Chapter 13); on both sides in the Cold War (Chapter 15); in Western exaggerations of the cold-blooded villainy of the Soviet intervention if Afghanistan and the long Soviet arms buildup (Chapter 2); in the tendency on both sides of the Cold War to assimilate the enemy-image to memories of Hitler and Nazi aggression (Chapter 12); in the worst-case thinking on both sides as to the power and hostility of the opponent (Chapters 3 and 10); in the many historical examples of aggression motivated not by cold-blooded ambition but mainly by fear (Chapter 8); in Deutsch's concept of a malignant process of hostile interaction, which brings out the worst on both sides and partly justifies each in being afraid of the other (Chapter 8); in the concept of tension and the elements of exaggerated fear, wounded pride, and anger that compose it (Chapter 8); in the concepts of projection (Chapter 10) and the injured-innocence mechanism (Chapter 12) that sustain the diabolical enemy-image; in the Western tendency to ignore the motives of self-interest that would deter the Soviet Union both from a nuclear first strike and from any cold-blooded invasion of Western Europe (Chapter 4); in the persistent tendency not to empathize with the longing for peace, the understandable fear, or the understandable anger on the other side (Chapter 11); and in the scenarios illustrating how a nuclear war might start on the basis of exaggerated fear (accidental war or desperate preemption) rather than deliberate desire for conquest (Chapter 5).

Two relationships of all this to arms control are clear. The causes of war lie deeper than the weapons with which it is fought (Chapter 6), but the process of negotiation, if done in good faith with a genuine effort to empathize and to reach fair agreements, is itself a major way to reduce the fear and anger elements in tension.

2. *The Soviets' myth of aggressive Western-and-Chinese encirclement.* Their fear is surely excessive. Arbatov insists that the USSR is heavily outgunned if all of its "potential enemies," including China and Japan, are taken into account (Chapter 3). His fear is understandable. We would be fearful too if surrounded by so many hostile neighbors, whose hostility must seem inexplicable to someone who could not admit even to himself that his country

had had a hand in creating it—inexplicable except on the basis of aggressively hostile intentions (Chapter 12, the injured-innocence mechanism). But that is precisely why it can be called a myth. What Arbatov and the great majority of his countrymen apparently cannot see is the genuinely defensive motives of the encircling countries. The encirclement exists, but it is not essentially aggressive. He does not have to fear that all of the USSR's potential enemies will pounce on it at once in a concerted attack. The ones that are farthest away from each other (e.g. China and Western Europe) probably would not even fight together in a war that the Soviet Union started.

The myth of aggressive encirclement is relevant to arms control in that the West should try to understand how natural it is (even if mistaken) for the Soviet Union to want all of the West's potentially aggressive arms to be taken into account, including those of Britain and France, in any systematic consideration of the East–West arms balance.

3. *The hawks' myth of Soviet strategic superiority.* Their fear also is surely excessive. Soviet conventional superiority is a fact. Soviet strategic superiority is not. It is a complex, ambiguous, controversial question (Chapter 3). Leslie Gelb's view deserves repetition (1982, p. 18), "The experts who look at all of these factors call the strategic balance a draw. Put another way, I have yet to meet a senior American military officer involved in this subject who would trade the American arsenal for the Soviet one. Only those experts who focus exclusively on Soviet superiority in land-based missiles think otherwise." Apparently the experts who "focus exclusively on Soviet superiority in land-based missiles" have been indulging in selective inattention, consciously or half-consciously, on a very large scale. They conveniently ignore the American superiority, qualitative if not quantitative, in the other two legs of the triad: submarine-launched ballistic missiles (SLBMs) and bombers. (For elaboration see Cox, 1982, chapter on "Misestimating Soviet Power"; Cordesman, 1982, pp. 41, 47, 49).

The resulting distortion is serious, since President Reagan has picked it up, speaks as if it is a self-evident fact, and has apparently convinced most of the American public that it is a fact. That means that not only he and his hand-picked advisers but probably a considerable majority of the American public would be dissatisfied with a freeze or any other agreement that did not change the existing balance and therefore, as he would probably put it, "left us in a position of inferiority."

4. *The Western rationalists' myth of Soviet nuclear restraint even after a possible war has started.* Western observers of the Soviet Union who (like this one) stress the mirror-image concept and the "human" side of the Soviet decision-makers are often unaware of an ominous aspect of Soviet military thinking that we should be taking with deadly seriousness: their all-or-none style of thinking about a possible major war. Although fully aware of the horrors of nuclear war and anxious to avoid it if they possibly can, the Soviet strategists have apparently decided that *if* they are "forced" to fight by a Western attack their response must be an immediate, all-out offensive-and-defensive "crushing rebuff" of the Western aggressors, including, if there are the slightest indications of a Western intention to resort to nuclear weapons, a preemptive counterforce attack on the United States. In that case they think they should in effect jump quickly to the top or near the top of the "escalation ladder" that many Western analysts have assumed to be fundamental in the thinking of strategists on both sides.

Those Western analysts have tended to assume that the Soviet decision-makers, being as rational as the Western analysts themselves and equally anxious to avoid the totally devastating city-busting type of nuclear war, would cling to the lower rungs of the ladder as long as possible, fighting some kind of limited nuclear war rather than courting total destruction by leaping quickly to the top or near it. The nuclear fighting might be limited to battlefield weapons, for instance, or to attacks on military targets (such as staging areas for troops about to invade Western Europe, supply depots, and transportation centers) other than the ultimate nation-destroying nuclear forces such as SS-18s, SS-19s and SS-20s. Therefore, they have reasoned, the United States should be prepared for various forms of "flexible response" that would deter the Soviet Union from escalating beyond whatever level they had already reached. Such a capability for flexible response would be expensive but has been seen as preferable to defeat by the USSR on any level of war, and immensely preferable to total nuclear destruction (Chapter 9). It and it alone would assure maximum "stability."

Such elaborate rational calculations now appear to suffer from a faulty underlying premise, namely that Soviet strategists are rational, in the terms in which Western analysts have defined rationality. There are important differences between their assumptions and ours, probably stemming especially from the more black-and-white, all-or-none character of their thinking and from the influence on it of the Soviet military experience in World War II. A group of Western analysts who have intensively studied the Soviet sources (including Fritz Ermarth, Benjamin Lambeth, and Edward Warner, whose writings have been reproduced in the fifth edition of Reichart and Sturm, 1982) have emphasized those underlying differences.

As they describe it the philosophy of the Soviet strategists is unabashedly a war-fighting rather than merely a war-deterring philosophy, differing in that respect from the thinking of Bernard Brodie (1946) and others in the West who have thought of nuclear war as so radically different from previous wars that almost the sole purpose of a nuclear capability should be to deter use of nuclear weapons by the other side. Soviet strategists do not counterpose war-fighting against war-deterring as many of us do; rather, they see a war-fighting capability as the best form of deterrence and, if worse comes to worst, the best way to survive (Garthoff, 1978). As Lambeth puts it, they have preferred to "stick to the more traditional notion that if you want peace prepare for war" (1982, p. 196); and Warner, stressing the Soviet lack of interest in Western definitions of stability, says that "in the Soviet view, the more powerful the USSR is, the more stable the international situation" (1982, p. 54). According to Ermarth "we should have been less hopeful that they would accept a nonthreatening form of parity and stability" (1982, p. 62). Richard Burt (1982) agrees:

> If Moscow does possess a concept of strategic stability it is not the one that has guided American defense policy or negotiation strategy at SALT. . . . Soviet strategic programs, from the deployment of countersilo ICBM forces to the orbiting of anti-satellite weapons, tend to reflect the preference for nuclear war-fighting found in Soviet literature. [p. 422]

None of this is necessarily a reason for Western negotiators to adopt the Soviet war-fighting emphasis or to judge specific proposals by that standard. In my judgment we *are* more rational in this respect and should stay that way. It is a reason, though, not to have unrealistic hopes of converting them to our concept of stability, and not to spend time trying to do so. Our negotiators can better spend their time urging specific proposals, such as deep cuts in the most dangerously destabilizing weapons, that we believe would be mutually beneficial in their frame of reference as well as in ours.

It is also a potent reason for us to avoid giving them the slightest reason to think they must preempt with their nuclear weapons and to plan our own forces with that in mind.

5. *The NATO myth of an American "nuclear umbrella."* Until 1957 the West European governments relied on the obviously enormous superiority of American nuclear weapons and on an implicit or explicit assurance that the United States would use those weapons against the USSR if it should actually invade Western Europe. They felt they could relax, more or less, under that nuclear "umbrella." The umbrella developed serious leaks when the Soviet Union launched its sputnik and successfully tested its first ICBM in 1957. Even though the leaks were well patched by America's regaining obvious nuclear superiority in the early and middle 1960s, they reappeared with the steady Soviet strategic progress and gaining of a potent retaliatory capability in the late 1960s and the 1970s (Smoke, 1982, pp. 115–16, 120–24).

Now, with the Soviet retaliatory capability at least equal to that of the United States, the umbrella is torn to shreds. Few people in their right mind would expect the United States to commit nuclear suicide by starting a nuclear exchange to save Western Europe (cf. Freedman, 1981–82; Burt, 1982, p. 421). The time has come for candor on that subject and for building a West European sense of security on a more honest and solid basis—namely, on a recognition of all the considerations of hard national self-interest that would keep the Soviet Union from wanting to invade Western Europe (Chapter 4), a recognition of all the considerations of self-interest that should lead the West and the USSR to a joint declaration condemning first use of nuclear weapons and to drastic restriction or abandonment of first-strike weapons (see below, pp. 310–11), and a steady maintaining of adequate conventional defense of Western Europe with full American cooperation (Chapters 7 and 17).

If the pretense of an umbrella is not abandoned, it will be a classical instance of the momentum of preexisting beliefs (Chapter 12).

6. *The nearly universal myth of peace through nuclear parity.* The "grotesque redundancy" of nuclear weapons today and the consequent opportunity on both sides to adopt safely a policy of minimal nuclear deterrence, unilaterally if multilateral cuts prove impossible, has been a main theme of this book (Chapters 6, 7, 12). It needs no repetition here. What needs repetition is the irrationality of the bland, unexamined assumption, still overwhelmingly predominant on both sides (and in the West predominant even among a great many liberal, peace-minded intellectuals), that parity—usually called "balance"—matters, in the nuclear as in the conventional area. It does not. Parity, apart from the equal need of both sides to maintain an invulnerable second-strike capability, is irrelevant. And if it is allowed to stand in the way of deep cuts it is dangerous. The West is aware that when two boys with matches are standing in a closed room with gasoline up to their ankles it does not matter which one has ten matches and which has five. Most of us have not yet fully seen the inevitable logical consequence that when arms control is being negotiated a "balance" in matches is irrelevant and that a ratio of ten to two, against oneself, could be cheerfully accepted.

THE BLIND SPOT: Not seeing the opponents' or the onlookers' perception of one's own country. Nearly everywhere there is a striking, and very dangerous, absence of empathy (Chapter 11). For us in the West the most critically important forms of it are our grossly inadequate recognition of the Soviet decision-makers' longing for peace (Chapter 4), their genuine fear of nuclear aggression by encircling enemies (Chapter 3 and 9), and their natural, expectable anger at some of the things we have done and are now doing (Chapters 8–12).

The importance of realistic empathy in arms control negotiations is obvious. It includes hard-nosed recognition of the ways in which opponents may be trying to deceive, outwit, or outmaneuver one's own side. More importantly, it includes recognition of the hierarchy of their goals and values—what they care about most and what they care about, but not so much. Creative, integrative bargaining requires, first, clear recognition of one's own hierarchy of goals, with firmness and persistence in seeking those at the top of the list, and then understanding of their hierarchy, in order to put the two together and play an intelligent mutual-benefit, positive-sum game (Pruitt, 1981; Fisher and Ury, 1981).

When we in the West think about the Soviet fear of us there is a key element that we often overlook completely. It is the fear we are now almost certainly creating by increasing our first-strike capability *more rapidly* than they are increasing theirs—and, from their point of view, needlessly.

History has shown that the rapidity of the upward change in an opponent's relative strength is perhaps even more important than its actual level as a cause of the kind of unhealthy fear that can lead to preventive or preemptive aggression. Germany's fear in 1914 of the increasing size of the Russian Army and of increasing encirclement of Germany by the Russian-French-British Entente, combining with Austrian disintegration to produce an acute future imbalance in Germany's disfavor, is an outstanding case in point. Another is our own recent and present fear of the Soviet Union's coming from behind in nuclear strength, overtaking us, and, as many of us have seen it, threatening to surpass us. At that stage the injured-innocence mechanism jumps into operation: "Since they know we don't threaten them, why are they threatening us?" (Chapter 12).

That is just the kind of anxiety we must be creating in Soviet minds now with our plans for a rapid increase throughout the 1980s in weapons that could be used in a first strike, such as the MX, the Pershing II, the cruise missile, and the Trident II, over and above what they apparently regard as a level of rough equivalence now. In a crisis, will that heightened level of fear and suspicion make them more likely to preempt (Chapters 4 and 5)? If so, isn't it one of the strongest reasons why arms negotiation now should, as a minimum, result in some kind of freeze?

Taking such psychological factors into account, what should our own priorities in arms negotiation be? The following six measures, in the following tentative order of importance, are suggested here:

1. *Deep cuts in destabilizing nuclear weapons*. Preferably they should consist of drastic, equal, visible destruction of such weapons (Admiral Gayler's proposal) in successive stages (cf. Charles Osgood's GRIT).

2. *A drastically lowered ratio of warheads to missiles*. Senator Gore's proposal. Its purpose, like that of deep cuts in destabilizing weapons, is to make a nuclear first strike less at-

tractive by greatly reducing the prospect that, with a first strike, either side could nearly eliminate the other's land-based first-strike capability.

3. *A joint no-first-use statement.* The Soviets have agreed; it's now up to us.

4. *A modified freeze agreement.* The psychological value of the freeze movement is great, as a way of giving a strong impetus to the government in good directions, but the wording of the freeze resolution passed by Congress in 1983 can be improved on.

5. *A comprehensive test ban* (CTB). The limited test ban agreed on in 1963 has not yet been extended to include underground tests. It should be.

6. *A tradeoff.* An example would be elimination of all or most of the Soviet SS-20s in return for elimination of all or most of the West's Pershing II and ground-launched cruise missiles (GLCMs). What West Europe fears most is the Soviet SS-20s, and what the Soviet Union fears most is the Pershing IIs and the GLCMs.

The rest of this chapter elaborates on some of the pros and cons of these six, from a psychological point of view.

Deep Cuts in Destabilizing Nuclear Weapons

The proposal of Admiral Gayler (pronounced "Gighler"; the *New York Times Magazine*, April 25, 1982) is perhaps the most creative and hopeful idea in the arms control area that anyone has contributed for many years. It deserves to be put first in any list of what we should aim for. As former commander-in-chief of United States forces in the Pacific and former director of the National Security Agency, his credentials are as impeccable as General Taylor's. His proposal actually solves (or largely solves) three crucial problems about which arms negotiators have wrangled endlessly: the problem of verification, the problem of equality (which should not be crucial but which is crucial, psychologically, as long as people think it is), and the problem of classification (e.g. which weapons should be counted as "strategic"). And it is, or should be, fully acceptable to both sides.

The Gayler proposal is this:

Let each side turn in an equal number of explosive nuclear devices. *Let each side choose* the weapons it wishes to turn in, whether missile warheads, bombs, or artillery shells. Each weapon would count the same—as one device. . . . A nuclear device is uniquely identifiable and can be counted without error when turned in; thus there is full verification without intrusive inspection in either country. Since each side chooses the weapons it wishes to turn in, there can be no problem about what is fair. And since all explosive fission devices count equally, we have no arguments about how the weapons should be classified. *Self-interest will make each side turn in its more vulnerable weapons. This is good.* As we now stand, both the United States and the Soviet Union have relatively vulnerable land-based strategic missiles, mounted in fixed silos. It would be logical for both sides to start giving up these weapons, while retaining their less vulnerable strategic bombers and virtually invulnerable nuclear-armed submarines. In this way, the temptation of either side to fire first in time of crisis, lest it lose its weapons to an enemy who attacks first, will be reduced. The ''hair trigger'' character of the nuclear forces, the most dangerous aspect of the present situation, will be eliminated. [Gayler, 1982, p. 49; emphasis added]

One possible objection arises immediately: Wouldn't each side, in addition to trying to retain its least vulnerable weapons, try to retain the biggest, most destructive ones? That objection is largely if not entirely answered by a technical fact that is not widely known. As Gayler puts it:

The essence of a nuclear weapon is its fissionable material. All else is mere supporting hardware—missile or cannon or airplane, guidance system or re-entry shield or arming and fusing. Moreover, all nuclear weapons have roughly the same amount of fissionable material. In a ''small'' weapon, the fission element accounts for the weapon's entire explosive yield; in a megaton-range weapon, which depends on fusion, a similar quantity of fissionable material acts only as the spark for the enormously greater succeeding explosion. Hence, in counting the weapons to be eliminated from the nuclear arsenals of both sides, all weapons can be treated alike. [p. 88]

Isn't this idea too momentous, and too new and startling, to be quickly agreed on? Probably it is. Again, though, Gayler has an answer. He proposes that a start be made by each side's turning in a relatively small number of weapons, perhaps fifty, to test the system and establish confidence. They would turn in some such number to a central body, perhaps a joint Soviet–American commission established for the purpose, perhaps with a third party brought in as referee. And the weapons need not be destroyed, though their neutralization should be visible to all. Their fissionable material could be converted to nuclear power for peaceful purposes (p. 49). Once confidence is established there could be agreement on a schedule according to which a very large reduction, "say 10,000 devices each," would be achieved.

There is some resemblance here to Charles Osgood's GRIT proposal (Graduated and Reciprocated Initiatives in Tension-reduction; Osgood, 1962). Osgood's proposal differs in that it does not require negotiation and agreement before starting. He suggests "initiatives" on our side—taking what could become the leadership of the world in a reversal of the malignant process of hostile interaction—that would at first be unilateral (yes, unilateral) in the justified hope that the other side would recognize such a tangible proof of the West's determination to reverse the arms race and would follow suit with initiatives of its own. There is at least one successful historical precedent in President Kennedy's initiatives after the Cuban missile crisis (Etzioni, 1970). The tension-reduction process could then acquire the kind of psychological momentum that the arms race now has.

There is ample reason to put Gayler's proposal first, in view of the probably great resistance of both America's leaders and the American public to any initiative that could be called unilateral and therefore, it would be generally assumed, risky. Gayler's proposal is *not* unilateral in any way. The public has not yet accepted the full practical consequences of the analogy of the boys with matches in the gasoline-filled room. However, if the Soviet side were to reject Gayler's proposal (it probably would not, if the proposal were properly presented), Osgood's GRIT would appear to represent the second-best chance for the human race to ensure its own survival.

A Drastically Lowered Ratio of Warheads to Missiles

A terrible mistake was made in the late 1960s (Lawrence Weiler and others argued vigorously against it) when we ourselves introduced and deployed that terribly destabilizing weapon, the MIRV. Henry Kissinger has fully recognized that mistake and has also virtually acknowledged that he himself was mistaken in pushing it at the time (1983; Drew, 1983a, p. 40). Before Kissinger climbed on the anti-MIRV bandwagon, Senator Gore had taken the lead in Congress to mobilize sentiment in favor of a drastic reduction and ultimate elimination of MIRVs and had made such headway that the idea was adopted in principle by the Scowcroft Commission appointed by Reagan in 1983, apparently with majority approval in Congress. (Incongruously, it was combined in a package with the MX—a MIRVed MX. The incongruity was widely noticed and is hard to explain; for a semi-explanation see Elizabeth Drew, 1983a and b.)

The logic behind the change in philosophy is not immediately evident, but it is convincing once it is seen. It is this:

First there is the basic principle that the danger of nuclear war is increased whenever either side is confronted by a nuclear arsenal on the other side that is both powerful and vulnerable. The power creates fear and the vulnerability creates a temptation to reduce the fear by striking first. That is what "destabilizing" means. A weapon that is both powerful and vulnerable is destabilizing. That is the principle underlying the urgent need for deep cuts in destabilizing weapons. It applies here too.

There is then some really simple arithmetic. A common rule of thumb in present military thinking is that two warheads are, on the average, under favorable conditions, needed to knock out one missile-launcher and the missile it contains. If an opponent has 1,000 launchers you need 2,000 warheads in order to knock out nearly all of them. The ratio—two to one in this case—is what matters. But with MIRVs each side can readily have as many as six warheads for every launcher on the other side. That is essentially the situation now. But if the ratio could be reduced to one-to-one by having only single-warhead "Midgetman" missiles, neither side would dare to strike first, since it would know that many launchers would be left over, even after its first strike, and that it would then be in terrible danger.

The chief valid argument against the Midgetman is probably its cost, which has been estimated as high as $50 billion over a period of years. But that is incomparably less than the cost of a nuclear war.

A Joint No-first-use Statement

Obviously, if neither side resorts to nuclear weapons first, there will be no nuclear war. Obviously too, if neither side resorts to nuclear weapons first *even if it thinks it is losing in a conventional war* (Chapter 5), there will be no nuclear war. There should be a clear-eyed comparison of those two disasters. Macho pride is entirely on the side of the "Masada complex," which chooses courageous national suicide rather than defeat. Common sense is on the other side today, and elementary morality is on the side of not choosing self-destruction when it could mean murdering most of the rest of the human race. But that is not the real issue.

The purpose of a no-first-use declaration has often been misunderstood. Some have quite naturally asked, "Could we expect the Soviet Union to believe us, just because we said we wouldn't be the first to do it? And could we believe them just because they said it?" The answer is no in both cases; neither side could or would rely solely on the other's words. There is no valid comparison between this and the fatuous Kellogg–Briand Peace Pact of the late 1920s.

The point is: *If* we have sincerely given up the obsolete and utterly crazy idea of being the first to cross the firebreak between conventional and nuclear war—obsolete and crazy now that the other side has such an overwhelming nuclear retaliatory capability—we could clear the air and reduce unnecessary suspicion by being willing to say so. The Soviets can legitimately reason: If the American are straining their economy in order to build many new first-strike weapons and aren't willing to join us even in *saying* they wouldn't use them, we can expect the worst.

Actually, of course, our actions rather than our words are what they will notice most and take most seriously. If we were to say we had renounced first use and at the same time were to continue to build the MX, the Pershing II, the land-based cruise missile, and Trident II, they would have every reason to distrust our words. What is likely to impress them, and should help mightily in reducing tension, is a combination of words and actions, each reinforcing the other.

There is also the major value of a genuine no-first-use policy, actions as well as words, in its psychological effect on ourselves. As long as neither is in line with common sense, the ideas of the American public on the subject are likely to remain befuddled, and we ourselves might in a time of crisis commit the worst of all blunders—and crimes.

(For a much more detailed arguing of the same case, see Bundy, Kennan, McNamara, and Smith, 1982; and for a German reply, see Kaiser, Leber, Mertes, and Schulze, 1982. For a French reply, Rose, 1982.)

A Modified Freeze Agreement

Unfortunately the startling success of the freeze movement in the United States can be attributed partly to the mildness of the freeze resolution in Congress. It asks for no cuts at all, let alone deep cuts, although without cuts the redundancy of nuclear weapons in the world will remain as grotesque as ever. It asks only for equal, bilateral agreement, with no challenging of the nearly universal assumption that both equality and bilateral agreement are essential. Surely on the level of political action that was wise. The leaders of the movement were right to ask for only that much, since they had to demonstrate that at least that much is already wanted by a considerable majority of the American people. Doing so made possible the unquestionable majority support that the movement needed in order to become a political power. Equally surely, though, the movement now needs to go further. It must educate and agitate for some things (such as the three discussed above) that could actually reverse the arms race and more effectively fend off the danger of nuclear war.

For those Americans who still doubt the wisdom of even such a mild agreement, the two chief sticking points are probably the question of verifiability and the question of our being, as President Reagan said, frozen into a position of inferiority. Both are important and need to be continually discussed. Both have been discussed at some length in this book, verifiability at the beginning of this chapter and the nonexistence of strategic inferiority in Chapter 3 and earlier in this chapter.

There remains the question of whether the freeze resolution in its present form can be improved without endangering its present Congressional support. It probably can, at least by recognizing more fully the transcendent importance of freezing, or cutting, the first-strike capability on both sides. The nature of present strength is more important than its overall level, and the nature of present weapons can be greatly improved from the standpoint of stability, even if their overall level remains the same.

A Comprehensive Test Ban (CTB)

One of President Kennedy's triumphs, during the brief period of relaxation following the Cuban missile crisis of 1962, was the limited test ban (LTB), which forbade nuclear explosions in the air, under water, or in outer space, leaving only underground tests still permissible. Apparently there have been no serious violations of the LTB since then. Why not finish now the job he began?

Although interest in the subject has waned, informed arms controllers still want to finish the job. Alva Myrdal, for instance, speaks of how the hopes of 1963 remain unfulfilled (1976, p. xxiv) and regrets that the public has been "too easily satisfied with driving the tests underground" (p. 95). Cox (1982) thinks a CTB is "very important" and discusses how feasible adequate verification now is. "The Soviets are prepared to sign such a treaty tomorrow. After years of haggling about adequacy of verification measures, an important breakthrough was made in 1978. The Soviet Union accepted, in principle, new procedures for verification proposed by the United States and Britain" (p. 171).

Resistance would probably come not from the Soviets but from our own military men, who might well be bent on testing the various new types of weaponry, especially weapons capable of a first strike, that are scheduled for development during the next few years. If a person assumes that we are behind and need to catch up, that argument makes some sense. If it is assumed that we are not or that parity in this respect does not matter, it makes no sense at all. In fact, the psychological danger of increasing unhealthy fear in the USSR, thereby increasing the likelihood that they would preempt at a time of crisis, seems much more important than any limitation of our deterrent power that an inability to test those weapons might entail. (The Soviets are developing new weapons too, and it is not certain that ours need testing more than theirs do.)

A Tradeoff of Long-range Theater
Nuclear Forces (LRTNF) in Europe

One such trade-off, for instance, would be elimination of all or most of the Soviet SS-20s in return for the nondeployment of the West's Pershing II and ground-launched cruise missiles (GLCMs). That would resemble President Reagan's ''zero option.'' A similar and probably much more negotiable trade would be the one Paul Nitze and Yuri Kvitsinsky tentatively agreed on in 1982, which was disapproved at that time by both governments. Many in Europe think the disapproval could be reconsidered. Still another is Andropov's recent proposal that Soviet SS-20s might be reduced, if no new American weapons were deployed, to approximately the level represented numerically by the British and French intermediate-range forces (INF).

There are many complexities here that cannot be gone into in a book of this type. Since both Western Europe and the western USSR were already subject to quick and total destruction by the ICBMs on each side, which can be as easily used at intermediate range as at intercontinental range, the military side of the whole issue is probably much less important than the psychological and political side. The Soviets would like to wean Western Europe away from its alliance with the United States by appearing to be more forthcoming than the Americans, and the Americans in the present Administration want the reverse, in order to consolidate the alliance while also ensuring the deployment of at least some of the cruise missiles if not also the Pershing IIs. There is room here for the playing of some interesting positive-sum games.

What peace-oriented Americans most need to keep in mind, though, is the speed and the incredible accuracy of the Pershing II, which understandably strike terror into the hearts of Soviet decision-makers who want at least their command-and-control system not to be totally destroyed in a first strike (Steinbruner, 1981–82). The argument that this greatly increases the anger and the unhealthy type of fear on the Soviet side, and consequently the danger of preemption in a crisis, is very strong. Cruise missiles are dangerous in a special way too; their accuracy, difficulty of detection, and uninspectable character raise acute questions about their desirability from the standpoint of peace, though probably not as much question as is raised by the inherently war-promoting nature of the Pershing II. The entire assumption of the present Administration that deployment of these new weapons is necessary in order to demonstrate Western ''resolve'' has to be challenged. A trade in which the SS-20s were greatly reduced, while we were able to slough off such dubious weapons, could represent an important increase in the chances of peace. (If we could eliminate the MX—a mutual-harm weapon if there ever was one—it would be even better.)

For a much more detailed treatment of various possible mutual-benefit tradeoffs, taking Soviet points of view into account, and for a wholesome reminder of the importance of not raising public hopes too high, as SALT I did, see Gelb (1983).

CHAPTER NINETEEN

Other Ways to Reduce Tension

One trouble with simple prescriptions for peace is that they usually sound like (and are) platitudes. In spite of that, or perhaps because of it, they often conflict or seem to conflict. Don't aggress, don't dominate, don't appease; be strong, be firm, be friendly; communicate, cooperate; combat injustice wherever it exists, but without interfering in the domestic affairs of other countries; build strong international organizations, but be sure they are the kind that doesn't diminish our independence too much.

Yet the subject could hardly be more important. The point has been made (Chapter 6) that even arms control, urgent as it is, is likely to be unattainable or unenforceable unless fairly drastic tension-reduction has already been achieved, mainly in other ways; and the broader point has been made (Chapter 8) that, in view of the present advanced state of East–West tension, drastic reduction of the tension is even more urgent than deterrence, if and when a choice has to be made between them.

Then how can we get real tension-reduction?

One approach that seems appropriate at this point is a longish list of many concrete things that can be done or not done, with references back to the chapters in which the rationale underlying them is discussed. That could provide many starting points for thinking of the most practical sort. Readers may want to add some of their own and subtract from the list the items they disagree with. The length of the list should then make it possible for each reader to make his or her own considered judgment of each item, with comparatively few inadvertent exclusions, and come up with a selected list of the ones that seem most important, that he or she can do something about, or both.

Dubious Assumptions

Since this is a psychological book, it is appropriate to focus first on our own thought processes, starting with a list of widely held assumptions that, in the light of this book's analysis, the reader may want to reject or revise before considering the concrete actions and nonactions that follow. The assumptions:

1. That an aggressive action by an opponent must stem from aggressive motives (Chapter 2)
2. That if an opponent is arming faster than we are its purpose must be aggression (Chapter 2)
3. That if we, in response, are now arming faster than the opponent, our purpose must be strictly defensive (Chapter 10, the moral self-image)
4. That the USSR now has more nuclear strength than the United States (Chapter 3)
5. That patriotism requires uncritical approval of whatever one's own country does (Chapter 10, the moral self-image)
6. That the badness of the Bad Guys is a reason not to talk with them (Chapter 12, blurred distinctions)
7. That a balance of power (defined as equality) promotes peace, even in the absence of tension-reduction (Chapters 6 and 12)
8. That civil strife in a Third World country is likely to be mainly due to Communist subversion (Chapters 10 and 12)
9. That all or most of the Third World is vital to the security of the United States (Chapter 17)
10. That anti-Communist dictators and oligarchies are our natural allies (Chapter 12)

Proposed Actions and Nonactions

- Studying intensively the history of our own times—for instance, high school and college courses in twentieth century world history, with special attention to the causes of wars (Chapters 13–16)

- Studying the art of negotiation—e.g. memoirs of diplomats and the more systematic recent work of scholars such as Walton and McKersie (1965), Dean Pruitt (1981), Roger Fisher (Fisher and Ury, 1981), Jeffrey Rubin (1982), and William Zartman (1978)
- Studying the arts of mediation through problem-solving and conflict-resolving workshops (Wedge, 1972; Kelman, 1972; Burton, 1979)
- Looking for things we can honestly approve of on the other side, such as the magnificent performance of the Soviet Union in World War II (Chapters 14 and 15)
- Taking a fresh look at things in our own history that opponents might honestly perceive as aggression and asking why we did them (Chapter 15)
- Considering various definitions of aggression and applying them evenhandedly to opponents' actions and our own (Chapter 15)
- Strengthening our own economy (Chapter 16)
- Energy-independence; developing an ability to get along without access to the oil of the Middle East if necessary (Chapters 15 and 16)
- Generous but discriminating economic aid to developing countries (Chapter 17)
- Increasing trade with the Soviet bloc (Chapter 16)
- Equal cooperation with the Soviet Union and China (Chapter 16)
- Avoiding the name-calling type of rhetoric, while being candid in discussing real current issues (Chapter 16)
- Promoting many kinds of exchanges; cordial welcoming of exchangees; tactful but candid discussion, with them, of peace-related issues (Chapters 11, 16)
- Candid but very limited discussion of hot issues, such as human rights and the emigration of Jews, that we can do little or nothing about (Chapter 15)
- Supporting all or nearly all of the specialized agencies of the U.N. (Chapter 16)
- Encouraging regional organizations such as the OAS, the OAU, and ASEAN (Chapter 16)
- Reviving discussion of the pros and cons of strong world organization (below, Chapter 20)

- Unofficial "Track-Two" diplomacy, coordinated with official diplomacy (Chapter 16)
- Language and culture study, especially Russian, Chinese, and Arabic (Chapter 16)
- No launch-on-warning policy (Chapter 5)
- No deployment of superfast, super-accurate weapons such as the Pershing II on the soil of Western Europe (Chapter 5)
- No intervention in civil wars unless the provocation is extremely great (Chapter 5)
- Absolutely no escalation of nonnuclear to nuclear war under any circumstances (Chapter 5), which means no first use of tactical, battlefield weapons, even if our side is losing
- A decision, in advance, that even loss of all access to Middle East oil would not justify a first crossing of the psychological firebreak between nonnuclear and nuclear war (Chapter 5)
- Arthur Cox's proposal that the United States and the USSR agree not to intervene with their own troops anywhere in certain defined parts of the Third World (1982, pp. 156–64; see also Chapter 5)
- Clarification, for ourselves and in all contacts with the Soviet Union, of the special dangers inherent in preventive war, preemptive war, and the human and computer errors that could lead to a mistaken perception that the other side was starting to preempt (Chapter 5)
- Especially urgent attention to peace in the Middle East, including consideration of drastic measures such as:

1. Taking fully into account Israel's security need, including its tiny size, its grotesquely hard-to-defend shape, and the momentum of Arab hostility, and compensating for those exceptional dangers in such ways as international policing, with Israeli participation, of border areas such as the West Bank, the Gaza Strip, the Golan Heights, Lebanon south of the Litani, and the eastern half of the Sinai. All heavy weapons, Israeli or other, could be prohibited in those areas (White, 1977).

2. Maintaining or reestablishing Arab sovereignty in all or nearly all of those border areas, in principle immediately and in practice as quickly as is at all feasible. This would be in accord with the spirit of Resolution 242 and the Camp David accords.

3. Working with the USSR again in the spirit of the Vance–Gromyko communiqué of 1977 (Chapter 15).

4. Bringing legitimate pressure to bear on Israel (e.g. withdrawal of military and/or economic aid) if necessary to achieve what the rest of the world would regard as a fair settlement (White, 1977).

5. Impressing on Israel, with special urgency, the terrible danger to the world if it engages again in preventive war, as it did in 1956 and 1982, or if it were to be the first to resort to nuclear weapons in another Arab–Israeli war (Chapter 5).

6. Improving American relations with Turkey, Iraq, and Iran.

7. Helping the USSR to save face if it withdraws from Afghanistan (Cox, 1982, p. 161).

CHAPTER TWENTY

Eventual World Federation

Jonathan Schell's prescriptions for preserving the human race can be summarized (all too briefly) in his words:

> The deterrence policy . . . is only a piece of repair work on the immeasurably more deeply entrenched system of national sovereignty. . . . The task facing the species is to shape a world politics that does not rely on violence. This task falls into two parts—two aims. The first is to save the world from extinction by eliminating nuclear weapons from the earth. . . . The second aim, which alone can provide a sure foundation for the first, is to create a political means by which the world can arrive at the decisions sovereign states previously arrived at through war'' (1982).

How right is he?

His first prescription—a world with literally no nuclear weapons—is probably too visionary to be a realistic goal for anyone now living. Even if a democratic world federation is achieved, it seems likely that for a long time the central authority will need to possess a certain minimum of nuclear strength in order to guard against the secret manufacture and use of such weapons by parts of the world that want to dominate the rest of it. On the other hand, his second prescription, which must mean some kind of effective world federation (though for some reason he avoids the word federation), seems extremely desirable as a basic answer to the problem of war, and quite possibly feasible if, during the next two or three decades, events move in certain ways. Its pros and cons and its feasibility or infeasibility therefore deserve careful discussion.

Its Advantages

Some of us once knew, but have half-forgotten, how strong the case for a democratic world federation, with minimum powers sufficient to prevent war, actually is (Cousins, 1945). These things count in its favor:

• What we have now is international anarchy. It is gang law. It is what the "law of the streets" would be if there were no policeman on the corner and no courts or judges backed by police. "International law," as it now exists, and if the word "law" is seriously meant, is a contradiction in terms. There can be no true law without law enforcement.

• We, the human race, live on a shrinking planet. Intercontinental ballistic missiles and the nuclear-armed submarines of both superpowers that are now roaming all the oceans have eliminated distance as a protective shield for the United States. They have made enforceable peace imperative and continued domination of the world by parochial national loyalties dangerous to the survival of all of us.

• Parochial national loyalties are the crux of the problem. A larger loyalty is essential. It is basically as ridiculous for the loyalties of Americans, Russians, and Chinese to be wholly bound up in the symbols of nationality as it would have been for citizens of Massachusetts, Pennsylvania, and Virginia, in the years when the Founding Fathers were creating a new nation, to cling to and identify with their states more than with the flag and Constitution of the United States of America.

• The economic burdens of trade barriers, of pollution, and of maldistribution and parochial control of vital resources could be greatly relieved by effective planning and cooperation. Moreover, the truly crushing economic burden of competitive armaments on a world scale, which is probably the chief factor now preventing a flourishing world economy, could be eliminated.

• The people to whom national governments are now responsible are nation-minded. To get reelected or to stay in power those governments have to conform, most of the time, to the nationalistic passions and misperceptions of their national constituencies. Yet the actions of governments in international affairs affect millions in nations other than their own and could condemn those millions to total destruction. Power for our species would mean that the entire human race (or at least the politically conscious parts of it), with their national antagonisms more or less canceling each other out, would become the constituency of the top leaders. To be reelected they would have to be acceptable to the whole, not to a part, of the world. Much the same could be said about educators and persons in the mass media, both of whom are in a sense now responsible to nationalistic constituencies.

• There is need for a federation much stronger than the U.N., in the ways most relevant to world peace. As keepers of the peace between major nations the League of Nations and the United Nations have both failed. Although they have often served peace in minor ways (e.g. policing Arab–Israeli borders from 1956 to 1967), they have done so only when the interests of no great power conflicted with what the situation seemed to call for (or, in the case of Korea, when the Soviet representative in the Security Council was absent). The very structure of the Security Council of the U.N., where the right to veto has been jealously guarded by both superpowers, guarantees futility in any crisis in which the interests of one major power, as perceived by that power, go against what most of the rest of the world wants.

• A world federation also has to be democratic in two ways: responsiveness to the majority of the world's people and decentralization—that is, regional autonomy and national autonomy wherever such autonomy does not seriously conflict with the interests of the majority, especially the imperative need for peace. The World Federalists' definition of their goal, "minimum powers adequate to preserve peace," makes sense. Given the growth of nationalism in the Third World in our century, and the relinquishment of colonial power by the Western colonial nations (at least in the sense of direct colonial control), the wisdom of letting each nation work out its own destiny, as far as possible, seems obvious.

The Case Against It

Three arguments have often been brought up against a strong world federation, in addition to the basic nationalistic (and rather obviously short-sighted) feeling that it would mean "being outvoted by foreigners, on matters of vital interest to us." The three are:

1. The federation might be dominated by the Third World, to the detriment of the First (the Western) World. The huge increase in the number of Third World members of the U.N., since

it was established in 1945, gives some substance to that argument.

2. It might be dominated by the advanced nations, which are far superior in wealth, science, technology, military power, education and political experience, though not necessarily in virtue. With the present economic stagnation of much of the Third World (inaccurately labeled the ''developing'' countries), that prospect seems a real one.

3. It might be dominated by one or the other of the superpowers. The record of the semidomination of the U.N., in its early years, by the United States, and of domination of other countries in Eastern Europe and elsewhere by the USSR, gives some substance to that argument also.

While all three points have value as indicators of dangers to be avoided if and when a stronger world federation is organized, they are not necessarily arguments against the kind of federation that could be organized if those dangers are kept in mind. Safeguards against the dangers might be set up, as the framers of the American Constitution did when they created checks and balances and when they let the House of Representatives reflect the relative populations of states, while the Senate preserved equal voting power for the states regardless of population. Their success demonstrates that it is not necessarily beyond the power of human ingenuity to frame such safeguards.

If that is done, the weight of the positive arguments seems far greater than that of the negative ones—*if* at any time in the future the whole enterprise seems feasible.

Could It Ever Occur?

That is the rub. The commonest argument against world federation is not that it is undesirable but that it could never be achieved and is therefore not worth further thought or action. ''It is a utopian dream,'' the argument runs, ''The forces of nationalism are too strong for it. Each nation will cling to its own sovereignty, jealously guarding it against the danger of being outvoted by 'a collection of foreigners.' Can you imagine the United States, for instance, agreeing to a World Constitution that would put predominant military power into the hands of something resembling the General Assembly of the U.N.—military power that then might be wielded by a Third World majority, perhaps in league with the Soviet Union, to reduce the United States to subservience and rob it of its unique natural riches? Can you imagine the Soviet Union, with its ingrained suspicion of the entire capitalist world, agreeing to a World Constitution that might allow it to be dominated by a coalition of Third World and capitalist nations, probably headed by the United States?''

The last point is surely a decisive argument against the feasibility of world federation *now* or in the foreseeable future. Without a very great reduction of tension, probably requiring decades, that is hardly conceivable. The emotional resistance of the Soviet leadership to a decisive strengthening of the United Nations, which they have perceived as mainly capitalist-dominated—a resistance that would be much greater if the proposal were to put real teeth into such an organization—has always been much greater than the resistance in the United States, Western Europe, or the Third World. There is no World Federalist movement in the USSR. Cord Meyer, an early outstanding leader of the American World Federalists, soon learned that lesson and may well have been wise when he decided that coping with the USSR now was more urgent than working toward a federated world in the more distant future.

On the other hand, neither their deeply ingrained suspicion of us nor ours of them is necessarily unchangeable. If either side makes a real effort to stop and reverse the present malignant process, those on the other side, with the great new fear of total nuclear destruction in the back of their minds, may welcome the reversal and do much to sustain it (Chapter 8). Isn't it dogmatic to say categorically that the one course of action that would most decisively strike at the roots of war must forever remain beyond the reach of the rationality and good will of a war-hating human species? Present trends point that way, but trends have changed, notably in the USSR after the death of Stalin, and the same could happen again.

Hans Morgenthau, the arch-"realist," has remarked on the paradox that, at a stage of world history when effective world organization has become more urgent than ever before, the forces of nationalism have made it more difficult to achieve than ever before. It would be hard to disagree with either of those points. But history is full of altered trends. In the long run there are two hopeful possibilities.

One is that the worldwide realistic *fear* of nuclear war that now exists could bear good fruit. Barbara Tuchman noted it as a radically new element in the situation, making dubious all predictions based only on the past. It could work powerfully in the coming years and bring drastic actions that have not yet been seen. Jonathan Schell sees that as the only hope. *If* agitation and education for the desirability of world federation are combined with basic forms of tension-reduction on both sides during the last two decades of our century, a great mellowing of attitudes in both superpowers seems well within the realm of possibility. That in turn might make a democratic world federation possible.

The other hopeful possibility rests on a view of a possible future that most of us have recoiled from even imagining. It is that after a nuclear war (yes—*after* a nuclear war) a world government of some kind could become not only possible but probable. The human beings who remained alive, even if they were no more than, say, 1 percent of the world's present population, could make a new start.

The hope rests partly on history. Two periods in our century have seen a high tide of world enthusiasm on behalf of organization for peace: the period just after World War I and the period just after World War II. In both periods the horrors of a great war were fresh in people's minds. The first resulted in the first great experiment in world organization, the League of Nations. The second resulted in the United Nations. If a Third World War should occur and not destroy everyone, that would be the time when a third and stronger such tide could flow, and when the people remaining would be most likely to summon the courage and the common sense to forge a world organization transcending national sovereignty and possessing at least the minimum powers sufficient to prevent war.

Most of us in the peace movement have been so obsessed with the catastrophe of nuclear war that our thoughts have stopped at the point of imagining a nuclear war that does or does not begin. That is undoubtedly where, if we are realistic, the emphasis ought to lie. Staving off a nuclear war is by far the most urgent task we confront. The reader will note that that task has been put first throughout this book and is confronted in twenty-one of its twenty-two chapters.

One good reason is the sheer uncertainty of what a nuclear war and its aftermath might be like. The war itself could be anything between destruction of one city on each side and destruction of all birds and mammals (including man) on the face of the earth, leaving, as Schell put it, ''a republic of insects and grass.'' He himself recognizes that uncertainty; he is usually careful to say that an all-out nuclear exchange could (not would) result in the extinction of human life on our planet. The aftermath is similarly uncertain. One result could be hundreds of small patches of miserably surviving human beings, mainly on the fringes of civilization, scrabbling for a Stone Age type of existence through hunting and rudimentary agriculture. Another would be a combination of that and a number of surviving nuclei of the nations that now exist. The forces of nationalism would surely continue to be strong and might well prevail over the tide of international feeling that is predicted here.

Or—perhaps most probable in view of the way both World War I and World War II ended—one side or the other could emerge terribly devastated (and a loser in that sense) but the decisive victor in terms of relative military power. In that sense of the word ''win,'' either a U.S.-led coalition or a USSR-led coalition could ''win.'' Those of us who really believe in our kind of democracy can have no doubt as to which would be better, but the opposite could occur. The USSR could emerge the victor and in that case could probably control, militarily, the entire Eurasian continent, all of the Eastern Hemisphere, or, conceivably, all of the world including, sooner or later, North America. The very high probability that the Soviets are not now thinking seriously of world domination as a realistic possibility that could be worth a war (Chapter 4) does not mean they would reject it if, as a result of a war they had not sought but had given their hearts' blood to win, they found themselves in possession of it. In that case there would be a ''world government''—a Soviet-dominated world government.

The hard-liners such as Colin Gray (1979) have a point when they insist that if such a war occurs it does matter which side ''wins'' in a military sense. Among other things, the chances that the human race might achieve a tolerably democratic form of world federation during the next century would in that case be slim. They would be slim also if, after generating enormous suffering and hatred, the war turned out to be a stalemate.

It would be quite otherwise if the non-Communist countries (including, let us say, Western Europe and Japan as well as the United States) were to ''win'' in that sense and if, between now and then, there were to have been much thinking and talking in them about the deeper causes of war and the desirability of a democratic world federation. The United Nations, excluding Germany and Japan, was the product of such a victory and such thinking in 1945 and 1946. Psychologically there would be nothing impossible about it, as there is with the proposal that the East–West conflict should now be replaced by a world federation. The anti-Communist nations (those that remained) would have been at least temporarily welded together by the struggle itself; psychologically they would still have a common enemy and a desire to hold the "war-making dictators" in check, as they did after each of the two great previous wars.

Surely it would then be wise, in the interest of lasting peace, to treat the defeated enemies humanely, as was done after World War II, and to welcome them as quickly as possible into full and equal membership in the federation—more quickly than Germany and Japan were admitted into the United Nations. The alternative—kicking the enemy when he is down, as was done after World War I—would in all probability increase, not decrease, the chances of World War IV.

But surely, too, the chances of World War IV would be more greatly increased if, even when offered such an opportunity to lay a solid basis for peace, the West were to slip back into the old anarchy of jealously sovereign nations.

It follows that thinking and talking about the pros and cons of a democratic world federation, now and from now on, would be worthwhile.

CHAPTER TWENTY-ONE

Persuading the American People

In Chapter 18 it was argued that these six measures should have priority as ways of preventing nuclear war:

1. Deep cuts in destabilizing nuclear weapons
2. A drastically lowered ratio of warheads to missiles
3. A joint no-first-use statement
4. A modified freeze agreement
5. A comprehensive test ban
6. A tradeoff such as simultaneous elimination of SS-20s, Pershing IIs, and ground-launched cruise missiles

Is there any hope that a majority of the American people, after incidents such as the shooting down of the Korean plane, might still be persuaded to accept such measures?

It is suggested here that there is—if those of us who believe in them use intelligently the art of persuasion.

That means, first of all, an understanding of what the thoughts and feelings of the American people are now—the less conscious thoughts and feelings as well as the more conscious ones.

The Anesthetic Fog

There is a mystery here. *Why* have most of the American people not yet seen clearly the urgency of the danger that to us, the peace activists, seems so plain? Are there unconscious psychological forces that keep them half-oblivious to what stares them in the face?

In some of the most powerful words spoken or written in our century, Jonathan Schell (1982) came close to saying that that is the case. The end of his book is this:

> If we reject our doom, and bend our efforts toward survival—if we arouse ourselves to the peril and act to forestall it, making ourselves the allies of life—then the anesthetic fog will lift; our

vision, no longer straining not to see the obvious, will sharpen; our will, finding secure ground to build on, will be restored; and we will take full and clear possession of life again. One day—and it is hard to believe that it will not be soon—we will make our choice. Either we will sink into the final coma and end it all or, as I trust and believe, we will awaken to the truth of our peril, a truth as great as life itself, and, like a person who has swallowed a lethal poison but shakes off his stupor at the last moment and vomits the poison up, we will break through the layers of our denials, put aside our faint-hearted excuses, and rise up to cleanse the earth of nuclear weapons.

What is the "anesthetic fog"? What is the "poison"? Why do so many of us "strain not to see the obvious"? Apart from suggestive metaphors such as "breaking through the layers of our denials," Schell does not clearly answer those questions. They need answers if we, the responsible peace activists in the United States, are to act intelligently to induce the kind of "vomiting" he regards as imperative.

It is clear, to begin with, that there has to be an acute emotional disturbance, even horror, if action as violent as vomiting is to occur. Detached intellectual analysis of the sort aspired to in this book is not enough. Goodwill and a vague longing for peace are not enough. Horror is needed. The peace movement cannot do without it. There is intense emotion in books like Schell's, in the eloquence of speakers like Helen Caldecott and Robert Lifton, and in films like *The Last Epidemic*. As a motivating force that kind of fear-arousal is essential. Even as an incentive to undertake thoroughgoing, detached intellectual analysis it is needed, since people rarely challenge the foundations of their own habitual perceptions, and take a long new look at the evidence, unless fear or frustration of some sort forces them to do so.

Immediately, though, we come to a daunting paradox. Horror can cut both ways. It can energize action but can also paralyze action. It can mobilize resources the individual did not know he possessed or cause his mind to shrink away from the horror itself and everything associated with it. The thought-avoiding reaction is, to use Lifton's term, "psychic numbness" and in Schell's terms, "layers of denials," an "anesthetic fog," "stupor," and "a straining not to see the obvious." It is the very "poison" he wants us to "vomit up."

There is in fact much reason to think that the unhealthy, thought-avoiding response has predominated almost from the very beginning of our atomic era. According to the survey data of Cottrell and Eberhardt (1948) the initial event, the destruction of Hiroshima and Nagasaki, was so dramatic, so awe-inspiring, that the knowledge of it reached almost every adult in the United States with unprecedented speed. Yet, from the time when the ill-conceived Baruch Plan failed in 1948 until the freeze movement began in earnest in 1981, there was amazingly little thought or discussion by the general public about such things as a freeze, deep cuts, no first use, the dangers inherent in MIRVs, and so on. The outburst of creative professional thinking on nuclear strategy in the years 1957–63 was the exception, not the rule, and it evoked so little response from the general public that even the principle of eliminating vulnerable first-strike weapons, which was the chief upshot of that outburst, was violated by the Congressional approval of a silo-based MX in 1983, without much public protest.

There is an urgent need, then, to learn more about the circumstances in which the reaction to a great danger is mainly a healthy facing up to the danger and doing something about it, and the circumstances in which the reaction is mainly an unhealthy avoidance of the entire subject. The success or failure of the present peace movement in the West could hinge mainly on the realism and discrimination of its answers to that question. Is it possible, for instance, that its recent primary emphasis on the colossal destructiveness of nuclear weapons has lasted long enough and that the primary emphasis should now be on what can be realistically done to prevent nuclear war?

The change in 1981 was that the promotion of a nuclear freeze provided something clear, practical, and socially acceptable to do. Awareness of the danger had been present—in the back of people's minds—since 1945 and had been reinforced in 1957 by the almost simultaneous appearance of the Soviet sputnik and the first Soviet testing of an ICBM, but without practical result. Now, for the first time, the gates of action were opened. People could now open their minds freely to emotion and feel that the emotion, instead of being bottled up and leading only to a sense of futility, might be allowed to flow freely, since now there was a mass movement that could even affect the policy of the government. The process became cumulative. It will be hard to bottle up *that* genie, now that it has been let out of the bottle, even though there may be temporary setbacks.

The data of experimental psychology offer some support to that interpretation. The pioneering experiment of Janis and Feshbach (1953) brought out the first, surprising evidence that "fear-arousing communication" might be counterproductive, presumably because the feeling of distaste could irrationally spread to include the action recommended to avoid the danger, as well as the danger that was to be avoided. Since then there have been a considerable number of experiments (especially by Leventhal, summarized by Freedman, Carlsmith and Sears, 1970, pp. 321–27; Tedeschi and Lindskold, 1976, pp. 328–30) generally supporting the opposite view that fear-arousal *is* usually effective, and the stronger the fear aroused, the more effective. Most relevant here, though, is the work of Janis (1967) indicating that the reaction to danger is more likely to be strong and realistic if there is a clear idea of acceptable things that can be done about it.

In sum, both the historical and the experimental evidence suggest that stressing the horror of nuclear war is likely to be effective *if* people are presented at the same time with types of preventive action that are clear, apparently practical, not too complicated, and acceptable in terms of their own values and the values of the people around them. Otherwise they are likely to be in a state of inner conflict and may turn away from the whole subject, especially if they are feeling an increasing distaste for the extremely unpleasant aspects of it.

Among other things, that means there should be a careful choice of the war-preventing actions that seem most feasible and that would not require a long and probably discouraging process of negotiation. Otherwise there will be discouragement and cynicism about the chances of rapid progress, putting a damper on the whole peace movement. For instance, a no-first-use policy could be established immediately, since the Soviets already want it. At the other extreme, it is doubtful that total elimination of nuclear weapons could ever be achieved (page 320), and almost certainly a world federation strong enough to prevent war between the major powers could not be achieved before the end of this century, if then (pages 323–24). But all six of the measures proposed at the beginning of this chapter probably (not certainly) pass this test.

The need to focus on actions that have at least some immediate acceptability also implies recognizing and respecting the more firmly held conscious values of the audience, such as their

need for enough strength to deter Soviet aggression against Western Europe and their need for verifiability in any arms control
agreement—and it implies taking very much into account their
less admirable and less conscious values such as macho pride
(Chapter 9). All six of the measures stressed in this chapter are
consistent with full recognition of the need to continue adequate
deterrence of a Soviet first strike by maintaining a potent second-
strike capability, and with the need for adequate conventional defense. The need for verifiability is also accepted.

It should be acknowledged that all of the proposed actions do
go against the cruder sort of macho pride. There is in them no insistence that America must be "number one" in military power
and prestige or that it should have the military power to intimidate the USSR and "prevail" in the many conflicts of interest
that are likely to arise. But that amount of acceptance of pride
limitation is the unavoidable minimum that any effective way of
averting nuclear war necessarily involves. There is a value tradeoff here, of the sort that Jervis insists should be candidly faced
(1976, pp. 128–42). *Some* pride limitation is the price of peace.

What about the proposal, made repeatedly in this book, that
either side could with safety cut back its nuclear arms, unilaterally if necessary, to no more than is judged necessary for a virtually invulnerable second-strike capability—perhaps a few nuclear-armed submarines and bombers? Does that fail the test of
adequate acceptability in the eyes of the American public?

Right now it almost certainly does. The tabooed word "unilateral," combined with the seemingly drastic nature of the proposal itself, is a major psychological handicap. That is why it was
not included in the list of six most immediately urgent measures
at the beginning of this chapter. There has been almost no public
agitation for it, though Kennan came close to it when, in present-
ing the case for his 50 percent across-the-board cut in nuclear
weapons, he said that "there would still be plenty of overkill
left—so much so that if the first operation were successful, I
would like to see a second one put in hand to rid us of at least
two-thirds of what would be left" (1981). But if the thing could in
fact be done safely and, by drastically reversing the nuclear arms
race, would greatly reduce the chance of nuclear war, why not?
Are we really so sure that the common sense of the American
people would not respond to something so sensible, even if it were

advocated by respected opinion leaders and the people had two or three years to get used to the idea? And even though a 79-to-16 percent majority now agree that "it doesn't matter if the United States or the Soviet Union is ahead in nuclear weapons because both sides have more than enough to destroy each other no matter who attacks first"?

Psychological Obstacles

While Jonathan Schell's "anesthetic fog" is probably the first and greatest obstacle to clear thinking about how to avert nuclear war, and to rational persuasion on that subject, there are at least three others.

The Illusion of Soviet Strategic Superiority

Leslie Gelb's (1982) summary is worth quoting again:

> The experts who look at all these factors call the strategic balance a draw. Put another way, I have yet to meet a senior American military officer involved in this subject who would trade the American arsenal for the Soviet one. Only those experts who focus exclusively on Soviet superiority in land-based missiles think otherwise. [p. 18]

The evidence on this point, consisting chiefly of America's superiority in its second-strike capability (submarines and bombers), is elaborated to some extent in Chapters 3 and 18. (As is emphasized in Chapter 3, this reassuring generalization does not apply to conventional weapons. Soviet superiority in that area is seldom questioned.)

If Gelb is right, most of the American public have been woefully misinformed, self-deluded, or both with regard to the strategic situation. They still tend to believe that the USSR is ahead not only in conventional but also in nuclear capability. For instance, a Roper poll in September and October 1980 (summarized in a State Department memorandum, March 1981), at the height of Ronald Reagan's presidential campaign, asked a cross-section of Americans whether they thought the United States was behind the USSR in nuclear strength, about even, or ahead. The results:

U.S. behind	43%
U.S. about even	29
U.S. ahead	15
Don't know	13

There is some reason to think the public now is less ready to grant Soviet nuclear superiority than it was then, since it has seen President Reagan's strenuous efforts to increase American nuclear strength. A *New York Times*/CBS poll in February 1983 showed 32 percent believing the USSR was ahead, as compared with a figure of 44 percent obtained in 1982.

As an instance of exaggerated fear—the opposite of wishful thinking—those findings are striking. The fact is also of fundamental importance to those who want to persuade the public of the value of genuine, drastic arms control. The question of which side is ahead has a startlingly great effect on whether the public supports a freeze. In a *New York Times*/CBS poll in May 1982 the central question and the replies to it were as follows:

"Do you favor or oppose the United States agreeing to a 'nuclear freeze' with the Soviet Union—that is, putting a stop to the testing, production and installation of additional nuclear weapons by both sides?"

Favor a freeze	72%
Oppose it	21
No opinion	7

In other words, when a freeze is described without raising the question of relative nuclear strength the public is overwhelmingly in favor of it. But when the wording is changed in a way that focuses attention on that factor the results are radically different:

"What if a nuclear freeze would result in the Soviet Union having somewhat greater nuclear strength . . .?"

Favor a freeze	30%
Oppose it	60
No opinion	10

There is an ambiguity in the word "greater"; was it understood to mean "greater than if there were no freeze" or "greater than that of the United States"? Nevertheless the finding is bad news for arms controllers. Now that the Reagan Administration is geared up to spend great amounts of money each year (much more than the USSR has ever spent annually in the past) on the development and production of new types of nuclear weapons and the means of their delivery (cruise missiles, MX, Trident II, Stealth bombers), it has a strong incentive to continue to depict that spending as necessitated by a present American nuclear inferiority and as only catching up with a menacing Soviet superiority. It can also oppose a freeze with the fully justified statement that a freeze would inhibit American expansion much more than Soviet expansion and therefore (depending again on what the public believes our present relative strength is) leave America in a position of continuing inferiority.

Therefore it is of critical importance for proponents of genuine and equal arms reductions to recognize how false the myth of Soviet nuclear superiority is (see especially Cox, 1982, Chapter 4), how justifiably alarmed the Soviet decision-makers must be becoming as a result of our present and planned buildup, and how urgent it therefore is, in the arms controllers' persuasive efforts, to have the facts and figures to demolish the myth.

A useful source of some of those facts and figures is Elizabeth Drew (1983a), who calculates that

> . . . the [American] defense budget grew by nearly 25% in real terms between 1980 and 1982, and it was on top of that that the Reagan Administration proposed to raise it by seven per cent a year for the four years following. . . . In terms of constant dollars (after inflation) the continuing increase in the Reagan defense budget is larger than the one the Reagan Administration itself proposed for the period from 1982 through 1986. And then, this year, the Reagan Administration ended up asking for a ten per cent increase in its defense budget for fiscal 1984. [p. 52]

In other words, if we assume a rough equality already in, say, 1980, the United States was jumping ahead in total defense expenditures at a rate that the USSR, with only half its Gross Annual Product, could hardly be expected to match. (According to CIA estimates published in 1980, covering the 1970–79 period: "Estimated in constant dollars, Soviet defense activities in-

creased at an average annual rate of three per cent." Quoted by
Cox, 1982, pp. 104–5, with the remark that during that period
the Soviet figure of 3 percent was "about the same" as the rate
"at which the United States and most of its NATO partners have
raised their military spending during each of the past five
years.")

The Diabolical Enemy-image

As we have seen, exaggerated fear is a product of two things, exaggerated perception of a potential enemy's strength and exaggerated perception of its aggressively hostile intentions. If either
is zero, the product is zero. In the case of the American public's
image of the USSR, both are exaggerated.

Compared with the facts and interpretations in this book, especially in Chapters 2, 4, and 15, a large majority of the American public have a simplistic Good Guys–Bad Guys picture of the
conflict between their country and the USSR. That has been true
since approximately 1946. For instance, in 1981 a Roper poll
(summarized in a State Department memorandum, December
1981) asked a national sample to choose between four statements
about "Russia's primary objective in world affairs." The results
were as follows:

A. "Russia seeks global domination and will risk a major war to achieve that domination if it can't be achieved by other means."	34%
B. "Russia seeks global domination but not at the expense of starting a major war."	35%
(Total: Global Domination)	69%
C. "Russia seeks to compete with the U.S. for more influence in different parts of the world."	18%
D. "Russia seeks only to protect itself against the possibility of attack by other countries."	6%
Don't know	7%

In a *Washington Post*/ABC News poll in April 1982, 80 percent
agreed with the statement that the Soviet Union would "try to
cheat on any nuclear freeze agreement and get an advantage over
the U.S." Only 13 percent disagreed.

It begins to look as if the general public's picture of the USSR
is even more diabolical than has been supposed by most of the

peace activists, who would naturally tend to attribute to the public an attitude not too different from their own and that of the people they know.

If the public's diabolical image is a considerable exaggeration of Soviet actions and intentions in the field of foreign policy, as our evidence indicates, it is an unnecessary obstacle to arms control in three ways: The public is too obsessively afraid of conventional Soviet aggression that they think might even demand a first-use nuclear response by us (Chapter 4); they expect Communist cheating to an extent that Einhorn's evidence (1981–82) does not justify (Chapter 18); and individuals who are more familiar with the evidence are too afraid to express their real view for fear of being labeled ''soft on Communism.'' With regard to that anxiety, the columnist Mary McGrory reports on how it recently operated in Congress: President Reagan ''had spectacular success with [his] approach on the MX missile, which was once as unpopular as jungle warfare and which now is well on the way to reality, because Democrats were stampeded into support by fear of what he would say about them if they didn't fall in line'' (1983; see also Drew, 1983b, pp. 69–75). It is not only presidents who can intimidate with expressed or implied accusations of ''soft on Communism''; many Americans know how easily friends, neighbors, and (most dangerously perhaps) employers can intimidate in the same way, and how a vague fear of such accusations can inhibit free expression even when the fear is not justified at all.

What can be done about it? How can this fundamental obstacle to peace be circumvented or overcome?

Certainly not by whitewashing the evils of Soviet totalitarianism, past and present. In the ways stressed by Conquest (1968), Solzhenitzyn (1973), and others, the Soviet government has not only betrayed the promise of the first, democratic revolution of 1917 but has greatly exceeded the evils of the Tsarist regime which that revolution overthrew. No one who has read the *Gulag Archipelago* or heard about the dissenters now incarcerated in Soviet hospitals for the insane could want evil of that magnitude to be glossed over. A whitewash is not the answer.

The practical answer is to make an immediate, sharp separation between the domestic policies of the Soviet government and the motives behind its foreign policy. Even a Bad Guy can prefer not to be incinerated, especially if he vividly remembers the burn he suffered in World War II. It is not necessary to attribute to the Soviet decision-makers a lack of power motivation, or goodwill toward us, or trustworthiness. It is necessary only to realize that, like us, they want to stay alive and have some common sense about how to do it (Chapters 2, 4, 10–12, and 18).

Macho Pride

A main thesis of this book has been that macho pride is probably second only to exaggerated fear of aggression by the Bad Guys as a motive underlying the policies that lead to unwanted war (Chapters 1, 9, and 16). Specifically it helps in explaining the intensity with which each side in the East–West conflict clings to the fetish of equality in nuclear weapons, in spite of the obviousness of nuclear redundancy and the irrelevance of nuclear strength above the level of an invulnerable second-strike capability (Chapters 12 and 17), in spite of the war-breeding character of the arms race itself (Chapters 8 and 16), and in spite of the economic instability and deprivation that the expense of more-than-minimal nuclear strength is now creating. That is good evidence that something more than exaggerated fear is at work here, under the surface of consciousness. On the subconscious level there must be a deep, unacknowledged need to "heroize" one's own country; and a Good Guys–Bad Guys picture, with the Good Guys being also Strong Guys who would win if the Bad Guys attack, is the simple way to achieve it.

What can be done about that obstacle to peace?

The fact that it is mainly subconscious rules out a crude frontal attack as an effective approach. To say to a hard-liner, "You are indulging in macho pride at the expense of both peace and prosperity," could evoke nothing but anger and the most scornful name-calling in return—especially if it happens to be true.

One alternative is obvious: to focus on the immense, colossally destructive harm that a single nuclear-armed submarine can do. That should be enough to satisfy, by duplicating them, the most self-inflating macho fantasies that lurk close to the surface of consciousness of the most macho-motivated hard-liner. Those tension-reducers who (like this one) genuinely believe in adequate nuclear deterrence should have no hesitation in saying so, stressing their agreement with others on that point, and being ready with facts as to how horribly destructive even the most minimal nuclear retaliation would actually be. If they also believe in adequate conventional arms (as this one does), that is fortunate too. They can then honestly stress their agreement, in principle, with all of those who want Western Europe to be adequately defended.

The same considerations rule out *ad hominem* attacks on the military. Unless very carefully stated, such attacks are likely to be inaccurate and unfair in any case. Many military men are more soberly aware of the nuclear danger, and have done more thinking about how to avoid it, than most civilians have. Even if the majority of them have an almost deliberately cultivated unwillingness to empathize with the human side of an enemy, they share that unwillingness with many millions of their civilian countrymen. As the reader may have noticed, there is in this book no general denunciation of "militarism"; on the contrary, there has been agreement with the judgment of Barbara Tuchman, Salvador de Madariaga, and others (Chapter 6) that fear and distrust create arms, much more than the other way around. In any case, denunciation of "militarism," especially if it is linked with war in a statement such as "I'm against war and militarism," is sure to antagonize not only most of the military men but also many of the great middle group of civilians who believe, as I do, that *some* military force is necessary for deterrence and who are precisely the group we want to persuade. If what we want to do away with is not all arms or all soldiers but only the present grotesque redundancy of nuclear arms, that is exactly what we should say.

Two well-established psychological principles are involved here. One is the principle, established by Carl Hovland and his colleagues at Yale University (Hovland, Lumsdaine, and Sheffield, 1949; Hovland, Janis, and Kelley, 1953) that when communicating with a skeptical audience it is better to use a "two-sided" than a one-sided approach—that is, if some points on the opposite side can be honestly granted, they should be. It is sometimes called the "yes-but technique." It is more effective, at least when the audience is skeptical at the outset, perhaps mainly because the listeners feel that the speaker is honest enough to grant some of the points that to the listener seem obvious. He is leveling with them and respecting their intelligence.

The other principle is somewhat similar. It too stems mainly from Hovland's laboratory at Yale. It is that persuasion is likely to be most effective when the persuader's message is decidedly different, but not *too* different, from what the listener already believes. If there is no clear difference the listener tends to assimilate what he hears to what he already thinks and perhaps to lose interest (Hovland and Pritzker, 1957); if the difference is too great he is likely to reject everything the persuader says, regarding him as crazy, irresponsible, or (in our present context) a dupe of the diabolical enemy (Hovland, Harvey, and Sherif, 1957). The ideal amount of difference is somewhere in between.

For those of us who want to persuade the middle majority of the American people to accept what we regard as the policies most essential for preventing nuclear war, both of these principles are relevant. There *is* a good case for both nuclear and conventional deterrence. In talking with those who believe in an even more extensive type of deterrence than we do, we are likely to be most effective when we can say, "Certainly I believe in deterrence, especially by conventional forces in Western Europe, and of course a good invulnerable nuclear force on submarines and bombers, *but,* in view of our present amount of overkill, it simply doesn't matter how much nuclear force we have above that minimum." That would be a "two-sided" approach, a "yes-but" approach; it would also represent a more moderate position, and therefore a much more widely and immediately acceptable one, than Jonathan Schell's magnificent last line: ". . . rise up to cleanse the earth of nuclear weapons."

In other words, it would make the six fairly drastic proposals on the first page of this chapter much more acceptable by assuring the listeners that both their fear and their pride were being respected.

Psychological Opportunities

In the opinion survey data there is one particularly bright spot for arms reducers. In a *Washington Post*/ABC News national poll in April 1982, the respondents were asked whether they agreed or disagreed with this statement:

> "It doesn't matter if the United States or the Soviet Union is ahead in nuclear weapons because both sides have more than enough to destroy each other no matter who attacks first."

Agree	79%
Disagree	16
No opinion	5

In other words, more than four out of five, among those with opinions, agreed essentially with George Kennan's proposition that there is a ''grotesque redundancy'' of nuclear weapons on both sides. Doesn't this mean that the American public is on the verge of accepting—with intelligent leadership in this direction—the idea that we might *unilaterally* cut back our nuclear arms to no more than a potent second-strike capability? Doesn't it look as if the American public, with more common sense than it has sometimes been given credit for, sees through what has been called here ''the myth of peace through nuclear parity''?

That does not necessarily follow. If the dread word ''unilateral'' had been used, the knee-jerk, unthinking reaction of most of the public might well have been to reject the practical implications of what they apparently believe. Yet this opens a vista of hope for arms reducers. If so many Americans are on the verge of seeing this momentous possibility, how much would it take for them to see the implications of what they already believe? What if several thousand arms reducers were to travel through the country asking everyone: ''Suppose we were to take the initiative to cut back to the minimum of nuclear arms that is really necessary. *You* know that what we have now is not necessary. Wouldn't that enable the Soviet Union, hard pressed economically as it is, and longing for peace as it must (after World War II), to breathe a long sigh of relief and at least partly follow suit? And wouldn't that enormously reduce the chance of the human race's committing suicide?''

Perhaps that would encounter so much resistance, based mainly on a macho revulsion against ''being weaker'' than our chief adversary—even in something as irrelevant as nuclear strength above the minimum—that no explicit change in American policy would occur. Perhaps an explicit and significant change would occur. But, at the very least, such a movement should cause our negotiators to be less rigid than they otherwise would be in clinging to the present U.S. version of what constitutes nuclear parity.

Another way to put it is that the American public is fully ready to grasp John Kenneth Galbraith's favorite metaphor: the two boys in a closed room with gasoline up to their ankles, squabbling over which has seven matches and which has six.

Another indication of a psychological opportunity is the evidence of a substantial movement of public opinion between early 1982 and the Korean airliner incident in September 1983. Support for a freeze increased from great to overwhelming. According to Barry Sussman of the *Washington Post*, the *Washington Post/ABC* News national poll in April 1983 showed 80 percent approving a freeze, as compared with 72 percent in May 1982 (in both cases, without bringing in the question of whether the USSR would benefit). On military spending there has been a striking reversal of earlier endorsements of military spending. Sussman (1983) reports a majority of 59 to 37 percent favoring cutting military spending to reduce the deficit, in contrast with February 1982, when such cuts were opposed by 53 to 41 percent (Sussman, 1982). There was also a clear and significant drop in public approval of President Reagan's handling of the Soviet Union. According to William Schmidt in the *New York Times* (1983), reporting on *New York Times/CBS* News polls, 62 percent in September 1981 said they approved his dealings with Moscow; by January 1983 the figure had dropped to 45 percent.

Probably the most significant of those figures is the indication that economic considerations are being increasingly taken into account as potent reasons for arms reductions. That too suggests tactics for arms control persuaders: Stress the economic reasons for arms reduction.

Obviously there has been a marked increase in American condemnation of the USSR, and in readiness to spend on nuclear weapons, as a result of the airliner incident. The movement toward genuine arms control has suffered a serious setback. At this writing, though, it is not yet clear whether the setback will be lasting. The figures cited above still suggest that another shift in the direction of real arms control can occur.

Education, as Distinguished from Persuasion

How can a *teacher* contribute legitimately to the prevention of war, including nuclear war?

It cannot be done by one-sided persuasion of the sort that this chapter has represented, which is appropriate for almost everyone else in a free country such as ours. A teacher's role is different. On all hotly controversial issues, such as a nuclear freeze or no first use, a teacher's role is primarily to present both sides or make it easy for students to be exposed to both sides, and to encourage independent, evidence-oriented, skeptical but open-minded thinking about both sides. Some rough conformity to the equal-time principle is essential.

Fortunately, that is precisely what is now most needed. If this book has demonstrated anything it has demonstrated the importance of empathy with both sides—defining empathy as simply understanding another's point of view, not sympathy or agreement—as a basis for realistic thinking about how to get peace. On all issues related to the East–West conflict that is the psychologically necessary first step. And it is something that almost anyone who ever plays a teacher's role—parents, preachers, writers, editors, directors of television programs, high school teachers, and college professors in various disciplines—can legitimately try to promote.

Concretely, there are several ways to do it. One is to recommend or require reading of Soviet writers such as Arbatov or Trofimenko (see References), along with militant Western writers such as Reagan or Weinberger. Another is to follow up such reading with very free discussion among the students themselves. Another—and in my teaching experience this is both the most valuable and the most enjoyed by the students—is role-playing by the students (Janis and King, 1954). The instructions may go somewhat like this: "One of you will be an American who is visiting Moscow, and who sits down in a bus next to a Russian who turns out to be a member of the Communist Party. He speaks excellent English. The other will be the Russian. Now flip a coin to decide which of you will be the American and which will be the Russian. . . . All right, now during the next eight minutes you will talk about foreign policy questions. The American will defend America's policies and the Russian will defend Soviet policies. Go ahead." In a small group with two hours to devote to the exercise it is possible for every student to play the Soviet role once; in a large group that privilege may have to be limited to those who volunteer. As a rule there are more than enough volunteers.

It's a game, and it's played with gusto.

CHAPTER TWENTY-TWO

Grounds for Hope

To maintain its own morale and momentum the peace movement needs realistic grounds for hope. There are such grounds, and they are a good deal more significant than some of us have realized.

They are not enough to justify the slightest complacency or relaxation of effort. The mushroom cloud and Jonathan Schell's nightmare vision of a possible—or probable—future are still there. Some of the reasons for a pessimistic view have been discussed at length in this book. Even the nearly universal desire for peace is not much of a safeguard, if the many forms of war-promoting misperception are fully taken into account. National publics as well as national leaders deceive themselves and perceive situations in ways that have often led to aggressive war that has not been recognized by them as aggression. Then are we, the human race, doomed to destroy ourselves?

We do not and cannot know. We can know only that there is enough light shining through the darkness to make it clear that those who are tempted to throw up their hands and stop trying are wrong. They are giving up too soon. There are these ten grounds for hope:

1. *The nearly universal desire for peace has reached a new level of urgency.* It was already strong in every country in 1914 (Chapter 13) and strong in the German people, though not in Hitler, at the outset of World War II (Chapter 14). Both were before Hiroshima. Since Hiroshima there has been no war between the superpowers or between any of the more advanced countries of Europe and Asia, perhaps chiefly because fear of the war's becoming nuclear has been so strong (a fear that has been much weaker among the less developed countries such as India–Pakistan, Ethiopia–Somalia, and Iran–Iraq).

Even though fear is a motive that can be misdirected by misperception of many kinds (Chapters 9–12), it is biologically an elemental force (Chapter 1), and the elemental physical fear of war itself is surely on the whole a major deterrent to war. As we have seen (Chapters 4, 15), it has been strong since World War II in the USSR, among the top decision-makers as well as the people—at least as strong as among their counterparts in the United States and probably stronger. We do not need to infer the contrary from their behavior in Afghanistan or from their arms buildup (Chapter 2).

2. *There is a new interest in the nature of misperception.* Up to now it has not gone very far, but the recent application of psychological concepts to international affairs, represented for instance by the young and vigorous International Society of Political Psychology and by many of the scholars cited in this book, is at least a hopeful sign.

3. *There has been no war between major powers for almost forty years.* Whether based on fear of nuclear destruction or not, that is a remarkable phenomenon. It resembles the ninety-nine-year peace among the major powers of Europe from 1815 to 1914 (broken significantly, but not catastrophically, by the Crimean War and the Franco-Prussian War). Both of those long periods of peace are a convincing answer to those who say that war is inevitable. If the peace that started in 1945 were to last as long as the one between Napoleon and World War I, it would last until 2044.

4. *The peace movement has grown with remarkable speed and has influenced the great majority in America as well as in Western Europe.* Its sudden grassroots blossoming in rural New England, its extension to physicians and other professional groups, the large majorities it has commanded in opinion polls (though fear of Soviet aggression remains stronger), the joining of it by the Catholic Church, and its obvious influence on Congress and on the rhetoric of the Reagan Administration—all of these are testimony to its vitality in the United States. Other peace movements have petered out and have evaporated in time of war, but that is not a fair test. The fair test is whether a peace movement helps to prevent war. And this movement seems different. The others had no Jonathan Schell.

The anesthetic fog is lifting.

5. *Communism no longer threatens the whole world (if it ever did).* In contrast with Orwell's prediction (or warning) of what the world might be like in 1984, both the Soviet Union and Communist China have evolved and mellowed since the days of Stalin. It has

been an irregular process in both cases and has left an essentially totalitarian government still in full control, but the mellowing has been real. In the Soviet Union after the death of Stalin in 1953, and up to the ousting of Khrushchev in 1964, there was a significant thaw. In some ways, notably openness to the West, the 1970s have witnessed a similar thaw. Many in the West are not aware or not fully aware of the recent change in the USSR, but, according to Robert Kaiser (1981), "In 1972 the Soviet Union was still cut off from most outside influences, still living in the isolation that Stalin established. Today that description no longer applies; Soviet society is much more open than it has been at any time since the 1920s" (pp. 502–3).

In China the end of the anti-intellectual Cultural Revolution, the presence of a powerful Soviet army on China's northern border, and the coming of Richard Nixon brought about a return to sane pragmatism and a readiness for good relations with the United States. Many Americans, amazed and pleased by China's apparent new friendliness, have probably even overinterpreted it as a basic change of heart. Thought control in China is still rigid and ruthless (Nagorski, 1981, pp. 683–87). But Mao's type of dedication to a revolutionizing of the world has apparently become, like that of Lenin, more or less a thing of the past.

The long-term loosening of the Kremlin's formerly tight control of Eastern Europe, including its recent obvious reluctance to crack down on Poland, is a favorable sign. The crackdown on Afghanistan is a decidedly unfavorable sign but, for reasons discussed in Chapter 2, does not necessarily imply a new aggressive policy. There, as in Poland, Hungary, Czechoslovakia, and elsewhere, the Soviet decision-makers have learned what a headache conquered lands can be, and in Cuba they have learned how expensive a client state can be.

In fact, for some twenty years Soviet Communism has been losing ground to nationalism in the world as a whole. We have lost ground to nationalism too whenever we pitted ourselves against it, in China, Vietnam, Iran, and elsewhere, but the Soviet Union has lost ground on a larger scale for somewhat the same reason, in China, Egypt, and Poland, for example, and it had lost important ground earlier in Yugoslavia. If these setbacks are seen along with the recent economic stagnation of the Soviet Union at home, the conclusion is clear: The wave of the present and future is not Communism; it is nationalism, in a hundred-odd peoples in a hundred-odd places, all rejecting domination by either the Soviet Union or the United States. We and the Soviet Union can hope for rapport with this nationalism—if we deserve it. Domination, no.

In relation to peace, an important conclusion follows: *We do not need to fear that we must go through a nuclear holocaust in order to save the world and ourselves from Soviet domination.* The tide of history has turned decisively against it. On that basic issue we can relax. We will not have to choose between being red and being dead. It looks as if the absolute worst that the Soviet Union could do to the West, short of war, would be to seize the Middle East's oil fields and in some degree "Finlandize" Western Europe—probably temporarily—but that would not be the end of the world. It would not be Soviet domination of the world or of the United States, and it would not be a nuclear holocaust, unless we ourselves are insane enough to be the first to unleash nuclear war.

Specifically, we can relax by relinquishing our fear of an inevitable domino process if Communists gain power in one or a few countries in the Third World. That fear was fundamental in getting us into Vietnam and keeping us there. Probably it had some validity in the 1960s. It was realistic to think that Laos and Cambodia, at least, and perhaps Thailand, would become Communist-controlled if Vietnam did. But fears of a much wider spread of Communism if we failed to stop it by force had little validity then and have less now. (For a review of all the assets the West has in the Third World if we do *not* appear to threaten national independence there, see Chapter 17.) There may well be *national* Communism or milder forms of Marxist socialism in a number of places, comparable to its forms in China, Vietnam, Yugoslavia, Cuba and Nicaragua, but not the monolithic world movement under Moscow's control that we legitimately feared in the 1950s, and not necessarily aggressively hostile to the United States.

In a longer time perspective—decades or generations rather than years—these additional trends are grounds for hope:

6. *The advanced countries of the West and the Far East also show signs of mellowing.* The democratic West has retreated from imperialism. It also behaved much better toward its defeated enemies after World War II than after World War I, and the result of that (plus the unconditionalness of their defeat) has been a major in-

crease of both peacefulness and democracy in both West Germany and Japan. Those two countries, which can perhaps be regarded as the swing countries in the world balance of power, are now full-fledged members of the relatively prosperous, educated, democratic, technologically advanced, and peace-oriented "West."

7. *Soviet–American relations improved, intermittently but greatly, between 1953 and about 1975. They could do it again.* There is probably enough momentum in the spiral—the malignant process of hostile interaction—that has existed since about 1975 to make any short-term prospect of improvement very dubious, especially since the Korean plane incident. However, the same could be said about the similarly long and frightening period of increasing tension between 1945 and 1953, and it was replaced, after the death of Stalin, by the much longer, more irregular period of improvement. That period was punctuated by crises (Hungary, Berlin, Cuba, Vietnam, Czechoslovakia, the SAC alert of 1973), but after each crisis there was a new period of relaxation and usually a better one. There is ample reason for hope that the same could occur again, though not necessarily soon (Chapter 15).

8. *Women are playing a larger role in American foreign policy.* If this book is right in its emphasis on macho pride as a cause of war (Chapter 9), then whatever may be said against the role of women in politics on other grounds, their influence on the macho policies that increase the danger of war should be wholesome. (Of course there are exceptions, such as Joan of Arc and Margaret Thatcher, but poll data confirm the general impression that on issues related to war and peace women tend to be less macho than men.)

9. *Young people tend to be less nationalistic than older ones, which suggests a long-term trend away from the macho type of nationalism.* The Vietnam era and the scorn of many young people at that time for "superpatriotism" are well known. There are some indications that it is a worldwide phenomenon and still has some vitality.

10. *Education has been increasing throughout the world, and (along with related factors such as travel and discussion) it is, as a rule, a factor for peace.* Education is a central factor in the "development cluster," which includes also economic development, health, and the Western type of democracy. There *is* evidence, especially since 1945, that that cluster is correlated with peace. It is true that in the less democratic countries education is usually co-opted to

serve strictly the purposes of the national government. That is to be expected and in general serves no peaceful purpose. That was preeminently true in Nazi Germany and is true now of the USSR, China, and most of the less developed countries. However, if the term "developing" turns out eventually to be appropriate in describing more than a few of the less developed countries (it is not appropriate now, since most of them are stagnant, retreating, or developing very slowly), education and its related factors seem likely to become a more broadening process. If so, the very long-term prospect for the world as a whole is toward more democracy, and with it a trend toward more mature, less chauvinistic forms of nationalism, with less danger of war.

Putting together the realistic grounds for short-term fear and for long-term hope, my conclusion is that we, the human race, should muster all the restraint, all the empathy, all the wisdom at our command, concentrating on short-term measures in order to get safely through the danger period immediately ahead, but should not despair of the longer future. If we, the human race, manage to get through the danger period without a major war, there is an excellent chance of relatively smooth sailing from then on. It may even be possible then to make strides toward the kind of strong international organization that would basically attack the causes of war.

References

ADORNO, THEODORE W.; ELSE FRENKEL-BRUNSWIK; DANIEL LEVINSON; and NEVITT SANFORD. *The Authoritarian Personality.* New York: Harper, 1950.

ALBERTINI, LUIGI. *The Origins of the War of 1914.* 3 vols. London: Oxford University Press, 1952–57.

ALLISON, GRAHAM T. *Essence of Decision: Explaining the Cuban Missile Crises.* Boston: Little, Brown, 1971.

ALMOND, GABRIEL. *The Appeals of Communism.* Princeton, N.J.: Princeton University Press, 1954.

ALMOND, GABRIEL, and JAMES S. COLEMAN. *The Politics of the Developing Areas.* Princeton, N.J.: Princeton University Press, 1960.

ARBATOV, GEORGY. "A Soviet Commentary." In Cox, Arthur M., *Russian Roulette: The Superpower Game.* New York: Times Books, 1982, pp. 173–99.

ARDREY, ROBERT. *African Genesis.* New York: Atheneum, 1963.

BALL, GEORGE W., "Reflections on a Heavy Year," *Foreign Affairs,* special issue, "America and the World, 1980," *59,* No. 3 (1981): 474–99.

BARGHOORN, FREDERICK. *The Soviet Image of the United States.* New York: Harcourt Brace, 1950.

BARNET, RICHARD J. *Roots of War: The Men and Institutions Behind U.S. Foreign Policy.* New York: Penguin Books, 1972.

———. "The Search for National Security," *The New Yorker,* April 27, 1981a, pp. 50–140.

———. "Why on Earth Would the Soviets Invade Europe?" *Washington Post,* November 22, 1981b, pp. C1, C5.

BAUER, RAYMOND; ALEX INKELES; and CLYDE KLUCKHOHN. *How the Soviet System Works.* Cambridge, Mass.: Harvard University Press, 1956.

BIALER, SEWERYN. "Poland and the Soviet Imperium," *Foreign Affairs,* special issue, "America and the World, 1980," *59,* No. 3 (1981): 522–39.

———. "The Soviets Really Need Their Nukes," *Washington Post,* May 8, 1983, p. B1.

BLAINEY, GEOFFREY. *The Causes of War.* New York: The Free Press, 1973.

BLAKER, JAMES, and ANDREW HAMILTON. *Assessing the NATO/Warsaw Pact Mili-*

tary Balance. Washington, D.C.: Congressional Budget Office, 1977. Reprinted with minor revisions in Reichart and Sturm (1982), pp. 333–50.

BLECHMAN, BARRY M. "Do Negotiated Arms Limitations Have a Future?" *Foreign Affairs,* Fall 1980. Reprinted with minor revisions in Reichart and Sturm (1982), pp. 408–19.

BRODIE, BERNARD. *Strategy in the Missile Age.* Princeton, N.J.: Princeton University Press, 1959.

————, ed. *The Absolute Weapon.* New York: Harcourt Brace, 1946.

BRONFENBRENNER, URIE. "The Mirror-image in Soviet American Relations," *Journal of Social Issues, 17,* No. 3 (1961): 45–56.

BULL, HEDLEY. *The Future of Strategic Deterrence.* London: International Institute for Strategic Studies, Autumn 1980, pp. 13–23. Reprinted with minor revisions in Reichart and Sturm (1982) as "The Prospects for Deterrence."

BUNDY, McGEORGE; GEORGE KENNAN; ROBERT McNAMARA; and GERARD SMITH. "Nuclear Weapons and the Atlantic Alliance," *Foreign Affairs, 60,* No. 4 (Spring 1982): 753–68.

BURNS, JOHN F. "The Emergence of Andropov," *New York Times Magazine,* February 27, 1983.

BURT, RICHARD. "The Relevance of Arms Control in the 1980s," *Daedalus,* Vol. *110,* No. 1, Winter 1981. Reprinted with minor revisions as "The Perils of Arms Control in the 1980s" in Reichart and Sturm (1982), pp. 419–31.

BURTON, JOHN. *Deviance, Terrorism and War: The Process of Solving Unsolved Social and Political Problems.* New York: St. Martin's Press, 1979.

BUTOW, ROBERT. *Tojo and the Coming of the War.* Princeton, N.J.: Princeton University Press, 1961.

BUTTERFIELD, HERBERT. *History and Human Relations.* London: Collins, 1951.

CANNON, WALTER B. *Bodily Changes in Pain, Hunger, Fear and Rage.* New York: Harper, 1963.

CANTRIL, HADLEY. *The Human Dimension: Experiences in Policy Research.* New Brunswick, N.J.: Rutgers University Press, 1967.

CARPENTER, C. RAY. "Behavior and Social Relations of the Howling Monkey," *Comparative Psychology Monthly,* Johns Hopkins University, 1934.

CLAUSEWITZ, CARL VON. *On War.* Paperback, Baltimore: Penguin Books, 1968. Original German version: *Vom Kriege,* Berlin, 1832.

CONQUEST, ROBERT. *The Great Terror: Stalin's Purge of the 1930s.* New York: Macmillan, 1968.

CORDESMAN, ANTHONY H. *Deterrence in the 1980s. Part I: American Strategic Forces and Extended Deterrence.* Adelphi Papers, No. 175. London: International Institute for Strategic Studies, 1982.

COTTRELL, LEONARD, and SYLVIA EBERHARDT. *American Opinion on World Affairs in the Atomic Age.* Princeton, N.J.: Princeton University Press, 1948.

COUSINS, NORMAN. "Modern Man Is Obsolete," *The Saturday Review,* August 1945. Reprinted in *The Saturday Review,* Aug. 1, 1970.

COX, ARTHUR M. *Russian Roulette: The Superpower Game.* New York: Times Books, 1982.

DEUTSCH, MORTON. *The Resolution of Conflict: Constructive and Destructive Processes.* New Haven: Yale University Press, 1973.

_____. "The Prevention of World War III: A Psychological Perspective," *Political Psychology, 4,* No. 1 (March 1983): 3–31.

DOLLARD, JOHN; LEONARD DOOB; NEAL MILLER; O. H. MOWRER; and ROBERT SEARS. *Frustration and Aggression.* New Haven: Yale University Press, 1939.

DREW, ELIZABETH. "A Political Journal." *The New Yorker,* May 9, 1983a, pp. 48–87, and June 20, 1983b, pp. 39–75.

EINHORN, ROBERT. "Treaty Compliance," *Foreign Policy, 45* (Winter 1981–82): 29–47.

EINSTEIN, ALBERT. Quoted by Cox (1982), p. 206.

ELON, AMOS, and SANA HASSAN. *Between Enemies: An Arab–Israeli Dialogue.* London: André Deutsch, 1974.

ERMARTH, FRITZ W. "Contrasts in American and Soviet Strategic Thought." In Reichart and Sturm (1982), pp. 61–70.

ETHEREDGE, LLOYD. "Hardball Politics: A Model," *Political Psychology, 1,* No. 1 (Spring 1979): 3–25.

ETZIONI, AMITAI. *The Hard Way to Peace: A New Strategy.* New York: Collier Books, 1962.

_____. "The Kennedy Experiment." In E. I. Megargee and J. E. Hokanson, eds., *The Dynamics of Aggression: Individual, Group and International Analyses.* New York: Harper and Row, 1970.

FAIRBANK, JOHN KING. *The United States and China.* Rev. ed. New York: Viking, 1958.

FAY, SIDNEY B. *The Origins of the World War.* 2 vols. New York: Free Press, 1966. Originally 1928, 1930.

FEIFER, GEORGE. "Russian Disorders: The Sick Man of Europe," *Harper's,* February 1981, pp. 41–55.

FESTINGER, LEON. *A Theory of Cognitive Dissonance.* New York: Harper, 1957.

FISCHER, FRITZ. *Germany's Aims in the First World War.* New York: Norton, 1967. Original German version: *Griff nach der Weltmacht,* Hamburg, 1961.

FISHER, ROGER, and WILLIAM URY. *Getting to YES: Negotiating Agreement Without Giving In.* Boston: Houghton Mifflin, 1981.

Fontaine, André. "Transatlantic Doubts and Dreams," *Foreign Affairs,* special issue, "America and the World, 1980," *59,* No. 3 (1981): 578–93.

Frank, Jerome. *Sanity and Survival: Psychological Aspects of War and Peace.* New York: Vintage Books, 1967. Rev. ed., 1982.

Freedman, Jonathan; J. Merrill Carlsmith; and David O. Sears. *Social Psychology.* Englewood Cliffs, N.J.: Prentice-Hall, 1970.

Freedman, Lawrence. "NATO Myths." *Foreign Policy, 45* (Winter 1981–82): 48–68.

Freud, Anna. *The Ego and the Mechanisms of Defense.* New York: International Universities Press, 1946.

Freud, Sigmund. *A General Introduction to Psychoanalysis.* London: Boni & Liveright, 1924. Citations are from American paperback edition, Doubleday Permabooks, 1953.

Fromm, Erich. *The Anatomy of Human Destructiveness.* New York: Holt, Rinehart & Winston, 1973.

Fulbright, Senator J. William. "The Fatal Arrogance of Power," *New York Times Magazine,* May 15, 1966.

Garthoff, Raymond L. "Mutual Deterrence and Strategic Arms Limitation in Soviet Policy," *International Security,* Summer 1978.

Gayler, Admiral Noel. "How to Break the Momentum of the Nuclear Arms Race," *New York Times Magazine,* April 25, 1982, pp. 48–88.

Gelb, Leslie H. "Nuclear Bargaining: The President's Options," *New York Times Magazine,* June 27, 1982.

————. "A Practical Way to Arms Control," *New York Times Magazine,* June 5, 1983, pp. 33–42.

George, Alexander L. *The Limits of Coercive Diplomacy.* Boston: Little, Brown, 1971.

George, Alexander, and Richard Smoke. *Deterrence in American Foreign Policy: Theory and Practice.* New York: Columbia University Press, 1974.

Gray, Colin. "Nuclear Strategy: The Case for a Theory of Victory," *International Security, 4,* No. 1 (Summer 1979): 54–87. Reprinted with minor revisions, under the title "What Deters? The Ability to Wage Nuclear War," in Reichart and Sturm (1982), pp. 171–87.

Guroff, Gregory, and Steven Grant. Washington, D.C., USICA study, "Soviet Elites: World View and Perceptions of the U.S." Summarized by Murrey Marder, *Washington Post,* October 25, 1981, p. A6.

Gottlieb, Sanford. *What About the Russians?* Northfield, Mass.: Student/Teacher Organization to Prevent Nuclear War, 1982.

Halle, Louis J. *The Cold War as History.* New York: Harper Colophon, 1967.

Harkabi, Yehoshafat. *Arab Attitudes to Israel.* Jerusalem: Israel Universities Press, 1971.

HAYAKAWA, SENATOR S. I. *Modern Guide to Synonyms*. New York: Funk & Wagnalls, 1968.

HEIDEN, KONRAD. *Der Fuehrer*. Boston: Houghton Mifflin, 1944.

HEIDER, FRITZ. *The Psychology of Interpersonal Relations*. New York: Wiley, 1958.

HERADSTVEIT, DANIEL. *The Arab–Israeli Conflict: Psychological Obstacles to Peace*. Oslo: Universitetsforlaget, 1979.

HERMANN, CHARLES F. *International Crises*. New York: Free Press, 1973.

HINTON, HAROLD C. *Communist China in World Politics*. Boston: Houghton Mifflin, 1966.

HITLER, ADOLF. *My New Order* (speeches). Ed. Raoul de Roussy de Sales. New York: Reynal and Hitchcock, 1941.

———. *Mein Kampf*. Cambridge, Mass.: Houghton Mifflin, Riverside Press, 1943 (originally 1925, 1927).

HOLBORN, HAJO. *A History of Modern Germany, 1840–1945*. New York: Knopf, 1969.

HOLSTI, OLE; ROBERT NORTH; and RICHARD BRODY. "Perception and Action in the 1914 Crisis." In Singer, (1968), pp. 123–58.

HORNEY, KAREN. *The Neurotic Personality of Our Time*. New York: Norton, 1937.

HOUGH, JERRY. "Why the Russians Invaded," *The Nation*, March 1, 1980, pp. 225–32.

HOVLAND, CARL; ARTHUR LUMSDAINE; and F. D. SHEFFIELD. *Experiments on Mass Communication*. Princeton, N.J.: Princeton University Press, 1949.

HOVLAND, CARL; IRVING JANIS; and HAROLD KELLEY. *Communication and Persuasion*. New Haven: Yale University Press, 1953.

HOVLAND, CARL, and H. A. PRITZKER. "Extent of Opinion Change as a Function of Amount of Change Advocated," *Journal of Abnormal and Social Psychology, 54* (1957): 257–61.

HOVLAND, CARL; O. J. HARVEY; and MUZAFER SHERIF. "Assimilation and Contrast Effects in Reactions to Communication and Attitude Change," *Journal of Abnormal and Social Psychology, 55* (1957): 244–52.

HOWARD, MICHAEL. "The Case for Keeping a Strong Conventional Arms Capability," letter to *The Times* (London), November 3, 1981. Quoted by Cox (1982), pp. 147, 210.

IKLÉ, FRED. "There's Reason for Our Caution About Dealing with the Soviets," *Washington Post*, August 17, 1982, p. A17.

INTERNATIONAL INSTITUTE FOR STRATEGIC STUDIES (IISS). *The Military Balance, 1982–83*. London, 1982.

JAMES, WILLIAM. *Psychology*. New York: Henry Holt, 1890.

JANIS, IRVING L. "Effects of Fear Arousal on Attitude Change: Recent Developments in Theory and Experimental Research." In Leonard Berkowitz, ed., *Advances in Experimental Social Psychology.* Vol. 3. New York: Academic Press, 1967.

_____. *Victims of Groupthink.* Boston: Houghton Mifflin, 1973.

JANIS, IRVING, and SEYMOUR FESHBACH. "Effects of Fear-arousing Communications," *Journal of Abnormal and Social Psychology, 48* (1953): 78–92.

JANIS, IRVING, and BERT L. KING. "The Influence of Role-playing on Opinion Change," *Journal of Abnormal and Social Psychology, 49* (1954): 211–18.

JAY, PETER. "Regionalism and Geopolitics," *Foreign Affairs,* special issue, "America and the World, 1979," *58,* No. 3 (1980): 485–514.

JERVIS, ROBERT. *Perception and Misperception in International Politics.* Princeton: Princeton University Press, 1976.

_____. "Why Nuclear Superiority Doesn't Matter," *Political Science Quarterly, 94* (Winter 1979–80): 617–33. Reprinted with minor revisions as "What Deters? The Ability to Inflict Assured Destruction," in Reichart and Sturm, (1982), pp. 161–70.

JONES, EDWARD, and RICHARD NISBETT. *The Actor and the Observer: Divergent Perceptions of the Causes of Behavior.* Morristown, N.J.: General Learning Press, 1971.

KAHN, HERMAN. *On Escalation: Metaphors and Scenarios.* New York: Praeger, 1965.

KAISER, KARL; GEORG LEBER; ALOIS MERTES; and FRANZ-JOSEF SCHULZE. "Nuclear Weapons and the Preservation of Peace: A German Response" (to Bundy *et al.*), *Foreign Affairs, 60,* No. 5 (Summer 1982): 1157–70.

KAISER, ROBERT G. *Russia: The People and the Power.* New York: Pocket Books, 1976.

_____. "U.S.–Soviet Relations: Goodbye to Détente," *Foreign Affairs* special issue, "America and the World, 1980," *59,* No. 3 (1981): 500–521.

KAPLOWITZ, NOEL. "Psychopolitical Dimensions of the Middle East Conflict," *Journal of Conflict Resolutions,* Vol. *20,* No. 2, June 1976.

KARPOVICH, M. "Russian Imperialism or Communist Aggression?" *New Leader,* June 4, 11, 1951. Reprinted in R. A. Goldwin, ed., *Readings in Russian Foreign Policy.* New York: Oxford University Press, 1959, pp. 657–66.

KEENY, SPURGEON M., JR., and WOLFGANG K. H. PANOFSKY. "MAD Versus NUTS: Can Doctrine or Weaponry Remedy the Mutual Hostage Relationship of the Superpowers?" *Foreign Affairs, 60,* No. 2 (Winter 1981–82): 287–304.

KELMAN, HERBERT C., ED. *International Behavior: A Social-psychological Analysis.* New York: Holt, Rinehart & Winston, 1965 (includes White, 1965).

_____. "The Problem-solving Workshop in Conflict Resolution." In R. L. Merritt, ed., *Communication in International Politics.* Urbana: University of Illinois Press, 1972.

KENNAN, GEORGE F. The Reith Lectures. Reprinted in *Memoirs: 1950–1963.* Boston: Little, Brown, 1972.

———. "Imprudent Response to the Afghanistan Crisis?" *Bulletin of the Atomic Scientists,* April 1980, pp. 7–9. Reprinted from *New York Times Magazine,* February 1, 1980.

———. Address on the occasion of his receiving the Albert Einstein Peace Prize, Washington, D.C., May 19, 1981. Quoted by Cox (1982), pp. 201–2.

———. *The Nuclear Delusion: Soviet–American Relations in the Atomic Age.* New York: Pantheon, 1982.

KERNBERG, OTTO. *Borderline Conditions and Pathological Narcissism.* New York: Jason Aronson, 1975.

KHRUSHCHEV, NIKITA. *For Victory in Peaceful Competition with Capitalism.* New York: Dutton, 1960.

———. *Khrushchev Remembers.* Trans. and ed., Strobe Talbott. Boston: Little, Brown, 1970.

KISSINGER, HENRY. *The Necessity for Choice: Prospects for American Foreign Policy.* New York: Harper, 1961.

———. "A New Approach to Arms Control," *Time,* Vol. *121,* March 21, 1983, pp. 24–26.

KNUTSON, JEANNE N., ED. *Handbook of Political Psychology.* San Francisco: Jossey-Bass, 1973.

KOHUT, HEINZ. *The Restoration of the Self.* New York: International Universities Press, 1977.

LAMBETH, BENJAMIN. "Soviet Strategic Conduct and the Prospects for Stability." R-2579-AF (Santa Monica: Rand Corp., December 1980). Reprinted with minor revisions as "What Deters? An Assessment of the Soviet View," in Reichart and Sturm (1982) pp. 188–98.

LASSWELL, HAROLD D. *Psychopathology and Politics.* Chicago: University of Chicago Press, 1930.

LEBOW, RICHARD NED. *Between Peace and War: The Nature of International Crisis.* Baltimore: Johns Hopkins Press, 1981.

LEITES, NATHAN. *A Study of Bolshevism.* New York: Free Press, 1953.

LELLOUCHE, PIERRE. "Europe and Her Defense," *Foreign Affairs, 60,* No. 1 (Spring 1981): 813–34.

LEWIN, KURT. *Field Theory in Social Science.* New York: Harper, 1951.

LORENZ, KONRAD. *On Aggression.* New York: Harcourt Brace, 1966.

LYONS, EUGENE. *Our Secret Allies.* New York: Duell, Sloan & Pearce, 1954.

MARDER, MURREY. "After 1962 Disgrace, Soviets Refuse to Yield on Troops," *Washington Post,* October 1, 1979, p. A2.

MARDER, MURREY. "Events Around Stalled SALT Illustrate Moscow-Washington Gulf." *Washington Post,* January 2, 1981, p. A14.

McGRORY, MARY. Column in *Washington Post,* July 5, 1983.

McNAMARA, ROBERT S. "The Military Role of Nuclear Weapons." *Foreign Affairs, 62* (1), Fall 1983, 59–80.

MORGENTHAU, HANS. *Politics Among Nations: The Struggle for Power and Peace.* 4th ed. New York: Knopf, 1967.

MYRDAL, ALVA. *The Game of Disarmament.* New York: Pantheon, 1976.

NAGORSKI, ANDREW. "East Asia in 1980," *Foreign Affairs,* special issue, "America and the World, 1980," *59,* 3 (1981): 667–95.

*New York Times/*CBS News Poll, May 19–23, reported in *New York Times,* May 30, 1982, pp. 1, 22.

NIEBUHR, REINHOLD. *Moral Man and Immoral Society.* New York: Scribner's, 1960.

NIKHONOV, ALEXEI (Institute of World Economy and International Relations, Moscow). Quoted by Marder, *Washington Post,* October 1, 1979, p. A2.

NITZE, PAUL. "Deterring Our Deterrent," *Foreign Policy, 25* (Winter 1976–77): 195–210.

————. "Strategy in the Decade of the 1980s," *Foreign Affairs, 59,* No. 1 (Fall 1980): 82–101.

NORTH, ROBERT C. "Perception and Action in the 1914 Crisis," *Journal of International Affairs,* No. 1, 1967.

NOVAK, JOSEPH. *The Future is Ours, Comrade.* Garden City, N.Y.: Doubleday, 1960.

ORGANSKI, A. F. K. *World Politics.* New York: Knopf, 1958.

OSGOOD, CHARLES E. *An Alternative to War or Surrender.* Urbana: University of Illinois Press, 1962.

OSGOOD, ROBERT E. *Limited War Revisited.* Boulder, Colo.: Westview Press, 1979. Quotations are from excerpts reprinted under the title "Limited War and Power Projection" in Reichart and Sturm (1982), pp. 373–82.

PARES, BERNARD. *A History of Russia.* 5th ed. New York: Knopf, 1947.

PAYNE, JAMES L. *The American Threat: The Fear of War as an Instrument of Foreign Policy.* Chicago: Markham, 1970.

Pentagon papers. Edited by Neil Sheehan and others. New York: New York Times Books, 1971. Citations are from the Bantam edition, 1971.

PERRY, HELEN S. "Selective Inattention as an Explanatory Concept for U.S. Public Attitudes Toward the Atomic Bomb," *Psychiatry, 17* (1954): 225–42.

PETROV, VLADIMIR. "New Dimensions of Soviet Foreign Policy." In Franklin D. Margiotta, ed., *Evolving Strategic Realities: Implications for U.S. Policymakers.* Washington, D.C., National Defense University Press, 1980, pp. 16–38.

PIAGET, JEAN. "Principal Factors Determining Intellectual Evolution from Childhood to Adult Life." In Piaget, *Factors Determining Human Behavior.* Cambridge, Mass.: Harvard University Press, 1937.

PONOMARYOV, B.; ANDREI GROMYKO; and V. KHVOSTOV. *History of Soviet Foreign Policy, 1945–1970.* Moscow: Progress Publishers, 1973.

PRUITT, DEAN G. *Negotiating Behavior.* New York: Academic Press, 1981.

REICHART, JOHN F., and STEVEN R. STURM, EDS. *American Defense Policy.* 5th ed. Baltimore: Johns Hopkins Press, 1982.

RICH, NORMAN. *Hitler's War Aims.* New York: Norton, 1973.

ROSE, FRANCOIS DE. "Inflexible Response," *Foreign Affairs, 61,* No. 1 (Fall 1982): 136–50.

ROSTOW, WALT W. *The Stages of Economic Growth: A Non-Communist Manifesto.* Cambridge, Mass.: Harvard University Press, 1960.

RUBIN, JEFFREY Z. *Dynamics of Third Party Intervention: Interdisciplinary Perspectives on International Conflict.* New York: Praeger, 1980.

SACHAR, HOWARD M. *A History of Israel.* New York: Knopf, 1976.

SCALAPINO, ROBERT A. "Asia at the End of the 1970s," *Foreign Affairs,* special issue, "America and the World, 1979," *58,* 3 (1980): 693–737.

SCHEER, ROBERT. *With Enough Shovels: Reagan, Bush, and Nuclear War.* New York: Random House, 1982.

SCHELL, JONATHAN. *The Fate of the Earth.* New York: Knopf, 1982.

SCHELLENBERG, JAMES A. *The Science of Conflict.* New York: Oxford University Press, 1982.

SCHLESINGER, JAMES. In *Department of Defense, Annual Report, F. Y. 1976 and F. Y. 1977.* Washington, D.C.: U.S. Govt. Printing Office, 1975. Quoted by Jervis (1982), p. 164.

SCHMIDT, WILLIAM E. "Poll Shows Lessening Fear the U.S. Military is Lagging," *New York Times,* February 6, 1983, p. 1. Reports "a recent *New York Times*/CBS News Poll."

SCHMITT, BERNADOTTE. *The Coming of the War, 1914.* 2 vols. New York and London: Scribner's, 1930.

SCOTT, JONATHAN F. *Five Weeks: The Surge of Public Opinion on the Eve of the Great War.* New York: John Day, 1927.

SHIRER, WILLIAM. *The Rise and Fall of the Third Reich.* New York: Simon & Schuster, 1960.

SHULMAN, MARSHALL D. *Stalin's Foreign Policy Reappraised.* New York: Atheneum, 1965. Originally Harvard University Press, 1963.

SIMON, HERBERT. *Models of Man.* New York: Wiley, 1957.

SINGER, J. DAVID, ED. *Quantitative International Politics: Insights and Evidence.* New York: The Free Press, 1968.

SMOKE, RICHARD. "The Evolution of American Defense Policy." In *Handbook of Political Science,* Vol. 8, *International Politics.* Ed. Fred I. Greenstein and Nelson Polsby. Reading, Mass.: Addison-Wesley, 1975. Reprinted with minor revisions in Reichart and Sturm (1982), pp. 94–135.

SNYDER, GLENN, and PAUL DIESING. *Conflict Among Nations.* Princeton, N.J.: Princeton University Press, 1977.

SOLZHENITSYN, ALEKSANDR I. *The Gulag Archipelago, 1918–1956: An Experiment in Literary Investigation.* 2 vols. New York: Harper & Row, 1973.

SONNENFELDT, HELMUT, and WILLIAM G. HYLAND. "Soviet Perspectives on Security." *Adelphi Paper 150.* London: International Institute of Strategic Studies, 1979.

STATE DEPARTMENT. *Briefing Memorandum,* March 9, 1981, "Public Attitudes Toward U.S.–Soviet Relations." From Dyess to Stoessel and Eagleburger, drafted by Alvin Richman and B. Roshco. Reports a series of Roper polls on relative military strength; only that of September–October 1980 deals specifically with nuclear capability. Unclassified.

STATE DEPARTMENT. *Information Memorandum,* December 2, 1981, "Despite Distrust of Soviet Intentions Majority of Americans Favor Negotiations." From Dean Fischer to the Secretary. Reports Roper polls from 1979 to 1981; drafted by Alvin Richman. Unclassified.

STEINBRUNER, JOHN D. "Nuclear Decapitation." *Foreign Policy, 45* (Winter 1981–82): 16–28.

STOESSINGER, JOHN. *Why Nations Go to War.* New York: St. Martin's Press, 1974.

STUBBING, RICHARD A. "The Imaginary Defense Gap: We Already Outspend Them." *Washington Post,* February 14, 1982, pp. C1, C4.

SULLIVAN, HARRY STACK. *The Interpersonal Theory of Psychiatry.* Ed. Helen Swick Perry and Mary Ladd Gawel. New York: Norton, 1953.

SUSSMAN, BARRY. Report on *Washington Post*/ABC News Poll, *Washington Post,* April 29, 1982, p. A17.

———. Report on *Washington Post*/ABC News Poll, *Washington Post,* February 1, 1983.

TALBOTT, STROBE. "Playing for the Future: Is the U.S. Making the Right Moves Toward Moscow in Arms Control?" *Time,* April 18, 1983, pp. 16–29.

TALBOTT, STROBE, and BRUCE NELAN. "The View from Red Square," *Time,* February 4, 1980, p. 18.

TAYLOR, A. J. P. *The Origins of the Second World War.* 2d ed. New York: Fawcett, Atheneum, 1961. Citations are from Fawcett edition.

———. *Europe: Grandeur and Decline.* Harmondsworth; Middlesex, England: Penguin Books, 1967. Original essays 1943–55.

TAYLOR, GENERAL MAXWELL. "With the Arms of Devastation Already in Hand, It Would Be Folly to Race the Russians Further," *International Herald-Tribune,* July 4, 1981. Originally written for the *Washington Post.*

TEDESCHI, JAMES T., and SVENN LINDSKOLD. *Social Psychology.* New York: Wiley, 1976.

TOLAND, JOHN. *Adolf Hitler.* New York: Ballantine, 1976.

TROFIMENKO, HENRY. "The Third World and the U.S.–Soviet Competition: A Soviet View," *Foreign Affairs, 59,* No. 5 (Summer 1981): 1021–40.

TUCHMAN, BARBARA. *The Guns of August.* New York: Macmillan, 1962. Citations from Bantam edition, 1976.

———. *Stillwell and the American Experience in China, 1911–45.* New York: Macmillan, 1970.

———. "The Alternative to Arms Control," *New York Times Magazine,* April 18, 1982.

TUCKER, ROBERT C. *The Soviet Political Mind.* New York: Praeger, 1963.

———. *Stalin as Revolutionary, 1879–1929: A Study in History and Personality.* New York: Norton, 1973. First volume of a three-volume biography.

TVERSKY, AMOS, and DANIEL KAHNEMAN. "Availability: A Heuristic for Judging Frequency and Probability," *Cognitive Psychology,* Vol. 5, 1973.

ULAM, ADAM B. *The Rivals: America and Russia Since World War II.* New York: The Viking Press, 1971.

WALTON, RICHARD E., and R. B. MCKERSIE. *A Behavioral Theory of Labor Negotiations.* New York: McGraw-Hill, 1965.

WALZER, MICHAEL. *Just and Unjust Wars: A Moral Argument with Historical Illustrations.* New York: Basic Books, 1977.

WARNER, EDWARD L. "Defense Policy of the Soviet Union." In Reichart and Sturm (1982), pp. 48–61.

WATTS, WILLIAM, and LLOYD FREE. *State of the Nation, 1976.* New York: Universe Books, a Potomac Associates Book, 1976.

WEDGE, BRYANT. "Mass Psychotherapy for Intergroup Conflict." In J. H. Masserman and J. J. Schwab, eds., *Man for Humanity.* Springfield, Ill.: Charles C. Thomas, 1972.

WHITE, RALPH K. "Hitler, Roosevelt and the Nature of War Propaganda," *Journal of Abnormal and Social Psychology, 44,* No. 2 (April 1949): 157–74.

———. "Soviet Perceptions of the U.S. and the U.S.S.R." In Kelman (1965), pp. 238–76.

———. "'Socialism' and 'Capitalism': An International Misunderstanding," *Foreign Affairs, 44* (1966): 216–28.

———. "Three Not-so-obvious Contributions of Psychology to Peace" (Lewin memorial address), *Journal of Social Issues, 25,* No. 4 (1969): 23–29.

_____. *Nobody Wanted War: Misperception in Vietnam and Other Wars.* Rev. ed. New York: Doubleday/Anchor, 1970.

_____. "Propaganda: Morally Questionable and Morally Unquestionable Techniques," *Annals of the American Academy of Political and Social Science, 398* (November 1971): 26–35.

_____. "Misperception in the Arab–Israeli Conflict," *Journal of Social Issues, 33,* No. 1 (1977): 190–221.

_____. "Empathizing with the Rulers of the USSR." *Political Psychology, 4,* No. 1 (March 1983): 121–37.

WHITNEY, CRAIG. "The View from the Kremlin," *New York Times Magazine,* April 20, 1980, pp. 30–91.

WOHLSTETTER, ALBERT. "The Delicate Balance of Terror," *Foreign Affairs, 37* (1959): 211–34.

WOLFE, BERTRAM. "Communist Ideology and Soviet Foreign Policy," *Foreign Affairs, 41* (1962): 152–70.

WOUK, HERMAN. *The Winds of War.* New York: Simon & Schuster, Pocket Books, 1973.

WRIGHT, QUINCY. *A Study of War.* Chicago: University of Chicago Press, 1942. Rev. abridged ed., 1964.

YANKELOVICH, DANIEL, and LARRY KAAGAN. "Assertive America," *Foreign Affairs,* special issue, "America and the World, 1980," *59,* No. 3 (1981): 696–713.

YARMOLINSKY, ADAM. Reply to question at symposium, "The Search for Global Security," Washington, D.C., May 18–19, 1981.

YOUNG, ANDREW. "The United States and Africa: Victory for Diplomacy." *Foreign Affairs,* special issue, "America and the World, 1980," *59,* No. 3 (1981): 648–65.

ZAMOSHKIN, YU. A., and E. YA. BATALOV, EDS. *Sovremyennoye Polyetyicheskoye Soznanyiye v S.Sh.A.* (Contemporary Political Consciousness in the U.S.A.). Moskva: Izdatyelstvo "Nauka," 1980.

ZARTMAN, I. W. "Negotiation as a Joint Decision-making Process," *Journal of Conflict Resolution, 21* (1977): 619–38. Reprinted in I. W. Zartman, ed., *The Negotiation Process.* Beverly Hills: Sage, 1978.

ZINNES, DINA. "The Expression and Perception of Hostility in Prewar Crisis: 1914." In Singer (1968), pp. 85–122.

Index

Accidental war, 54–56, 299
Acheson, Dean, 71, 72, 227n
Adenauer, Konrad, 101
Adler, Alfred, 123
Adlerian process of compensation, 138, 156, 158
Adorno, Theodore W., 125
Afghanistan, 13, 14–21, 36, 42, 43, 45–46, 48–50, 60, 98, 102, 115, 120, 125, 129, 143, 144, 154, 181, 204, 237, 242–244, 261, 263, 282, 285, 286, 296, 299, 319, 345, 346
Agadir crisis (1911), 93, 121
Agent orange, 18
Aggression, 3, 14n, 128–134, 200–202, 238–249, 255–257, 273–274, 278, 290–291, 299, 316
Air reconnaissance, 29–30
Albania, 243
Albertini, Luigi, 208
Algeciras Conference, 192
Algeria, 121, 286
Allies, close relations with, 280–284
Allison, Graham T., 133
Almond, Gabriel, 125, 291
Alsace-Lorraine, 121, 150, 191, 196, 199, 204, 206, 207, 212
Amin, Hafizullah, 16–18, 296
Andropov, Yuri, 23, 35, 43, 237, 256, 282, 313
Angell, Norman, 2
Anger, 82, 88, 90, 91, 128–134, 136, 163–165, 200–202, 260, 262, 268, 269, 296, 299
Angola, 42, 49–50, 60, 102, 164, 165, 237, 247, 285
Antiballistic missile (ABM), 236

Antitank weapons, 41
Appeasement, 6, 100, 105, 174, 205, 215, 216, 221, 222, 255–256, 262, 273
Arab–Israeli conflict, 60, 95, 97–99, 115, 116, 121, 129, 152–153, 163, 164, 167, 257, 274, 283–284, 293–294, 318–319
Arbatov, Georgy, 14n, 22–24, 34–35, 47, 50n, 178–180, 203, 227n, 299, 300, 343
Ardrey, Robert, 2, 152
Argentina, 49, 121, 149, 165
Aristotle, 109n
Arms-against-an-innocent-self mechanism, 84–86
Arms control, 295–314
Arms-makers, 266
Arms race, 21–23, 68
Arms reduction agreements, 67, 75–79
Arnold, Matthew, 298
Association of Southeast Asian Nations (ASEAN), 317
Assured destruction (AD), 110
Attribution, 172–175, 262
Australia, 280
Austria-Hungary, 60, 73, 93, 96, 114, 120, 132, 136, 148, 150, 156–158, 182, 190, 192–194, 196, 197, 199–202, 206–208, 217, 222, 248, 264

Balance of power, 27, 67, 69–75, 248, 259, 267, 280, 316
Ball, George, 283
Bandung Conference, 43
Bangladesh, 150

Barghoorn, Frederick, 143
Barnet, Richard J., 43, 44, 45, 50n, 126–127
Baruch Plan, 330
Batalov, E. Ya., 227n
Battlefield nuclear weapons, 41–42, 172, 318
Bauer, Raymond, 144
Bay of Pigs, 27, 145, 235, 241, 245, 246, 252, 291, 296
Beck, Jozef, 217
Begin, Menachem, 152, 241, 247, 252
Belgium, 102, 114, 121, 194–196, 204, 218, 280
Beneš, Eduard, 217
Berchtold, Count Leopold von, 200
Berlin crises, 15, 36, 71, 151, 164, 232, 234–235, 243–244, 253
Berlin-to-Baghdad railway, 94, 156–157, 193, 208
Bethmann-Hollweg, Theobald von, 72, 193, 194, 200, 203
Bialer, Seweryn, 51, 125, 155, 282, 286
Biological weapons, 18, 297, 298
Biological Weapons Convention (BWC), 297
Bismarck, Otto von, 73, 101, 129, 190, 191, 247
Black-top enemy image, 180
Blainey, Geoffrey, 269
Blaker, James, 24, 41
Blame, projection of, 138
Blechman, Barry, 60n, 68–69
Blitzkrieg, 218
Blurred distinctions, 172–175, 262, 316
Boer war, 69, 191, 208
Bolsheviks, 146, 213, 228
Bosnia-Herzegovina, 150, 192, 199, 204, 207, 261
Brandt, Willy, 236
Brazil, 49, 165, 267
Brest-Litovsk, Treaty of, 228
Brezhnev, Leonid, 39, 60, 129, 233, 237, 256, 295
Brinkmanship, 73
Brodie, Bernard, 110, 234, 302

Brody, Richard, 198
Bronfenbrenner, Urie, 10
Buffer territory, 12–13, 20, 44, 46
Bulgaria, 243
Bull, Hedley, 111n
Bundy, McGeorge, 40, 311
Bunsen, Christian von, 200, 201
Burns, John F., 43
Burt, Richard, 60n, 302, 303
Burton, John, 317
Butow, Robert, 99
Butterfield, Herbert, 162–163, 176

Caldecott, Helen, 329
Cambodia, 2, 42, 49, 50, 150, 164, 237, 247, 285, 290
Camp David accords, 318
Canada, 280
Cannon, Walter B., 91
Cantril, Hadley, 145, 177, 246, 291
Capitalism, 263–264
Carlsmith, J. Merrill, 331
Carpenter, C. Ray, 152
Carter, Jimmy, 16, 20, 47, 278, 282, 284, 295
Carter Doctrine, 47, 285
Carthage, 247
Castro, Fidel, 145, 235, 246, 291
Causes of War, The (Blainey), 269
Central Intelligence Agency (CIA), 97
Chamberlain, Neville, 100, 174, 196, 215, 216, 222–224
Chauvinism, 121, 122n
Chess game analogy, 38–40, 44, 46, 160
Chiang Kai-shek, 232, 245, 252, 292
Chile, 49, 165, 252
China, 20, 26, 29, 35, 42, 59, 71, 150, 236, 285, 287, 346
Churchill, Sir Winston, 3, 6, 105, 231
Civil wars, intervention in, 56–60
Classification problem, 306
Clausewitz, Carl von, 201, 278
Coleman, James S., 291
Communism, 263, 267, 286, 292, 345–347

Communist Manifesto, The (Marx and Engels), 170, 228
Comprehensive Test Ban (CTB), 306, 312, 328
Compulsive acts, 117–118
Congo, 267
Conquest, Robert, 337
Conventional forces, 22–24, 32–33, 38, 68, 80–81, 83, 85, 273, 277, 333
Cordesman, Anthony, 31n, 32, 300
Cottrell, Leonard, 330
Cousins, Norman, 321
Cox, Arthur M., 23n, 31n, 40, 41, 42, 44, 55, 172, 227n, 300, 312, 318, 319, 335, 336
Crimean war, 345
Cruise missiles, 66, 84, 94, 95, 237, 247, 305, 306, 313, 335
Crystal Night, 216
Cuba, 36, 42, 43, 49, 60, 287
Cuban missile crisis, 15, 26–28, 65, 94, 95, 121, 164, 165, 235, 246, 247, 253, 254, 296, 308
Cultural lag, 170
Curzon Line, 217, 218, 230
Cyprus, 46, 121, 150
Czechoslovakia, 36, 43, 45, 46, 48, 60, 98, 115, 120, 131, 154, 164, 212, 215–217, 223, 232, 236, 241, 243, 244, 275, 285

Daladier, Edouard, 215, 222, 224
Danzig, 150, 212, 217, 218, 220
Defensively motivated aggression, 53–54, 96–100, 197, 238
Delcassé, Théophile, 192, 199, 204, 207
Dembo, Tamara, 173
Democracy, 263–265, 279, 288
Denial, 142, 157
Denmark, 218, 280
Destabilizing nuclear weapons, deep cuts in, 305, 306–309, 328
Détente, 15, 16, 20, 81, 101, 164, 165, 236, 254
Deterrence, 24, 71, 76; *see also* Minimal deterrence

limitation of conventional, 109–112
slippages in, 102–103
tension-reduction and, 104–106
Deutsch, Morton, 83, 88, 92–93, 299
"Devil theory" of war, 3–4
Diabolical enemy-image, 67, 77, 88, 118, 133–134, 137, 138–142, 145, 161, 166, 176, 177, 202–203, 207, 247, 249, 260, 296, 299, 336–337
Diem, Ngo Dinh, 14, 15, 17, 252, 292
Diesing, Paul, 133, 227n
Diplomatic recognition, 251
Dollard, John, 130, 137
Dominican Republic, 49, 60, 85, 165, 252
Domino theory, 267, 347
Doob, Leonard, 130, 137
Drew, Elizabeth, 309, 335, 337
Driving forces, 82
Dual Alliance, 191, 192
Dulles, John Foster, 147, 177, 251, 292

Eastern Europe, Soviet takeover of (1944–48), 97, 114–115, 143, 171, 241, 243, 258, 262
East Germany, 243, 287
Eberhardt, Sylvia, 330
Economic aid, 287, 293, 317
Economic motives, 265–269
Economic strength, 279–280
Education, 342–343, 348
Edward VII, King of England, 101
Egypt, 98, 102, 115, 234, 287, 288, 346
Einhorn, Robert, 296–298, 337
Einstein, Albert, 172
Eisenhower, Dwight D., 234, 235
Eisner, Kurt, 213
Elon, Amos, 167
El Salvador, 49, 164, 165, 252, 290, 292
Emergency reaction, 91
Empathy, realistic, 160–167, 207, 304

Empire-building, 120
Empire-keeping, 120–121
Encirclement, 12, 20, 25, 29, 35, 203–204, 299–300, 304, 305
Engels, Friedrich, 170, 228
Equality, problem of, 306
Ermath, Fritz W., 110, 302
Errors
  subconsciously motivated, 138–159
  unmotivated, cognitive, 168–185, 262–263
Estonia, 217, 243
Etheredge, Lloyd, 123
Ethiopia, 42, 49, 50, 60, 102, 164, 214, 221, 237, 247, 285
Etzioni, Amitai, 87, 88, 93, 119, 308
Eurocommunism, 285
Exaggerated anger, 136
Exaggerated fear, 113, 114–120, 128, 132, 136, 139, 196, 260, 296, 299
Exchanges, 251, 317

Fairbank, John King, 245
Falkland Islands, 2, 121, 149, 151, 274
False moral pride, 166
Fashoda crisis (1898), 101, 191
Fay, Sidney B., 96, 198, 199, 201, 206
Fear, 3, 21, 25, 28–29, 37, 48, 65–66, 80, 82–84, 88, 89, 91, 98, 197, 198, 262, 269, 304, 305, 344–345
  exaggerated, 113, 114–120, 128, 132, 136, 139, 196, 260, 296, 299
  realistic, 112–114
Feifer, George, 84, 124, 144
Feshbach, Seymour, 331
Festinger, Leon, 168
Finland, 44, 217, 229, 258
Finlandization thesis, 43, 44–45
First-strike capability, 38–40, 84, 85, 110, 172, 303, 305–306, 310, 332
Fischer, Fritz, 199

Fisher, Roger, 304, 317
Five Weeks: A Study of the Surge of Public Opinion on the Eve of the Great War (Scott), 201
Flexible response, 109–111, 301
Fontaine, André, 227n, 282, 283
Fourteen Points, 211, 212
France, 73, 280
  balance of power, 70, 72
  Ruhr, occupation of, 213
  Suez crisis, 121, 234
  Versailles Treaty, 97, 225–226
  in Vietnam, 121
  West Germany and, 101
  in World War I, 93, 96, 102, 158, 182, 190–192, 194–198, 203, 204, 207, 208, 263, 264, 305
  in World War II, 145, 215, 216, 218, 219, 223–226, 248, 278–279
Franco, Francisco, 215, 222
Franco-Prussian war, 69, 121, 190, 345
Frank, Jerome, 10
Franz Ferdinand, Archduke of Austria, 129, 132, 134, 137, 156, 193, 198, 260
Free, Lloyd, 26n, 122, 145, 246, 264, 291
Freedman, Jonathan, 331
Freedman, Lawrence, 303
Free-floating anxiety, 131, 137–140
Frenkel-Brunswik, Else, 125
Freud, Anna, 123
Freud, Sigmund, 2, 112–114, 117, 122, 128, 131–132, 137–139, 156, 158
Fromm, Erich, 131
Führer principle, 264, 265
Fulbright, J. William, 6, 105
Fury, 91

Galbraith, John Kenneth, 341
Garthoff, Raymond, 35, 302
Gayler, Admiral Noel, 305–308
Gaza strip, 150, 294, 318
Gelb, Leslie, 297, 300, 314, 333
Geneva Summit Conference (1955), 233

George, Alexander L., 102, 111*n*
Germany
  balance of power, 69–70, 72
  Versailles Treaty and, 97, 211–213, 225–226
  in World War I, 73, 93–94, 96, 102, 114, 120, 129, 136, 148, 150, 155–158, 182, 190–204, 206–208, 211, 248, 260–264, 305
  in World War II, 106, 114, 120, 145, 148, 210–226, 229
Ghana, 286
Gladstone, William, 100
Goebbels, Joseph, 263
Golan Heights, 318
Good Guys–Bad Guys thinking, 3, 29, 31, 33, 109–112, 139–142, 165–166, 168–170, 173–175, 178, 180, 238, 316, 336–338
Goodman, Ellen, 29
Gore, Albert, 305, 309
Gottlieb, Sanford, 39, 51
Grandeur, delusions of, 123–124, 125, 203, 256, 265, 274
Grant, Steven, 20
Gray, Colin, 110, 326
Great Britain, 280
  balance of power, 70, 72
  in Boer war, 191, 208
  in Falklands dispute, 121, 149
  Suez crisis, 121, 234
  in World War I, 93–94, 102, 129, 155, 158, 182, 191–196, 199, 203, 204, 206, 208, 262–264, 305
  in World War II, 106, 145, 215, 216, 218–220, 223, 224, 231, 261, 278–279
Great Illusion, The (Angell), 2
Great Purges, 257
Greece, 59, 165, 232, 247, 274
Grey, Sir Edward, 194, 195, 203, 261
Grim realism, 141–142
GRIT (Graduated and Reciprocated Initiatives in Tension-reduction), 87, 104, 305, 308
Gromyko, Andrei, 16, 51, 227*n*

Ground-launched cruise missile (GLCM), 66, 306, 310, 313
Guatemala, 49, 60, 85, 165, 247, 252
Guerrilla movements, 102
Guilt, 139, 140, 238, 239
Guinea, 286
Gulag Archipelago, 10, 164, 170, 229, 258
Guroff, Gregory, 20
Guyana, 286

Hacha, Emil, 217
Hague Conference, First, 75
Halle, Louis J., 12, 227*n*
Hamilton, Andrew, 24, 41
Hard Way to Peace, The (Etzioni), 87
Harkabi, Yehoshafat, 168
Harvey, O. J., 340
Hassan, Sana, 167
Hate, 128–134, 163–165
Heiden, Konrad, 123
Heider, Fritz, 168, 173
Heradstveit, Daniel, 168
Hermann, Charles F., 133
Hilsman, Roger, 26, 145
Hindenburg, Paul von, 214
Hinton, Harold C., 245
Hiroshima, 231, 332
Hitler, Adolf, 3, 4, 21, 70, 72, 100, 106, 120, 123–124, 126, 129–131, 145, 146, 148, 174, 189, 205, 229, 230, 239, 241, 248, 249, 256, 260–265, 268, 278–279
Holborn, Hajo, 197
Holland, 218, 280
Holocaust, 131, 216
Holsti, Ole, 198
Horney, Karen, 90, 123
Hostility, 89, 91
Hough, Jerry, 20, 25
Hovland, Carl, 339–340
Howard, Michael, 283
Humiliation, 26, 27
Humility, 166
Hungary, 36, 43, 45, 46, 48, 60, 98, 115, 120, 154, 164, 233–234, 243, 244, 275, 287

Hyland, William, 25

Ideology, 263–265
Iklé, Fred, 56, 297, 298
Illusion, 145–148
India, 60, 150, 274
Indonesia, 85, 247, 267, 287
Inferiority complex, 123, 138
Injured-innocence mechanism, 84–
    86, 176–177, 262, 299, 300,
    305
Inkeles, Alex, 144
Insecurity, 10–14, 21, 25, 84, 177
Interactive concept of tension, 88
Intercontinental ballistic missile
    (ICBM), 26, 234
International Institute of Strategic
    Studies, 31n, 35
International Physicians for the
    Prevention of Nuclear War, 40
International Society of Political
    Psychology, 109n, 345
Iran, 2, 45, 46, 48, 49, 60, 71, 85,
    97, 102, 115, 121, 148–149,
    165, 245–247, 274, 282, 319
Iraq, 2, 45, 46, 48, 49, 60, 121,
    148–149, 165, 274, 286, 319
"Iron Curtain" speech (Churchill),
    231
Irrationality, 123
Islam, 46, 48
Israel, 27, 46, 48, 60, 98, 99, 115,
    121, 129, 152–153, 163, 241,
    280
Italy, 204, 221, 280

Jackson–Vanik amendment, 16
James, William, 155, 159
Janis, Irving, 39, 133, 331, 339,
    343
Japan, 74, 280, 285, 287, 348
    China, relations with, 98–99,
        215, 222, 249
    Manchuria, seizure of, 214
    Pearl Harbor, 39, 73, 100, 102,
        129, 145, 202, 219, 230, 248,
        249, 262
    in World War II, 148, 150, 231
Jay, Peter, 276, 283, 292–293

Jervis, Robert, 45, 74, 99, 105, 110,
    111n, 137–138, 147, 149, 163,
    168, 332
Jews, 129–131, 164, 216, 237, 260,
    262, 317
Johnson, Lyndon B., 18, 126
Jones, Edward, 172, 175
Jordan, 49, 85, 165
Judea, 121, 152–153

Kaagan, Larry, 26n, 122n, 127–128
Kahn, Herman, 110, 234
Kahneman, Daniel, 100
Kaiser, Karl, 311
Kaiser, Robert G., 11, 25, 35, 51–
    52, 84, 85, 124, 125, 144,
    227n, 286, 287, 346
Kaplowitz, Noel, 168
Karmal, Babrak, 17, 18
Karpovich, M., 12
Kashmir, 150, 242
Keeny, Spurgeon M., Jr., 110
Kelley, Harold, 339
Kellogg-Briand Peace Pact, 310
Kelman, Herbert C., 317
Kennan, George F., 11, 20, 25, 40,
    111, 113, 116–117, 155, 183,
    227n, 245, 298, 311, 332, 341
Kennedy, John F., 27, 121, 145,
    234, 235, 253, 254, 308
Kernberg, Otto, 123
Khomeini, Ayatollah, 46, 48
Khrushchev, Nikita, 37, 39, 42, 72,
    124, 147, 174, 177, 183, 227n,
    233–235, 244, 256
Khrushchev Remembers (Talbott), 12
Khvostov, V., 227n
Kim Il Sung, 244
King, Bert L., 39, 343
Kissinger, Henry A., 25, 60, 110,
    125, 234, 254, 292, 309
Kluckhohn, Clyde, 144
Knutson, Jeanne, 109n
Kohut, Heinz, 123
Korea, 49, 60, 85
Korean airliner incident, 14, 28–30,
    65, 122, 164, 175, 202, 237,
    247, 342, 348
Korean war, 43, 59, 71, 72, 94, 102,

121, 148, 153, 165, 232–233,
243–245, 252, 261
Kun, Bela, 213
Kuwait, 45
Kvitsinsky, Yuri, 313

Lambeth, Benjamin, 44, 302
Languages, 288, 318
Laos, 49, 150, 165, 290
Lasswell, Harold, 109n
Last Epidemic, The, 329
Latvia, 217, 243
Launch-on-warning policy, 55, 56,
318
League of Nations, 213, 214, 221,
229, 322, 325
Disarmament Conference (1932–
33), 75
Lebanon, 2, 60, 99, 150, 163, 318
Leber, Georg, 311
Lebow, Richard Ned, 26, 73, 111n,
133, 227n
Leites, Nathan, 125
Lellouche, Pierre, 44
Lend-Lease, 230, 250
Lenin, V. I., 228, 264, 267, 268
Leventhal, 331
Leviné, 213
Levinson, Daniel, 125
Lewin, Kurt, 82, 152, 173, 175
Lichnowsky, Karl, 155
Lifton, Robert Jay, 171, 329
Limited nuclear war, 41–42, 172,
318
Limited Test Ban Treaty (1963), 75,
235, 306, 312
Lindskold, Svenn, 331
Lithuania, 217, 243
Lorenz, Konrad, 2, 152
Louis XIV, King of France, 248
Ludendorff, Erich, 211, 221
Lumsdaine, Arthur, 339
Lusitania, 195
Luxemburg, Rosa, 213
Lyons, Eugene, 146

MacArthur, Douglas, 71, 231, 233
Macedonia, 150

Machiavelli, Niccolò, 109n
Macho pride, 11, 26, 28, 90, 91, 99,
119–128, 132, 141–142, 152,
156, 158, 166, 198–200, 260,
268, 269, 296, 310, 332, 338–
340, 348
Madariaga, Salvador de, 6, 78, 339
Malenkov, Georgi, 233
Male potency, symbolism of, 128
Malignant process of hostile interac-
tion, 92–96, 206, 207, 238,
250, 255–256, 259, 296, 299,
348
Malvinas, 121, 151, 274
Manchuria, 214, 231, 233
Mao Tse-tung, 174, 232
Marder, Murrey, 295
Maritime Provinces of Siberia,
150–151
Marne, battle of the, 195
Marshall Plan, 213, 225, 232, 250,
253
Marx, Karl, 170, 174, 228
Marxism, 289
Marxism-Leninism, 125
Masada complex, 62, 310
McGrory, Mary, 337
McKersie, R. B., 317
McNamara, Robert, 40, 234, 311
Mein Kampf (Hitler), 213, 269
Meir, Golda, 237
Mensheviks, 228
Mertes, Alois, 311
Meyer, Cord, 324
Midgetman missile, 309
Militarism, 339
Military-industrial complex, 4, 16,
266
Miller, Neal, 130, 137
Minimal deterrence, 80–86
forms of, 273–294
Mirror-image conflicts, 256–257,
264, 301
MIRV missile, 247, 297, 309
Missiles to warheads, ratio of, 305–
306, 308–309, 328
Modified freeze agreement, 306,
311–312
Moltke, Helmuth von, 206

Moral Man and Immoral Society
(Niebuhr), 143
Moral pride, 166
Moral self-image, 88, 142–144,
147, 161, 247, 260, 290, 316
Morgenthau, Hans, 324
Morocco crisis (first), 192, 199,
208, 268
Morocco crisis (second), 93, 192,
199, 208, 268
Mowrer, O. H., 130–131, 137
Munich, 58, 100, 106, 215, 216,
222, 278–279
Mussolini, Benito, 214–216, 222,
256, 265
Mutual-benefit tradeoffs, 313–314,
328
Mutually assured destruction
(MAD), 110–111
MX missile, 66, 247, 297, 305, 309,
310, 314, 330, 335, 337
Myrdal, Alva, 312

Nagasaki, 231, 330
Nagorski, Andrew, 287, 346
Nagy, Imré, 244
Namibia, 290
Napalm, 18
Napoleon I, 248
Napoleon III, 73, 74, 190
Narcissism, 90, 123
Nasser, Gamal Abdel, 234
Nationalism, 286, 322, 323, 326,
346–349
National sovereignty, 171, 258–259
Naval forces, 22
Nazi–Soviet Pact, 216–217, 219,
229, 258
Negotiation, 78–79
Nelan, Bruce, 12, 19–20, 35
Neurotic anxiety, 112, 114–119,
131, 140
New Zealand, 280
Nicaragua, 42, 49, 95, 164, 165,
267
Niebuhr, Reinhold, 120, 143, 239
Nigeria, 267
Nikhonov, Alexei, 227n, 295
Nisbett, Richard, 172, 175

Nitze, Paul, 46–47, 49, 51, 110,
281, 313
Nixon, Richard M., 15, 60, 81,
236, 237, 254, 284, 346
No-first-use-policy, 306, 310–311,
328, 331
North, Robert, 198, 203
North Atlantic Treaty Organization
(NATO), 22–24, 41, 232
Northern Ireland, 121, 151
Norway, 218, 280
Novak, Joseph, 125
Nuclear decapitation, 55
Nuclear freeze, 1, 183–185, 305,
306, 311–312, 328, 330, 334–
335, 342
Nuclear umbrella, myth of, 303
Nuclear war, scenarios for outbreak
of, 54–65

Oder-Neisse line, 236
Ogaden province, 151, 242
Ogarkov, Nikolai, 39
Oil, 45–48, 63–65, 266, 279, 347
Oman, 165
On-site inspection, 297
Organization of African Unity
(OAU), 317
Organization of American States
(OAS), 317
Organization for Economic Coop-
eration and Development
(OECD), 281
Organski, A. F. K., 71–72
Osgood, Charles, 87, 88, 93, 104,
305
Osgood, Robert, 127
Overconfidence, 145, 146, 148–
150, 161, 196, 249, 261, 275
Overkill, 111, 113, 117, 183–185,
266
Overlapping territorial self-images,
150–154, 261

Pakistan, 60, 274
Palestine, 152–153, 283
Palestine Liberation Organization
(PLO), 99, 129, 283

Panic, 91
Panovsky, Wolfgang K. H., 110
Paranoia, 29, 82, 84, 112, 123–126, 203, 257
Pares, Bernard, 12, 227n
Parity, 67, 69–75, 155, 172, 182–185, 275–277, 304
Patriotism, 316
Payne, James L., 278
Peaceful co-existence, 264
Pearl Harbor, 39, 73, 100, 102, 129, 145, 202, 230, 262
Peloponnesian War, 247
Pentagon Papers, 17, 98, 267
Perception and Misperception in International Politics (Jervis), 137
Perceptual lag, 170–171
Perry, Helen Swick, 159
Persecution, delusions of, 123–124, 203, 256, 265
Pershing II missile, 38, 55, 56, 66, 84, 85, 94, 95, 247, 305, 306, 310, 313, 314, 318
Petrov, Vladimir, 19
Philippine Islands, 49, 60, 165
Piaget, Jean, 177
Plato, 109n
Poland, 43, 102, 103, 145, 164, 195, 211, 212, 216–218, 229, 230, 237, 243, 247, 261, 286, 287, 346
Polish Corridor, 150, 212, 217, 220, 225, 226, 261
Ponomaryov, B., 227n
Positive reinforcement, 251
Potsdam Conference, 231
Preexisting beliefs, 137, 168–171, 262, 303
Prenuclear beliefs, 171–172
Pride: see Macho pride; Wounded pride
Pritzker, H. A., 340
Projection, 122, 142, 144, 156–158, 176, 177
Propaganda, credulous acceptance of, 178–180, 262–263
"Pro-us" illusion, 145–148, 155, 161, 177, 261
Pruitt, Dean G., 304, 317

Quemoy, 150, 165, 242, 246, 252

Rapacki Plan, 251
Rationality, 117–119
Rationalization, 138–140, 142–144, 156–158, 176, 247
Reagan, Ronald, 1, 33, 87, 155, 163, 275, 282, 300, 333, 334, 342
Realistic fear, 112–114
Reichart, John F., 31n, 110, 302
Reparations, 212–213, 225
Repression, 122, 156, 158
Resistance, 122, 156, 158
Resolution 242, 236, 318
Resolve, 273–274, 277–279
Restraining forces, 82
Rhee, Syngman, 233, 244
Rhineland, 212, 215, 221, 226
Rich, Norman, 263
Rivals, The (Ulam), 11
Role-playing, 161, 166
Rome, 247
Roosevelt, Franklin D., 202, 216, 222, 224, 229, 231, 264
Rose, François de, 311
Rostow, Walt, 281
Rubin, Jeffrey, 317
Ruhr Valley, 213, 225
Rumania, 243
Russell, Bertrand, 71
Russia
    balance of power, 70, 72
    in World War I, 93, 96, 102, 148, 158, 182, 191, 194–198, 200, 203, 204, 206, 208, 211, 248, 261–263, 305
Russia: The People and the Power (Kaiser), 11, 124
Russian Roulette: The Superpower Game (Cox), 55
Russo-Japanese war, 69, 192

Saar valley, 212, 214, 226
SAC-alert (1973), 60, 65, 129, 165, 237, 246
Sachar, Howard M., 97, 98, 241
Sadat, Anwar el-, 288
SALT I, 75, 236, 296, 314

SALT II, 16, 75, 165, 237, 251, 253, 282, 295–297
Samaria, 121, 152–153
Sanford, Nevitt, 125
Satellite reconnaissance, 26, 30
Saudi Arabia, 45, 60, 165, 283, 285, 287
Scalapino, Robert A., 286, 287
Scapegoat phenomenon, 132
Scenarios for outbreak of nuclear war, 54–65
Scheer, Robert, 44
Schell, Jonathan, 1, 76–77, 171, 258–259, 320, 325, 326, 328–329, 340, 344
Schellenberg, James, 269
Schlesinger, James, 24, 110
Schlieffen Plan, 155, 194
Schmidt, William E., 342
Schmitt, Bernadotte, 200, 201
Schulze, Franz-Josef, 311
Schuschnigg, Kurt von, 215, 217
Science of Conflict, The (Schellenberg), 269
Scott, Jonathan F., 201
Scowcroft Commission, 309
Sears, Robert, 131, 137, 331
Second-strike capability, 22, 40, 77, 110, 111, 234, 273, 275, 277, 304, 332, 333, 338
Secrecy, 29
Selective attention, 155, 159, 204
Selective inattention, 142, 153, 154–159, 161–162, 170, 204, 247, 261
Self-assertion, 127–128
Self-preservation, 3
Self-respect, 119, 120
Serbia, 96, 114, 132, 136–137, 156, 192–194, 196, 200–202, 206, 261, 262
Shah of Iran, 97, 115, 245, 246, 252, 284, 292
Shatt el-Arab, 151, 242
Sheffield, F. D., 339
Sherif, Muzafer, 340
Shirer, William, 223
Shulman, Marshall D., 97, 227n, 258

Siege mentality, 35, 66
Simon, Herbert, 133
Sinai, 121, 150, 318
Six-Day War (1967), 115, 129, 236, 241
Smith, Gerard, 40, 311
Smoke, Richard, 102, 111n, 227n, 303
Snyder, Glenn, 133, 227n
Socialism, 263–265, 279, 286, 292
Social reinforcement of beliefs, 170
Solzhenitzyn, Aleksandr, 174, 337
Somalia, 49, 60, 286
Sonnenfeldt, Helmut, 25
South Africa, 280, 293–294
South Yemen, 43, 95, 285
Soviet arms buildup, 13, 21–28, 85, 94, 95, 129, 164, 176, 181–182, 299, 345
Soviet Political Mind, The (Tucker), 11, 126
Spain, 165
Spanish Armada, 247
Spanish civil war, 59, 215, 222
Spinoza, Baruch, 238
Sputnik, 234, 303
SS-18s, 301
SS-19s, 301
SS-20s, 40, 41, 85, 94, 95, 301, 306, 313, 314
Stalin, Joseph, 10, 126, 129, 130, 164, 170, 171, 174, 216–217, 228–231, 233, 239, 250, 257–258, 265
Stalingrad, battle of, 219, 230
Stealth bombers, 335
Steinbruner, John D., 32, 55, 313
Stoessinger, John, 148, 248, 249, 289, 291
Strait of Tiran, 253
Strategic Arms Limitation Talks: see SALT I; SALT II
Strength, 273–277
Stubbing, Richard A., 23n
Study of War, A (Wright), 269
Sturm, Steven R., 31n, 110, 302
Subconsciously motivated errors, 138–159
Submarine-launched ballistic mis-

sile (SLBM), 80, 300
Substantial equivalence, 275
Sudetenland, 150, 212, 215, 216, 222–223, 226, 242, 261
Suez crisis (1956), 121, 234
Sufficiency, 81, 275
Sullivan, Harry Stack, 122, 158
Superiority, 22, 31–36, 67–69, 123, 172, 300, 333–336
Sussman, Barry, 342
Syracuse, 247

Taiwan (Formosa), 150, 151, 232, 242, 245
Talbott, Strobe, 12, 19, 20, 25, 35, 297
Taylor, A. J. P., 97, 189, 222, 223, 225
Taylor, Maxwell, 40, 41, 43, 274, 275
Tedeschi, James T., 331
Tension, psychological meaning of, 87–92
Tension-reduction, 78–79, 82, 256
  arms reduction agreements without, 75–79
  balance of power without, 69–75
  case for drastic, 87–106
  defensively motivated aggression, 96–100
  deterrence and, 104–106
  feasibility of, 100–101
  forms of drastic, 295–314
  malignant process of hostile interaction, 92–96
  military superiority without, 67–69
  slippages in deterrence, 102–103
Territorial self-images, overlapping, 150–154, 261
Territory-regaining, 121
Test-ban agreement (1963), 75, 235, 306, 312
Thailand, 267
Theater Nuclear Forces (TNF), 282
Third World, 49–51, 124, 176, 267, 284–294, 316, 318, 322–323
Tito, Marshal, 174, 243
Tocqueville, Alexis de, 109n

Toland, John, 218
Toller, Ernst, 213
Trade, 43, 253, 317
Tradeoffs, 306, 313–314, 328
Trends, extrapolation of, 180–182, 263
Trident II, 305, 310, 335
Triple Alliance, 191, 204
Triple Entente, 73
Trofimenko, Henry, 47, 48, 227n, 343
Trotsky, Leon, 146, 228
Truman, Harry S., 231, 232
Truman Doctrine, 232
Tuchman, Barbara, 6, 75, 78, 96, 197–199, 203, 206, 245, 259, 325, 339
Tucker, Robert C., 11, 25, 126, 227n, 257
Turkey, 27, 46, 60, 121, 232, 247, 274, 319
Tversky, Amos, 100

U-2 spy plane incident, 29–30, 235, 247, 296
Ulam, Adam B., 11, 25, 227n, 245
United Nations, 240, 254, 317, 322, 324, 327
Universalization, 178
Unmotivated, cognitive errors, 168–185, 262–263
Upper Silesia, 212
Ury, William, 304, 317

Vance, Cyrus, 16, 282
Vance–Gromyko communiqué (1977), 95, 251, 253, 284, 318
Venezuela, 49
Verification measures, 306, 312
Versailles, Treaty of, 70, 97, 195, 211–213, 225–226, 260
Vicarious guilt, 140
Viet Cong, 146, 147, 236, 242, 249
Vietnam, 42, 43, 49, 85, 286, 287
Vietnam war, 14–15, 17–18, 43, 59, 98, 102, 115, 126, 143, 145–147, 153, 165, 236, 241, 242, 245–247, 249, 252, 261, 267, 274, 289–290, 347

Vladivostok agreement, 94, 284

Walton, Richard E., 317
Walzer, Michael, 240
Warheads to missiles, ratio of, 305–306, 308–309, 328
Warner, Edward L., 110, 302
War-promoting motives, 109–134
War-promoting perceptions, 135–159
Wars of liberation, 43
Washington Naval Conference, 75
Watts, William, 26n, 122
Weapons-in-use image, 75–76, 77
Weapons-serving-as-a-deterrent image, 76, 78
Wedge, Bryant, 317
Weiler, Lawrence, 308
Weimar Republic, 213, 214
Weinberger, Caspar, 343
West Bank, 150, 152–153, 241, 252, 290, 294, 318
West Gemany, 40–41, 101, 280, 348
White, Ralph K., 10, 17, 34, 97, 98, 116, 144–146, 149, 167, 170, 176, 180, 236, 241, 242, 247, 264, 265, 284, 288, 289, 318, 319
Whitney, Craig, 11–12, 19, 20, 25, 35
Why Nations Go to War (Stoessinger), 248
Wilhelm II, Kaiser, 72, 74, 155, 190, 191, 193, 194, 198–201, 203–206, 208, 260, 261
Wilson, Woodrow, 120, 211, 213
Wishful thinking, 33, 34, 147, 148
Wohlstetter, Albert, 110, 234
Wolfe, Bertram, 125, 126

Women, 348
World federation, 1, 320–327, 331
World War I, 69, 189–209; *see also names of countries*
  condensed history of, 190–196
  possibility of prevention of, 205–209
  psychological parallels with the East–West conflict, 196–205
World War II, 37, 39, 70, 100, 189, 211–226, 273–274; *see also names of countries*
  condensed history of, 210–220
  possibility of prevention of, 220–226
Worst-case thinking, 33, 34, 68, 74, 84, 138, 139, 148–150, 161, 261, 275, 299
Wouk, Herman, 221
Wounded pride, 26, 90, 299
Wright, Quincy, 269

Yalta conference, 231
Yankelovich, Daniel, 26n, 122n, 127–128
Yarmolinsky, Adam, 297
Yellow rain, 298
Yemen, 49, 50, 164, 237, 247
"Yes-but technique," 339, 340
Young, Andrew, 285, 287, 293, 294
Youth, 348
Yugoslavia, 60, 232, 243, 286, 346

Zaïre, 49, 165
Zamoshkin, Yu. A., 227n
Zartman, William, 317
Zimmermann telegram, 129
Zinnes, Dina, 89, 90, 198
"Zionist expansionism," 129, 163

Date Due

FEB 1 3 1986

UML 735